Pro Ubuntu Server Administration

Sander van Vugt

Apress®

Pro Ubuntu Server Administration

Copyright © 2009 by Sander van Vugt

ISBN-13 (pbk): 978-1-4302-1622-3

ISBN-13 (electronic): 978-1-4302-1623-0

Lead Editor: Frank Pohlmann
Technical Reviewer: Samuel Cuella
Editorial Board: Clay Andres, Steve Anglin, Mark Beckner, Ewan Buckingham, Tony Campbell, Gary Cornell, Jonathan Gennick, Michelle Lowman, Matthew Moodie, Jeffrey Pepper, Frank Pohlmann, Ben Renow-Clarke, Dominic Shakeshaft, Matt Wade, Tom Welsh
Project Manager: Beth Christmas
Copy Editor: Bill McManus
Associate Production Director: Kari Brooks-Copony
Production Editor: Elizabeth Berry
Compositor: Linda Weidemann
Proofreader: Liz Welch
Indexer: Becky Hornyak
Artist: April Milne
Cover Designer: Kurt Krames
Manufacturing Director: Tom Debolski

Distributed to the book trade worldwide by Springer-Verlag New York, Inc., 233 Spring Street, 6th Floor, New York, NY 10013. Phone 1-800-SPRINGER, fax 201-348-4505, e-mail orders-ny@springer-sbm.com, or visit http://www.springeronline.com.

For information on translations, please contact Apress directly at 2855 Telegraph Avenue, Suite 600, Berkeley, CA 94705. Phone 510-549-5930, fax 510-549-5939, e-mail info@apress.com, or visit http://www.apress.com.

Apress and friends of ED books may be purchased in bulk for academic, corporate, or promotional use. eBook versions and licenses are also available for most titles. For more information, reference our Special Bulk Sales–eBook Licensing web page at http://www.apress.com/info/bulksales.

This book is dedicated to Florence.
And the next, and the next, and all of them, always.

Contents at a Glance

Foreword xv

About the Author. xvii

About the Technical Reviewer xix

Introduction xxi

CHAPTER 1   Performing an Advanced Ubuntu Server Installation 1

CHAPTER 2   Using Ubuntu Server for System Imaging 29

CHAPTER 3   Performance Monitoring 45

CHAPTER 4   Performance Optimization 83

CHAPTER 5   Advanced File System Management 109

CHAPTER 6   Network Monitoring 131

CHAPTER 7   Creating an Open Source SAN 161

CHAPTER 8   Configuring OpenLDAP 197

CHAPTER 9   Integrating Samba 231

CHAPTER 10   Configuring Ubuntu Server As a Mail Server 249

CHAPTER 11   Managing Ubuntu Server Security 281

CHAPTER 12   Configuring Ubuntu Server As a VPN Server 303

CHAPTER 13   Configuring Kerberos and NTP on Ubuntu Server 321

CHAPTER 14   Ubuntu Server Troubleshooting 343

INDEX 383

Contents

Foreword xv

About the Author. xvii

About the Technical Reviewer xix

Introduction xxi

CHAPTER 1   Performing an Advanced Ubuntu Server Installation 1

What's So Special About an Enterprise Installation?. 1

    Server Hardware 2

    Connection to a SAN 2

    Authentication Handling 3

Preparing for the Installation in a Network 3

    Which RAID? 4

    Choosing a File System 5

Installing Ubuntu Server 7

    Starting the Installation. 8

    Creating a Software-Based RAID Solution. 9

    Creating LVM Logical Volumes on Top of a

        Software RAID Device 16

    Completing the Installation. 22

Post-Installation Tasks 24

    Setting Up NIC Bonding. 24

    Setting Up Multipathing. 26

Summary. 28

▮CHAPTER 2   **Using Ubuntu Server for System Imaging** 29

Setting Up a Clonezilla Imaging Server 29

Setting Up Diskless Remote Boot in Linux 30

    Installing the DRBL Software 31

    Configuring the DRBL Software 32

Setting Up the DHCP Server 33

Completing Clonezilla Configuration 35

Configuring the Clients for Cloning 36

    Setting Up the Server for Cloning 37

    Cloning the Client 39

Summary 43

▮CHAPTER 3   **Performance Monitoring** 45

Interpreting What Your Computer Is Doing: top 45

    CPU Monitoring with top 46

    CPU Performance Monitoring 48

    Memory Monitoring with top 49

    Process Monitoring with top 50

Analyzing CPU Performance 51

Finding Memory Problems 57

Monitoring Storage Performance 65

Monitoring Network Performance 72

Performance Baselining 80

Summary 81

▮CHAPTER 4   **Performance Optimization** 83

Strategies for Optimizing Performance 83

    About /proc and sysctl 83

    Applying a Simple Test 85

CPU Tuning 87

    Understanding CPU Performance 87

    Optimizing CPU Performance 88

Tuning Memory 91
    Understanding Memory Performance. 91
    Optimizing Memory Usage 92
Tuning Storage Performance. 96
    Understanding Storage Performance 96
    Optimizing the I/O Scheduler 97
    Optimizing Reads. 98
Network Tuning 98
    Tuning Kernel Parameters 98
    Optimizing TCP/IP 100
    Some Hints on Samba and NFS Performance Optimization 105
    Generic Network Performance Optimization Tips. 106
Summary. 107

CHAPTER 5   **Advanced File System Management** 109

Understanding File Systems 109
    Inodes and Directories 110
    Superblocks, Inode Bitmaps, and Block Bitmaps. 112
    Journaling 114
    Indexing. 115
Optimizing File Systems. 116
    Optimizing Ext2/Ext3 116
    Tuning XFS 124
    What About ReiserFS?. 128
Summary. 130

CHAPTER 6   **Network Monitoring**. 131

Starting with Nagios 131
Configuring Nagios 135
    Location of the Configuration Files 135
    The Master Configuration File: nagios.cfg. 136
    Creating Essential Nagios Configuration Files. 138

Installing NRPE. 152

    Configuring NRPE on the Monitored Server. 152

    Configuring the Nagios Server to Use NRPE 154

Managing Nagios. 155

Summary. 159

CHAPTER 7   **Creating an Open Source SAN**. 161

Preparing Your Open Source SAN. 163

    Hardware Requirements. 163

    Installing Required Software 163

Setting Up the Distributed Replicated Block Device 164

Accessing the SAN with iSCSI. 169

    Configuring the iSCSI Target 169

    Configuring the iSCSI Initiator 173

Setting Up Heartbeat. 175

    Setting Up the Base Cluster from /etc/ha.d/ha.cf. 175

    Configuring Cluster Resources 180

    Backing Up the Cluster Configuration. 187

    Configuring STONITH. 191

Heartbeat Beyond the Open Source SAN. 194

Summary. 195

CHAPTER 8   **Configuring OpenLDAP** 197

Using the LDAP Directory. 197

Introducing OpenLDAP 201

Configuring OpenLDAP. 202

    Installing OpenLDAP 202

    Configuring the Server 203

    Adding Information to the LDAP Database. 215

    Using ldapsearch to Verify Your Configuration 217

Using LDAP Management Commands. 220

    Modifying Entries in the LDAP Database 221

    Deleting Entries from the LDAP Database. 222

    Changing a Password 222

Logging In to an LDAP Server 223

    Configuring PAM for LDAP Authentication. 223

    Setting Up nsswitch.conf to Find LDAP Services 228

    Testing LDAP Client Connectivity 230

Summary. 230

CHAPTER 9   **Integrating Samba** 231

Setting Up Samba the Easy Way. 231

    Creating a Local Directory to Share 232

    Applying Permissions to the Local Directory. 232

    Defining the Share. 232

    Creating a Samba User Account 235

    Testing Access to the Share. 235

Integrating Samba with LDAP 236

    Preparing Samba to Talk to LDAP. 236

    Preparing LDAP to Work with Samba. 237

    Telling Samba to Use LDAP 238

Using Samba As a Primary Domain Controller 241

    Changing the Samba Configuration File. 241

    Creating Workstation Accounts 243

Integrating Samba in Active Directory 244

    Making Samba a Member of the Active Directory Domain. 244

    Using Kerberos to Make Samba a Member of Active Directory. . .245

Authenticating Linux Users on Windows with Winbind. 245

Summary. 247

■CHAPTER 10   **Configuring Ubuntu Server As a Mail Server** 249

Understanding the Components of a Mail Solution 249
Configuring the Postfix MTA 250
    Handling Inbound and Outbound Mail 251
    Installing Postfix and Configuring the Initial Settings. 256
    Configuring Postfix Further. 257
    Managing Postfix Components 262
    Configuring the Master Daemon 263
    Configuring Global Settings 264
    Configuring a Simple Postfix Mail Server. 267
    Tuning Postfix with Lookup Tables 269
    Using Postfix Management Tools 273
Receiving E-mail Using IMAP or POP3. 274
    Fetching E-mail Using Cyrus IMAPd 275
    Filtering Incoming E-mail with procmail 278
    Getting E-mail with POP3 Using Qpopper 279
Summary. 280

■CHAPTER 11   **Managing Ubuntu Server Security** 281

Managing Cryptography 281
    Introduction to SSL 282
    Public and Private Keys. 282
    The Need for a Certificate Authority 283
    Creating a Certificate Authority and Server Certificates 284
Securing Applications with AppArmor 290
    AppArmor Components. 290
    Installing and Starting AppArmor 293
    Creating and Managing AppArmor Profiles 294
    Updating a Profile. 299
    Monitoring AppArmor's Status. 299
Summary. 302

CHAPTER 12   Configuring Ubuntu Server As a VPN Server 303

Installing and Configuring OpenVPN 303
    VPN Networking 304
    Generating Certificates 305
Configuring the VPN Server 313
Configuring a Linux VPN Client 316
    Configuring Windows Clients 320
Summary 320

CHAPTER 13   Configuring Kerberos and NTP on Ubuntu Server 321

Configuring an NTP Time Server 321
    How NTP Works 322
    Customizing Your NTP Server 327
Understanding Kerberos 329
Installing and Configuring Kerberos 330
Configuring the Kerberos Server 332
    Configuring Generic Kerberos Settings 332
    Configuring the KDC Settings 335
Configuring the Kerberos Client 339
    Configuring Simple Kerberos Applications 339
    Logging In with Kerberos 340
Summary 341

CHAPTER 14   Ubuntu Server Troubleshooting 343

Identifying the Problem 344
Troubleshooting Tools 351
    Working with init=/bin/bash 351
    Rescue a Broken System 353
    Working with a Knoppix Rescue CD 357

Common Problems and How to Fix Them 360
    Grub Errors 361
    No Master Boot Record 364
    Partition Problems 365
    LVM Logical Volume Problems 368
    Kernel Problems 375
    File System Problems 378
    Lost Administrator Password 380
Summary 381

▪INDEX 383

Foreword

Several months ago, we received a post to the `ubuntu-server` mailing list from Sander van Vugt. Sander explained that he was writing an advanced book on Ubuntu Server administration, as well as a second edition of his *Beginning Ubuntu Server Administration*. Sander solicited ideas and asked for feedback. Though several books have been published on Ubuntu Server Edition, this is the first time, to my knowledge, that feedback has been sought from the Ubuntu Server community. We are grateful for the chance to help, and some of the suggestions made by Ubuntu Server Edition's developers and users appear in the pages of this book.

This book covers Ubuntu 8.04 LTS Server Edition, sometimes referred to by its codename "Hardy Heron." Ubuntu releases an LTS (Long Term Support) edition about every two years. The LTS designation indicates that this release will be maintained and supported for five years by Canonical Ltd., the commercial sponsor of Ubuntu. By focusing on the LTS edition, Sander ensures that this book will be a useful addition to your library.

I am thankful to Sander for writing a book targeted at professional administrators. I think that it comes at a perfect time for Ubuntu Server Edition. We worked hard to make Ubuntu 8.04 our most enterprise-ready version yet, and this book is targeted at the enterprise administrators who need to know about Ubuntu Server's advanced features. Among the new and updated features are the following:

- Integrated host firewalling to protect Internet-facing servers

- Added AppArmor policies and increased kernel hardening

- Increased range of storage capabilities, including iSCSI and DRBD

- Sun's OpenJDK, new to Ubuntu Server in the Ubuntu 8.04 distribution

- Active Directory integration, provided by Likewise Open

- Added KVM virtualization support

I think the fact that this book is focused on the enterprise users, that it covers the LTS edition, and that Sander asked for Ubuntu Server community feedback all add up to making this a good book. I hope that it is useful to you, and helps you in your adoption of Ubuntu Server Edition.

One last word about the Ubuntu Server community. Though Ubuntu has a corporate sponsor, a large portion of the work is done by the community. Who is the community? Anyone who submits a bug report, helps package applications, writes documentation, answers questions from other users on the mailing list or IRC, or helps testing. We would love for you to get involved and help us make Ubuntu Server even better than it is now. I encourage you to visit `https://wiki.ubuntu.com/ServerTeam/` for more information.

Rick Clark
Engineering Manager, Ubuntu Server Edition

About the Author

SANDER VAN VUGT is an independent trainer and consultant who lives in the Netherlands and works in the extended EMEA (Europe, Middle East, and Africa) area. He specializes in Linux high availability, storage solutions, and performance problems, and has successfully implemented Linux clusters across the globe. Sander has written several books about Linux-related subjects, including *The Definitive Guide to SUSE Linux Enterprise Server* (Apress, 2006) and *Beginning Ubuntu Server Administration* (Apress, 2008).

Sander's articles can be found on several international web sites and in magazines such as *SearchEnterpriseLinux.com*, *Linux Journal*, and *Linux Magazine*. He works as a volunteer for the Linux Professional Institute (LPI), contributing topics for different certification levels. Most important, Sander is the father of Alex and Franck, and is the loving husband of Florence. For more information, consult Sander's web site: www.sandervanvugt.com. Sander can be reached by e-mail at mail@sandervanvugt.com.

About the Technical Reviewer

SAMUEL CUELLA, born in 1985, currently is an IT student and works as a Linux/Solaris trainer. Samuel taught the complete Mandriva certification program in China (JUST University) and also teaches Linux for LPI certification training. He is a Novell Certified Linux Professional (CLP).

Introduction

This book is about advanced Ubuntu Server administration. In this book you will read about topics that normally are of interest to experienced administrators. The typical reader of this book will already know how to handle basic tasks such as managing files, users, permissions, and services such as Apache and Samba.

I have written this book around some major themes. First of them is administering Ubuntu Server in the data center. This theme covers typical issues that you'll encounter only when installing Ubuntu Server in an enterprise environment, such as connecting the server to the SAN or configuring Ubuntu Server as a Clonezilla imaging server. You'll also learn how to set up high availability for services running on Ubuntu Server.

The second major theme is performance and troubleshooting. There is a chapter about performance monitoring and analysis, which is followed by a chapter about performance optimization. You'll also find a chapter about file system monitoring and optimization. The last chapter in the book provides extensive coverage of Ubuntu Server troubleshooting.

The next theme comprises advanced options offered by network services. You'll learn how to set up an OpenLDAP Directory server, how to connect your Samba server to that Directory server, and how to configure Ubuntu Server as a mail server.

The last theme is security. This starts with an introduction to OpenSSL and the configuration of a certificate authority. The chapter on OpenVPN delves further into the topic of certificates, and the chapter on Kerberos shows how you can use Kerberos to set up secure authentication for different services. You'll also find some in-depth information about the configuration of AppArmor to protect your applications.

I hope that this book meets your requirements and that you enjoy reading it as much as I have enjoyed writing it!

CHAPTER 1

■ ■ ■

Performing an Advanced Ubuntu Server Installation

Installing Ubuntu Server with RAID

You know how to install Ubuntu Server. There are, however, some additional challenges that you may face when installing Ubuntu Server in a network. Most important of those challenges is that your server may need a software-based RAID solution. If you want to configure your server with software RAID, and especially if you want to use LVM volumes on top of that, installing Ubuntu Server can be quite hard. In this chapter you'll learn all you need to know about such an installation.

What's So Special About an Enterprise Installation?

You may ask: what's the big deal about an enterprise network installation of Ubuntu Server versus a "normal" Ubuntu Server installation? There are some important differences when installing Ubuntu Server in an enterprise environment in which other servers are used as well, as this section explains. First, take a look at the recommended minimal installation requirements for a normal server installation:

- 256 MB of RAM

- 500 MHz CPU

- 4 GB hard drive

- Optical drive

The next few sections discuss some of the most significant differences between a network installation and a simple stand-alone installation.

Server Hardware

The first major difference between a demo installation in your test network and an enterprise network installation is in the server hardware itself. When setting up a server in an enterprise environment, you probably want some redundancy. You can implement that redundancy by making sure that some devices have a backup available. For example, most data-center-grade servers have a dual power supply, two network cards, and at least two hard disks. The advantage? If one breaks, the server can start using the other. And the big deal is that all of this happens automatically.

Some of the setup of this redundant hardware is done in the hardware itself. I don't cover that in this book. Some setup can be software based as well. For example, the use of software RAID, or NIC teaming (also known as NIC bonding), makes sure that two network boards are presented as one single network interface. The purpose of that? It can add redundancy to your network card, or if you prefer, it can increase performance because two network cards bundled together can handle twice the workload of a single network card working alone.

Connection to a SAN

Next, your server may be connected to a storage area network (SAN). If you've never worked with a SAN before, no worries—just consider it a bunch of external disks for the moment. Chapter 7 covers in depth setting up Ubuntu Server as a SAN. Typically, a specialized network card called a host bus adapter (HBA) takes care of the connection to a SAN. Such a host adapter may use iSCSI, which sends SCSI packets encapsulated in IP over a copper-based network, or it may be a Fibre Channel card, using an expensive Fibre Channel infrastructure.

If your server is connected to a SAN, you normally would want to have some redundancy in the SAN as well. This redundancy is implemented by using multiple HBAs that connect to the SAN using different network connections. Now, there is something unique about this scenario. Normally, when the HBA in your server connects to the SAN, it gets an additional storage device. For instance, if you have a local hard disk in your server, you would normally see it as the device /dev/sda. If just one HBA connects to the shared storage on the SAN, the HBA would offer your server access to an external hard drive, which would be seen by your server as a new storage device, typically /dev/sdb.

Now imagine the situation in which two different HBAs use separate network connections to connect to the same shared storage area on the SAN. Each of the two HBAs would give you an additional external device, so you would see an additional /dev/sdb and /dev/sdc. There is one problem with that, though: both /dev/sdb and /dev/sdc would refer to the same storage device! That normally is not a good idea, and that is where multipath comes in. When using multipath, an additional kernel module is loaded. The purpose of this module is to tell the operating system that the devices /dev/sdb and /dev/sdc (in this example) are just the same device. As you can understand, when connecting your server to a redundant SAN, the configuration of multipath is an absolute requirement.

Authentication Handling

One last difference when installing your server in a network environment is that typically you would implement an external authentication mechanism. If you have only one server, it makes perfect sense to handle user authentication on that server itself. However, if you have more than one server, it makes sense to use a service that takes care of authentication for you at a centralized location in the network. This refers to a server that has already been set up in the network for this purpose. Such a service might be your LDAP server or a Microsoft Active Directory environment. The Ubuntu Server installation process helps you to set that up as well. In the next section you'll read all about it.

Preparing for the Installation in a Network

You now know what to take care of when installing Ubuntu Server in a network environment. So let's talk about the installation itself. In this section you'll read how a typical server installation in a network environment takes place. I'll assume that you have installed Ubuntu Server before, so I'll be rather brief on the obvious parts, and more in depth with regard to the advanced parts of the installation. Before you start the actual installation, you should understand what I'm going to install here for purposes of demonstration.

The server that you are going to read about in this section has the following properties:

- Two quad-core processors

- 8 GB of RAM

- Five disks

- Two Gigabit Ethernet network boards

Note You may not have the hardware described here available. That's no problem, because you can create a configuration like this rather easily using virtualization software like VMware. Okay, it's a problem to create two virtual CPUs with quad core each, and it will be a problem allocating 8 GB of RAM in most situations as well, but processors and RAM don't make that big of a difference when performing the installation anyway. The focus here is on disk and network setup. And using a free virtualization solution like VMware Server, you can just create as many disks and as many Ethernet network boards as you like.

It's fine if your server has additional properties, but from the installation perspective, having the preceding list of properties really is all that matters. Before you insert the installation CD and start the installation, it helps to make a plan. Most important is the planning of your disk setup. In a typical server installation, what you want above all is redundancy and performance at the same time. This means that if a disk breaks, the other disks should take over immediately. To reach this goal, you would probably want to work with some kind of RAID setup.

Which RAID?

There are two ways to set up RAID on your server: hardware based and software based. If your server has a hardware RAID controller, you should consult the documentation for that controller. Every RAID controller is different, and there is no generic way in which I can describe how to set that up. If your server does not have hardware RAID, you can use a software-based RAID solution. Software RAID often does not offer the same level of performance as hardware RAID, but the advantage is that you don't have to pay anything extra to use it. When implementing software RAID, the following four methods are of interest:

- *RAID 0*: This RAID method is referred to as disk striping. Actually, RAID 0 just bundles two disks together. This is excellent for performance, because you have two controllers that can handle the data flow simultaneously, but RAID 0 is not built for redundancy and fault tolerance. If one disk in a RAID 0 array breaks, you can't access any data on the array anymore.

- *RAID 1*: RAID 1 is all about disk mirroring. One disk is used as the active disk and handles all I/O; the other disk is used only as a hot backup disk. Everything that happens on the active disk happens on the backup disk as well, so at all times, the backup disk will be the same. Therefore, if the active disk fails, the backup disk can take over easily. This is a very safe method of working, but it doesn't offer the best performance. Therefore, especially if you are in an environment in which lots of files are written to the storage devices, you either should not use RAID 1 or should create a RAID 1 array that uses two controllers to increase write speed on the RAID. For rather static volumes, however, RAID 1 is an excellent solution.

- *RAID 10*: RAID 10 offers you the best of both worlds: it's RAID 0 with RAID 1 behind it. So, you have excellent performance and excellent fault tolerance at the same time. There is one disadvantage, though: you need a minimum of four disks to set it up.

- *RAID 5*: If you need to write huge amounts of data, RAID 5 is what you need. To set up RAID 5, you need a minimum of three disks. When a file is written, it is spread over two of the three disks, and the third disk is used to write parity information for this file. Based on this parity information, if something goes wrong with one of the disks in the RAID 5 array, the RAID software is always able to reconstruct the data in a very fast way. To promote optimal performance, in RAID 5 the parity information is spread over all the disks in the array. So there is no dedicated disk that stores this information, and that promotes very good performance as well.

Note The parity information that is used in a RAID setup creates some kind of a checksum for all files on the RAID. If a disk in the RAID gets lost, the original file can be reconstructed based on the parity information.

Apart from the RAID technologies mentioned here, there are other RAID solutions as well. However, everything else relates in some way to the techniques mentioned here. In the example that I'll show in this chapter, you will install a server that has a RAID 1 array for the system files and a RAID 5 array to store data files.

On top of the RAID arrays, you need some disk storage mechanism as well. Basically, there are two options: use logical volumes or use traditional partitions. Especially for data volumes, it is a very clever idea to use logical partitions. Not only are these easily resizable, but they also offer the snapshot feature. Using snapshot technology makes it a lot easier to make a backup of open files. Most backup programs have a problem backing up files that are in use, whereas if you use snapshot technology, you can freeze the status of your volumes, which allows you to back up anything on the snapshot. Also, when using logical volumes, you can go far beyond the maximum of 16 partitions that you can create when using traditional partitions. The one disadvantage is that you can't boot from a logical volume.

Choosing a File System

Next, you need to consider what you want to do on top of these logical volumes. In all cases, you need to format the logical volume so that a file system is created that allows you to store files on your server. Typically, the following file systems are available:

- *Ext2*: The traditional Linux file system since shortly after Linux was created. It is very stable, but does not offer journaling functionality, which means that it can take a (very) long time to repair the file system in case of problems. Use Ext2 on small volumes that are mainly read-only.

- *Ext3*: Basically, Ext3 is just Ext2 with journaling added to it. Journaling allows you to recover very fast in case problems do occur. Ext3 is a good solution to store data, but it is not the best file system when you are using many (read: more than about 5,000) files in one directory. The indexing methodology used in Ext3 is rather limited.

- *XFS*: XFS was created by supercomputer manufacturer SGI as an open source file system. The most important property of XFS is that it is meant for "large." That means large files, large amounts of data, and large file systems. XFS also is a complete 64-bit file system. It has some excellent tuning options as well, a journal, and a very well-tuned index. All that makes XFS currently the best solution to store data files.

- *ReiserFS*: In the late 1990s Hans Reiser created ReiserFS, a revolutionary file system that was organized in a totally different way compared to the early file systems that were available at that time. Because of this completely new approach, ReiserFS offered supreme performance, especially in environments in which many small files had to be handled. Some other (minor) issues were addressed as well and that made it a very nice file system for data volumes. However, kernel support for ReiserFS has never been great and that has lead to stability issues. In specific environments in which many large files need to be handled, ReiserFS may still be a good choice, but be aware that ReiserFS is not very stable and you will have problems with it sooner or later.

- *JFS*: Journaled File System was developed by IBM as one of the first file systems that offered journaling. The development of this file system has stopped, however, and therefore I don't recommend its use on new servers.

Based on the preceding information, you should now be capable of creating a blueprint for the disk layout that your server is going to use. Table 1-1 provides an overview of what I'm going to install on my server in this chapter. The items in parentheses are recommended sizes when working from a VMware test environment or any other test environment in which available storage is limited.

■**Note** Chapter 4 covers advanced file system management tasks. ReiserFS management is included as well. Normally I wouldn't recommend using ReiserFS anymore, but to make it easier for you to apply the contents of Chapter 4, in the example setup, I'm setting up a ReiserFS file system as well.

Table 1-1. *Blueprint of Server Disk Layout*

Directory	Size	File System	Storage Back End	Storage Device
/boot	100 MB (50 MB)	Ext2	Primary partition	RAID 1
/	20 GB (5 GB)	Ext3	LVM volume	RAID 1
/var	5 GB (1 GB)	XFS	LVM volume	RAID 1
/tmp	1 GB (1 GB)	ReiserFS	LVM volume	RAID 1
/srv	50 GB (1 GB)	XFS	LVM volume	RAID 5
/home	50 GB (1 GB)	XFS	LVM volume	RAID 5

Now that we've done our homework, it's time to start. In the next section you'll read how to actually install this configuration.

Installing Ubuntu Server

One more check to do before you start the actual installation: Ubuntu Server is available in 64- and 32-bit versions. To get the most out of your server hardware, make sure to use a 64-bit version of Ubuntu Server. For instance, 32-bit Ubuntu can't address more than 4 GB of RAM, and even if you use the special PAE (Physical Address Extension) version of the kernel that uses 36 bits instead of the default 32 bits to address memory, you can't go beyond 32 GB of RAM. When using 64 bits, however, you can address exabytes of memory, which is probably enough for the next couple of years. To use a 64-bit version of the operating system, your drivers must be available in 64-bit versions as well. In some cases, that may be a problem. So it's best to do some research and check if drivers for your hardware devices are available in 64-bit versions. If they are, use 64 bits; otherwise use 32 bits.

■**Note** To understand what I'm covering in this book, it doesn't really matter whether you're using the 32-bit or 64-bit Ubuntu server version. Using a different version of the operating system doesn't change much the way in which you will work with Ubuntu Server.

Starting the Installation

This section describes how to perform the first steps of the installation:

1. Boot your server from the installation media and select the installation language that you want to use. For non-US-based installations, don't forget to use the F3 button from the initial installation window to set your local keyboard layout.

2. After you specify your local settings, the installation program shows the available network interface cards that it has found and asks you to select a primary network board, as shown in Figure 1-1. Because NIC teaming, which is needed to add both network cards to one interface, is not supported by the installation program, just select your first network board and press Enter.

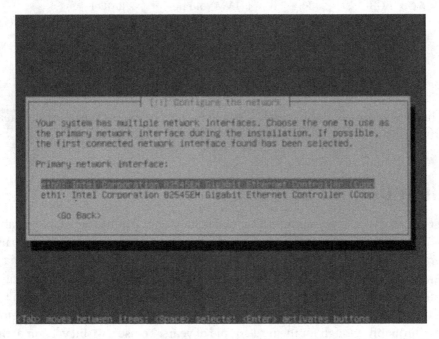

Figure 1-1. *NIC teaming is not supported by the installation program, so just press Enter to configure the first Ethernet interface using DHCP.*

3. Enter a name for your server. The default name Ubuntu is probably not sufficient, so make sure to specify something unique.

4. Select your time zone and wait for the Partition Disks interface to appear.

Creating a Software-Based RAID Solution

This section describes how to set up Ubuntu Server using software RAID to provide for maximal redundancy. Using software RAID helps you to get the best performance and redundancy if no hardware-based RAID solution is available.

1. From the Partition Disks screen, select Manual and press Enter. Make sure not to select the Guided option, which is the default, as you can see in Figure 1-2. You next see an overview of all disk devices that the installer has found, as shown in Figure 1-3.

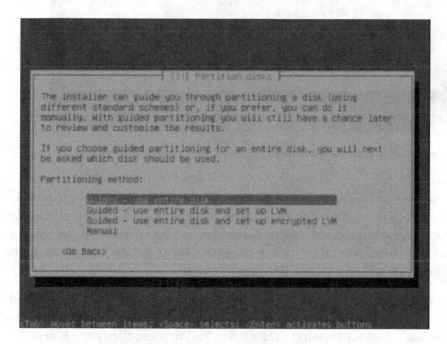

Figure 1-2. *Don't press Enter to accept default values in this screen!*

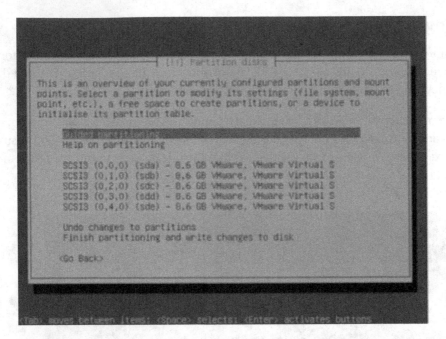

Figure 1-3. *The installer gives an overview of all available disk devices.*

2. From the overview in Figure 1-3, you have to select all disk devices one by one (this means that you have to perform this step five times). If there is nothing on the disks yet, the installer will ask you if it needs to set up a partition table. Select Yes and then press Enter. After you have done this, the result will look similar to the screen shown in Figure 1-4.

3. Select the first FREE SPACE indicator that you see (as shown in Figure 1-4) and press Enter. You'll see the Partition Disks interface shown in Figure 1-5. From this interface, make sure to select Create a New Partition and then press Enter.

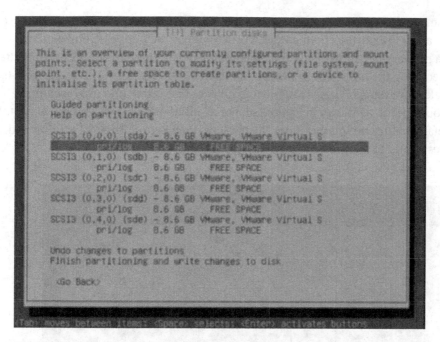

Figure 1-4. *Before proceeding, make sure that you see something similar to this.*

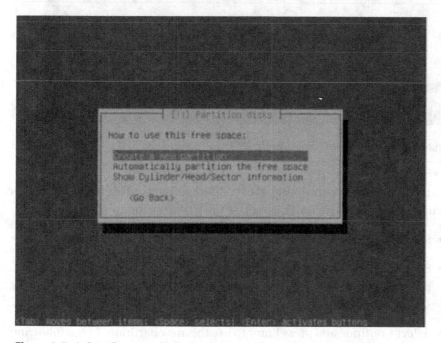

Figure 1-5. *Select Create a New Partition and press Enter to continue.*

4. The installer asks what partition size you want to use. On the first device only, create a 100 MB partition, which you will use later as the boot partition, and make
it a primary partition that is at the beginning of your hard disks. Press Enter after
specifying the partition size, which takes you to the screen shown in Figure 1-6.
Make sure that you specify to use it as an Ext2 file system and use /boot as the
mount point, as shown in Figure 1-6. For all other parameters, you can accept the
default values on this partition. Next, select Done Setting Up the Partition and
press Enter to proceed.

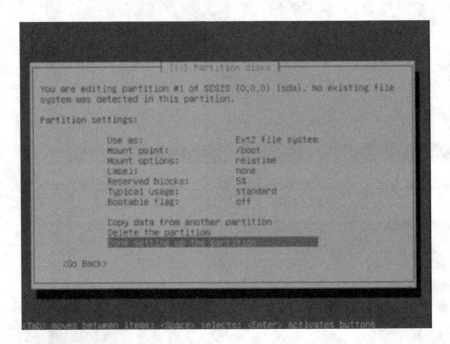

Figure 1-6. *Make a boot partition first.*

5. Next, you must set up the free space that remains on the first hard disk as space to
be used by the software RAID. To set up the partition, follow these steps:

- Select the next FREE SPACE indicator and press Enter to proceed.

- Select Create a New Partition and accept the partition size that the installation
program suggests. Write this size down, because you'll need to use exactly the
same size on the second hard disk.

- Select Continue and press Enter to use this new partition. In the following
screen, select it to be a primary partition.

- In the partition settings window (the screen shown in Figure 1-6), specify that the partition should be used as a physical volume for RAID, as shown in Figure 1-7.

- Select Done Setting Up the Partition.

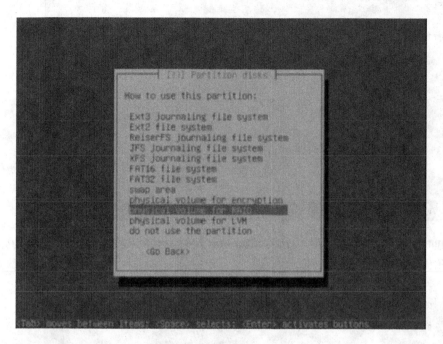

Figure 1-7. *Select Physical Volume for RAID to mark the partition as usable for software RAID.*

6. Repeat the procedure from Step 5 for the free space on all other disk devices. On the second disk, the partition should be the exact same size as the RAID partition on disk 1, and on all other disks, you can use all available disk space. When finished, the Partition Disks screen should look similar to Figure 1-8.

7. Still from within the partition overview, select the option Configure Software RAID (at the top of the screen) and press Enter. This takes you to the screen shown in Figure 1-9. Select Yes and press Enter to write the current partitioning to your hard disks.

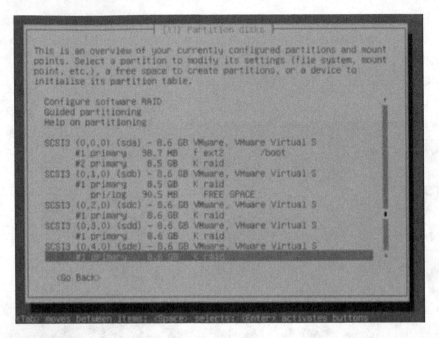

Figure 1-8. *After setting up all partitions that you want to use in your RAID setup, the Partition Disks screen looks like this.*

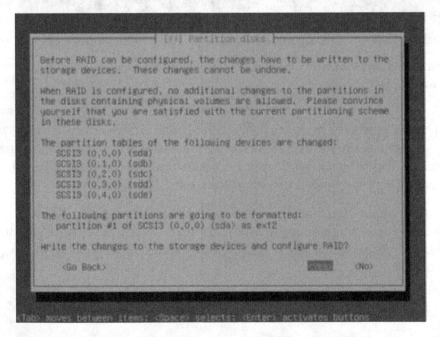

Figure 1-9. *Before creating the RAID sets, you need to write the partitions to disk.*

8. The installer takes you automatically to the Multidisk utility, which helps you to create the RAID device. From there, select Create MD Device and press Enter. Next, select from the three different RAID types that are supported by this utility (see Figure 1-10): RAID 0, RAID 1, and RAID 5. In this procedure, I show you how to create a RAID 1 set and a RAID 5 set, so first select RAID1 and press Enter.

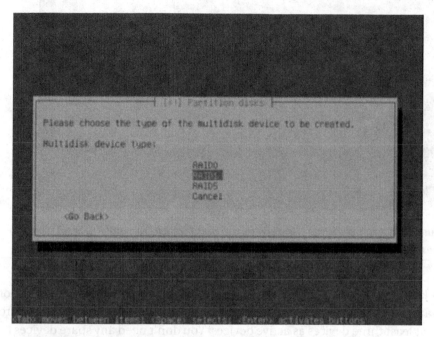

Figure 1-10. *First make the RAID 1 array for your operating system files.*

9. Specify the number of active devices that you want to use. For a RAID 1 array, this would typically be two devices. This value is added by default, so select Continue and press Enter to proceed.

10. Indicate how many spare devices you want to use. In RAID 1, there are no spare devices, so accept the value of 0, which is entered by default, select Continue, and press Enter.

11. To complete the RAID setup, you need to add partitions that you've marked as RAID partitions to the RAID set. Make sure to select /dev/sda2 and /dev/sdb1 (see Figure 1-11) and then select Continue and press Enter.

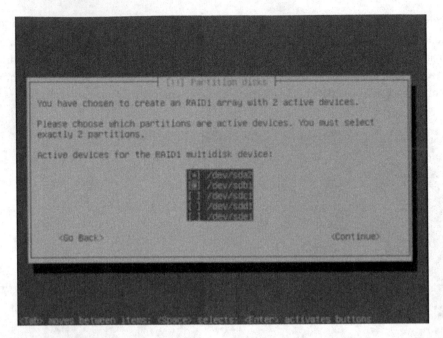

Figure 1-11. *After selecting the devices you want to add to your RAID set, select Continue and press Enter.*

12. Back in the main RAID configuration menu, select Create MD Device once more to create the RAID 5 array. Now add all remaining devices to this array. Make sure to use at least three devices as active devices. You don't need any spare devices here. When you're back in the main RAID menu, select Finish and press Enter to write the RAID configuration to your server's hard drive.

Creating LVM Logical Volumes on Top of a Software RAID Device

You now have set up two software RAID devices. These devices can be used just as you would use a normal hard disk as a storage device. On a hard disk, you can set up traditional partitions, as well as LVM logical volumes. For maximal flexibility, it is a good idea to use LVM logical volumes. In this section you'll learn how to set them up on top of the software RAID devices you've just created. This procedure also works if you are using hardware RAID; just use the hardware RAID device names instead of the md device names used in this procedure.

1. You now automatically return to the main menu, in which you'll see the two RAID devices that you've just created. Select the size specification that you see directly under the RAID 0 device (see Figure 1-12) and press Enter to start putting some logical volumes on the device. This brings you to the Partition Disks interface that you've seen a couple of times before.

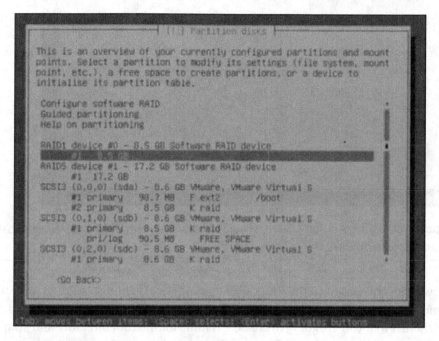

Figure 1-12. *Select the size specification under the name of the RAID device and press Enter.*

2. From the Partition Disks interface, change the status of the partition from Do Not Use to Use As. Press Enter, select Physical Volume for LVM, and press Enter again. Next, back in the Partition Disks interface, select Done Setting Up the Partition and press Enter. In the Partition Disks interface, the first RAID device now is marked as an LVM volume. Repeat Steps 1 and 2 from this procedure to make the other RAID device usable as an LVM device as well. After doing this successfully, the Partition Disks interface should look similar to Figure 1-13.

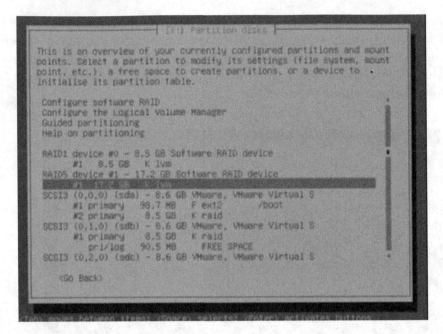

Figure 1-13. *Before you start to create logical volumes, your Partition Disks interface should look similar to this.*

3. Now that you've marked the RAID devices as physical volumes in the LVM setup, which makes them usable for LVM, it's time to put some LVM logical volumes on them. First, you are going to create a volume for the root directory and swap space and put that on the RAID 1 array. Next, you'll create the /var, /home, and /tmp volumes on the RAID 5 array. Start by selecting the option Configure the Logical Volume Manager (press Enter). In the overview, you should see that there currently are two physical volumes available. To create the highest possible redundancy, you'll create a volume group on each of them. To do this, from the interface that you see in Figure 1-14, select Create Volume Group and press Enter.

4. Next, you need to provide a name for the volume group you want to create. In this scenario, because you want a volume group that is clearly divided between two physical storage devices, I suggest using the names of these devices for the volume group name. So make a volume group with the name RAID1 on the RAID 1 array, and next create a volume group with the name RAID5 on the RAID 5 array. After creating the volume group, select the storage device on which you want to create it. As you can see in Figure 1-15, the names of these storage devices will be /dev/md0 for the first RAID device and /dev/md1 for the second RAID device. Make sure that you create both volume groups now. After selecting the storage device, select Continue and press Enter.

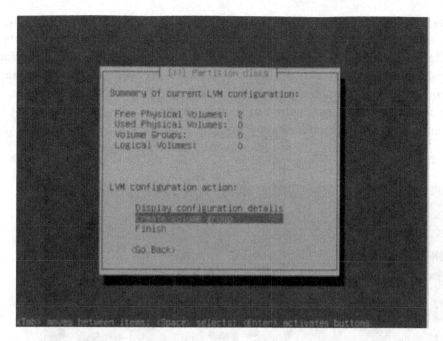

Figure 1-14. *Select Create Volume Group and press Enter to start defining a volume group.*

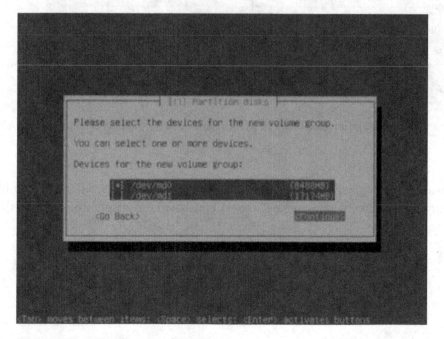

Figure 1-15. *Select the storage device that you want to use, select Continue, and press Enter.*

5. You next see a summary of the current LVM configuration that shows that you now have two volume groups. From here, select Create Logical Volume and press Enter. This gives you a list of all existing volume groups. Select the volume group in which you want to create the logical volume and press Enter. Next, enter the name of the logical volume you want to create and proceed to the next step. In the following screen (see Figure 1-16), enter the size of the logical volume that you want to create. It's a good idea never to use all available disk space; this gives you the flexibility to resize easily at a later stage. Select Continue and press Enter.

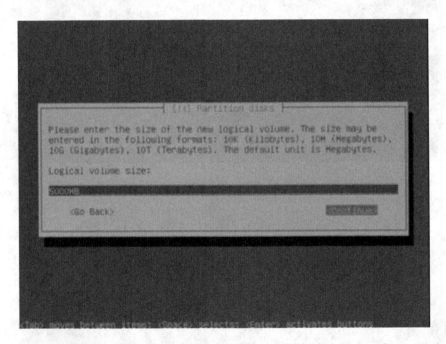

Figure 1-16. *It's a good idea never to use all available disk space when creating the logical volumes.*

6. Create all the logical volumes that you want to use, and then, from the LVM summary screen, shown in Figure 1-17, select Finish and press Enter to complete this procedure.

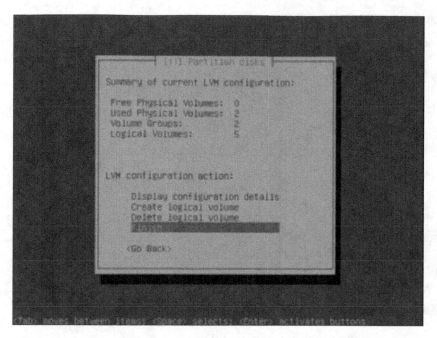

Figure 1-17. *After creating all logical volumes, select Finish and press Enter to complete this part of the procedure.*

7. At this stage you have created the RAID devices, put some logical volume groups on top of them, and created the logical volumes that you want to use in the volume groups. Now it's time for the final step: you need to put some file systems in the volume groups. To do this, select the logical volumes one by one. From the Partition Disks interface, which should now look similar to that shown in Figure 1-18, you can easily recognize by their names the logical volumes that you've created. Select the line that marks the free space that is available on the logical volumes and press Enter.

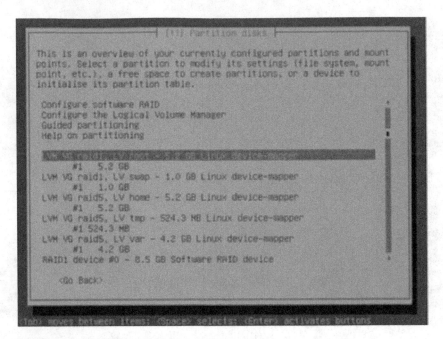

Figure 1-18. *Select the logical volumes one by one to put a file system on them.*

8. You are now back in the overview screen of the Partition Disks interface. Select the line labeled Use As and select the file system that you want to use on this logical volume. After selecting the file system, select the directory on which you want to mount this volume. Next, select Done Setting Up the Partition and press Enter. Repeat this procedure for all the logical volumes that you have created. After doing this for all your volumes, select Finish Partitioning and Write Changes to Disk and press Enter. This writes the disk layout that you have created and brings you to the next step of the procedure.

Completing the Installation

Now that you've set up the disk layout for your server, it's time to complete the installation. This includes creating a user account, specifying where to authenticate, and selecting one or more of the predefined installation patterns for your server. In the following procedure, you'll learn what's involved.

1. As you probably already know, on Ubuntu server you won't work as root by default. Therefore, you are asked to enter the name of a new user that will be created now. Your first name might not be a bad idea. Make sure this user has a password as well.

2. If you need a proxy server to access the outside world, you can now enter the data that you need to access this proxy server. You'll do this as a URL. This can be a basic URL, but you can also use a URL that includes a username and password. For instance, if a special user account server1 with the password p@ssw0rd needs to authenticate on the proxy with the name squid that is reachable on port 3120, the line you enter looks as follows: http://server1:p@ssw0rd@squid:3120. If no proxy information is needed, you can just skip this field and leave it empty.

3. Select one or more of the installation patterns available for your server. This is not an important option, because later you can install all software packages that are offered here. Now the software is copied to your server. Wait until this is completed.

4. You'll now see a message that installation is complete (see Figure 1-19). Press Enter now to boot into your new system.

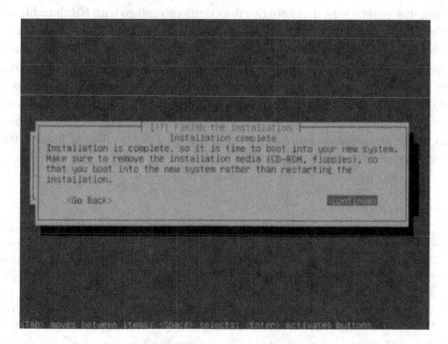

Figure 1-19. *When the installation is completed, press Enter to start the installed system.*

Post-Installation Tasks

Now you have a functional instance of Ubuntu Server, but you are not done yet. In a typical data-center installation, a server has several network cards, and to get the best out of these network cards, you probably want to set up NIC bonding. You can configure NIC bonding in two ways: for maximal redundancy or for maximal performance. Your enterprise server might connect to a SAN as well. This adds another requirement: setting up multipathing. The next two subsections describe how to accomplish these tasks.

Setting Up NIC Bonding

Even the most basic network servers have at least two network cards. Some models even have four or more network cards installed. This not only is useful if you want to connect your server to several networks at the same time, but also enables you to use these multiple network cards to increase performance or redundancy. The technique used for this is referred to as NIC bonding. Using NIC bonding, you'll get a new network device that typically has the name bond0. Two of the physical network cards are assigned to this device. When setting up NIC bonding, you don't work with eth0 and eth1 anymore; you'll work with bond0 instead. That means that the IP address is assigned to bond0 as well.

Speaking in a general way, there are two directions you can go with NIC bonding. When setting it up for redundancy, one of the network cards will be active, whereas the other one is on standby and takes over only if the active network card fails. This enables fault tolerance on the network connection for your server. In the high-performance setup, the two network cards in the bonding configuration work together to handle the work load. That means that you could create a 2 gigabit connection by bundling two 1-GB network cards. In the following procedure you'll learn how to set up NIC bonding on Ubuntu Server. But before starting, take a look at the list in Table 1-2 of the different options that you can use when setting up NIC bonding.

Table 1-2. *NIC Bonding Options*

Option	Use
mode=0	This mode enables round robin. That means that packets are transmitted in a sequential way between the network cards assigned to the bonding interface. Using this option, you'll get load balancing and redundancy at the same time.
mode=1	Using this mode, one of the network cards is active and the other one is passive. This enables fault tolerance, but doesn't do anything for performance.
mode=2	This mode divides the work load between associated devices, but tries to keep a network connection on the same device as long as possible. This offers redundancy and load balancing at the same time, but with better performance than mode=0. Because this mode is also more complicated, it is more prone to errors.

Option	Use
mode=3	Use this mode to transmit everything on all slave devices. This mode provides fault tolerance with the shortest recovery times; a network card may fail without service interruption.
mode=4	This mode uses IEEE 802.3ad Dynamic Link aggregation. This bundles the network cards in the bond device as one, but does require additional configuration on the network switch.
mode=5	This mode distributes connections to the network cards in the bond device, thus enabling load balancing. One of the major advantages to using this mode is that no additional configuration is needed on the switch.

The following procedure explains how to set up NIC bonding:

1. Create a module alias in /etc/modprobe.d/aliases, as shown in Listing 1-1. This makes sure that the right kernel module is loaded when setting up NIC bonding. Make sure that the names of the kernel devices for eth0 and eth1 in Listing 1-1 are replaced by the real module names needed for your network cards. Because the bonding is between eth0 and eth1 only, you don't need to do anything on eth2 here.

Listing 1-1. *Use /etc/modprobe.d/aliases to Load the Correct Kernel Modules*

```
# Append to the bottom of this file:
alias bond0 bonding
alias eth0 e100
alias eth1 e100
alias eth2 e100
options bonding mode=0 miimon=100
```

2. In the /etc/modprobe/arch directory, you'll find a file that contains settings for your specific kernel architecture (see Listing 1-2). For instance, if you are using an i386 kernel, the name of this file is i386. Edit this file to make sure the right options are loaded for the bonding device.

Listing 1-2. *Edit the /etc/modprobe.d/arch/i386 File to Contain the Correct Bonding Options*

```
# Append to the bottom of this file:
alias bond0 bonding
options bonding mode=0 miimon=100 downdelay=20
```

3. As a final step, you need to modify the file that contains the configuration of your network card to create the bond0 device and its properties. The example in Listing 1-3 shows what the content of this file looks like. Make sure to change server-specific settings, such as the MAC address used in this example.

Listing 1-3. *Change the /etc/network/interfaces File to Create the bond0 Device*

```
# This file describes the network interfaces available on your system
# and how to activate them. For more information, see interfaces(5).
# The loopback network interface
auto lo
iface lo inet loopback
# The primary network interface
#auto eth0
#iface eth0 inet static
#    address 192.168.0.120
#    netmask 255.255.255.0
#    network 192.168.0.0
#    broadcast 192.168.0.255
#    gateway 192.168.0.1
auto bond0
iface bond0 inet static
    address 192.168.0.120
    netmask 255.255.255.0
    network 192.168.0.0
    broadcast 192.168.0.255
    gateway 192.168.0.1
    hwaddress ether 00:03:B3:48:50:2C
    post-up ifenslave bond0 eth0 eth1
```

This completes all required steps to set up the bond device. To verify that it comes up when your server starts, reboot your server now.

Setting Up Multipathing

A server in a data center is often connected to a SAN. To avoid having a single point of failure, your server probably has two HBAs that are configured to two storage networks that connect to the same SAN filer (see Figure 1-20).

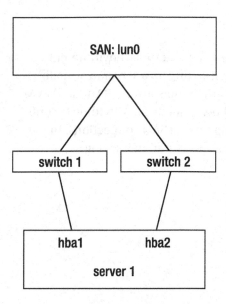

Figure 1-20. *Schematic overview of the way a server is connected to the SAN*

This redundancy in the SAN connections would normally produce an undesirable result. Let's say your server has a redundant connection to one LUN on the SAN. For the moment, consider the SAN to be a black box, and a LUN to be some storage that is allocated in a logical group on the SAN, like you would use partitions on hard drives. See Chapter 7 for information on how to set up a SAN yourself. The server would see this LUN via both the first and second HBAs. Because the server normally has no way of determining that it sees the same device on the SAN twice, it would offer you two new devices—for instance, /dev/sdb coming via the first HBA, and /dev/sdc coming via the second HBA. As you can imagine, this is not good.

To prevent your server from getting two devices, you should use multipathing. Initializing this is not too difficult; Ubuntu Server has a multipath daemon that you can load to take care of this problem. Installing it is a really simple two-step procedure:

1. Use apt-get install multipath-tools to install the multipath software.

2. Enter the command /etc/init.d/multipathd to start the multipath process, and make sure that it automatically restarts when you restart your server.

The result of these two steps is that you'll get a new storage device. Use fdisk -l or lsscsi to find out what the name of this device is. This storage device refers to your SAN. When setting up partitions on the SAN, make sure to use this storage device, and not the /dev/sdb and /dev/sdc devices that your server also still gives you.

Summary

In this chapter you have learned how to set up a server in an enterprise environment. As you have seen, this is quite a different approach from setting up a server in a small business or home environment. You have learned how to set up software RAID, and LVM logical volumes on top of that. You have also learned how to set up NIC bonding for optimized network card performance, and multipath for optimized SAN connections. In the next chapter you'll learn how to set up Ubuntu Server for workstation imaging.

■ ■ ■

## CHAPTER 2

Using Ubuntu Server for System Imaging
Clonezilla on Ubuntu Server

In the first chapter of this book, you read how to perform an enterprise network installation of Ubuntu Server. The topic of this chapter is somewhat related to installation of Ubuntu Server. In this chapter you'll learn how to set up a Clonezilla imaging server. There may be several reasons why you would want to set up such a server. The most important of them is that working with workstation images reduces help desk expenses. If after a minimal period of troubleshooting it turns out that repairing a workstation is going to take too long, it's much faster just to restore the image of that workstation. Of course, this assumes that all work-related files will be written to some other server first. In this chapter you'll learn how to set up Clonezilla for imaging.

Setting Up a Clonezilla Imaging Server

The Clonezilla imaging server is currently the most popular open source imaging solution. It has two versions, a stand-alone version and a server version. Whereas the stand-alone version does well to make and restore images of single machines, you'll need the server version if you need to make images of multiple systems. In its current version, up to 40 workstations can be imaged simultaneously using a method that uses broadcast or multicast to ensure optimal use of network bandwidth.

Before installing the required software, make sure that your environment is set up for imaging. Basically, it comes down to two elements:

- A fast dedicated network for imaging (you do absolutely want Gigabit or better). This means that you need a second network card installed on your server and a dedicated Ethernet network connected to that network card.

- Workstations that can boot from the network card (PXE boot). All modern network cards support PXE boot, so that shouldn't be a problem. Just make sure that you enable network boot in the BIOS of your workstation.

I'll assume that you have both elements. If not, save yourself a great deal of hassle and make sure that these are in place before you start.

Setting Up Diskless Remote Boot in Linux

To use Clonezilla in a server environment, you need to set up diskless remote boot first. The solution for that is Diskless Remote Boot in Linux (DRBL); you can download it from http://drbl.sourceforge.net/one4all. Before setting up DRBL, you must set up the network interface card. Assuming that you've just installed on your Ubuntu 8.04 server a second network card for use with DRBL and the network card hasn't been set up yet, follow this procedure to set up the second network card:

1. Using root permissions, open the file /etc/network/interfaces.

2. To add a second network card that is meant to be used for Clonezilla only, add the following information to the file. Of course, you are free to use any IP information that you want to use.

   ```
   auto eth1
   iface eth1 inet static
           address 10.0.0.10
           netmask 255.255.255.0
           network 10.0.0.0
           broadcast 10.0.0.255
   ```

3. Restart the network to activate the new configuration. Don't forget to make sure that your new network card (you should see it as eth1) really is available.

Installing the DRBL Software

Now that the network is prepared, you can install the DRBL software. It is a good idea to use Ubuntu's secure apt to do this, so you first need to download the DRBL GPG key and install it. Use the following two commands to do that:

```
wget http://drbl.nchc.org.tw/GPG-KEY-DRBL
apt-key add GPG-KEY-DRBL
```

Next, you need to change the /etc/apt/sources.list file to add the new installation sources that allow you to add the DRBL software and keep it up to date. Make sure to add the following two lines to the sources.list file:

```
deb http://free.nchc.org.tw/ubuntu hardy main restricted universe multiverse
deb http://free.nchc.org.tw/drbl-core drbl stable
```

Next, execute the following commands to install the software:

```
apt-get update
apt-get install drbl
```

Depending on the speed of your Internet connection, this may take a while. After this command has finished execution, all required software is downloaded but nothing is installed yet.

When you run the apt-get install drbl command, the installation program asks the following questions, the recommend answers to which are provided:

1. Do you want to install some network boot images for different Linux distributions? Doing so would download more than 100 MB from the Internet to allow you to perform an easy installation of workstations. Normally, you don't need to do this, so press Enter to accept the default value No and proceed.

2. Do you want serial console output for typical clients? Unless you know you do need it, choose the default option, which is No.

3. What kind of kernel do you want to use on the clients to do imaging? Typically, you would choose option 1, which offers i586 and better. Option 0 is for old, pre-Pentium clients only, and option 2 is only for if your CPU is the same on the DRBL server and clients. This would typically not be the case, so choose 1 here and proceed.

4. Do you want to upgrade your operating system? Assuming you don't need to do that at this point, press Enter to accept the default value of No. Go have a cup of coffee now, because several megabytes of files need to be downloaded at this stage.

Configuring the DRBL Software

After the download is finished, you can start the configuration. I'll assume that your DRBL server has two network interfaces (see Figure 2-1): eth0, which is used for normal Internet and user traffic, and eth1, which is used for DRBL. eth1 is configured with the IP address 10.0.0.10 in this example; of course, you are free to use any other address range you like. Do make sure, however, that you are using a 24-bit subnet mask, because otherwise the broadcast/multicast performance will be very bad.

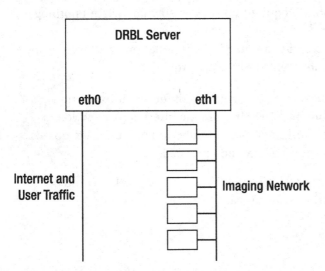

Figure 2-1. *Schematic overview of the imaging network*

Now to configure DRBL, use the /opt/drbl/sbin/drblpush -i command. This will set up your server. Setting up your server this way is easy, because the program will detect almost all settings automatically.

The first couple of questions ask you about the DNS configuration you want to use. Pay attention when you're asked which network card is used for your Internet connection; specify the correct card here, or else you'll have DRBL traffic on that card. After you select the Internet interface, the DRBL interface is selected automatically.

Next, you can populate the database of your DRBL server with the MAC addresses of the clients. How does this work? Press Y to tell DRBL that it should start collecting MAC addresses now.

Finally, start up all the client computers one by one and make sure they boot from their network card. As indicated in the menu, press 1 to find out if all the clients have been found. Once you are confident that all clients have been detected, press 2 to finish collecting MAC addresses of connected clients and quit. The advantage of doing this is that you can bind particular configurations to particular workstations. You are not required to do this, though. Without the fixed MAC address to IP address connection, DRBL also works well. And after all, you have more flexibility if you don't have to create fixed IP address to MAC address mappings first.

■**Note** You also can use DRBL to boot workstations with a Ubuntu image. The software even allows you to store private configuration environments on the server for each of these workstations. If you want to go this way, it is a very good idea to make a mapping between IP addresses and MAC addresses of the workstations. If you just want to do imaging, there is no reason to create this mapping.

Setting Up the DHCP Server

In the next step (see Listing 2-1), the DRBL program asks you whether you want the DHCP server, which is configured automatically, to hand out the same IP address to clients at all times. This is useful if you want the same client to work with the same configuration at all times. If this is the case, press Y; otherwise, press Enter to continue. In case you do want the clients to work with the same IP addresses at all times, their MAC addresses must be stored in a configuration file. The DRBL setup program creates this file automatically for you. Just press Enter to accept the default name for this file.

Listing 2-1. *The DRBL Program Sets Up a DHCP Server Automatically*

```
Do you want to let the DHCP service in DRBL server offer same IP address to the
client every time when client boots (If you want this function, you have to
collect the MAC addresses of clients, and save them in file(s) (as in the
previous procedure)). This is for the clients connected to DRBL server's
ethernet network interface eth1 ?
[y/N]
```

Next, you must specify the IP address that the DHCP server will hand out for the first client. You do this by specifying the last byte only (see Listing 2-2). So, for example, if you are on the network 10.0.0.0/24 and you want the first client to have the IP address 10.0.0.101, just enter 101 here. A DHCP range will then be configured automatically. Press Y to accept this range. You will see an overview of the network configuration of your DRBL server. Happy with it? Then press Enter to continue.

Listing 2-2. *Specify How the DHCP Range to Be Used Must Be Configured*

```
*******************************************************
Do you want to let the DHCP service in DRBL server offer same IP address to the
client every time when client boots (If you want this function, you have to collect
the MAC addresses of clients, and save them in file(s) (as in the previous
procedure)). This is for the clients connected to DRBL server's ethernet network
interface eth1 ?
[y/N] n
*******************************************************
OK! Let's continue, we will set the IP address of clients by "first boot gets IP
first" instead of fixed one!
*******************************************************
What is the initial number do you want to use in the last set of digits in the IP
(i.e. the initial value of d in the IP address a.b.c.d) for DRBL clients connected
to this ethernet port eth1.
[1]
```

Once the DHCP server has been fully configured, the configuration program tells you what the DRBL network should currently look like (see Listing 2-3). Check that this is what you expected, and if it is, proceed with the configuration.

Listing 2-3. *The DRBL Setup Program Shows What It Is Going to Configure*

```
The Layout for your DRBL environment:
*****************************************************
         NIC    NIC IP                 Clients
+-----------------------------+
|        DRBL SERVER          |
|                             |
|   +-- [eth0] 192.168.1.60 +- to WAN
|                             |
|   +-- [eth1] 10.0.0.111 +- to clients group 1 [ 12 clients, their IP
|                             |                  from 10.0.0.50 - 10.0.0.61]
+-----------------------------+
*****************************************************
Total clients: 12
*****************************************************
Press Enter to continue...
```

Next you need to specify which DRBL mode you want to use. There are two different scenarios here. First, you can use DRBL to provide each client with a boot image that you'll use to give them a useable operating system. Do this at all times, because it gives you a complete working environment available on the client, and that may be useful if you need to set additional parameters from the client's PXE-delivered operating system.

During the next step, specify that you want to use full Clonezilla mode. This provides everything a client needs to boot and do its work in the Clonezilla environment, which enables you to do easy workstation imaging.

Completing Clonezilla Configuration

Now you are getting to the next step of the configuration. You need to assign a directory that can be used by Clonezilla. I suggest using a rather large storage device, formatting it with XFS, and mounting it on a directory; /clonezilla might be suitable. Do not use ReiserFS for this file system, because it isn't very stable. Also make sure that your /etc/fstab file is modified to activate this directory the next time your server boots. To configure this, follow these steps:

1. Assuming that you have a dedicated hard disk with an existing partition on it, which is reachable via the device /dev/sdb1, use mkfs.xfs /dev/sdb1 to format the device with the XFS file system.

2. Use mkdir /clonezilla to create the Clonezilla directory.

3. Make sure your /etc/fstab includes the following line to mount the Clonezilla directory automatically:

```
/dev/sdb1       /clonezilla      xfs        defauls    0   0
```

After you specify which file system to use, the configuration program asks you if you want to set a password as well. If you use a password, only authenticated clients can use Clonezilla services. Do what fits your situation best here.

Now the installer asks if you want to define a boot prompt for clients. It may be a good idea to do so, so that your clients have the option to specify what they want to do when booting with an image they've obtained from the DRBL server. A default timeout of 7 seconds is generated for this boot prompt. If this is not enough time, change it in the next step. Following that, just press Enter to specify that you don't want to see a graphical boot menu on the client computers.

Next the configuration program asks if you want to use the DRBL server as a NAT server. If you just want to use Clonezilla for cloning, select No here. For the next three questions, press Enter to select the default options. This will start the Clonezilla DHCP server, and all related services. At this stage, you can use PXE boot on the clients to boot them into the Clonezilla server.

Configuring the Clients for Cloning

Now that you've set up a basic Clonezilla environment, you are going to use the drbl-client-switch command to add the appropriate Clonezilla options to the boot menu, thus enabling end users to specify what they want to do on their client workstations. You can configure the environment in different ways—for fully automatic setup, or in such a way that the administrator starts the cloning process manually after using PXE boot on the client. First you'll learn how to use the drbl-client-switch command to set up the server, and then you'll learn how to start cloning on the clients.

Setting Up the Server for Cloning

The following procedure, typically a one-time-only procedure, allows you to set up the Clonezilla server for cloning:

1. On the server (either by SSH or directly), start the `/opt/drbl/sbin/drbl-client-switch` command to access the screen shown in Figure 2-2.

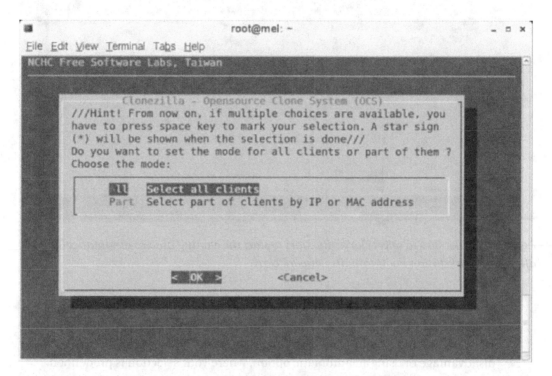

Figure 2-2. *You can set up imaging for all nodes, or for a limited selection of nodes only.*

2. Specify in what mode your client will be starting automatically. Assuming that you'll be using PXE boot only when you want to clone the client, select the option `clonezilla-start`, as shown in Figure 2-3. This automatically starts the cloning engine.

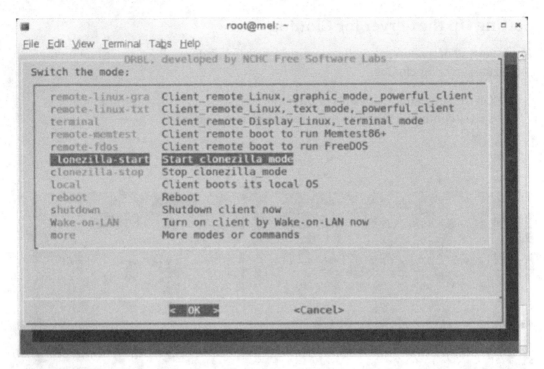

Figure 2-3. *Make sure to select clonezilla-start to start the cloning process automatically after your workstation boots from its network card.*

3. You can now select an option to start a clone or restore process automatically (see Figure 2-4). After you choose one of these automatic options, Clonezilla will use multicast mode, thus allowing you to clone at the highest possible speed. The disadvantage of using an automatic option, where your selection is predefined, is that you'll always need to run the `drbl-client-switch` command before every major job. The alternative is to use the option `select-in-client`, which uses unicast but gives more flexibility from within the client. Because it is more flexible, I'll use this option.

4. Specify what to offer as the default client boot option. Make sure to select the option `-y1`, which halts to show you the boot menu. In the next and last screen, select `-p reboot`, which will reboot the client machine automatically after it has been cloned.

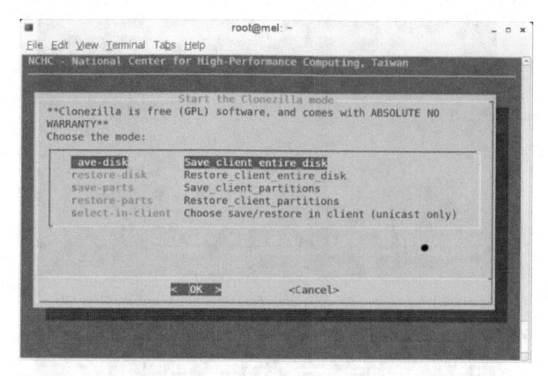

Figure 2-4. *For optimal performance, use one of the first four options; for optimal flexibility, use the select-in-client option.*

Cloning the Client

Now that everything is set up, you are ready to start cloning your client:

1. Make sure the workstation that you want to boot boots from its network card. You'll see the DRBL boot menu, with the Clonezilla option selected by default (see Figure 2-5). Make sure your workstation boots this option.

2. From the Clonezilla menu, you can choose from two different options, as shown in Figure 2-6. Use the option device-image to write an image file to the Clonezilla server. The device-device option is useful only if you want to clone the contents of a hard drive to an external storage device. This doesn't write an image file; it just clones your hard drive to the selected storage device. Any storage device can be used for this purpose, as long as it is at least as big as the hard drive you want to clone.

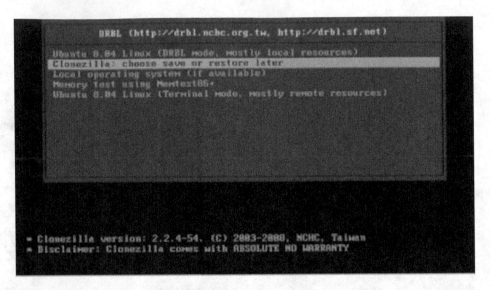

Figure 2-5. *When booting the workstation from the network card, the Clonezilla option automatically pops up.*

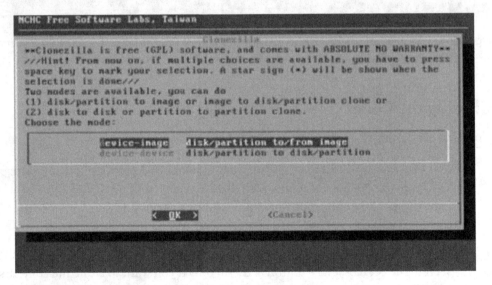

Figure 2-6. *Use the device-image option to write the cloned disk to an image file on the Clonezilla server.*

3. Specify what action you want to take (see Figure 2-7). The most important options are savedisk, which clones the entire disk to the image file, and restoredisk, which restores the client from an image file. The other two options allow you to save and restore individual partitions only.

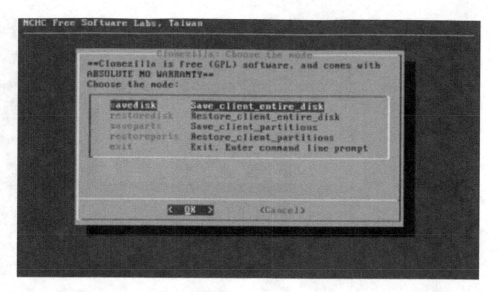

Figure 2-7. *Select savedisk to write the contents of the entire hard drive to an image file.*

4. Specify what priority should be used. The default priority fits well; it will try the ntfsclone program, which obviously is for NTFS file systems only; if you're not using NTFS, it tries partimage, and if that also doesn't work, it will use the (very slow) dd command to clone the disk. Count on that to take a couple of hours, though, because dd is rather inefficient.

5. Make sure that the option is selected that forces the client to wait before cloning. This option makes sure that nothing will happen by accident, and as you can imagine, that's rather important.

6. In the following screen, you need to specify what command you want to use to compress the cloned image. The default value, which uses gzip, will do rather well here. Following that, you need to give a name to save the image (see Figure 2-8). This is very important, because when restoring the original state of your hard drive, this image name will be the only thing that you've got. So, make sure that all your machines have a unique name, and use that machine name (appended by the date on which you've created the image if you'd like) to store the image.

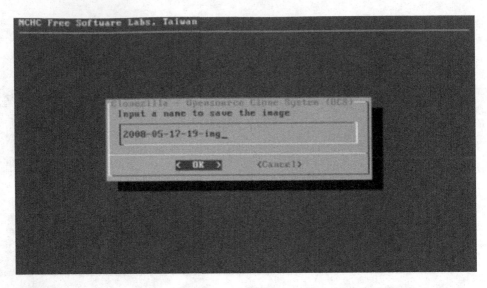

Figure 2-8. *Make sure to use something more descriptive than the default name for your image.*

7. Select the hard disk(s) that you want to clone (see Figure 2-9). Typically only one disk will be offered, but if the machine you're cloning has more than one hard drive, you can clone all of them with Clonezilla.

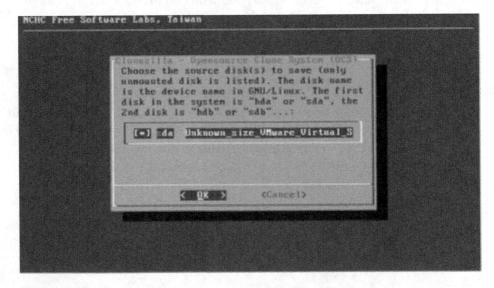

Figure 2-9. *Select all disks that you want to include in your image.*

That's all. The cloning process will start now. Be patient, because it can take some time to complete.

Summary

In this chapter you've learned how to use Ubuntu Server as a system imaging solution. This is a very useful solution that allows you to recover from problems on workstations fast and easily. In the next chapter you'll learn all about performance monitoring on Ubuntu Server.

CHAPTER 3

■ ■ ■

Performance Monitoring
Finding Performance Problems on Ubuntu Server

Running a server is one thing. Running a server that works well is something else. On a server whose default settings haven't been changed since installation, things may just go terribly wrong from a performance perspective. Finding a performance problem on a Linux server is not that easy. You need to know what your computer is doing and how to interpret performance monitoring data. In this chapter you'll learn how to do just that.

To give you a head start, you'll have a look at top first. Though almost everyone already knows how to use the top utility, few know how to really interpret the data that top provides. The top utility is a very good starting place when analyzing performance on your server. It gives you a good indication of what component is causing performance problems in your server. After looking at top, we'll consider some advanced utilities that help to identify performance problems on particular devices. Specifically, we'll look at performance monitoring on the CPU, memory, storage, and network.

Interpreting What Your Computer Is Doing: top

Before you start to look at the details produced by performance monitoring, you should have a general overview of the current state of your server. The top utility is an excellent tool to help you with that. As an example for discussion, let's start by looking at a server that is restoring a workstation from an image file, using the Clonezilla imaging solution. The top output in Listing 3-1 shows how busy the server is that is doing the restoration.

Listing 3-1. *Analyzing top on a Somewhat Busy Server*

```
top - 09:19:12 up 21 min,  3 users,  load average: 0.55, 0.21, 0.13
Tasks: 140 total,   1 running, 139 sleeping,   0 stopped,   0 zombie
Cpu(s):  0.0%us,  1.0%sy,  0.0%ni, 90.1%id,  3.9%wa,  0.0%hi,  5.0%si,  0.0%st
Mem:   4083276k total,   989152k used,  3094124k free,    15712k buffers
Swap:  2097144k total,        0k used,  2097144k free,   862884k cached

  PID USER      PR  NI  VIRT  RES  SHR S %CPU %MEM    TIME+  COMMAND
 5350 root      20   0     0    0    0 S    0  0.0  0:00.05 nfsd
 5356 root      20   0     0    0    0 S    0  0.0  0:00.07 nfsd
 5359 root      20   0     0    0    0 S    0  0.0  0:00.08 nfsd
    1 root      20   0  1804  760  548 S    0  0.0  0:01.19 init
    2 root      15  -5     0    0    0 S    0  0.0  0:00.00 kthreadd
    3 root      RT  -5     0    0    0 S    0  0.0  0:00.00 migration/0
    4 root      15  -5     0    0    0 S    0  0.0  0:00.00 ksoftirqd/0
    5 root      RT  -5     0    0    0 S    0  0.0  0:00.00 watchdog/0
    6 root      RT  -5     0    0    0 S    0  0.0  0:00.00 migration/1
    7 root      15  -5     0    0    0 S    0  0.0  0:00.00 ksoftirqd/1
    8 root      RT  -5     0    0    0 S    0  0.0  0:00.00 watchdog/1
    9 root      15  -5     0    0    0 S    0  0.0  0:00.00 events/0
   10 root      15  -5     0    0    0 S    0  0.0  0:00.00 events/1
   11 root      15  -5     0    0    0 S    0  0.0  0:00.00 khelper
   46 root      15  -5     0    0    0 S    0  0.0  0:00.00 kblockd/0
   47 root      15  -5     0    0    0 S    0  0.0  0:00.00 kblockd/1
   50 root      15  -5     0    0    0 S    0  0.0  0:00.00 kacpid
```

CPU Monitoring with top

When analyzing performance, you start at the first line of the top output. The load average parameters are of particular interest. There are three of them, indicating the load average for the last 1 minute, the last 5 minutes, and the last 15 minutes. The anchor value is 1.00. You will see 1.00 on a one-CPU system any time that all CPU cycles are fully utilized but no processes are waiting in the queue. 1.00 is the anchor value for each CPU core in your system. So, for example, on a dual-CPU, quad-core system, the anchor value would be 8.00.

■**Note** The load average is for your system, not for your CPU. It is perfectly possible to have a load average far above 1.00 even while your CPU is doing next to nothing.

Having a system that works exactly at the anchor value may be good, but it isn't the best solution in all cases. You need to understand more about the nature of a typical workload before you can determine whether or not a workload of 1.00 is good.

Consider, for example, a task that is running completely on one CPU, without causing overhead in memory or other critical system components. You can force such a task by entering the following line of code at the dash prompt:

```
while true; do true; done
```

This task will completely claim the CPU, thus causing a workload of 1.00. However, because this is a task that doesn't do any I/O, the task does not have waiting times; therefore, for a task like this, 1.00 is considered a heavy workload. You can compare this to a task that is I/O intensive, such as a task in which your complete hard drive is copied to the null device. This task will also easily contribute to a workload that is higher than 1.00, but because there is a lot of waiting for I/O involved, it's not as bad as the while true task from the preceding example line. So, basically, the load average line doesn't give too much useful information. When you see that your server's CPU is quite busy, you should find out why it is that busy. By default, top gives a summary for all CPUs in your server; if you press 1 on your keyboard, top will show a line for each CPU core in your server. All modern servers are multicore, so you should apply this option. It not only gives you information about the multiprocessing environment, but also shows you the performance indicators for individual processors and the processes that use them. Listing 3-2 shows an example in which usage statistics are provided on a dual-core server.

Listing 3-2. *Monitoring Performance on a Dual-Core Server*

```
top - 09:34:14 up 36 min,  3 users,  load average: 0.31, 0.55, 0.42
Tasks: 140 total,   1 running, 139 sleeping,   0 stopped,   0 zombie
Cpu0  :  0.3%us,  0.8%sy,  0.0%ni, 92.8%id,  2.7%wa,  0.0%hi,  3.5%si,  0.0%st
Cpu1  :  0.2%us,  0.7%sy,  0.0%ni, 97.3%id,  1.8%wa,  0.0%hi,  0.0%si,  0.0%st
Mem:   4083276k total,  3937288k used,   145988k free,      672k buffers
Swap:  2097144k total,      156k used,  2096988k free,  3822700k cached

PID USER      PR  NI  VIRT  RES  SHR S %CPU %MEM    TIME+  COMMAND
  1 root      20   0  1804  760  548 S    0  0.0   0:01.19 init
  2 root      15  -5     0    0    0 S    0  0.0   0:00.00 kthreadd
  3 root      RT  -5     0    0    0 S    0  0.0   0:00.00 migration/0
  4 root      15  -5     0    0    0 S    0  0.0   0:00.01 ksoftirqd/0
  5 root      RT  -5     0    0    0 S    0  0.0   0:00.00 watchdog/0
  6 root      RT  -5     0    0    0 S    0  0.0   0:00.00 migration/1
  7 root      15  -5     0    0    0 S    0  0.0   0:00.02 ksoftirqd/1
  8 root      RT  -5     0    0    0 S    0  0.0   0:00.00 watchdog/1
```

```
  9 root    15  -5    0    0    0 S    0   0.0   0:00.02 events/0
 10 root    15  -5    0    0    0 S    0   0.0   0:00.00 events/1
 11 root    15  -5    0    0    0 S    0   0.0   0:00.00 khelper
 46 root    15  -5    0    0    0 S    0   0.0   0:00.00 kblockd/0
 47 root    15  -5    0    0    0 S    0   0.0   0:00.00 kblockd/1
 50 root    15  -5    0    0    0 S    0   0.0   0:00.00 kacpid
 51 root    15  -5    0    0    0 S    0   0.0   0:00.00 kacpi_notify
137 root    15  -5    0    0    0 S    0   0.0   0:00.00 kseriod
```

The output in Listing 3-2 provides information that you can use for CPU performance monitoring, memory monitoring and process monitoring, as described in the following subsections.

CPU Performance Monitoring

When you are trying to determine what your server is doing exactly, the CPU lines (Cpu0 and Cpu1 in Listing 3-2) are important indicators. They enable you to monitor CPU performance, divided into different performance categories. The following list summarizes these categories:

- us: Refers to the workload in user space. Typically, this relates to running processes that don't perform many system calls, such as I/O requests or requests to hardware resources. If you see a high load here, that means your server is heavily used by applications.

- sy: Refers to the work that is done in system space. These are important tasks in which the kernel of your operating system is involved as well. Load average in system space should in general not be too high. It is elevated when running processes that don't perform many system calls (I/O tasks and so on) or when the kernel is handling many IRQs or doing many scheduling tasks.

- ni: Relates to the number of jobs that have been started with an adjusted nice value.

- id: Indicates how busy the idle loop is. This special loop indicates the amount of time that your CPU is doing nothing. Therefore, a high percentage in the idle loop means the CPU is not too busy.

- wa: Refers to the amount of time that your CPU is waiting for I/O. This is an important indicator. If the value is often above 30 percent, that could indicate a problem on the I/O channel that involves storage and network performance. See the sections "Monitoring Storage Performance" and "Monitoring Network Performance" later in this chapter to find out what may be happening.

- hi: Relates to the time the CPU has spent handling hardware interrupts. You will see some utilization here when a device is particularly busy (optical drives do stress this parameter from time to time), but normally you won't ever see it above a few percentage points.

- si: Relates to software interrupts. Typically, these are lower-priority interrupts that are created by the kernel. You will probably never see a high utilization in this field.

- st: Relates to an environment in which virtualization is used. In some virtual environments, the hypervisor (which is responsible for allocating time to virtual machines) can take ("steal," hence "st") CPU time to give it to virtual machines. If this happens, you will see some utilization in the st field. If the utilization here starts getting really high, you should consider offloading virtual machines from your server.

Memory Monitoring with top

The second type of information provided by top, as shown in Listing 3-2, is information about memory and swap usage. The Mem line contains four parameters:

- total: The total amount of physical memory installed in your server.

- used: The amount of memory that is currently in use by devices or processes. See also the information about the buffers and cached parameters (cached is discussed following this list).

- free: The amount of memory that is not in use. On a typical server that is operational for more than a couple of hours, you will always see that this value is rather low.

- buffers: The write cache that your server uses. All data that a server has to write to disk is written to the write cache first. From there, the disk controller takes care of this data when it has time to write it. The advantage of using the write cache is that, from the perspective of the end-user process, the data is written, so the application the user is using does not need to wait anymore. This buffer cache, however, is memory that is used for nonessential purposes, and when an application needs more memory and can't allocate that from the pool of free memory, the write cache can be written to disk (flushed) so that memory that was used by the write cache is available for other purposes. When this parameter is getting really high (several hundreds of megabytes), it may indicate a failing storage subsystem.

In the Swap line you can find one parameter that doesn't relate to swap, cached. This parameter relates to the number of files that are currently stocked in cache. When a user requests a file from the server, the file normally has to be read from the hard disk. Because a hard disk is much slower than RAM, this process causes major delays. For that reason, every time after fetching a file from the server hard drive, the file is stored in cache. This is a read cache and has one purpose only: to speed up reads. When memory that is currently allocated to the read cache is needed for other purposes, the read cache can be freed immediately so that more memory can be added to the pool of available ("free") memory. Your server will typically see a (very) high amount of cached memory, which, especially if your server is used for reads mostly, is considered good, because it will speed up your server. If your server is used for reads mostly and this parameter falls below 40 percent of total available memory, you will most likely see a performance slow-down. Add more RAM if this happens.

Swap and cache are distinctly different. Whereas cache is a part of RAM that is used to speed up disk access, swap is a part of disk space that is used to emulate RAM on a hard disk. For this purpose, Linux typically uses a swap partition, which you created when installing your server. If your server starts using swap, that is bad in most cases, because it is about 1,000 times slower than RAM. Some applications (particularly Oracle apps) always work with swap, and if you are using such an application, usage of swap is not necessarily bad because it improves the performance of the application. In all other cases, you should start worrying if more than a few megabytes of swap is used. In Chapter 4, you'll learn what you can do if your server starts swapping too soon.

Process Monitoring with top

The last part of the top output is reserved for information about the most active processes. You'll see the following parameters regarding these processes:

- PID: The process ID of the process.

- USER: The user identity used to start the process.

- PR: The priority of the process. The priority of any process is determined automatically, and the process with the highest priority is eligible to be run first because it is first in the queue of runnable processes. Some processes run with a real-time priority, which is indicated as RT. Processes with this priority can claim CPU cycles in real time, which means that they will always have highest priority.

- NI: The nice value with which the process was started.

- VIRT: The amount of memory that was claimed by the process when it first started. This is *not* the same as swap space. Virtual memory in Linux is the total amount of memory that is used.

- RES: The amount of the process memory that is effectively in RAM (RES is short for "resident memory"). The difference between VIRT and RES is the amount of the process memory that has been reserved for future use by the process. The process does not need this memory at this instant, but it may need it in a second. It's just a view of the swap mechanism.

- SHR: The amount of memory this process shares with another process.

- S: The status of a process.

- %CPU: The percentage of CPU time this process is using. You will normally see the process with the highest CPU utilization at the top of this list.

- %MEM: The percentage of memory this process has claimed.

- TIME+: The total amount of time that this process has been using CPU cycles.

- COMMAND: The name of the command that relates to this process.

Analyzing CPU Performance

The top utility offers a good starting point for performance tuning. However, if you really need to dig deep into a performance problem, top does not offer enough information, so you need more advanced tools. In this section you'll learn how to find out more about CPU performance-related problems.

Most people tend to start analyzing a performance problem at the CPU, because they think CPU performance is the most important factor on a server. In most situations, this is not true. Assuming that you have a newer CPU, not an old 486-based CPU, you will hardly ever see a performance problem that really is related to the CPU. In most cases, a problem that looks like it is caused by the CPU is caused by something else. For instance, your CPU may just be waiting for data to be transferred from the network device.

To monitor what is happening on your CPU, you should know something about the conceptual background of process handling, starting with the run queue. Before being served by the CPU, every process enters the run queue. Once it is in the run queue, a process can be runnable or blocked. A *runnable process* is a process that is competing for CPU time. The Linux scheduler decides which runnable process to run next based on the current priority of the process. A *blocked process* doesn't compete for CPU time. It is just waiting for data from some I/O device or system call to arrive. When looking at the system load as provided by utilities like uptime or top, you will see a number that indicates the load requested by runnable and blocked processes, as in the following example using the uptime utility:

```
root@mel:~# uptime
11:29:17 up 21 min,  1 user,  load average: 0.00, 0.00, 0.05
```

A modern Linux system is always a multitasking system. This is true for every processor architecture that can be used, because the Linux kernel constantly switches between different processes. In order to perform this switch, the CPU needs to save all the context information for the old process and retrieve context information for the new process.

The performance price for these context switches is heavy. In an ideal world, you need to make sure that the number of context switches is limited to a certain extent. You can do this by using a multicore CPU architecture, a server with multiple CPUs, or a combination of both. Another solution is to offload processes from a server that is too busy. Processes that are serviced by the kernel scheduler, however, are not the only cause of context switching. Hardware interrupts, caused by hardware devices demanding the CPU's attention, are another important source of context switching.

As an administrator, it is a good idea to compare the number of CPU context switches with the number of interrupts. This gives you an idea of how they relate, but cannot be used as an absolute performance indicator. In my experience, about ten times as many context switches as interrupts is fine; if there are many more context switches per interrupt, it may indicate that your server has a performance problem that is caused by too many processes competing for CPU power. If this is the case, you will be able to verify a rather high workload for those processes with top as well.

■Note Ubuntu Server uses a tickless kernel. That means that the timer interrupt is not included in the interrupt listing. Older kernels included those ticks in the interrupt listing, and you may find that to be true on other versions of Ubuntu Linux. If this is the case, the interrupt value normally is much higher than the number of context switches.

To get an overview of the number of context switches and timer interrupts, you can use vmstat -s. Listing 3-3 shows example output of this command. In this example, the performance behavior of the server is pretty normal, as the number of context switches is about ten times as high as the number of interrupts.

Listing 3-3. *The Relationship Between Interrupts and Context Switches Gives an Idea of What Your Server Is Doing*

```
root@mel:~# vmstat -s
    2075408  total memory
    1892160  used memory
     899644  active memory
     932312  inactive memory
```

```
    183248  free memory
    189836  buffer memory
   1444256  swap cache
   1052216  total swap
       100  used swap
   1052116  free swap
   3353499  non-nice user cpu ticks
     20898  nice user cpu ticks
   1027734  system cpu ticks
1742271887  idle cpu ticks
   3862983  IO-wait cpu ticks
      7332  IRQ cpu ticks
     39741  softirq cpu ticks
         0  steal cpu ticks
  26602325  pages paged in
  94786274  pages paged out
         7  pages swapped in
        28  pages swapped out
  17289263  interrupts
 190266247  CPU context switches
1209543415  boot time
    423309  forks
```

Another performance indicator for what is happening on your CPU is the interrupt counter, which you can find in the file /proc/interrupts. The kernel receives interrupts from devices that need the CPU's attention. It is important for the system administrator to know how many interrupts there are, because if the number is very high, the kernel will spend a lot of time servicing them, and other processes will get less attention. Listing 3-4 shows the contents of the /proc/interrupts file, which gives a precise overview of every interrupt the kernel has handled since startup.

Listing 3-4. */proc/interrupts Shows Exactly How Many of Each Interrupt Have Been Handled*

```
root@mel:~# cat /proc/interrupts
        CPU0    CPU1
   0:    85      0    IO-APIC-edge      timer
   1:     2      0    IO-APIC-edge      i8042
   7:     0      0    IO-APIC-edge      parport0
   8:     3      0    IO-APIC-edge      rtc
   9:     1      0    IO-APIC-fasteoi   acpi
  12:     4      0    IO-APIC-edge      i8042
  16:     9      0    IO-APIC-fasteoi   uhci_hcd:usb1, heci
```

```
 17:      0        0    IO-APIC-fasteoi   libata
 18:    414        0    IO-APIC-fasteoi   uhci_hcd:usb5, ehci_hcd:usb6, eth1
 19: 16130        0    IO-APIC-fasteoi   uhci_hcd:usb4, ohci1394, libata, libata
 21:      0        0    IO-APIC-fasteoi   uhci_hcd:usb2
 22:    250        0    IO-APIC-fasteoi   uhci_hcd:usb3, ehci_hcd:usb7
 23:    199        0    IO-APIC-fasteoi   HDA Intel
217:   2168        0    PCI-MSI-edge      eth0
NMI:      0        0    Non-maskable interrupts
LOC:  21208    57442    Local timer interrupts
RES:    149      325    Rescheduling interrupts
CAL:    134      376    function call interrupts
TLB:     12      137    TLB shootdowns
TRM:      0        0    Thermal event interrupts
SPU:      0        0    Spurious interrupts
ERR:      0
MIS:      0
```

In a multi-CPU or multicore environment, there can be some very specific performance-related problems. One of the major problems in such environments is that processes are served by different CPUs. Every time a process switches between CPUs, the information in cache has to be switched as well. You pay a high performance price for this. The top utility can provide information about the CPU that was last used by any process, but you need to switch this on. To do that, from the top utility, first use the f command and then j. This switches on the option Last used cpu (SMP) for an SMP environment. Listing 3-5 shows the interface from which you can do this.

Listing 3-5. *Switching Different Options On or Off in top*

```
Current Fields:  AEHIOQTWKNMbcdfgjplrsuvyzX  for window 1:Def
Toggle fields via field letter, type any other key to return

* A: PID     = Process Id         u: nFLT    = Page Fault count
* E: USER    = User Name          v: nDRT    = Dirty Pages count
* H: PR      = Priority           y: WCHAN   = Sleeping in Function
* I: NI      = Nice value         z: Flags   = Task Flags <sched.h>
* O: VIRT    = Virtual Image (kb)  * X: COMMAND = Command name/line
* Q: RES     = Resident size (kb)
* T: SHR     = Shared Mem size (kb)  Flags field:
* W: S       = Process Status     0x00000001  PF_ALIGNWARN
```

```
* K: %CPU    = CPU usage            0x00000002  PF_STARTING
* N: %MEM    = Memory usage (RES)   0x00000004  PF_EXITING
* M: TIME+   = CPU Time, hundredths 0x00000040  PF_FORKNOEXEC
  b: PPID    = Parent Process Pid   0x00000100  PF_SUPERPRIV
  c: RUSER   = Real user name       0x00000200  PF_DUMPCORE
  d: UID     = User Id              0x00000400  PF_SIGNALED
  f: GROUP   = Group Name           0x00000800  PF_MEMALLOC
  g: TTY     = Controlling Tty      0x00002000  PF_FREE_PAGES (2.5)
  j: P       = Last used cpu (SMP)  0x00008000  debug flag (2.5)
  p: SWAP    = Swapped size (kb)    0x00024000  special threads (2.5)
  l: TIME    = CPU Time             0x001D0000  special states (2.5)
  r: CODE    = Code size (kb)       0x00100000  PF_USEDFPU (thru 2.4)
  s: DATA    = Data+Stack size (kb)
```

After switching on the Last used CPU (SMP) option, you will see the column P in top that displays the number of the CPU that was last used by a process.

To monitor CPU utilization, top offers a very good starting point. If that doesn't give you enough information, try the vmstat utility as well. You may need to install this package first, using apt-get install sysstat. With vmstat you can get a nice, detailed view of what is happening on your server. Of special interest is the cpu section, which contains the five most important parameters on CPU usage:

- cs: The number of context switches

- us: The percentage of time the CPU has spent in user space

- sy: The percentage of time the CPU has spent in system space

- id: The percentage of CPU utilization in the idle loop

- wa: The percentage of utilization the CPU was waiting for I/O

There are two ways to use vmstat. Probably the most useful way to run it is in sample mode. In this mode, a sample is taken every *n* seconds, where you specify the number of seconds for the sample as an option when starting vmstat. Running performance monitoring utilities in this way is always good, because it shows you progress over a given amount of time. You may find it useful as well to run vmstat for a given amount of time only. For instance, Listing 3-6 shows output of a vmstat command that takes a sample 30 times with a 2-second interval between samples. This was started by entering the command vmstat 2 30.

Listing 3-6. *In Sample Mode, vmstat Can Give You Trending Information*

```
root@mel:~# vmstat 2 30
procs -----------memory---------- ---swap-- -----io---- -system-- ----cpu----
 r  b   swpd     free   buff  cache   si   so    bi   bo    in    cs  us  sy  id  wa
 0  0      0  3893820  23716  57180    0    0     6    3     1    24   0   0 100   0
 0  0      0  3893556  23848  57148    0    0    42   82    89   216   0   0  99   1
 0  0      0  3893552  23848  57248    0    0     0    0     2    40   0   0 100   0
 0  0      0  3893552  23848  57248    0    0     0    0     2    39   0   0 100   0
 0  0      0  3893552  23848  57248    0    0     0   34    11    44   0   0 100   0
 0  0      0  3891452  23856  59312    0    0  1086    8  1424  2839   0   1  98   0
 0  0      0  3888672  23856  62260    0    0  1424    0  2272  4532   0   2  98   0
 0  0      0  3888688  23856  62260    0    0     0    0     2    39   0   0 100   0
 0  0      0  3888688  23856  62260    0    0     0    8     3    41   0   0 100   0
 0  0      0  3888688  23856  62260    0    0     0    0     2    39   0   0 100   0
 0  0      0  3888688  23856  62260    0    0     0    0     2    39   0   0 100   0
 0  0      0  3882988  24304  67000    0    0  2586   52  4079  2851   0   4  77  20
 0  0      0  3881260  24388  68280    0    0   662    0  1954  2616   0   2  96   2
 0  0      0  3879532  24604  69808    0    0   872   48  2752  3575   0   3  88   9
 0  0      0  3879000  24692  70400    0    0   320    0  1752  2773   0   1  95   4
 0  0      0  3878444  24724  70952    0    0   308    0   852  1125   0   1  95   5
 0  0      0  3878444  24724  70952    0    0     0   40     8    39   0   0 100   0
 0  0      0  3878320  24724  70952    0    0     0    6     3    45   0   0 100   0
 0  0      0  3878320  24724  70952    0    0     0    0     2    38   0   0 100   0
 0  0      0  3878204  24768  70960    0    0     4   34    70   163   0   0 100   0
 0  0      0  3878204  24768  70960    0    0     0    0     2    39   0   0 100   0
 r  b   swpd     free   buff  cache   si   so    bi   bo    in    cs  us  sy  id  wa
 0  0      0  3878204  24772  70956    0    0    10    6   150   332   0   0  99   0
 0  0      0  3876628  24868  72812    0    0   792    0  3148  4065   0   3  88   8
 0  0      0  3874276  25184  74140    0    0   844   12  5856  7399   0   4  84  12
 0  0      0  3872916  25276  75544    0    0   688   22  2146  1619   0   2  90   9
 0  0      0  3872916  25276  75544    0    0     0    0     2    39   0   0 100   0
 0  0      0  3872916  25276  75544    0    0     0  302    15    44   0   0 100   0
 0  0      0  3872916  25276  75544    0    0     0    0     2    39   0   0 100   0
 0  0      0  3872916  25276  75544    0    0     0    0     2    38   0   0 100   0
 0  0      0  3872916  25276  75544    0    0     0    0     2    45   0   0 100   0
```

Another useful way to run vmstat is with the option -s. In this mode, vmstat shows you all the statistics since the system booted. As you can see in Listing 3-6, apart from the CPU-related options, vmstat also shows information about processors, memory, swap, I/O, and the system. These options are covered later in this chapter.

Finding Memory Problems

Memory is very important on a server, possibly more important than CPU. The CPU can work smoothly only if processes are ready in memory and can be offered from there; if this is not the case, the server has to get its data from the I/O channel, which is about 1,000 times slower to access than memory. From the processor's point of view, even system RAM is relatively slow. Therefore, modern server processors have large amounts of cache, which is even faster than memory.

You have read earlier in this chapter how to interpret basic memory statistics provided by top, so I will not cover them again in this section. Instead, I cover some more-advanced memory-related information. First, you should know that in memory a default page size is used. On an i386 system, typically 4 KB pages are used. This means that everything that happens, happens in chunks of 4 KB. There is nothing wrong with that if you have a server handling large amounts of small files. If, however, your server handles huge files, it is highly inefficient if only these small 4 KB pages are used. For that purpose, huge pages can be used, with a size of up to 2 MB. You'll learn how to set these up in Chapter 4.

If a server runs out of memory, it resorts to using swap memory. Swap memory is emulated RAM on your server's hard drive. Because the hard disk is involved in swapping, you should avoid it at all times; access times to a hard drive are about 1,000 times slower than access times to RAM. If your server is slow, swap usage is the first thing to look at. You can do this by using the command free -m. This gives you an overview similar to the output shown in Listing 3-7.

Listing 3-7. *free -m Provides Information About Swap Usage*

```
root@mel:~# free -m
                total    used    free    shared    buffers    cached
Mem:            3987     3841    146     0         9          3719
-/+ buffers/cache:       112     3875
Swap:           2047     0       2047
```

As you can see, on the server from which this sample is taken, nothing is wrong—there is no swap usage at all, and that is good.

On the other hand, if you see that your server is swapping, the next thing you need to know is how actively it is swapping. The vmstat utility provides useful information about this. This utility provides swap information in the si (swap in) and so (swap out) columns. If you see no swap activity at all, that's fine. In that case, swap space has been allocated but is not used. If, however, you do see significant activity in these columns, you're in trouble. This means that swap space is not only allocated, but also being used, and that will really slow down your server. The solution? Reduce the workload on this server. To do this, you must make sure that you move processes that use lots of memory to another server, and that is where top comes in handy. In the %MEM column, top gives information about memory usage. Find the most active process and make sure that it loads somewhere else.

When swapping memory pages in and out, your server uses the difference between active and inactive memory. *Inactive memory* is memory that hasn't been used for some time, whereas *active memory* is memory that has been used recently. When moving memory blocks from RAM to swap, the kernel makes sure that only blocks from inactive memory are moved. You can see statistics about active and inactive memory by using vmstat -s. In the example in Listing 3-8, you can see that the amount of active memory is relatively small compared to the amount of inactive memory.

Listing 3-8. *Use vmstat -s to Get Statistics About Active vs. Inactive Memory*

```
root@mel:~# vmstat -s
      4083276 K total memory
      3933264 K used memory
        90904 K active memory
      3786488 K inactive memory
       150012 K free memory
         7436 K buffer memory
      3812208 K swap cache
      2097144 K total swap
            0 K used swap
      2097144 K free swap
          796 non-nice user cpu ticks
            0 nice user cpu ticks
         1564 system cpu ticks
        84025 idle cpu ticks
         4366 IO-wait cpu ticks
            0 IRQ cpu ticks
         2939 softirq cpu ticks
            0 stolen cpu ticks
      3993666 pages paged in
        20167 pages paged out
            0 pages swapped in
            0 pages swapped out
        44656 interrupts
       438610 CPU context switches
   1213553859 boot time
         5671 forks
```

Another issue that you should be aware of is that on 32-bit processors, there is
a problem accessing memory above 1 GB directly. To make it possible to access this
memory anyway, Linux uses high and low memory. High memory is not accessible
directly by the kernel, so typically user-space programs are loaded here. The kernel can
only address low memory directly. On 64-bit processors, this difference does not exist.
Some Linux kernels have a problem addressing memory on servers with 4 GB or more of
memory. On those kernels, you'll see about 3.2 GB of RAM only. Ubuntu Server, however,
addresses this issue by using a kernel with Physical Address Extensions (PAEs) by default.
These kernels can address as much as 16 GB of RAM.

When analyzing memory usage, you should take into account the memory that is used by the kernel itself as well. This is called *slab memory*. You can see the amount of slab memory currently in use in the /proc/meminfo file. Listing 3-9 gives an example of the contents of this file, which gives you detailed information about memory usage.

Listing 3-9. */proc/meminfo Gives Detailed Information About Memory Usage*

```
root@mel:~# cat /proc/meminfo
MemTotal:       4083276 kB
MemFree:         149444 kB
Buffers:           8460 kB
Cached:         3811544 kB
SwapCached:           0 kB
Active:           74112 kB
Inactive:       3803568 kB
HighTotal:      3209420 kB
HighFree:          8104 kB
LowTotal:        873856 kB
LowFree:         141340 kB
SwapTotal:      2097144 kB
SwapFree:       2097144 kB
Dirty:               80 kB
Writeback:            0 kB
AnonPages:        57716 kB
Mapped:           12692 kB
Slab:             18456 kB
SReclaimable:      4968 kB
SUnreclaim:       13488 kB
PageTables:        1356 kB
NFS_Unstable:         0 kB
Bounce:               0 kB
CommitLimit:    4138780 kB
Committed_AS:    648972 kB
VmallocTotal:    118776 kB
VmallocUsed:       8060 kB
VmallocChunk:    110240 kB
HugePages_Total:      0
HugePages_Free:       0
HugePages_Rsvd:       0
HugePages_Surp:       0
Hugepagesize:      2048 kB
```

In Listing 3-9, you can see that the amount of memory that is used by the Linux kernel is relatively small. But what exactly does it mean that about 18 MB is used by the kernel? If you need more details about that, you may like the slabtop utility. This utility provides information about the different parts (referred to as *objects*) of the kernel and what exactly they are doing. For normal performance analysis purposes, the SIZE and NAME columns are the most interesting ones. The other columns are of interest mainly to programmers and kernel developers and are therefore not described in this chapter. In Listing 3-10, you can see an example of information provided by slabtop.

Listing 3-10. *slabtop Provides Information About Kernel Memory Usage*

```
root@mel:~# slabtop
 Active / Total Objects (% used)    : 85855 / 88550 (97.0%)
 Active / Total Slabs (% used)      : 4120 / 4120 (100.0%)
 Active / Total Caches (% used)     : 58 / 74 (78.4%)
 Active / Total Size (% used)       : 17234.85K / 17887.11K (96.4%)
 Minimum / Average / Maximum Object : 0.01K / 0.20K / 8.00K

  OBJS ACTIVE   USE OBJ SIZE  SLABS OBJ/SLAB CACHE SIZE NAME
 16198  16193   99%   0.29K   1246       13       4984K radix_tree_node
 13260  13260  100%   0.05K    156       85        624K sysfs_dir_cache
 12090  12082   99%   0.13K    403       30       1612K dentry
  6144   6144  100%   0.01K     12      512         48K kmalloc-8
  5120   4619   90%   0.02K     20      256         80K kmalloc-16
  3968   3836   96%   0.06K     62       64        248K kmalloc-64
  3360   3357   99%   0.33K    280       12       1120K inode_cache
  3216   3216  100%   0.48K    402        8       1608K ext3_inode_cache
  3212   2456   76%   0.05K     44       73        176K buffer_head
  3168   3168  100%   0.43K    352        9       1408K shmem_inode_cache
  2714   2649   97%   0.09K     59       46        236K vm_area_struct
  2380   2229   93%   0.02K     14      170         56K Acpi-Namespace
  2048   2047   99%   0.03K     16      128         64K kmalloc-32
  1785   1641   91%   0.19K     85       21        340K kmalloc-192
  1472    937   63%   0.12K     46       32        184K kmalloc-128
  1112   1095   98%   0.50K    139        8        556K kmalloc-512
```

The most interesting information you get from slabtop is the amount of memory a particular slab is using. If this amount of memory seems too high, there may be something wrong with this module and you might need to update your kernel. The slabtop utility may also be able to help you find information on how much resources a certain kernel module is using. For instance, you'll find information about the caches your file system drivers are using, and this may indicate that it is better to use another file system after all.

When tuning memory utilization, another utility that you should never forget is ps. The advantage of ps is that it gives memory usage information on all processes on your server, and it is easy to grep on its result to find information about particular processes. To monitor memory usage, the ps aux command is very useful. It gives memory information in the VSZ and RSS columns. VSZ provides information about the virtual memory that is used. This relates to the total amount of memory that is claimed by a process. RSS refers to the amount of hardware memory that is in use. Listing 3-11 gives an example of some lines of ps aux output.

Listing 3-11. *ps aux Gives Memory Usage Information for Particular Processes*

```
root@mel:~# ps aux
USER        PID %CPU %MEM    VSZ   RSS TTY      STAT START   TIME COMMAND
root          1  0.0  0.0   2844  1692 ?        Ss   14:17   0:01 /sbin/init
root          2  0.0  0.0      0     0 ?        S<   14:17   0:00 [kthreadd]
root          3  0.0  0.0      0     0 ?        S<   14:17   0:00 [migration/0]
root          4  0.0  0.0      0     0 ?        S<   14:17   0:00 [ksoftirqd/0]
root          5  0.0  0.0      0     0 ?        S<   14:17   0:00 [watchdog/0]
root          6  0.0  0.0      0     0 ?        S<   14:17   0:00 [migration/1]
...
www-data   5574  0.0  0.0 235244  4024 ?        Sl   14:18   0:00 /usr/sbin/apach
root       5637  0.0  0.0   2568  1216 tty1     Ss   14:18   0:00 /bin/login --
root       5638  0.0  0.0   4192  1764 tty1     S+   14:18   0:00 -bash
root       5658  0.0  0.0   8052  2496 ?        Ss   14:25   0:00 sshd: root@pts/
root       5661  0.0  0.0   4176  1736 pts/0    Ss   14:25   0:00 -bash
root       5719  0.0  0.0   3632  1036 pts/0    R+   15:00   0:00 ps aux
```

When looking at the output of ps aux, you may notice that there are two different kinds of processes. The names of some are between square brackets, whereas the names of others are not. If the name of a process is between square brackets, the process is part of the kernel. All other processes are "normal" processes.

If you need more information about a process and what exactly it is doing, there are two ways to get that information. First, you can check the /proc directory for the particular process; for instance, /proc/5658 gives information for the process with PID 5658. In this directory, you'll find the maps file that gives some more insight into how memory is mapped for this process. As you can see in Listing 3-12, this information is rather detailed. It includes the exact memory addresses this process is using and even tells you about subroutines and libraries that are related to this process.

Listing 3-12. */proc/PID/maps Gives Detailed Information on Memory Utilization of Particular Processes*

```
root@mel:~# cat /proc/5658/maps
b7781000-b78c1000 rw-s 00000000 00:09 14414    /dev/zero (deleted)
b78c1000-b78c4000 r-xp 00000000 fe:00 5808329 /lib/security/pam_limits.so
b78c4000-b78c5000 rw-p 00002000 fe:00 5808329 /lib/security/pam_limits.so
b78c5000-b78c7000 r-xp 00000000 fe:00 5808334 /lib/security/pam_mail.so
b78c7000-b78c8000 rw-p 00001000 fe:00 5808334 /lib/security/pam_mail.so
b78c8000-b78d3000 r-xp 00000000 fe:00 5808351 /lib/security/pam_unix.so
b78d3000-b78d4000 rw-p 0000b000 fe:00 5808351 /lib/security/pam_unix.so
b78d4000-b78e0000 rw-p b78d4000 00:00 0
...
b7eb7000-b7eb8000 r-xp 00000000 fe:00 5808338 /lib/security/pam_nologin.so
b7eb8000-b7eb9000 rw-p 00000000 fe:00 5808338 /lib/security/pam_nologin.so
b7eb9000-b7ebb000 rw-p b7eb9000 00:00 0
b7ebb000-b7ebc000 r-xp b7ebb000 00:00 0         [vdso]
b7ebc000-b7ed6000 r-xp 00000000 fe:00 5808145 /lib/ld-2.7.so
b7ed6000-b7ed8000 rw-p 00019000 fe:00 5808145 /lib/ld-2.7.so
b7ed8000-b7f31000 r-xp 00000000 fe:00 1077630 /usr/sbin/sshd
b7f31000-b7f33000 rw-p 00059000 fe:00 1077630 /usr/sbin/sshd
b7f33000-b7f5b000 rw-p b7f33000 00:00 0         [heap]
bff9a000-bffaf000 rw-p bffeb000 00:00 0         [stack]
```

Another way of finding out what particular processes are doing is to use the pmap command. This command mines the /proc/PID/maps file to provide information about subprocesses that have memory in use. Also, it adds a summary of memory usage, as displayed by ps aux. Listing 3-13 gives an impression of the output of this utility.

Listing 3-13. *pmap Mines /proc/PID/maps to Provide Its Information*

```
root@mel:~# pmap -d 5658
5658:   sshd: root@pts/0
Address     Kbytes Mode  Offset           Device    Mapping
b7781000     1280 rw-s- 0000000000000000 000:00009 zero (deleted)
b78c1000       12 r-x-- 0000000000000000 0fe:00000 pam_limits.so
b78c4000        4 rw--- 0000000000002000 0fe:00000 pam_limits.so
b78c5000        8 r-x-- 0000000000000000 0fe:00000 pam_mail.so
b78c7000        4 rw--- 0000000000001000 0fe:00000 pam_mail.so
b78c8000       44 r-x-- 0000000000000000 0fe:00000 pam_unix.so
b78d3000        4 rw--- 000000000000b000 0fe:00000 pam_unix.so
b78d4000       48 rw--- 00000000b78d4000 000:00000 [ anon ]
```

```
b78e0000      16 r-x-- 0000000000000000 0fe:00000 libnss_dns-2.7.so
b78e4000       8 rw--- 0000000000003000 0fe:00000 libnss_dns-2.7.so
b78e6000      12 r-x-- 0000000000000000 0fe:00000 pam_env.so
b78e9000       4 rw--- 0000000000002000 0fe:00000 pam_env.so
b78eb000    1280 rw-s- 0000000000000000 000:00009 zero (deleted)
b7a3b000      36 r-x-- 0000000000000000 0fe:00000 libnss_files-2.7.so
b7a44000       8 rw--- 0000000000008000 0fe:00000 libnss_files-2.7.so
b7a46000      32 r-x-- 0000000000000000 0fe:00000 libnss_nis-2.7.so
b7a4e000       8 rw--- 0000000000007000 0fe:00000 libnss_nis-2.7.so
b7a50000      28 r-x-- 0000000000000000 0fe:00000 libnss_compat-2.7.so
b7a57000       8 rw--- 0000000000006000 0fe:00000 libnss_compat-2.7.so
b7a59000       8 rw--- 00000000b7a59000 000:00000   [ anon ]
b7a5b000       8 r-x-- 0000000000000000 0fe:00000 libkeyutils-1.2.so
b7a5d000       4 rw--- 0000000000001000 0fe:00000 libkeyutils-1.2.so
b7a5e000      28 r-x-- 0000000000000000 0fe:00000 libkrb5support.so.0.1
b7a65000       4 rw--- 0000000000006000 0fe:00000 libkrb5support.so.0.1
b7a66000    1316 r-x-- 0000000000000000 0fe:00000 libc-2.7.so
b7baf000       4 r---- 0000000000149000 0fe:00000 libc-2.7.so
b7bb0000       8 rw--- 000000000014a000 0fe:00000 libc-2.7.so
b7bb2000      12 rw--- 00000000b7bb2000 000:00000   [ anon ]
b7bb5000       8 r-x-- 0000000000000000 0fe:00000 libcom_err.so.2.1
b7bb7000       4 rw--- 0000000000001000 0fe:00000 libcom_err.so.2.1
b7bb8000     136 r-x-- 0000000000000000 0fe:00000 libk5crypto.so.3.1
b7bda000       4 rw--- 0000000000022000 0fe:00000 libk5crypto.so.3.1
b7bdb000       4 rw--- 00000000b7bdb000 000:00000   [ anon ]
b7bdc000     556 r-x-- 0000000000000000 0fe:00000 libkrb5.so.3.3
b7c67000       8 rw--- 000000000008a000 0fe:00000 libkrb5.so.3.3
b7c69000     160 r-x-- 0000000000000000 0fe:00000 libgssapi_krb5.so.2.2
b7c91000       4 rw--- 0000000000028000 0fe:00000 libgssapi_krb5.so.2.2
b7c92000      36 r-x-- 0000000000000000 0fe:00000 libcrypt-2.7.so
b7c9b000       8 rw--- 0000000000008000 0fe:00000 libcrypt-2.7.so
b7c9d000    1 56 rw--- 00000000b7c9d000 000:00000   [ anon ]
b7cc4000      80 r-x-- 0000000000000000 0fe:00000 libnsl-2.7.so
b7cd8000       8 rw--- 0000000000013000 0fe:00000 libnsl-2.7.so
b7cda000       8 rw--- 00000000b7cda000 000:00000   [ anon ]
b7cdc000      80 r-x-- 0000000000000000 0fe:00000 libz.so.1.2.3.3
b7cf0000       4 rw--- 0000000000013000 0fe:00000 libz.so.1.2.3.3
b7cf1000       8 r-x-- 0000000000000000 0fe:00000 libutil-2.7.so
b7cf3000       8 rw--- 0000000000001000 0fe:00000 libutil-2.7.so
b7cf5000       4 rw--- 00000000b7cf5000 000:00000   [ anon ]
b7cf6000    1192 r-x-- 0000000000000000 0fe:00000 libcrypto.so.0.9.8
b7e20000      84 rw--- 0000000000129000 0fe:00000 libcrypto.so.0.9.8
```

```
b7e35000      12 rw--- 00000000b7e35000 000:00000  [ anon ]
b7e38000      60 r-x-- 0000000000000000 0fe:00000  libresolv-2.7.so
b7e47000       8 rw--- 000000000000f000 0fe:00000  libresolv-2.7.so
b7e49000       8 rw--- 00000000b7e49000 000:00000  [ anon ]
b7e4b000     208 r-x-- 0000000000000000 0fe:00000  libdbus-1.so.3.4.0
b7e7f000       8 rw--- 0000000000033000 0fe:00000  libdbus-1.so.3.4.0
b7e81000       8 r-x-- 0000000000000000 0fe:00000  libck-connector.so.0.0.0
b7e83000       4 rw--- 0000000000001000 0fe:00000  libck-connector.so.0.0.0
b7e84000      92 r-x-- 0000000000000000 0fe:00000  libselinux.so.1
b7e9b000       8 rw--- 0000000000016000 0fe:00000  libselinux.so.1
b7e9d000       8 r-x-- 0000000000000000 0fe:00000  libdl-2.7.so
b7e9f000       8 rw--- 0000000000001000 0fe:00000  libdl-2.7.so
b7ea1000       4 rw--- 00000000b7ea1000 000:00000  [ anon ]
b7ea2000      36 r-x-- 0000000000000000 0fe:00000  libpam.so.0.81.6
b7eab000       4 rw--- 0000000000008000 0fe:00000  libpam.so.0.81.6
b7eac000      28 r-x-- 0000000000000000 0fe:00000  libwrap.so.0.7.6
b7eb3000       4 rw--- 0000000000007000 0fe:00000  libwrap.so.0.7.6
b7eb5000       4 r-x-- 0000000000000000 0fe:00000  pam_motd.so
b7eb6000       4 rw--- 0000000000000000 0fe:00000  pam_motd.so
b7eb7000       4 r-x-- 0000000000000000 0fe:00000  pam_nologin.so
b7eb8000       4 rw--- 0000000000000000 0fe:00000  pam_nologin.so
b7eb9000       8 rw--- 00000000b7eb9000 000:00000  [ anon ]
b7ebb000       4 r-x-- 00000000b7ebb000 000:00000  [ anon ]
b7ebc000     104 r-x-- 0000000000000000 0fe:00000  ld-2.7.so
b7ed6000       8 rw--- 0000000000019000 0fe:00000  ld-2.7.so
b7ed8000     356 r-x-- 0000000000000000 0fe:00000  sshd
b7f31000       8 rw--- 0000000000059000 0fe:00000  sshd
b7f33000     160 rw--- 00000000b7f33000 000:00000  [ anon ]
bff9a000      84 rw--- 00000000bffeb000 000:00000  [ stack ]
mapped: 8052K    writeable/private: 780K    shared: 2560K
```

One of the advantages of the pmap command is that it gives detailed information about the order in which a process does its work. You can see calls to external libraries, as well as additional memory allocation (malloc) requests that the program is making, as reflected in the lines that have [anon] at the end.

Monitoring Storage Performance

One of the hardest things to do properly is to monitor storage utilization. The reason is that the storage channel typically is at the end of the chain. Other elements in your server can have a positive or negative influence on storage performance. For instance, if your server is low on memory, that will be reflected in storage performance, because if your server doesn't have enough memory, there can't be a lot of cache and buffers, and thus your server has more work to do on the storage channel. Likewise, a slow CPU can have a negative impact on storage performance, because the queue of runnable processes can't be cleared fast enough. Therefore, before jumping to the conclusion that you have bad performance on the storage channel, you need to take other factors into consideration as well.

It is generally hard to optimize storage performance on a server. The best behavior really depends on the kind of workload your server typically has. For instance, a server that has a lot of reads has different needs from those of a server that does mainly writes. A server that is doing writes most of the time may benefit from a storage channel with many disks, because more controllers can work on clearing the write buffer cache from memory. If, however, your server is mainly reading data, the effect of having many disks is just the opposite. Because of the large number of disks, seek times will increase and therefore performance will be negatively impacted.

The following are some indicators that you are experiencing storage performance problems:

- Memory buffers and cache are heavily used but CPU utilization is low.

- Disk or controller utilization is high.

- Network response times are long but network utilization is low.

Before you try to understand storage performance, there is another factor that you should consider: the way that disk activity typically takes place. First, a storage device generally handles large sequential transfers better than it handles small random transfers. The reason is that, in memory, you can configure read-ahead and write buffers, which means that the storage controller is likely to go to the next block to which it needs to go. If your server handles small files mostly, read-ahead buffers have no effect at all, or might even slow down your server. In Chapter 5, you will learn how to optimize your server for such a workload.

From the perspective of which tools to use, there are two tools that really count when doing disk performance analysis. Before you read about these tools, however, you should be aware of the shortcomings of analyzing disk performance. The most important problem is that the Linux kernel does not track I/O of a process. This means that there are no tools that help you find which process is causing all disk I/O traffic. You can only try to deduce what process is causing a high I/O load, by analyzing other factors such as memory utilization and CPU utilization of that particular process.

The best tool to start your disk performance analysis is vmstat. This tool has a couple of options that help you see what is happening on a particular disk device, such as -d, which gives you statistics for individual disks, and -p, which gives partition performance statistics. As you already know, you can use vmstat with an interval parameter and a count parameter. Listing 3-14 shows the result of the command vmstat -d, which gives detailed information on storage utilization for all disk devices on your server.

Listing 3-14. *vmstat Is the Best Utility to Get Information About Storage Utilization*

```
root@mel:~# vmstat -d
disk- ------------reads------------ ------------writes----------- -----IO------
       total merged  sectors    ms  total merged  sectors    ms cur  sec
  ram0     0      0        0     0      0      0        0     0   0    0
  ...
   sda  3469   8759    91610 10320   1417    442    14850  2010   0    8
   sdb  4165   7895    94614 16790   2001    611    20860  2440   0   14
   sr0     0      0        0     0      0      0        0     0   0    0
   md0 22597      0   180800     0   4475      0    35740     0   0    0
  dm-0 13700      0   109594 58070    200      0     1600   110   0   11
  dm-1   104      0      832   960      0      0        0     0   0    0
  dm-2  8092      0    64736 20070   4135      0    33080  5520   0    9
  dm-3   289      0     2165  2860     66      0      514     0   0    0
  dm-4   173      0     1209  1400     66      0      514     0   0    0
  ...
   sdf     0      0        0     0      0      0        0     0   0    0
 loop0     0      0        0     0      0      0        0     0   0    0
 loop7     0      0        0     0      0      0        0     0   0    0
```

The output of this command shows detailed statistics about the reads and writes that have occurred on a disk. The following parameters are displayed when using vmstat -d:

- reads: total: Total number of reads requested.

- reads: merged: Total number of adjacent locations that have been merged to improve performance. This is the result of the read ahead parameter. High numbers are good here, because a high number means that within the same read request, a couple of adjacent blocks have been read as well.

- reads: sectors: Total number of disk sectors that have been read.

- reads: ms: Total time spent reading from disk.

- writes: total: Total number of writes.

- writes: merged: Total number of writes to adjacent sectors.

- writes: sectors: Total number of sectors that have been written.

- writes: ms: Total time, in milliseconds, your system has spent writing data.

- IO: cur: Total number of I/O requests currently in progress.

- IO: sec: Total amount of time spent waiting for I/O to complete.

Another way of monitoring disk performance with vmstat is by running vmstat in sample mode. For instance, vmstat 2 15 will run 15 samples with a 2-second interval. Listing 3-15 shows the result of this command.

Listing 3-15. *Sample Mode Provides a Real-Time Impression of Disk Utilization*

```
root@mel:~# vmstat 2 15
procs -----------memory---------- ---swap-- -----io---- -system-- ----cpu----
 r  b   swpd   free     buff   cache    si  so    bi  bo    in    cs  us sy id wa
 0  0      0 3666400  14344  292496    0   0    56   4   579    70   0  0 99  0
 0  0      0 3645452  14344  313680    0   0 10560   0 12046  2189   0  4 94  2
 0 13      0 3623364  14344  335772    0   0 11040   0 12127  2221   0  6 92  2
 0  0      0 3602032  14380  356880    0   0 10560  18 12255  2323   0  7 90  3
 0  0      0 3582048  14380  377124    0   0 10080   0 11525  2089   0  4 93  3
 0  0      0 3561076  14380  398160    0   0 10560  24 12069  2141   0  5 91  4
 0  0      0 3539652  14380  419280    0   0 10560   0 11913  2209   0  4 92  4
 0  0      0 3518016  14380  440336    0   0 10560   0 11632  2226   0  7 90  3
 0  0      0 3498756  14380  459600    0   0  9600   0 10822  2455   0  4 92  3
 0  0      0 3477832  14380  480800    0   0 10560   0 12011  2279   0  3 94  2
 0  0      0 3456600  14380  501840    0   0 10560   0 12078  2670   0  3 94  3
 0  0      0 3435636  14380  523044    0   0 10560   0 12106  1850   0  3 93  4
 0  0      0 3414824  14380  544016    0   0 10560   0 11989  1731   0  3 92  4
 0  0      0 3393516  14380  565136    0   0 10560   0 11919  1965   0  6 92  2
 0  0      0 3370920  14380  587216    0   0 11040   0 12378  2020   0  5 90  4
```

The columns that count in Listing 3-15 are the io: bi and io: bo columns, because they show you the number of blocks that came in from the storage channel (bi) and the number of blocks that were written to the storage channel (bo). In Listing 3-15, it is pretty clear that the server is busy servicing some heavy read requests and is doing nearly no writes at all. You should be aware, however, that it is not always this easy. In some situations you will find that some clients are performing heavy read requests while your server shows next to no activity in the io: bi column. If that happens, the reason probably is that the data that was read is still in cache.

Another tool to monitor performance on the storage channel is iostat. It provides an overview per device of the number of reads and writes. In the example in Listing 3-16, you can see the following device parameters being displayed:

- tps: Number of transactions (reads plus writes) handled per second

- Blk_read/s: Number of blocks read per second

- Blk_wrtn/s: Rate of disk blocks written per second

- Blk_read: Total number of blocks read since startup

- Blk_wrtn: Total number of blocks written since startup

Listing 3-16. *iostat Provides Information About the Number of Blocks Read and Written per Second*

```
root@mel:~# iostat
Linux 2.6.24-16-server (mel)    06/16/2008
```

avg-cpu:	%user	%nice	%system	%iowait	%steal	%idle
	0.12	0.00	1.12	0.94	0.00	97.82

Device:	tps	Blk_read/s	Blk_wrtn/s	Blk_read	Blk_wrtn
sda	9.83	2056.55	5.72	7354218	20466
sdb	8.98	2057.60	7.97	7357950	28508
md0	515.83	4112.64	13.70	14706744	49004
dm-0	5.57	43.13	1.47	154218	5264
dm-1	0.03	0.23	0.00	832	0
dm-2	3.76	18.18	11.94	65016	42680
dm-3	0.10	0.61	0.14	2165	514
dm-4	506.29	4049.86	0.14	14482249	514

If iostat doesn't give you enough detail, you can use the -x option as well. This option gives lots of information, and therefore doesn't fit on the screen nicely in most cases. Listing 3-17 shows an example of iostat -x being used.

Listing 3-17. *iostat -x Provides Much Information About What Is Happening on the Storage Channel*

```
root@mel:~# iostat -x
Linux 2.6.24-16-server (mel)    06/16/2008

avg-cpu:  %user   %nice %system %iowait  %steal   %idle
          0.11    0.00    1.63    1.24    0.00   97.02

Device:          rrqm/s   wrqm/s     r/s     w/s   rsec/s   wsec/s➡
 avgrq-sz avgqu-sz   await  svctm   %util
sda              367.98     0.22   13.53    0.44  3135.15     5.23➡
   224.91    0.03    1.87    1.15    1.60
sdb              369.60     0.28   11.91    0.63  3136.05     7.26➡
   250.64    0.03    2.09    1.39    1.74
md0                0.00     0.00  783.82    1.56  6269.87    12.50➡
     8.00    0.00    0.00    0.00    0.00
dm-0               0.00     0.00    4.71    0.16    37.65     1.28➡
     8.00    0.02    4.56    0.80    0.39
dm-1               0.00     0.00    0.03    0.01             0.20➡
     0.08    8.00    0.00    7.27    3.29    0.01
dm-2               0.00     0.00    1.98    1.36    15.83    10.88➡
     8.00    0.01    2.04    0.73    0.24
dm-3               0.00     0.00    0.07    0.02             0.53➡
     0.13    7.55    0.00    8.06    1.52    0.01
dm-4               0.00     0.00  776.98    0.02  6215.11     0.13➡
     8.00    2.20    2.83    0.02    1.38
```

When you use the -x option, iostat gives you the following information:

- rrqm/s: Reads per second merged before issued to disk. Compare this to the information in the r/s column to find out how much you gain in efficiency because of read ahead.

- wrqm/s: Writes per second merged before issued to disk. Compare this to the w/s parameter to see how much performance gain you have because of write ahead.

- r/s: The number of real reads per second.

- w/s: The number of real writes per second.

- rsec/s: The number of 512-byte sectors read per second.

- wsec: The number of 512-byte sectors written per second.

- avgrq-sz: The average size of files requested from disk. This is an important parameter because, based on the information that you get, you can optimize your file system accordingly (see Chapter 4 for more information on that).

- avgqu-sz: The average size of the disk request queue. This should be low at all times, because it gives the number of pending disk requests. If there is a high number here, that means that the performance of your storage channel cannot cope with the performance of your network.

- await: The average waiting time, in milliseconds. This is the time the request has been waiting in the I/O queue plus the time that it actually took to service this request. This parameter should also be low in all cases.

- svctm: The average service time, in milliseconds. This is the time it took before a request could be submitted to disk. If this parameter is below a few milliseconds (never more than 10 ms), nothing is wrong on your server. However, if this parameter is higher than that, something is wrong and you should consider doing some storage optimization.

- %util: The percentage of CPU utilization that was related to I/O.

As you can see, iostat -x is an important command to find out what's happening on your storage channel. The only thing it doesn't give is information about what processes are responsible for the I/O on your server. The Linux kernel does not provide a direct way of finding that information, but by using the lsof (list open files) command, you can at least find the names of files that are open on a device. And with the names of the files, you'll find the names of related processes as well. In Listing 3-18 you can see how lsof nicely puts all this information in its output.

Listing 3-18. *lsof Is Useful for Finding the Processes Working on a Given Device*

```
root@mel:~# lsof /var
COMMAND     PID    USER      FD    TYPE DEVICE  SIZE     NODE   NAME
rpc.statd   4764   statd     cwd   DIR  254,2   256      3655   /var/lib/nfs
syslogd     5054   syslog    1w    REG  254,2   392438   3624   /var/log/auth.log
smbd        5494   root      6u    REG  254,2   8192     1400➡
 /var/lib/samba/secrets.tdb
smbd        5494   root      14u   REG  254,2   4096     1440➡
 /var/lib/samba/ntdrivers.tdb
smbd        5494   root      15u   REG  254,2   4096     1403➡
 /var/lib/samba/group_mapping.tdb
smbd        5494   root      16u   REG  254,2   4096     1407➡
 /var/lib/samba/account_policy.tdb
smbd        5494   root      17u   REG  254,2   4096     1441➡
 /var/lib/samba/ntprinters.tdb
smbd        5494   root      18u   REG  254,2   696      1445➡
 /var/lib/samba/ntforms.tdb
dhcpd3      5528   dhcpd     6w    REG  254,2   4424     3571➡
 /var/lib/dhcp3/dhcpd.leases
atd         5549   daemon    cwd   DIR  254,2   72       1216➡
 /var/spool/cron/atjobs
cron        5560   root      cwd   DIR  254,2   120      1214   /var/spool/cron
apache2     5582   root      2w    REG  254,2   2370     3466➡
 /var/log/apache2/error.log
apache2     5582   root      7w    REG  254,2   0        2720➡
 /var/log/apache2/access.log
apache2     5583   www-data  2w    REG  254,2   2370     3466   /var/log/apache2/error.log
apache2     5583   www-data  7w    REG  254,2   0        2720➡
 /var/log/apache2/access.log
apache2     5589   www-data  2w    REG  254,2   2370     3466   /var/log/apache2/error.log
apache2     5589   www-data  7w    REG  254,2   0        2720➡
 /var/log/apache2/access.log
apache2     5593   www-data  2w    REG  254,2   2370     3466   /var/log/apache2/error.log
apache2     5593   www-data  7w    REG  254,2   0        2720➡
 /var/log/apache2/access.log
```

Monitoring Network Performance

On a typical server, network performance is as important as disk, memory, and CPU performance. After all, the data has to be delivered over the network to the end user. The problem, however, is that things aren't always as they seem. In some cases a network problem can be caused by misconfiguration in server RAM. If, for example, packets get dropped on the network, the reason may very well be that your server doesn't have enough buffers reserved for receiving packets, which may be because your server is low on memory. Again, everything is related, and your task is to find the real cause of the troubles.

When considering network performance, there are different kinds of information to be analyzed. As you know, several layers of communication are used on the network. If you want to analyze a problem with your Samba server, that requires a completely different approach from analyzing a problem with dropped packets. A good network performance analysis always goes from the bottom up. That means that you first need to check what is happening at the physical layer, and then go up through the Ethernet, IP, TCP/UDP, and protocol layers.

When analyzing network performance, always start by checking the network interface itself. Good old ifconfig offers excellent statistics to do just that. For instance, consider Listing 3-19, which gives the result of ifconfig on the eth1 network interface.

Listing 3-19. *Use ifconfig to See What Is Happening on Your Network Board*

```
root@mel:~# ifconfig eth1
eth1      Link encap:Ethernet  HWaddr 00:0c:f6:3f:5d:bb
          inet addr:10.0.0.10  Bcast:10.0.0.255  Mask:255.255.255.0
          inet6 addr: fe80::20c:f6ff:fe3f:5dbb/64 Scope:Link
          UP BROADCAST RUNNING MULTICAST  MTU:1500  Metric:1
          RX packets:7815390 errors:0 dropped:0 overruns:0 frame:0
          TX packets:12427826 errors:0 dropped:0 overruns:0 carrier:0
          collisions:0 txqueuelen:1000
          RX bytes:588058984 (560.8 MB)  TX bytes:1526947171 (1.4 GB)
          Interrupt:18 Base address:0xe800
```

As you can see from Listing 3-19, the eth1 network board has been quite busy, with 560 MB of received data and 1.4 GB of transmitted data. This is the total overview of what your server has been doing since it started up, so you will see that these statistics can be much higher for a server that has been up and running for a long time. You can also see that IPv6 (inet6) has been enabled for this network card. There's nothing wrong with that, but if you don't use IPv6, there's no reason why it should be enabled.

Next, in the lines RX packets and TX packets, you can see send (transmit, TX) and receive (RX) statistics. It's not especially the number of packets that is of interest here, but mainly the number of erroneous packets. In fact, all of these parameters should be 0 at all times. If you see anything else, you should check what is going on. The following error indicators are displayed using ifconfig:

- errors: Represents the number of packets that had an error. Typically, this is due to bad cabling or a duplex mismatch. In modern networks, duplex settings are detected automatically, and most of the time that goes quite well, so if you see an increasing number here, it might be a good idea to replace the patch cable to your server.

- dropped: A packet gets dropped if the server has no memory available to receive it. Dropped packets will also occur on a server that runs out of memory, so make sure that you have enough physical memory installed in your server.

- overruns: An overrun will occur if your NIC gets overwhelmed with packets. If you are using up-to-date hardware, overruns may indicate that someone is doing a denial-of-service attack on your server.

- frame: A frame error is an error caused by a physical problem in the packet, such as a CRC error. You may see this error on a server with a bad connection link.

- carrier: The carrier is the electrical wave that is used for modulation of the signal. It really is the component that carries the data over your network. The error counter should be 0 at all times, and if it isn't, you probably have a physical problem with the network board, so it's time to replace the network board itself.

- collisions: You might see this error in an Ethernet network in which a hub is used instead of a switch. Modern switches make packet collisions impossible, so you will probably never see this error anymore.

If you see a problem when using ifconfig, the next step should be to check your network board settings. You can use ethtool to do this. The problem with ethtool is that it's not supported for each network board. So, in some situations, ethtool will show you next to nothing. In other cases, it will give you detailed information, as you can see in Listing 3-20.

Listing 3-20. *Use ethtool to Check Settings of Your Network Board*

```
root@mel:~# ethtool eth1
Settings for eth1:
        Supported ports: [ TP ]
        Supported link modes:   10baseT/Half 10baseT/Full
                                100baseT/Half 100baseT/Full
                                1000baseT/Full
        Supports auto-negotiation: Yes
        Advertised link modes:  10baseT/Half 10baseT/Full
                                100baseT/Half 100baseT/Full
                                1000baseT/Full
        Advertised auto-negotiation: Yes
        Speed: 1000Mb/s
        Duplex: Full
        Port: Twisted Pair
        PHYAD: 0
        Transceiver: internal
        Auto-negotiation: on
        Supports Wake-on: pumbg
        Wake-on: g
        Current message level: 0x00000033 (51)
        Link detected: yes
```

Typically, just a few parameters from the ethtool output are of interest, the Speed and Duplex settings. They show you how your network board is talking to other nodes. If you see, for example, that your server is set to full duplex, whereas all other nodes in your network use half duplex, you've found your problem and know what you need to fix.

Another nice tool to monitor what is happening on the network is IPTraf (start it by entering iptraf). This is a real-time monitoring tool that shows what is happening on the network from a graphical interface. When you start it, it shows you a license agreement window. From that window, press a key to continue to the IPTraf main menu, which you can see in Figure 3-1.

Before you launch IPTraf from this menu, choose the Configure option. From there, you can specify what exactly you want to see and how you want it to be displayed. For instance, a useful setting to change is the additional port range. By default, IPTraf shows activity on privileged TCP/UDP ports only. If you have a specific application that you want to monitor and it doesn't use one of these privileged ports, select Additional Ports from the configuration interface (see Figure 3-2) and specify additional ports that you want to monitor.

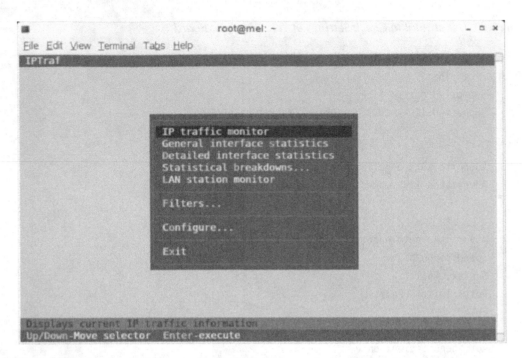

Figure 3-1. *IPTraf works from a menu to show you real-time network usage statistics.*

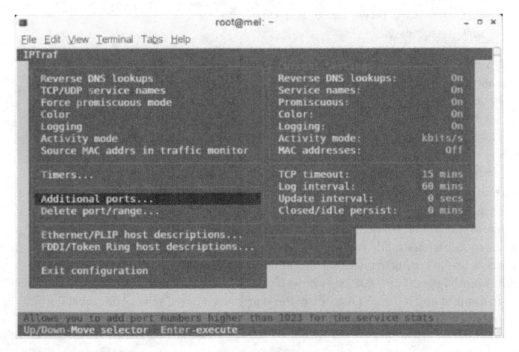

Figure 3-2. *Use the Additional Ports option from the configuration interface to monitor nonprivileged ports as well.*

After telling `iptraf` how to do its work, from the main menu use the IP Traffic Monitor option to start the tool. You can next select on which interface you want to listen, or just press Enter to listen on all interfaces. Next, IPTraf asks you in which file you want to write log information. You should be aware that it isn't always a good choice to configure logging, because logging may fill up your file systems quite fast. In case you don't want to log, press Ctrl+X now. This will start the IPTraf interface, which displays everything that is happening on your server and on what port exactly it is happening (see Figure 3-3).

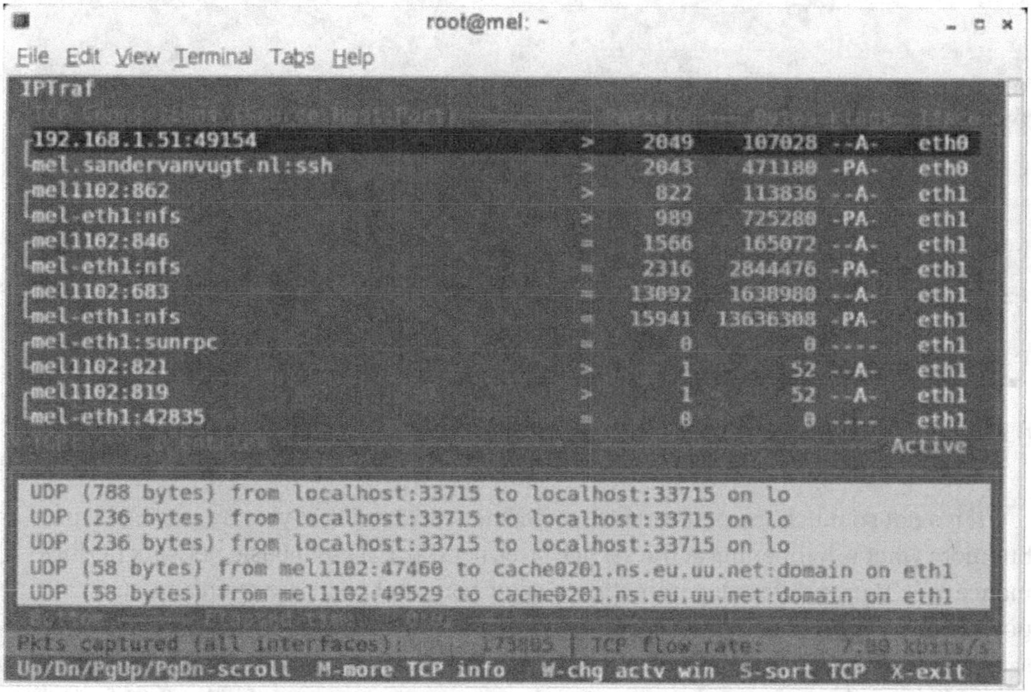

Figure 3-3. *IPTraf gives a real-time overview of what is happening on your server's network boards.*

Apart from the real-time overview of what is happening on the network, IPTraf also offers the LAN station monitor, shown in Figure 3-4. This interface is a great help in finding workstations that cause a lot of network load. For instance, you can use this to find the workstation that is doing video streaming or online gaming.

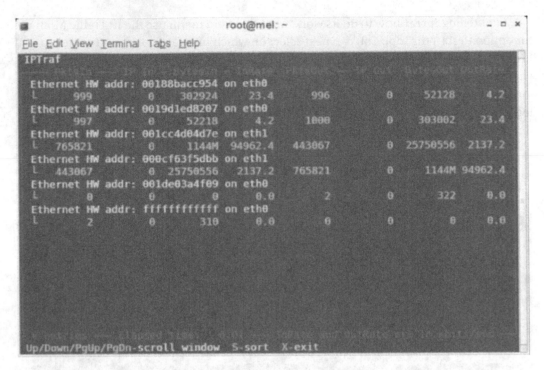

Figure 3-4. *The LAN station monitor shows the most active LAN station at the top of the list.*

If it's not so much the performance on the network card that you are interested in, but more what is happening at the service level, netstat is a good basic network performance tool. It uses different parameters to show you what ports are open and on what ports your server sees activity. My personal favorite way of using netstat is by issuing the netstat -tulpn command. This gives an overview of all listening ports on the server and even tells you what other node is connected to a particular port. See Listing 3-21 for an overview.

Listing 3-21. *netstat Enables You to See Which Ports Are Listening on Your Server and Who Is Connected*

```
root@mel:~# netstat -tulpn
Active Internet connections (only servers)
Proto Recv-Q Send-Q Local Address    Foreign Address  State    PID/Program name
tcp        0      0 0.0.0.0:2049     0.0.0.0:*        LISTEN   -
tcp        0      0 0.0.0.0:675      0.0.0.0:*        LISTEN   5162/rpc.ypxfrd
tcp        0      0 0.0.0.0:139      0.0.0.0:*        LISTEN   5419/smbd
tcp        0      0 0.0.0.0:683      0.0.0.0:*        LISTEN   5170/ypbind
```

```
tcp     0     0 0.0.0.0:111      0.0.0.0:*      LISTEN     4748/portmap
tcp     0     0 0.0.0.0:80       0.0.0.0:*      LISTEN     5582/apache2
tcp     0     0 0.0.0.0:42835    0.0.0.0:*      LISTEN     5398/rpc.mountd
tcp     0     0 127.0.0.1:5432   0.0.0.0:*      LISTEN     5197/postgres
tcp     0     0 127.0.0.1:6010   0.0.0.0:*      LISTEN     5938/1
tcp     0     0 0.0.0.0:33242    0.0.0.0:*      LISTEN     -
tcp     0     0 0.0.0.0:60026    0.0.0.0:*      LISTEN     4764/rpc.statd
tcp     0     0 0.0.0.0:443      0.0.0.0:*      LISTEN     5290/apache2
tcp     0     0 0.0.0.0:445      0.0.0.0:*      LISTEN     5419/smbd
tcp     0     0 0.0.0.0:669      0.0.0.0:*      LISTEN     5156/ypserv
tcp6    0     0 :::22            :::*           LISTEN     5117/sshd
tcp6    0     0 ::1:6010         :::*           LISTEN     5938/1
udp     0     0 0.0.0.0:2049     0.0.0.0:*                 -
udp     0     0 192.168.1.99:137 0.0.0.0:*                 5417/nmbd
udp     0     0 10.0.0.10:137    0.0.0.0:*                 5417/nmbd
udp     0     0 0.0.0.0:137      0.0.0.0:*                 5417/nmbd
udp     0     0 192.168.1.99:138 0.0.0.0:*                 5417/nmbd
udp     0     0 10.0.0.10:138    0.0.0.0:*                 5417/nmbd
udp     0     0 0.0.0.0:138      0.0.0.0:*                 5417/nmbd
udp     0     0 0.0.0.0:668      0.0.0.0:*                 5156/ypserv
udp     0     0 0.0.0.0:671      0.0.0.0:*                 5159/rpc.yppasswdd
udp     0     0 0.0.0.0:674      0.0.0.0:*                 5162/rpc.ypxfrd
udp     0     0 0.0.0.0:682      0.0.0.0:*                 5170/ypbind
udp     0     0 0.0.0.0:683      0.0.0.0:*                 5170/ypbind
udp     0     0 0.0.0.0:45750    0.0.0.0:*                 -
udp     0     0 0.0.0.0:700      0.0.0.0:*                 4764/rpc.statd
udp     0     0 0.0.0.0:67       0.0.0.0:*                 5528/dhcpd3
udp     0     0 0.0.0.0:69       0.0.0.0:*                 5428/in.tftpd
udp     0     0 0.0.0.0:35016    0.0.0.0:*                 4764/rpc.statd
udp     0     0 0.0.0.0:45010    0.0.0.0:*                 5398/rpc.mountd
udp     0     0 0.0.0.0:111      0.0.0.0:*                 4748/portmap
udp     0     0 10.0.0.10:123    0.0.0.0:*                 4563/ntpd
udp     0     0 192.168.1.99:123 0.0.0.0:*                 4563/ntpd
udp     0     0 127.0.0.1:123    0.0.0.0:*                 4563/ntpd
udp     0     0 0.0.0.0:123      0.0.0.0:*                 4563/ntpd
udp6    0     0 fe80::219:d1ff:feed:123  :::*              4563/ntpd
udp6    0     0 fe80::20c:f6ff:fe3f:123  :::*              4563/ntpd
udp6    0     0 ::1:123          :::*                      4563/ntpd
udp6    0     0 :::123           :::*                      4563/ntpd
```

When using `netstat`, quite a few options are available. The following is an overview of the most interesting ones:

- `-p`: Shows the PID of the program that has opened a port

- `-c`: Updates the display every second

- `-s`: Shows statistics for IP, UDP, TCP, and ICMP

- `-t`: Shows TCP sockets

- `-u`: Shows UDP sockets

- `-w`: Shows RAW sockets

- `-l`: Shows listening ports

- `-n`: Resolves addresses to names

Many other tools are available to monitor the network as well, but most of them are beyond the scope of this chapter because they are protocol or service specific; thus, they won't help you as much in finding performance problems on the network. However, I want to mention one very simple performance testing method that I personally use at all times when analyzing a performance problem. Because all that counts when analyzing network performance is how fast your network can copy data from and to your server, I like to measure that by creating a big file (1 GB, for example) and copying it over the network. To measure time, I use a `time` command that gives a clear impression of how long it really took to copy the file. For instance, `time scp server:/bigfile /localdir` will end with a summary of the total time it took to copy the file over. This is an excellent test, especially when you start optimizing performance, because it will show you immediately whether you reached your goals or not.

Performance Baselining

The purpose of a performance baseline is to establish what exactly is happening on your server and what level of performance is normal at any given moment in time. By establishing a performance baseline that is based on the long-term statistics for your server, it is easier to interpret the performance data that you'll find at any given moment in time. To do performance baselining, you can use tools like Nagios, which also includes an alerting function that will send you a message when a threshold is passed. To give you the perfect impression of what your server is doing, it's a good idea to implement a baselining tool as well. In Chapter 6, you'll read more about utilities that you can use for this purpose.

Summary

In this chapter you have learned how to monitor performance on your server. Now you can understand what really is happening on a server that isn't performing well. Next, you need to do something with that information. In Chapter 4 you will learn how to tune performance parameters to get the best out of your server.

■ ■ ■

## CHAPTER 4

Performance Optimization
Tuning Ubuntu Server
Like a Racing Car

No matter on which kind of server you install it, Ubuntu Server will always be installed with the same settings. To give an example, the area of reserved memory in RAM for packets coming in to the network board will always be the same, no matter if your server has 128 MB or 128 GB of RAM. As you can guess, there's something to gain here! In this chapter you'll read about performance optimization. We'll explore what possibilities there are to optimize performance of the CPU, RAM, storage, and network. I'll also give a few hints on optimizing performance for network services like Samba and NFS. If everything goes well, at the end of this chapter, your server will be performing a lot better.

Strategies for Optimizing Performance

You can look at performance optimization in two different ways. For some people, it just means changing some parameters and seeing what happens. That is not the best approach. A much better approach is to start with performance monitoring first. This will give you some crystal-clear ideas about what exactly is happening with performance on your server. Before optimizing anything, you should know what exactly to optimize. For example, if the network performs badly, you should know whether the problems are caused by the network or caused by an insufficient amount of memory allocated for the network packets coming in and going out. So make sure you know what to optimize.

About /proc and sysctl

Once you know what to optimize, it comes down to actually doing it. In many situations, optimizing performance means writing a parameter to the /proc file system. This file system is created by the kernel when your server boots up, and normally contains the settings that your kernel is working with. Under /proc/sys, you'll find many system parameters that can be changed. The easy way to change system parameters is to echo the new value to the configuration file. For example, the /proc/sys/vm/swappiness file contains a value that indicates how willing your server is to swap. The range of this value is 0 to 100; a low value means that your server will avoid swapping as long as possible, whereas a high value means that your server is more willing to swap. The default value in this file is 60. If you think your server is too eager to swap, you could change this value, using

```
echo "30" > /proc/sys/vm/swappiness
```

This method works well, but there is a problem. As soon as your server restarts, you will lose this value. So, the better solution is to store it in a configuration file and make sure that configuration file is read when your server boots up again. A configuration file exists for this purpose, named /etc/sysctl.conf. When booting, your server starts the procps service that reads this configuration file and applies all settings in it. So, to make it easier for you to apply the same settings again and again, put them in this configuration file. There is a small syntax difference, though.

In /etc/sysctl.conf, you refer to files that exist in the /proc/sys hierarchy. So the name of the file you are referring to is relative to this directory. Also, instead of using a slash as the separator between directory, subdirectories, and files, it is common to use a dot (even if the slash is accepted as well). That means that to apply the change to the swappiness parameter previously introduced, you would include the following line in /etc/sysctl.conf:

```
vm.swappiness=30
```

This setting would be applied only the next time that your server reboots. Instead of just writing it to the configuration file, you can apply it to the current sysctl settings as well. To do that, use the sysctl command; the following command can be used to apply this setting immediately:

```
sysctl vm.swappiness=30
```

In fact, using this solution does exactly the same thing as using the echo "30" > /proc/sys/vm/swappiness command. The most practical way of applying these settings is to write them to /etc/sysctl.conf first, and then activate them using sysctl -p /etc/sysctl.conf. Once the settings are activated in this way, you can also get an overview of all current sysctl settings, using sysctl -a. Listing 4-1 shows a partial example of the output of this command.

Listing 4-1. *sysctl -a Shows All Current sysctl Settings*

```
fs.inode-nr = 11997      300
fs.inode-state = 11997   300     0        0        0        0        0
fs.file-nr = 832         0       365313
fs.file-max = 365313
fs.dentry-state = 13406 8519     45       0        0        0
fs.overflowuid = 65534
fs.overflowgid = 65534
fs.leases-enable = 1
fs.dir-notify-enable = 1
fs.lease-break-time = 45
fs.aio-nr = 0
fs.aio-max-nr = 65536
fs.inotify.max_user_instances = 128
fs.inotify.max_user_watches = 524288
fs.inotify.max_queued_events = 16384
...
sunrpc.udp_slot_table_entries = 16
sunrpc.tcp_slot_table_entries = 16
sunrpc.min_resvport = 665
sunrpc.max_resvport = 1023
```

The output of sysctl -a can be somewhat overwhelming. I recommend using it in combination with grep to find the information you need. For example, sysctl -a | grep xfs would show you only lines that have the text xfs in their output.

Applying a Simple Test

Although sysctl and its configuration file sysctl.conf are very useful tools to change performance-related settings, you should thoroughly test your changes before applying them. Before you write a parameter to the system, make sure that it really is the parameter you need. The big question, though, is how to know that for sure. Even if not valid in all cases, I like to do a small test with a 1 GB file to find out what exactly the effect of a parameter is. First, I create a 1 GB file, using the following:

```
dd if=/dev/zero of=/root/1GBfile bs=1M count=1024
```

By copying this file around and measuring the time it takes to copy it, you can get a pretty good idea of the effect of some of the parameters. Many tasks you perform on your Linux server are I/O-related, so this simple test can give you an impression of whether or not there is any improvement after you have tuned performance. To measure the time it takes to copy this file, use the time command, followed by cp, as in time cp /root/1GBfile /tmp. In Listing 4-2, you can see an example of what this looks like when measuring I/O performance on your server. In this example, I'm using the time command to measure how much time it took to complete a given command. The output of time gives three parameters:

- real: The real time, in seconds, it took to complete the command. This includes waiting time as well.

- user: The time spent in user space that was required to complete the command.

- sys: The time spent in system space to complete the command.

Listing 4-2. *Use time to Measure Performance While Copying a File*

```
root@mel:~# dd if=/dev/zero of=/root/1GBfile bs=1M count=1024
1024+0 records in
1024+0 records out
1073741824 bytes (1.1 GB) copied, 7.75989 s, 138 MB/s
root@mel:~# time cp 1GBfile /tmp

real    0m8.644s
user    0m0.050s
sys     0m2.950s
```

When doing a test like this, though, it is important to interpret it in the right way. Consider for example Listing 4-3, in which the same command was repeated a few seconds later.

Listing 4-3. *The Same Test, 10 Seconds Later*

```
root@mel:~# time cp 1GBfile /tmp

real    0m7.998s
user    0m0.060s
sys     0m3.230s
```

As you can see, it now performs about two-thirds of a second faster than the first time the command was used. Is this the result of a performance parameter that I've changed in between? No, but let's have a look at the result of free -m, as shown in Listing 4-4.

Listing 4-4. *Cache Also Plays an Important Role in Performance*

```
root@mel:~# free -m
                total    used    free    shared    buffers    cached
Mem:            3987     2246    1741    0         17         2108
-/+ buffers/cache:       119     3867
Swap:           2047     0       2047
```

Any idea what has happened here? The entire 1 GB file was put in cache. As you can see, free -m shows almost 2 GB of data in cache that wasn't there before and that has an influence on the time it takes to copy a large file around.

So what lesson is there to learn? Performance optimization is complex. You have to take into account multiple factors that all have their influence on the performance of your server. Only when this is done the right way will you truly see how your server performs and whether or not you have succeeded in improving its performance. If you're not looking at the data properly, you may miss things and think that you have improved performance, while in reality you might have made it worse.

■**Caution** Performance tuning is complicated. If you miss a piece of information, the performance penalty for your server may be severe. Only apply the knowledge from this chapter if you feel confident about your assumptions. If you don't feel confident, don't change anything, but instead ask an expert for his opinion.

CPU Tuning

Assuming that you have applied all the lessons from Chapter 3 and have a clear picture of what is wrong with the utilization of your server, it is time to start optimizing. In this section you'll learn what you can do to optimize the performance of your server's CPU. First, you'll learn about aspects of the inner workings of the CPU that are important when trying to optimize performance parameters for the CPU. Then, you'll read about several common techniques to optimize CPU utilization.

Understanding CPU Performance

To be able to tune the CPU, you should know what is important with regard to this part of your system. To understand CPU performance, you should know about the thread scheduler. This part of the kernel makes sure that all process threads get an equal number of CPU cycles. Because most processes will do some I/O as well, it's not a problem that the scheduler puts process threads on hold momentarily. While not being served by the CPU, the process thread can wait for I/O. The fact that the process is doing that while being put on hold by the scheduler increases its efficiency. The scheduler operates by using fairness, meaning that all threads are moving forward using equal time segments. By using fairness, the scheduler makes sure there is not too much latency.

The scheduling process is pretty simple in a single-CPU core environment. Naturally, it is more complicated in a multicore environment. To work in a multi-CPU or multicore environment, your server uses a specialized symmetric multiprocessing (SMP) kernel. If needed, this kernel is installed automatically. In an SMP environment, the scheduler should make sure that some kind of load balancing is used. This means that process threads are spread over all available CPU cores. In fact, if a program is not written using a multithreaded or multiprocessor architecture, the kernel could only run this monolithic program on a dedicated CPU core. The kernel is only able to dispatch threads or processes on CPU cores, so only multithreaded processes could have their execution flow dispatched on distinct CPU cores. For example, if the Apache Web Server is compiled using the legacy mono-process architecture, it will take one CPU core. If it is compiled with the multiprocessor or multithreaded model, all processes and threads will run at the same time on the different CPU threads.

A specific concern in a multi-CPU environment is to ensure that the scheduler prevents processes and threads from being moved to other CPU cores. Moving a process means that the information the process has written in the CPU cache has to be moved as well, and that is a relatively expensive procedure.

You may think that a server will benefit if you install multiple CPU cores, but this is not true. When working on multiple cores, chances increase that processes swap around between cores, taking their cached information with them, which slows down performance in a multiprocessing environment. In two specific situations, you can benefit from a multiprocessing environment:

- When using virtualization, you can pin virtual machines to a particular CPU core.

- When using an application that is written for an SMP environment (for example, Oracle), the kernel will be able to dispatch all the threads and processes on the different cores efficiently.

Optimizing CPU Performance

CPU performance optimization is really just about doing two things: prioritizing processes and optimizing the SMP environment. Every process gets a static priority from the scheduler. The scheduler can differentiate between real-time (RT) processes and normal processes, but if a process falls into one of these categories, it will be equal to all other processes in the same category. That means the priority of RT processes is higher than the priority of normal processes, but also that it is not possible to differentiate between differ-ent RT processes. Be aware, though, that some RT processes (most of them are part of the Linux kernel) will run with highest priority, whereas the rest of the available CPU cycles have to be divided between the other processes. In that procedure, it's all about fairness: the longer a process is waiting, the higher its priority will be.

The way that the scheduler does its work is not tunable by any parameter in the /proc file system. The only way to tune it is by changing the values for some parameters that are defined in the kernel source file kernel/sched.c. Because this is a difficult procedure that in most situations doesn't give any benefits, I strongly advise against it. Another reason why you shouldn't do it is that, in modern Linux systems, there is another, much more efficient method to do this: use the nice command.

Adjusting Process Priority Using nice

You probably already know how the nice command works. It has a range that goes from -20 to 19. The lower the nice value of a process, the higher its priority. So a process that has a nice value of -20 will always get the highest possible priority. I strongly advice against using -20, because if the process that runs with this nice value is a very busy pro-cess, you risk other processes not being served at all anymore. This could even result in a crash of your server, so be careful with -20. If ever you want to adjust the nice value of a process, do it by using increments of 5. So if you want to increase the priority of the pro-cess using PID 1234, try using renice, as follows:

```
renice -5 1234
```

See if the process performs better now, and if it doesn't, renice it to -10, but never go beyond the value of -15, because you risk making your server completely dysfunctional. If ever you feel the need to increase process priority of a process beyond -15, your server probably just is overloaded and there are other measures to take. In that case, you may benefit from one of the following options:

- Check which processes are started when you boot your server. You can use the sysvconfig utility to display a list of all services and their current startup status. You may have some processes that you don't really need. Remove them from your runlevels.

- See if processes are competing for CPU cycles. You can do this by looking at the output of top. If you see several processes that are very busy, they definitely are competing for CPU cycles. If this is the case, try offloading one or more processes to another server.

- Look at the wait time for your CPU. If the wait time, as shown by the wa parameter in top, is high, the problem might not be process related, but rather storage related.

- If it is mainly one process that is very busy, thus preventing other processes from doing their work, see if you can run it on a multicore server. In that scenario, the busy process can just claim one of the cores completely (given that it is developed using the multiprocessing model), while all vital system processes are served by the other core.

Optimizing SMP Environments

If you are working in an SMP environment, one important utility to use to improve performance is the taskset command. You can use taskset to set CPU affinity for a process to one or more CPUs. The result is that your process is less likely to be moved to another CPU. The taskset command uses a hexadecimal bitmask to specify which CPU to use. In this bitmap, the value 0x1 refers to CPU0, 0x2 refers to CPU1, 0x4 refers to CPU2, 0x8 refers to CPU3, and so on.

■**Note** I follow the default Linux way of referring to CPU numbers, in which CPU0 is the first CPU, CPU1 the second, and so on.

So if you have a command that you would like to bind to CPUs 2 and 3, you would use the following command:

```
taskset 0xC somecommand
```

■**Note** If you are surprised about the 0xC in the preceding command, the number used by taskset is a hexadecimal number. CPUs 2 (hexadecimal value 4) and 3 (hexadecimal value 8) make up the value of 12, which, when written in a hexadecimal way, equals C.

You can also use taskset on running processes, by using the -p option. With this option, you can refer to the PID of a process; for instance,

```
taskset 0x3 7034
```

would set the affinity of the process using PID 7034 to CPUs 0 and 1.

You can specify CPU affinity for IRQs as well. To do this, you can use the same bit-mask that you use with `taskset`. Every interrupt has a subdirectory in /proc/irq/, and in that subdirectory there is a file with the name `smp_affinity`. So, for example, if your IRQ 5 is producing a very high workload (check /proc/interrupts to see if this is the case) and you therefore want that IRQ to work on CPU1, use the following command:

```
echo 0x2 > /proc/irq/3/smp_affinity
```

Tuning Memory

System memory is a very important part of a computer. It functions as a buffer between CPU and I/O. By tuning memory, you can really get the best out of it. Linux works with the concept of virtual memory, which is the total of all usable memory available on a server. You can tune the working of virtual memory by writing to the /proc/sys/vm directory. This directory contains lots of parameters that help you to tune the way your server's memory is used. As always when tuning the performance of a server, there are no solutions that work in all cases. Use the parameters in /proc/sys/vm with caution and use them one by one. Only by tuning each parameter individually will you be able to deter-mine whether you really got better memory performance.

Understanding Memory Performance

In a Linux system, virtual memory is used for many purposes. First, there are processes that claim their amount of memory. When tuning memory consumption for processes, it helps to know how these processes allocate memory. For instance, a database server that allocates large amounts of system memory when starting up has different needs from those of a mail server that works with small files only. Also, each process has its own memory space, which may not be addressed by other processes. The kernel ensures that this never happens.

When a process is created, using the `fork()` system call (which basically creates a child process from the parent), the kernel creates a virtual address space for the process. The virtual address space used by a process is made up of pages. These pages have a fixed size of 4 KB on a 32-bit system. On a 64-bit server, you can choose between 4, 8, 16, 32, and 64 KB pages.

Another important aspect of memory usage is caching. Your system includes a read cache and a write cache, and the way in which you tune a server that handles mostly read requests differs from the way in which you tune a server that handles write requests.

Optimizing Memory Usage

Basically, there are two kinds of servers: servers that run a heavy application that allocates lots of memory, and servers that offer services and therefore are accessed frequently by users. Depending on the kind of server you use, you can follow a different optimization approach. Three items are of specific interest with regard to this issue: the configuration of huge pages, the optimization of the write cache, and the optimization of inter-process communication.

Configuring Huge Pages

If your server is a heavily used application server, it may benefit from using large pages, also referred to as huge pages. A huge page by default is 2 MB. Using huge pages may be useful to improve performance in high-performance computing and with memory-intensive applications. By default, no huge pages are allocated, because they would be a waste on a server that doesn't need them. Typically, you set them from the Grub boot loader when you're starting your server. Later on, you can check the number of huge pages in use from the /proc/sys/vm/nr_hugepages parameter. The following procedure summarizes how to set huge pages:

1. Using an editor, open the Grub menu configuration file in /boot/grub/menu.lst.

2. Find the part of the configuration file that defines how your system should boot. It looks like the example in Listing 4-5.

Listing 4-5. *The Boot Section in /boot/grub/menu.lst*

```
title           Ubuntu 8.04, kernel 2.6.24-16-server
root            (hd0,0)
kernel          /vmlinuz-2.6.24-16-server root=/dev/mapper/system-root➥
 ro quiet splash\ hugepages=64
initrd          /initrd.img-2.6.24-16-server
quiet
```

3. In the kernel line, make sure that you enable huge pages, by using the parameter hugepages=nn. In Listing 4-5, I have defined the number of huge pages for this server to be 64.

4. Save your settings and reboot your server to activate them.

Be careful, though, when allocating huge pages. All memory pages that are allocated as huge pages are no longer available for other purposes, and if your server needs a heavy read or write cache, you will suffer from allocating too many huge pages immediately. If you find out that this is the case, you can change the number of huge pages currently in use by writing to the /proc/sys/vm/nr_hugepages parameter. Your server will pick up this new number of huge pages immediately.

Optimizing Write Cache

The parameters described in this section all relate to the buffer cache. As discussed earlier, your server maintains a write cache. By putting data in that write cache, the server can delay writing data. This is useful for more than one reason. Imagine that just after committing the write request to the server, another write request is made. It will be easier for the server to handle that write request if the data is not yet written to disk but is still in memory. You may also want to tune the write cache to balance between the amount of memory reserved for reading and the amount that is reserved for writing data.

The first relevant parameter is in /proc/sys/vm/dirty_ratio. This parameter is used to define the maximum percentage of memory that is used for the write cache. When the percentage of buffer cache in use exceeds this parameter, your server will write memory from the buffer cache to disk as soon as possible. The default of 10 percent works fine for an average server, but in some situations you may want to increase or decrease the amount of memory used here.

Related to dirty_ratio are the dirty_expire_centisecs and dirty_writeback_centisecs parameters, also in /proc/sys/vm. These parameters determine when data in the write cache expires and has to be written to disk, even if the write cache hasn't reached the threshold as defined in dirty_ratio yet. By using these parameters, you reduce the chances of losing data when a power outage occurs on your server. On the contrary, if you want to use power more efficiently, it is useful to give both these parameters the value of 0, which actually disables them and keeps data as long as possible in the write cache. This is useful for laptop computers, because your hard disk needs to spin up in order to write this data, and that takes a lot of power; turning off both of these parameters delays writing to hard disk as long as possible, which is good if you want to limit power consumption.

The last parameter that is related to writing data is nr_pdflush_threads. This parameter helps in determining the number of threads the kernel launches for writing data from the buffer cache. Understanding it is easy: having more of these threads means faster write back. So if you have the idea that buffer cache on your server is not cleared fast enough, increase the value of pdflush_threads using the following command:

```
sysctl -w vm.nr_pdflush_threads=4
```

When using this option, do respect the limitations. By default, the minimal value of pdflush_threads is set to 2 and the maximum is 8.

Next, there is the issue of overcommitting memory. By default, every process tends to claim more memory than it really needs. This is good, because it makes the process faster. If the process already has some spare memory available, it can access it much faster when it needs it, because it doesn't have to ask the kernel if it has some more memory available. To tune the behavior of overcommitting memory, you can write to the /proc/sys/vm/overcommit_memory parameter. Its default value is 0, which means that the kernel checks if it still has memory available before granting it. If that doesn't give you the performance you need, you can consider changing the value to 1, which forces the system to think there is enough memory in all cases. This is good for performance of memory-intensive tasks, but may result in processes getting killed automatically. You can also use the value of 2, which means that the kernel fails the memory request if there is not enough memory available. The minimal amount of memory that is available is specified in the /proc/sys/vm/overcommit_ratio parameter, which by default is set to 50 percent of available RAM. Using the value of 2 makes sure that your server will never run out of available memory by granting memory that is demanded by a process that needs huge amounts of memory (on a server with 16 GB of RAM, the memory allocation request would be denied only if more than 8 GB was requested by one single process).

Another nice parameter is /proc/sys/vm/swappiness. This indicates how eager the process is to start swapping out memory pages. A high value means that your server will swap very fast, and a low value means that the server will wait some more before starting to swap. The default value of 60 does well in most situations. If you still think your server starts swapping too fast, set it to a somewhat lower value, like 30.

Optimizing Inter-Process Communication

The last relevant parameters are those related to shared memory. Shared memory is a memory area that the Linux kernel or Linux applications can use to make communication between processes (also known as Inter-Process Communication, or IPC) as fast as possible. The cool thing about shared memory is that the kernel is not involved in the communication between the processes using it, and data doesn't even have to be copied because the memory areas can be addressed directly. To get an idea of shared memory–related settings your server is currently using, use the ipcs -lm command, as shown in Listing 4-6.

Listing 4-6. *Use ipcs -lm to View Shared Memory Settings*

```
root@mel:~# ipcs -lm

------ Shared Memory Limits --------
max number of segments = 4096
max seg size (kbytes) = 32768
max total shared memory (kbytes) = 8388608
min seg size (bytes) = 1
```

If your applications are written to use shared memory, you can benefit from tuning some of its parameters. If, on the contrary, your applications don't use share memory, it doesn't make a difference if you change the shared memory–related parameters. One of the best-known examples of an application that uses shared memory is Oracle. To find out whether shared memory is used on your server and, if so, in what amount it is used, use the ipcs -m command. Listing 4-7 shows an example of its output on a server where just one shared memory segment is used.

Listing 4-7. *Use ipcs -m to Find Out if Your Server Is Using Shared Memory Segments*

```
root@mel:~# ipcs -m

------ Shared Memory Segments --------
key          shmid     owner      perms     bytes       nattch    status
0x0052e2c1 0           postgres   600       29368320    4
```

The first parameter that is related to shared memory is shmmax. This defines the maximum size, in bytes, of a single shared memory segment that a Linux process can allocate. You can see the current setting in the configuration file /proc/sys/kernel/shmmax:

```
root@mel:~# cat /proc/sys/kernel/shmmax
33554432
```

This sample was taken from a system that has 4 GB of RAM. The shmmax setting was automatically created to allow processes to allocate up to about 3.3 GB of RAM. It doesn't make sense to tune the parameter to use all available RAM, because RAM has to be used for other purposes as well.

The second parameter that is related to shared memory is shmmni, which is not, as you might think, the minimal size of shared memory segments, but rather the maximum number of shared memory segments that your kernel can allocate. You can get the default value from /proc/sys/kernel/shmmni; it should be set to 4096. If you run an application that relies heavily on the use of shared memory, you may benefit from increasing this parameter; for instance:

```
sysctl -w kernel.shmmni=8192
```

The last parameter related to shared memory is shmall. It is set in /proc/sys/kernel/shmall and defines the total number of shared memory pages that can be used system wide. Normally, the value should be set to the value of shmmax, divided by the current page size your server is using. On a 32-bit processor, finding the page size is easy—it is always set to 4096. On a 64-bit computer, you can use the getconf command to determine the current page size:

```
# getconf PAGE_SIZE
4096
```

If the shmall parameter doesn't contain a value that is big enough for your application, change it as needed. For instance, use the following command:

```
sysctl -w kernel.shmall=2097152
```

Tuning Storage Performance

The third element in the chain of Linux performance is the storage channel. Performance optimization on this channel can be divided in two categories: file system performance and I/O buffer performance. File system optimization is dealt with in Chapter 5, so this section focuses on I/O optimization that is not directly related to the file system.

Understanding Storage Performance

To determine what happens with I/O on your server, Linux uses the I/O scheduler. This kernel component sits between the block layer that communicates directly with the file systems and the device drivers, as depicted in Figure 4-1. The block layer generates I/O requests for the file systems and passes those requests to the I/O scheduler. This scheduler in turn transforms the request and passes it to the low-level drivers. The drivers forward the request to the actual storage devices. If you want to optimize storage performance, optimizing the I/O scheduler is an important part of that.

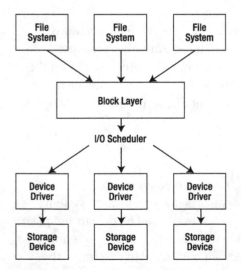

Figure 4-1. *The I/O scheduler sits between the file systems and the actual devices.*

Optimizing the I/O Scheduler

Working with an I/O scheduler makes your computer more flexible. The I/O scheduler can prioritize I/O requests and reduce the amount of time needed to search for data on the hard disk. Also, the I/O scheduler makes sure that a request is handled before it times out. An important goal of the I/O scheduler is to make hard disk seek times more efficient. The scheduler does this by collecting requests before really committing them to disk. Because of this approach, the scheduler can do its work more efficiently. For instance, it may choose to order requests before committing them to disk, which makes hard disk seeks more efficient.

When optimizing the performance of the I/O scheduler, there is a dilemma: you can optimize read performance or write performance, but not both at the same time. Optimizing read performance means that write performance will be not as good, whereas optimizing write performance means you have to pay a price in read performance. So before you start to optimize the I/O scheduler, you should really analyze what type of workload is generated by your server.

There are four different ways for the I/O scheduler to do its work:

- When you choose Complete Fair Queueing (cfq), the I/O scheduler tries to allocate I/O bandwidth fairly. This approach offers a good solution for machines with mixed workloads and offers the best compromise between latency and throughput. Latency is relevant in an environment in which a lot of data is read, and throughput is relevant in an environment in which there are a lot of file writes.

- The Deadline scheduler (deadline) works with five different I/O queues and therefore is very capable of differentiating between read requests and write requests. It does this by merging write actions and sorting them, which allows them to get written to disk faster. When using this scheduler, read requests will get a higher priority. Write requests do not have a deadline and, therefore, data to be written can remain in cache for a longer period. This scheduler does well in environments in which both good read and good write performance is required but reads have a bit higher priority. This scheduler does particularly well in database environments.

- The Noop scheduler (noop) performs only minimal merging functions on your data. Because there is no sorting, this scheduler has minimal overhead. This scheduler was developed for non-disk-based block devices, such as memory devices. It also does well on storage media that have extensive caching.

- The Anticipatory scheduler (anticipatory) tries to reduce read response times. It does so by introducing a controlled delay in all read requests. This increases the possibility that another read request can be handled in the same I/O request and therefore makes reads more efficient.

There are two ways to change the current I/O scheduler. You can echo a new value to the /sys/block/<YOURDEVICE>/queue/scheduler file. Alternatively, you can set it as a boot parameter, using elevator=yourscheduler at the Grub prompt or in the Grub menu. The choices are noop, anticipatory, deadline, and cfq.

Optimizing Reads

Another way to optimize how your server works is by tuning read requests. This is something that you can do on a per-disk basis. First, there is read_ahead, which can be tuned in /sys/block/<YOURDEVICE>/queue/read_ahead_kb. On a default Ubuntu Server installation, this parameter is set to 128 KB. If you have slow disks, you can optimize your read performance by using a higher value; 512 KB, for instance, is a good option. Also, you can tune the number of outstanding read requests by using /sys/block/<YOURDEVICE>/queue/nr_requests. The default value for this parameter also is set to 128, but a higher value may optimize your server in a significant way. Try 512, or even 1024, to get the best read performance, but do always observe whether it introduces too much latency while writing files.

■**Note** Optimizing read performance works well but be aware that, while making read performance better, you'll also introduce latency on writes. In general, there is nothing against that, but if your server loses power, all data that is still in memory buffers and hasn't been written yet will be lost.

Network Tuning

Among the most difficult items to tune is network performance, because multiple layers are used in networking. First, there are buffers on the network card itself that deal with physical packets. Next, there is the TCP/IP protocol stack, and then the application stack. All layers work together, and tuning one will have its consequences at the other layers. While tuning the network, always work upward in the protocol stack. That is, start by tuning the packets themselves, then tune the TCP/IP stack, and after that have a look at the service stacks that are in use on your server.

Tuning Kernel Parameters

While it initializes, the kernel sets some parameters automatically, based on the amount of memory that is available on your server. So the good news is that in many situations, there is no work to be done here. Some parameters, however, by default are not set in the most optimal way, so there is some performance to gain there.

For every network connection, the kernel allocates a socket. The socket is the end-to-end line of communication. Each socket has a receive buffer and a send buffer, also known as the read (receive) and write (send) buffers. These buffers are very important; if they are full, no more data can be processed, so data will be dropped. This will have important consequences for the performance of your server, because if data is dropped, it needs to be processed again.

The basis of all reserved sockets on the network comes from two /proc tunables:

```
/proc/sys/net/core/wmem_default
/proc/sys/net/core/rmem_default
```

All kernel-based sockets are reserved from these sockets. However, if a socket is TCP based, the settings in here are overwritten by TCP-specific parameters, in particular the tcp_rmem and tcp_wmem parameters. The upcoming section "Tuning TCP Read and Write Buffers" give more details on how to optimize those parameters.

The values of wmem_default and rmem_default are set automatically when your server boots. If, however, you suffer from dropped packets, you may benefit from increasing them. In many cases the values that are used by default are rather low. To set them, tune the following parameters in /etc/sysctl.conf:

```
net.core.wmem_default
net.core.rmem_default
```

Especially if you have dropped packets, try doubling them to find out if it leads to a better network performance.

Related to the default read and write buffer sizes are the maximum read and write buffer sizes, rmem_max and wmem_max. These are also calculated automatically when your server boots up, but for many situations are far too low. For instance, on a server that has 4 GB of RAM, the sizes of these are set to 128 KB only! You may benefit from changing their values to 8 MB instead:

```
sysctl -w net.core.rmem_max=8388608
sysctl -w net.core.wmem_max=8388608
```

When increasing the read and write buffer sizes, you also have to increase the maximum number of incoming packets that can be queued. This is set in netdev_max_backlog. The default value is set to 1000, which is not enough for very busy servers. Try increasing it to a much higher value, like 8000, especially if you suffer from long latency times on your network, or if there are lots of dropped packets:

```
sysctl -w net.core.netdev_max_backlog=8000
```

Apart from the maximum number of incoming packets that your server can queue, there also is a maximum number of incoming connections that can be accepted. You can set this parameter from the somaxconn file in /proc:

```
sysctl -w net.core.somaxconn=512
```

By tuning this parameter, you will limit the number of new connections that are dropped.

Optimizing TCP/IP

Up to now, you have tuned kernel buffers for network sockets only. These are generic parameters. If you are working with TCP, some specific tunables are available as well. Sometimes the options are related; if they are, the option that is higher in the protocol stack will always win. That is, a TCP tunable will overwrite a generic tunable. Most of the TCP tunables by default have a value that is too low. Chances are that you can gain a lot by increasing them. All relevant options are in /proc/sys/net/ipv4, as you can see in Listing 4-8.

Listing 4-8. *Set All IP-Related Parameters by Adding the Value You Want to Use in /proc/sys/ net/ipv4*

```
root@mel:/proc/sys/net/ipv4# ls
cipso_cache_bucket_size          tcp_dma_copybreak
cipso_cache_enable               tcp_dsack
cipso_rbm_optfmt                 tcp_ecn
cipso_rbm_strictvalid            tcp_fack
conf                             tcp_fin_timeout
icmp_echo_ignore_all             tcp_frto
icmp_echo_ignore_broadcasts      tcp_frto_response
icmp_errors_use_inbound_ifaddr   tcp_keepalive_intvl
icmp_ignore_bogus_error_responses tcp_keepalive_probes
icmp_ratelimit                   tcp_keepalive_time
icmp_ratemask                    tcp_low_latency
igmp_max_memberships             tcp_max_orphans
igmp_max_msf                     tcp_max_ssthresh
inet_peer_gc_maxtime             tcp_max_syn_backlog
inet_peer_gc_mintime             tcp_max_tw_buckets
inet_peer_maxttl                 tcp_mem
inet_peer_minttl                 tcp_moderate_rcvbuf
inet_peer_threshold              tcp_mtu_probing
```

ip_default_ttl

ip_dynaddr

ip_forward

ipfrag_high_thresh

ipfrag_low_thresh

ipfrag_max_dist

ipfrag_secret_interval

ipfrag_time

ip_local_port_range

ip_nonlocal_bind

ip_no_pmtu_disc

neigh

netfilter

route

tcp_abc

tcp_abort_on_overflow

tcp_adv_win_scale

tcp_allowed_congestion_control

tcp_app_win

tcp_available_congestion_control

tcp_base_mss

tcp_congestion_control

tcp_no_metrics_save

tcp_orphan_retries

tcp_reordering

tcp_retrans_collapse

tcp_retries1

tcp_retries2

tcp_rfc1337

tcp_rmem

tcp_sack

tcp_slow_start_after_idle

tcp_stdurg

tcp_synack_retries

tcp_syncookies

tcp_syn_retries

tcp_timestamps

tcp_tso_win_divisor

tcp_tw_recycle

tcp_tw_reuse

tcp_window_scaling

tcp_wmem

tcp_workaround_signed_windows

Tuning TCP Read and Write Buffers

A good place to start to optimize network performance is to tune the TCP read buffer size and write buffer size. By tuning them, you modify the amount of memory reserved for incoming (read) and outgoing (write) packets. These values are written to tcp_rmem and tcp_wmem. The kernel tries to allocate the best possible values for these parameters when it boots, but in some cases it doesn't work out that well. An indication of this is, for example, if your network suffers from dropped packets. If that happens, you can change the minimum size, the default size, and the maximum size of these buffers. Notice that each of these two parameters contains three values at the same time, for minimal, default, and maximal size. In general there is no need to tune the minimal size. Tuning the default size can be interesting, though. This is the buffer size that will be available when your server boots. By tuning it, you will ensure that your server works with the correct values straight away, and that you won't have to do any extra work. Tuning the maximum size is important, as it defines the upper threshold above which packets will get dropped. In Listing 4-9 you can see the default settings for these parameters on my server that has 4 GB of RAM.

Listing 4-9. *Default Settings for TCP Read and Write Buffers*

```
root@mel:~# cat /proc/sys/net/ipv4/tcp_rmem
4096    87380    4194304
root@mel:~# cat /proc/sys/net/ipv4/tcp_wmem
4096    16384    4194304
```

In this example, the maximum size is quite good, and 4 MB is available as the maximum size for read and write buffers. The default write buffer size, though, is limited. Imagine that you want to tune these parameters in a way that the default write buffer size is as big as the default read buffer size, and the maximum for both parameters is set to 8 MB. You could do that by using the next two commands:

```
sysctl -w net.ipv4.tcp_rmem="4096 87380 8388608"
sysctl -w net.ipv4.tcp_wmem="4096 87380 8388608"
```

Before tuning options like these, you should always check the availability of memory on your server. All memory that is allocated for TCP read and write buffers can't be used for other purposes anymore, so you might cause problems in other areas while tuning these. However, if you use a modern server that has gigabytes of RAM, this problem will not be relevant for you.

Tuning TCP Acknowledgments

Another useful set of parameters in /proc/sys/net/ipv4 is related to TCP's use of acknowledgments. TCP uses acknowledgments to confirm that certain packets have been received. Let's have a look at an example to understand how this works. Imagine that the sender in a TCP connection sends a series of packets, numbered 1,2,3,4,5,6,7,8,9,10. Now imagine that the receiver receives all of them, with the exception of packet 5. In the default setting, the receiver would acknowledge receiving up to packet 4, in which case the sender would send packets 5,6,7,8,9,10 again. This is a waste of bandwidth, because packets 6,7,8,9,10 have been received correctly already and will be sent again.

To handle this acknowledgment traffic in a more efficient way, the setting /proc/sys/net/ipv4/tcp_sack is enabled (has the value of 1). That means in cases like the preceding example, only missing packets have to be sent again and not the complete packet stream. For the sake of your network bandwidth, that is good, because only those packets that really need to be retransmitted are retransmitted. So if your bandwidth is low, you should always leave /proc/sys/net/ipv4/tcp_sack on. If, however, you are on a fast network, there is a downside. When using this parameter, packets may come in out of order, in which case you need larger TCP receive buffers to keep all the packets until they can be defragmented and put in the right order. That means that using this parameter involves more memory being reserved. From that perspective, on fast network connections, you better switch it off. To switch it off, use the following:

```
sysctl -w net.ipv4.tcp_sack=0
```

When disabling TCP selective acknowledgments as just discussed, you should also disable two related parameters: tcp_dsack and tcp_fack. These parameters enable selective acknowledgments for specific packet types. If tcp_sack is enabled, these should be on as well, and if tcp_sack is disabled, make sure these are off. To enable them, use the following two commands:

```
sysctl -w net.ipv4.tcp_dsack=0
sysctl -w net.ipv4.tcp_fack=0
```

If you prefer to work with selective acknowledgments, you can also tune the amount of memory that is reserved to buffer incoming packets that have to be put in the right order. With tcp_sack on, these buffers need to be bigger than they need to be if tcp_sack is off. This is because more packets need to be held in the buffer, waiting for all packets to be received, before your server can process them. Two parameters relate to this, ipfrag_low_thresh and ipfrag_high_thresh. When the number that is specified in ipfrag_high_thresh is reached, new packets to be defragmented are dropped until the server reaches ipfrag_low_tresh. Make sure the value of both of these parameters is set high enough at all times if your server uses selective acknowledgments. The following values are reasonable for most servers:

```
sysctl -w net.ipv4.ipfrag_low_thresh=393216
sysctl -w net.ipv4.ipfrag_high_thresh=524288
```

Optimizing Connections

Next in /proc/sys/net/ipv4 is the length of the TCP Syn queue that is created for each port. The idea is that all incoming connections are queued until they can be serviced. As you can probably guess, when the queue is full, connections get dropped. The situation is that the tcp_max_syn_backlog parameter that manages these per-port queues has a default value that is too low, as only 1024 bytes are reserved for each port. For good performance, it is better to allocate 8192 bytes per port. I recommend always using the value 8192 for this parameter, to make sure that your server won't suffer from lost packets:

```
sysctl -w net.ipv4.tcp_max_syn_backlog=8192
```

Also, there are some options that relate to the time an established connection is maintained. The idea is that every connection that your server has to keep alive uses resources. If your server is a very busy server, at a given moment, it will be out of resources and tell new incoming clients that no resources are available. Because a client can easily reestablish a connection in most cases, you probably want to tune your server in a way that it detects failing connections as soon as possible.

The first parameter that relates to maintaining connections is tcp_synack_retries. This parameter defines the number of times the kernel will send a response to an incoming new connection request. The default value is 5. Given the current quality of network connections, 3 is probably enough. So use the following to change it:

```
sysctl -w net.ipv4.tcp_synack_retries=3
```

Next is the tcp_retries2 option. This relates to the number of times the server tries to resend data to a remote host that has an established session. Because it is inconvenient for a client computer if a connection is dropped, the default value, 15, is a lot higher than the default value for tcp_synack_retries. However, retrying it 15 times means that all that time your server can't use its resources for something else. Therefore, better decrease this parameter to a more reasonable value of 5:

```
sysctl -w net.ipv4.tcp_retries2=5
```

The parameters just mentioned relate to sessions that appear to be gone. Another area where you can do some optimization is in maintaining inactive sessions. By default, a TCP session can remain idle forever. You probably don't want that, so use the tcp_keepalive_time option to determine how long an established inactive session will be maintained. By default, this will be 7200 seconds (2 hours). If your server tends to run out of resources, limit it to a considerably shorter period of time:

```
sysctl -w net.ipv4.tcp_keepalive_time=900
```

Related to keepalive_time is the number of packets that your server sends before deciding that a connection is dead. You can manage this by using the tcp_keepalive_probes parameter. By default, nine packets are sent before a server is considered dead. Change this value to 3 if you want to terminate dead connections faster:

```
sysctl -w net.ipv4.tcp_keepalive_probes=3
```

Related to the number of keepalive probes is the interval you want to use to send these probes. By default, that happens every 75 seconds. So even with three probes, it still takes more than 3 minutes before your server can see that a connection has really failed. To bring this period back, give the tcp_keepalive_intvl parameter the value of 15:

```
sysctl -w net.ipv4.tcp_keepalive_intvl=15
```

To complete the story about maintaining connections, we need two more parameters. By default, the kernel waits a little before reusing a socket. If you run a busy server, performance will benefit from switching this feature off. To do this, use the following two commands:

```
sysctl -w net.ipv4.tcp_tw_reuse=1
sysctl -w net.ipv4.tcp_tw_recycle=1
```

Some Hints on Samba and NFS Performance Optimization

In Linux environments, there are two file servers that really matter. First, there is NFS. NFS is a kernel-integrated file server, simple and therefore very fast, but not particularly secure. With NFS version 4, some security features have been added to NFS, but because in version 4 NFS isn't simple anymore, few companies really use it. The tips in this chapter are all version 3 related.

Samba is the open source implementation of the Windows Server Message Block (SMB) protocol that is used for file sharing in Windows environments. Because most users use Windows, Samba is a very popular file server. You can even use it with Apple or Linux clients, because they also include a Samba client stack.

■**Note** Modern Linux kernels can use two different modules for the Samba client: the older smbfs and the newer cifs. If it is available, use the cifs kernel module at all times, because it performs much better than the older smbfs module.

Optimizing NFS Performance

The first performance optimization parameters for NFS that almost everyone uses are the rsize and wsize options. These are client options, used when mounting an NFS share. If the MTU size on your network is set to 9000 bytes, make sure to use an rsize and wsize of 8192 bytes. The following line shows how to mount an NFS file server using these options:

```
mount -t nfs -o rsize=8192,wsize=8192 myserver:/myshare /mydirectory
```

The next choice in NFS performance optimization is whether to use sync or async. These are options when exporting a mount on the NFS server. The default choice is to export a mount with the sync option. This means that incoming data is written to disk before the NFS server confirms. This is safe, but it also is rather slow. If you are willing to take the risk of losing some data when your server crashes, and get a better write performance in exchange, use the `async` flag. The following example line from `/etc/exports` shows how to use it:

```
/myshare      *(rw,async,root_squash)
```

Optimizing Samba Performance

As is the case for NFS, there also are some performance parameters that you can use to increase Samba server performance. Unless stated otherwise, you should set these parameters in `/etc/samba/smb.conf`. The first of them is the socket option `tcp_nodelay`, which can be used in combination with the IP Type of Service (TOS) option. If your Samba server serves clients on the LAN, use the following:

```
socket options = IPTOS_LOWDELAY TCP_NODELAY
```

If your server is serving Samba clients over a WAN connection, better use the following:

```
socket options = IPTOS_THROUGHPUT TCP_NODELAY
```

The next setting to consider is the maximum transmit size. Normally, your client negotiates with the server to determine what maximum size to use for packets. You can set the maximum size the server will allow by using the `xmit` option in `smb.conf`. The interesting thing is that you might think that bigger is always better, but this is not the case. If your clients perform badly, try a value smaller than the default of 65536; for instance:

```
xmit = 32768
```

When using this parameter, don't set it too low. 4096 really is the minimal value to use, but you probably never want to go that low.

Apart from the options mentioned here, Samba has many other tuning options. Check `man smb.conf` for more information.

Generic Network Performance Optimization Tips

Until now, we have discussed kernel parameters only. There are also some more-generic hints to consider when optimizing performance on the network. You probably already have applied all of them, but just to be sure, let's repeat some of the most important tips:

- Make sure you have the latest network driver modules.

- Use network card teaming to double performance of the network card in your server.

- Check Ethernet configuration settings, such as the frame size, MTU, speed, and duplex mode on your network. Make sure all devices involved in network communications use the same settings.

- If supported by all devices in your network, use 9000-byte jumbo frames. This reduces the number of packets sent over the network, thereby reducing the overhead that is caused by sending all those packets, the result of which is a speedier network overall.

Summary

In this chapter you have learned how to tune performance of your server. Even if modern Linux kernels are quite good in automatically setting the best performance-related parameters, there is always room for improvement. Performance optimization can be cumbersome work, though, in which many elements are involved, not only parts of your server. In the next chapter you'll learn more about advanced file system management.

CHAPTER 5

■ ■ ■

Advanced File System Management

Getting the Best Out of Your File Systems

File system management is among the first things that you do when you start using Ubuntu Server. When you installed Ubuntu Server, you had to select a default file system. At that time, you probably didn't consider advanced file system options. If you didn't, this chapter will help you to configure those options. This chapter first provides an in-depth look at the way a server file system is organized, so that you understand what tasks your file system has to perform. This discussion also considers key concepts such as journaling and indexing. Following that, you'll learn how to tune and optimize the relevant Ubuntu file systems.

Understanding File Systems

A file system is the structure that is used to access logical blocks on a storage device. For Linux, different file systems are available, of which Ext2, Ext3, XFS, and, to some extent, ReiserFS are the most important. All have in common the way in which they organize logical blocks on the storage device. Another commonality is that inodes and directories play a key role in allocating files on all four file systems. Despite these common elements, each file system has some properties that distinguish it from the others. In this section you will read both about the properties that all file systems have in common and about the most important differences.

Inodes and Directories

The basic building block of a file system is the logical block. This is a storage unit your
file system is using. Typically, it exists on a logical volume or a traditional partition (see
Chapter 1 for more information). To access the data blocks, the file system collects information about where the blocks of any given file are stored. This information is written
to the inode. Every file on a Linux file system has an inode, and the inode contains the
almost complete administrative record of your files. To give you a better idea of what an
inode is, Listing 5-1 shows the contents of an inode as it exists on an Ext2 file system, as
shown with the debugfs utility. Use the following procedure to display this information:

1. Make sure files on the file system cannot be accessed while working in debugfs.
   You could consider remounting the file system using mount -o remount,ro
   /yourfilesystem. However, if you have installed your server according to the guide-
   lines in Chapter 1, remounting is not necessary. You will have an Ext2-formatted
   /boot. If necessary, use the mount command to find out which device it is using (this
   should be /dev/hda1 or /dev/sda1) and proceed.

2. Open a directory on the device that you want to monitor and use the ls -i command to display a list of all file names and their inode numbers. Every file has one
   inode that contains its complete administrative record. Note the inode number,
   because you will need it in step 4 of this procedure.

3. Use the debugfs command to access the file system on your device in debug mode.
   For example, if your file system is /dev/sda1, you would use debugfs /dev/sda1.

4. Use the stat command that is available in the file system debugger to show the
   contents of the inode. When done, use exit to close the debugfs environment.

Listing 5-1. *The Ext2/Ext3 debugfs Tool Allows You to Show the Contents of an Inode*

```
root@mel:/boot# debugfs /dev/sda1
debugfs 1.40.8 (13-Mar-2008)
debugfs: stat <19>
Inode: 19   Type: regular   Mode:  0644   Flags: 0x0   Generation: 2632480000
User:    0   Group:    0   Size: 8211957
File ACL: 0    Directory ACL: 0
Links: 1   Blockcount: 16106
Fragment: Address: 0    Number: 0    Size: 0
ctime: 0x48176267 -- Tue Apr 29 14:01:11 2008
atime: 0x485ea3e9 -- Sun Jun 22 15:11:37 2008
mtime: 0x48176267 -- Tue Apr 29 14:01:11 2008
```

```
BLOCKS:
(0-11):22749-22760, (IND):22761, (12-267):22762-23017, (DIND):23018,➡
   (IND):23019, (268-523):23020-23275, (IND):23276, (524-779):23277-23532,➡
   (IND):23533, (780-1035):23534-23789, (IND):23790, (1036-1291):23791-24046,➡
   (IND):24047, (1292-1547):24048-24303, (IND):24304, (1548-1803):24305-24560,➡
   (IND):24561, (1804-1818):24562-24576, (1819-2059):25097-25337, (IND):25338,➡
   (2060-2315):25339-25594, (IND):25595, (2316-2571):25596-25851, (IND):25852,➡
   (2572-2827):25853-26108, (IND):26109, (2828-3083):26110-26365, (IND):26366,➡
   (3084-3339):26367-26622, (IND):26623, (3340-3595):26624-26879, (IND):26880,➡
   (3596-3851):26881-27136, (IND):27137, (3852-4107):27138-27393, (IND):27394,➡
   (4108-4363):27395-27650, (IND):27651, (4364-4619):27652-27907, (IND):27908,➡
   (4620-4875):27909-28164, (IND):28165, (4876-5131):28166-28421, (IND):28422,➡
   (5132-5387):28423-28678, (IND):28679, (5388-5643):28680-28935, (IND):28936,➡
   (5644-5899):28937-29192, (IND):29193, (5900-6155):29194-29449, (IND):29450,➡
   (6156-6411):29451-29706, (IND):29707, (6412-6667):29708-29963, (IND):29964,➡
   (6668-6923):29965-30220, (IND):30221, (6924-7179):30222-30477, (IND):
```

If you look closely at the information that is displayed by using debugfs, you'll see that it basically is the same information that is displayed when using ls -l on a given file. The only difference is that in this output you can see the blocks that are in use by your file as well, and that may come in handy when restoring a file that has been deleted by accident.

The interesting thing about the inode is that it contains no information about the name of the file, because, from the perspective of the operating system, the name is not important. Names are for human users and they can't normally handle inodes too well. To store names, Linux uses a directory tree.

A directory is a special kind of file, containing a list of files that are in the directory, plus the inode that is needed to access these files. Directories themselves have an inode number as well; the only directory that has a fixed inode is /. This guarantees that your file system can always start locating files.

If, for example, a user wants to read the file /etc/hosts, the operating system will first look in the root directory (which always is found at the same location) for the inode of the directory /etc. Once it has the inode for /etc, it can check what blocks are used by this inode. Once the blocks of the directory are found, the file system can see what files are in the directory. Next, it checks which inode it needs to open the /etc/hosts file. It then uses that inode to open the file and present the data to the user. This procedure works the same for every file system that can be used.

In a very basic file system such as Ext2, the procedure works exactly in the way just described. Advanced file systems may offer options to make the process of allocating files somewhat easier. For instance, the file system may work with extents. An *extent* is a large number of contiguous blocks allocated by the file system as one unit. This makes handling large files a lot easier. Since 2006, there is a patch that enhances Ext3 to support extent allocation. You can see the result immediately when comparing the result of Listing 5-1 with Listing 5-2. This is the inode for the same file after it has been copied from the Ext2 volume to the Ext3 volume. As you can see, it has many fewer blocks to manage.

Listing 5-2. *A File System Supporting Extents Has Fewer Individual Blocks to Manage and Thus Is Faster*

```
root@mel:/# debugfs /dev/system/root
debugfs 1.40.8 (13-Mar-2008)
debugfs:  stat <24580>

Inode: 24580   Type: regular    Mode:  0644   Flags: 0x0   Generation: 2026345315
User:     0   Group:      0   Size: 8211957
File ACL: 0    Directory ACL: 0
Links: 1   Blockcount: 16064
Fragment: Address: 0    Number: 0     Size: 0
ctime: 0x487238ee -- Mon Jul  7 11:40:30 2008
atime: 0x487238ee -- Mon Jul  7 11:40:30 2008
mtime: 0x487238ee -- Mon Jul  7 11:40:30 2008
BLOCKS:
(0-11):106496-106507, (IND):106508, (12-1035):106509-107532, ➥
(DIND):107533, (IND):107534, (1036-2004):107535-108503
TOTAL: 2008
(END)
```

A file system may use other techniques to work faster as well, such as allocation groups. By using allocation groups, a file system divides the available space into chunks and manages each chunk of disk space individually. By doing this, the file system can achieve a much higher I/O performance. All Linux file systems use this technique; some even use the allocation group to store backups of vital file system administration data.

Superblocks, Inode Bitmaps, and Block Bitmaps

To mount a file system, you need a file system superblock. Typically, this is the first block on a file system and contains generic information about the file system. You can make it visible using the stats command from a debugfs environment. Listing 5-3 shows you what it looks like for an Ext3 file system.

Listing 5-3. *Example of an Ext3 Superblock*

```
root@mel:~# debugfs /dev/system/root
debugfs 1.40.8 (13-Mar-2008)
debugfs: stats
Filesystem volume name:    <none>
Last mounted on:           <not available>
Filesystem UUID:           d40645e2-412e-485e-9225-8e7f87b9f568
Filesystem magic number:   0xEF53
Filesystem revision #:     1 (dynamic)
Filesystem features:       has_journal ext_attr resize_inode dir_index➡
 filetype needs_recovery sparse_super large_file
Filesystem flags:          signed_directory_hash
Default mount options:     (none)
Filesystem state:          clean
Errors behavior:           Continue
Filesystem OS type:        Linux
Inode count:               6553600
Block count:               26214400
Reserved block count:      1310720
Free blocks:               23856347
Free inodes:               6478467
First block:               0
Block size:                4096
Fragment size:             4096
Reserved GDT blocks:       1017
Blocks per group:          32768
Fragments per group:       32768
```

Without superblock, you cannot mount the file system; therefore, most file systems keep backup superblocks at different locations in the file system. In that case, if the real file system gets broken, you can mount using the backup superblock and still access the file system anyway.

Apart from the superblocks, the file system contains an inode bitmap and a block bitmap. By using these bitmaps, the file system driver can determine easily if a given block or inode is available. When creating a file, the inode and blocks used by the file are marked as in use, and when deleting a file, they are marked as available and thus can be overwritten by new files.

After the inode and block bitmaps sits the inode table. This contains the administrative information of all files on your file system. Since it normally is big (an inode is at least 128 bytes), there is no backup of the inode table.

Journaling

With the exception of Ext2, all current Linux file systems support journaling. The journal is used to track changes of files as well as metadata. The goal of using a journal is to make sure that transactions are processed properly, especially if a power outage occurs. In that case, the file system will check the journal when it comes back up again and, depending on the journaling style that is configured, do a rollback of the original data or a check on the data that was open when the server crashed. Using a journal is essential on large file systems to which lots of files get written. Only if a file system is very small, or writes hardly ever occur on the file system, can you configure the file system without a journal.

■**Tip** An average journal takes about 40 MB of disk space. If you need to configure a very small file system, such as the 100 MB /boot partition, it doesn't make sense to create a journal on it. Use Ext2 in those cases.

In Chapter 4, you read about the scheduler and how it can be used to reorder read and write requests. Using the scheduler can give you a great performance benefit. When using a journal, however, there is a problem: write commands cannot be reordered. The reason is that, to use reordering, data has to be kept in cache longer, whereas the purpose of a journal is to ensure data security, which means that data has to be written as soon as possible.

To avoid reordering, a journal file system should use barriers. This ensures that the disk cache is flushed immediately, which ensures that the journal gets updated properly. Barriers are enabled by default, but they may slow down the write process. If you want your server to perform write operations as fast as possible, and at the same time you are willing to take an increased risk of data loss, you should switch barriers off. To switch off barriers, add a mount option. Each file system needs a different option:

- XFS uses nobarrier.

- Ext3 uses barrier=0.

- ReiserFS uses barrier=none.

Journaling offers three different journaling modes. All of these are specified as options while mounting the file system, which allows you to use different journaling modes on different file systems.

- `data=ordered`: When using this option, only metadata is journaled and barriers are enabled by default. This way, data is forced to be written to hard disk as fast as possible, which reduces the chances of things going wrong. This journaling mode uses the optimal balance between performance and data security.

- `data=writeback`: If you want the best possible performance, use this option. This option only journals metadata, but does not guarantee data integrity. This means that, based on the information in the journal, when your server crashes, the file system can try to repair the data but may fail, in which case you will end up with the old data (dating from before the moment that you initialized the write action) after a system crash. This option at least guarantees fast recovery after a system crash, which is sufficient for many environments.

- `data=journal`: If you want the best guarantees for your data, use this option. When using this option, data and metadata is journaled. This ensures the best data integrity, but gives bad performance because all data has to be written twice. It has to be written to the journal first, and then to the disk when it is committed to disk. If you need this journaling option, you should always make sure that the journal is written to a dedicated disk. Every file system has options to accomplish that.

Indexing

When file systems were still small, no indexing was used. An index wasn't necessary to get a file from a list of a few hundred files. Nowadays, directories can contain many thousands, sometimes even millions, of files; to manage so many files, an index is essential.

Basically, there are two approaches to indexing. The easiest approach is to add an index to a directory. This approach is used by the Ext3 file system: it adds an index to all directories and thus makes the file system faster when many files exist in a directory. However, this is not the best approach to indexing.

For optimal performance, it is better to work with a balanced tree (also referred to as b-tree) that is integrated into the heart of the file system itself. In such a balanced tree, every file is a node in the tree and every node can have child nodes. Because every file is represented in the indexing tree, the file system is capable of finding files very quickly, no matter how many files there are in a directory. Using a b-tree for indexing also makes the file system a lot more complicated. If things go wrong, the risk exists that you will have to rebuild the entire file system, and that can take a lot of time. In this process, you even risk losing all data on your file system. Therefore, when choosing a file system that is built on top of a b-tree index, make sure it is a stable file system. Currently, XFS and ReiserFS have an internal b-tree index. Of these two, ReiserFS isn't considered a very stable file system, so better use XFS if you want indexing.

Optimizing File Systems

Every file system has its own options for optimization. In fact, the presence or absence of a particular option may be a reason to prefer or avoid a given file system in particular situations. Speaking in general, Ext3/Ext3 is a fantastic generic file system. It is stable and very good in environments in which not too much data is written. XFS is a very dynamic file system with lots of tuning options that make it an excellent candidate for handling large amounts of data. ReiserFS should be avoided. Its main developer, Hans Reiser, is in prison for second-degree murder, so the future of ReiserFS is currently very uncertain. Regardless, it is covered later in the chapter just in case you are stuck using a ReiserFS file system.

Optimizing Ext2/Ext3

Before the arrival of journaling file systems, Ext2 was the default file system on all Linux distributions. It was released in 1993 as a successor to the old and somewhat buggy Ext file system. Ext2 was successful for a few years, until the release of Ext3 in the late 1990s. Initially, there was only one difference between Ext2 and Ext3: Ext3 has a journal, whereas Ext2 doesn't have one. Over time, patches have enhanced Ext3 some more. For instance, Ext3 has directory indexing and works with extents, neither of which is the case for Ext2. The successor of Ext3 is Ext4. This file system is already well on its way toward release, but because it is not included in Ubuntu Server 8.04, I won't cover it in this book.

On a current Linux server, it isn't really a dilemma whether you should use Ext2 or Ext3. In almost all cases you want to use Ext3, because it has more features. Choose Ext2 only if you specifically don't want a journal, perhaps because your file system is too small to host a journal. For example, this is the case for the /boot file system. Because Ext2 and Ext3 are almost completely compatible, I'll cover Ext3 optimization in the rest of this subsection.

Creating Ext2/Ext3

While creating an Ext3 file system, you can pass many options to it. Even if you don't pass any options, some options will be applied automatically from the /etc/mke2fs.conf configuration file. In this file, you can include default options for Ext2 and Ext3. Listing 5-4 shows you what the contents of this file look like.

Listing 5-4. *Use /etc/mke2fs.conf to Specify Default Options to Always Use when Creating an Ext3 File System*

```
root@mel:~# cat /etc/mke2fs.conf
[defaults]
        base_features = sparse_super,filetype,resize_inode,dir_index,ext_attr
        blocksize = 4096
        inode_size = 128
        inode_ratio = 16384

[fs_types]
        small = {
                blocksize = 1024
                inode_size = 128
                inode_ratio = 4096
        }
        floppy = {
                blocksize = 1024
                inode_size = 128
                inode_ratio = 8192
        }
        news = {
                inode_ratio = 4096
        }
        largefile = {
                inode_ratio = 1048576
        }
        largefile4 = {
                inode_ratio = 4194304
        }
```

For a complete overview of options that you can use when creating an Ext3 file system, use the man page of mkfs.ext3. Table 5-1 covers only the most useful options.

Table 5-1. *Most Useful mkfs.ext3 Options*

Option	Description
-c	This option checks the device for bad blocks. Use it if you don't trust the device and are unable to buy a new storage device. By default, a fast read-only test is performed when using this option. If you want to perform a faster read/write test, use -cc.
-g blocks_per_group	Ext3 organizes its file system in block groups. By using block groups, the file system can perform operations in parallel, which increases general file system performance. If you want more tasks on your file system to run simultaneously, use fewer blocks per block group. You should consider, however, that when creating the Ext3 file system, the optimal number of blocks per block group is calculated automatically, so it may not make sense to use this option.
-J device=external-journal	Use this option if you want to use an external journal. You should always use this option if you want to apply the data=journal mount option, because it allows for much better performance. If you want to use this option, you must create an external journal first. You would normally do that using the -O journal_dev option. For instance, use mkfs.ext3 -O journal_dev /dev/sdb1 to make /dev/sdb1 your journal device. Next, you can create the file system that uses the external journal by using the command mkfs.ext3 -J device=/dev/sdb1.
-N number_of_inodes	When creating an Ext3 file system, Ext3 creates a fixed number of inodes. By default, this would be half the number of data blocks available on the file system. The problem is that when all inodes are used, you cannot create new files, even if you still have lots of blocks available. If you know beforehand that you are going to work with many small files, or many large files, it may be useful to change the number of inodes by using this option. Be aware that it is not possible to change the number of inodes once the file system has been created. Note that Ext2/Ext3 is not capable of allocating new inodes dynamically. If this capability is important to you, use XFS instead, because it will automatically create new inodes as needed.
-O dir_index	Use this feature to create a directory index on Ext3 file systems. This enables indexing and therefore makes your file system a lot more scalable.
-S	This is a remarkable option that lets you write superblock and group descriptors only. Use this option if all of the superblocks and backup superblocks are corrupted and you want to recover the file system anyway. This option does not touch the inode table or the inode and block bitmaps, so it will recover your file system in some cases. You might make the situation worse, however, so only use this option as a last resort.

Mounting Ext2/Ext3

To activate a file system, you have to mount it. While mounting it, you can use specific mount options to determine how the file system must be activated. Table 5-2 lists and describes the most useful Ext2/Ext3 mount options.

Table 5-2. *Most Useful Ext2/Ext3 Mount Options*

Option	Description
check=none	Ext2/Ext3 is checked automatically from time to time. If you want to prevent your file system from being checked at any time (which may take a long time to complete), use this option.
sb=superblock	Use this option to specify the superblock that you want to use when mounting the Ext2/Ext3 file system. By default, an Ext2/Ext3 file system creates some backup superblocks. Use dump2fs to find out where they are. In most cases, you will have a backup superblock on block 32768. To use this superblock, you need to specify it as a 1 KB block unit. Because the file system by default uses 4 KB blocks in almost all cases, you should multiply the number 32768 by 4. So, to mount it, use mount sb=131072 /dev/something /somewhere.
noload	This option tells an Ext3 file system not to load the journal when mounting.
data=journal, data=ordered, data=writeback	Use this option to specify what kind of journaling you want to use. The different options were discussed in the "Journaling" section earlier in this chapter.
commit=n	This option is used to synchronize data and metadata every *n* seconds. The default value is 5; use 0 to disable automatic sync completely.

Analyzing and Repairing Ext2/Ext3

If you happen to encounter problems on your Ext2/Ext3 file system, the file system offers some commands that can help you to analyze and repair the file system, as described in this section.

e2fsck

e2fsck is a file system check utility that works on both Ext2 and Ext3. If you think something might be wrong with your file system, run e2fsck. You should make sure, though, that the file system on which you run it is not currently mounted. Because this is hard to accomplish if you want to run it on your root file system, it is not a bad idea to use the automatic check that occurs every once in a while when mounting an Ext2/Ext3 file system. This check is on by default, so don't switch it off.

When you run e2fsck on an Ext3 file system, the utility will check the journal and repair any inconsistencies. Only if the superblock indicates that there is a problem with the file system will the utility check data as well. On Ext2, e2fsck will always check data, because this is the only option. Normally, e2fsck will automatically repair all errors it finds, unless an error requires human intervention, in which case e2fsck will notify you so that you can use one of the advanced options by hand. Table 5-3 provides an overview of the most useful options that e2fsck has to offer.

Table 5-3. *Most Useful e2fsck Options*

Option	Description
-b superblock	Use this option to read one of the backup superblocks. Unlike when using the mount command, you can refer to the normal block position where the file system can find the backup superblock, which is block 32768 in most cases.
-c	This option lets e2fsck check for bad blocks. If it finds them, it will write them to a specific inode reserved for this purpose. In the future, the file system will avoid using any of these blocks. Be aware, though, that bad blocks are often an indication of real problems on your hard drive. Use the -c option with e2fsck as a temporary solution until you can replace your hard drive.
-f	Use this option to force checking, even if the file system seems to be without problems.
-j external_journal	Use this option to specify where the external journal can be found. You'll need this option if your file system uses an external journal.
-p	This option tells fsck to automatically repair everything that can be repaired without human intervention.
-y	This option assumes an answer of yes to all questions. This goes further than default -p behavior and will also automatically enter yes to questions that normally require human intervention.

dumpe2fs and tune2fs

In some situations, e2fsck may not do its work properly. In such cases, two useful utilities to analyze a little bit further what is happening are dumpe2fs and tune2fs. dumpe2fs dumps the contents of the superblock and the information about all block group descriptors (see Listing 5-5). On large file systems, e2fsck will give you huge amounts of output. If you just want to see information from the superblock, use it with the -h option, which makes it more readable.

Listing 5-5. *dumpe2fs Shows the Contents of the Superblock and All Group Descriptors*

```
Filesystem volume name:     <none>
Last mounted on:            <not available>
Filesystem UUID:            3babfd35-de36-4c81-9fb9-1a988d548927
Filesystem magic number:    0xEF53
Filesystem revision #:      1 (dynamic)
Filesystem features:        filetype sparse_super
Default mount options:      (none)
Filesystem state:           not clean
Errors behavior:            Continue
Filesystem OS type:         Linux
Inode count:                490560
Block count:                979933
Reserved block count:       48996
Free blocks:                898773
Free inodes:                490529
First block:                1
Block size:                 1024
Fragment size:              1024
Blocks per group:           8192
Fragments per group:        8192
Inodes per group:           4088
Inode blocks per group:     511
Last mount time:            Tue Jul  8 02:58:33 2008
Last write time:            Tue Jul  8 02:58:33 2008
Mount count:                1
Maximum mount count:        30
Last checked:               Tue Jul  8 02:58:16 2008
Check interval:             0 (<none>)
Reserved blocks uid:        0 (user root)
Reserved blocks gid:        0 (group root)
First inode:                11
Inode size:                 128
```

```
Group 0: (Blocks 1-8192)
  Primary superblock at 1, Group descriptors at 2-5
  Block bitmap at 6 (+5), Inode bitmap at 7 (+6)
  Inode table at 8-518 (+7)
  2029 free blocks, 4070 free inodes, 2 directories
  Free blocks: 532-2560
  Free inodes: 17, 20-4088
Group 1: (Blocks 8193-16384)
  Backup superblock at 8193, Group descriptors at 8194-8197
  Block bitmap at 8198 (+5), Inode bitmap at 8199 (+6)
  Inode table at 8200-8710 (+7)
  2095 free blocks, 4088 free inodes, 0 directories
  Free blocks: 14290-16384
  Free inodes: 4089-8176
Group 2: (Blocks 16385-24576)
  Block bitmap at 16385 (+0), Inode bitmap at 16386 (+1)
  Inode table at 16392-16902 (+7)
  5749 free blocks, 4088 free inodes, 0 directories
  Free blocks: 16387-16391, 16903-22646
  Free inodes: 8177-12264
```

If you see a parameter that you don't like when using dumpe2fs, you can use tune2fs to change it. Basically, tune2fs works on the same options as mkfs.ext3, so you won't have a hard time understanding its options. Consult the man page for more details on tune2fs.

debugfs

If you really are ready for a deep dive into your file system, debugfs is the utility you need. Make sure that you use it on an unmounted file system only. The debugfs tool works at a very deep level and may severely interfere with other processes that try to access files while you are debugging them. So, if necessary, take your live CD and use debugfs from there.

After starting debugfs, you'll find yourself in the debugfs interface, which offers some specific commands. You will also recognize some generic Linux commands that you know from a bash environment, but, as you will find out, they work a bit differently in a debugfs environment. For example, the ls command in debugfs shows you not only file names, but also the number of blocks in use by this item and the inode of this item, which is very useful information if you really need to start troubleshooting (see Listing 5-6).

Listing 5-6. *The ls Command in debugfs Works Differently*

```
root@mel:/# debugfs /dev/system/root
debugfs 1.40.8 (13-Mar-2008)
debugfs: ls



 2 (12) .   2 (12) ..   11 (20) lost+found    6135809 (12) var
4202497 (12) boot   5095425 (12) srv    335873 (12) etc
2924545 (16) media   24577 (16) cdrom    24578 (20) initrd.img
5808129 (12) lib   1073153 (12) usr   1417217 (12) bin
5865473 (12) dev   1966081 (12) home   1572865 (12) mnt
6168577 (12) proc   6086657 (12) root   2277377 (12) sbin
4947969 (12) tmp    360449 (12) sys   5586945 (12) opt
1302529 (16) initrd    24579 (16) vmlinuz    4808705 (16) tftpboot
2949121 (20) clonezilla    1785857 (12) isos
24580 (36) initrd.img-2.6.24-16-server    24581 (3692) .335873
(END)
```

In case you are wondering how this information may be useful to you, imagine a situation where you can't access one of the directories in the root file system anymore. This information gives you the inode that contains the administrative data on the item. Next, you can dump the inode from the debugfs interface to a normal file. For instance, the command dump <24580> /24580 would create a file with the name 24580 in the root of your file system and fill that with the contents of inode 24580. That allows you to access the data that file occupies again and may help in troubleshooting.

This information may also help when recovering deleted files. Imagine that a user tells you that he has created three files, /home/user/file1, /home/user/file2, and /home/user/file3, but has accidentally deleted file2 and desperately needs to get it back. The first thing you can do is use the lsdel command from the debugfs interface. Chances are it will give you a list of deleted inodes, including their original size and deletion time. Listing 5-7 shows an example.

Listing 5-7. *The lsdel Command in debugfs Gives You an Overview of Deleted Files*

```
root@mel:/# debugfs /dev/sda1
debugfs 1.40.8 (13-Mar-2008)
debugfs: lsdel
```

```
 Inode  Owner  Mode    Size     Blocks   Time deleted
233029      0 100644  16384      17/      17 Sun Jul  6 11:27:49 2008
233030      0 100644  16384      17/      17 Sun Jul  6 15:41:01 2008
           17      0 100644      814       1/       1 Tue Jul   8 06:33:45 2008
3 deleted inodes found.
(END)
```

As Listing 5-7 demonstrates, in the information that lsdel gives you, you can see the inode number, original owner, size in blocks, and, most important, the time the file was deleted. Based on that information, it's easy to recover the original file. If it was the file in inode 233030, from the debugfs interface, use dump <233030> /originalfile to recover it. Unfortunately, due to some differences between Ext2 and Ext3, lsdel works well on Ext2 but rarely works well on Ext3. In that case, you have to use some more advanced techniques.

Given the fact that the user in our example has created some files, it may be interesting to see what inodes were used. Let's say file1 still uses inode 123, file2 uses 127, and file3 is removed, so you can't find that information anymore. Chances are, however, that the inode that file3 has used was not too far away from inode 127, so you can try to dump all inodes between inode 128 and 140. Chances are that this will allow you to recover the original file, thanks to dumpe2fs.

There are many other commands available from debugfs as well. The help command from within the debugfs interface will give you a complete list. I recommend that you check out these commands and try to get an impression of the possibilities they offer, because you may need to use them some day.

Tuning XFS

The best feature of XFS is its scalability. The file system is completely 64 bits, which allows for use of file systems with sizes up to 9 exabytes (that is, 9 million terabytes). It is organized in a well-structured way that makes it a very fast file system. In an XFS file system, three different sections can be used for data storage. Most important of these is the data section. This is the only section that is created by default. The other two sections are the log section and the real-time section.

Organization of the XFS File System

The data section contains data blocks, and file system metadata (the administrative data) as well. Like Ext3, XFS uses different allocation groups. These block groups are created automatically when using mkfs.xfs, and sizes are calculated based on the size of the file system. Using these block groups is good for performance, because working with several block groups allows the file system to perform actions in parallel.

One of the most important parameters when creating an XFS file system is the number of allocation groups created. The default value performs well, but for better performance, it is a good idea to increase the number of block allocation groups. This is what you should do if the file system is very write intensive and sufficient memory is available. If the server in question doesn't have much available memory, using too many block groups is bad for performance. Also, when using a large number of block groups, you should make sure that there is enough available disk space in the file system at all times. When the file system is almost full, the file system will allocate lots of CPU cycles to handle all the simultaneous requests from the different block allocation groups. Fortunately, you can always use the xfs_growfs command to grow an XFS file system if necessary.

The log section is used as a file system journal. Changes in file system metadata are stored in it until the file system has time to commit these changes to the data section. When the file system crashes, upon mount, the file system can read incomplete transactions from this log section and recover the file system in a fast way. In the default setting, the log section is included in the data section. For better performance, you can choose to put it outside of the data section, which allows you to put it on another medium as well.

The real-time section is a unique property of the XFS file system. This section is used by files that have to be written to disk as fast as possible—in real time. To mark a file as a real-time file, use the xfsctl function. This function is not available as a command-line utility; instead, you have to implement it in the tools that you are writing to handle data on the XFS file system. If a file is real time, it will never be stored in memory buffers before writing it to disk, but rather will be written without further delay. This is an excellent way of preventing file system corruption.

Setting XFS Properties

To set properties for the XFS file system, you need to specify them when creating the file system. Creating an XFS file system with default settings is not too hard; the following command, for instance, is used to format /dev/sda1 as an XFS file system:

```
mkfs.xfs /dev/sda1
```

This command would format the file system as XFS with an internal log section, without a real-time section. If you would like to put the log section on a different device, which leads to better performance, use the following:

```
mkfs.xfs -l logdev=/dev/sdb1,size=10000b /dev/sda1
```

With this command, a 10,000-block log section is created on /dev/sdb1.

An important setting when creating the XFS file system is the number of allocation groups that you want to create. Depending on the file system size that you are using, the number of allocation groups is set automatically; use the xfs_info command to find out the number of allocation groups set on your file system. Listing 5-8 shows the agcount (number of allocation groups) parameter, which is set to 16, and the agsize (size per allocation group), which is set to 1,638,400 blocks.

Listing 5-8. *Showing XFS File System Information with xfs_info*

```
root@mel:~# xfs_info /srv
meta-data=/dev/mapper/system-srv isize=256      agcount=16, agsize=1638400 blks
          =                       sectsz=512     attr=0
data      =                       bsize=4096     blocks=26214400, imaxpct=25
          =                       sunit=0        swidth=0 blks, unwritten=1
naming    =version 2             bsize=4096
log       =internal              bsize=4096     blocks=12800, version  =1
          =                       sectsz=512     sunit=0 blks, lazy-count=0
realtime  =none                  extsz=4096     blocks=0, rtextents=0
```

To increase performance for this file system, you can change the number of allocation groups to 32, for example. You would do this by using the agcount=32 option when creating the file system. The complete command to do this for a file system that you want to create on /dev/sda1 is

```
mkfs.xfs -f -d agcount=32
```

You do not need to calculate the size of the allocation groups, because that will be calculated automatically. In the preceding command, you can see that the option -f is used, which is required in certain cases; mkfs.xfs will not write to the device if it suspects that a file system already exists on that device. So, if you want to re-create an XFS file system, make sure that you use the option -f.

Managing the XFS File System

Before storing files on your XFS file system, you need to mount it. XFS has some specific mount options. Among the most important option is allocsize, which specifies how much data to allocate for each file that you want to write. By using this parameter, you can avoid fragmentation and thus get better performance out of the file system. The default value of 64 KB does well for average workloads, but if you are putting large files on the file system, it may make sense to increase the allocsize parameter considerably. For instance, a 512 MB allocsize is good for multimedia solutions, such as Internet broadcasting. Valid values reach from 4 KB to 1 GB, with power of 2 increments. Use this mount option at all times, because it will make your XFS file system perform much better.

The second option that is wise to use when mounting the file system is a rather generic one that you can use for other file system as well: noatime makes sure that the access time of files is not modified every time a file is accessed. It is a good idea to use this parameter in write-intensive environments, because writing a new access time to the file system every time a file is accessed has a high performance price.

A third important mount option is barrier. This option is important if you want to make sure that files are written properly to hard disk. On modern disk systems, a file is not written directly to the hard drive, but to a write cache instead. When the file has been written to these in-memory buffers, the file system is informed that the file has been written, whereas in fact it hasn't been. If at that moment the server crashes, the modifications to the file will get lost. When using the barrier option, you can force the file system to write modifications to on-disk write buffers, instead of to in-memory write buffers, thus ensuring that the file really is written to disk. There's only one condition: your disk must have a cache that can be used for writing files, but that is the case on almost all modern hard drives.

Once mounted, you will see that many file system utilities have an XFS alternative. For instance, if you use man -k xfs to search the man pages for all commands that relate to XFS, you'll see that numerous commands are available. The function of some commands is not too hard to figure out. For example, if you have worked with fsck, you will have no problem using xfs_repair to repair the XFS file system. And if you have resized a file system before, you'll find that it's not too hard to resize an XFS file system using xfs_growfs. XFS has some very specific utilities as well, the most significant of which are described next:

- xfs rtcp: As previously discussed, when creating an XFS file system, you can specify that a real-time section be created as well. Files that are written to this section are written there without using the disk cache mechanism, which helps you to prevent file system corruption. If you want, you can copy files to that section directly, using the xfs_rtcp command. When using this command, you can even specify that a fixed extend size must be used. For the rest, xfs_rtcp works like an ordinary file copy command.

- xfsdump: You have probably worked with tar to create backups before. When using XFS, the xfsdump command is the most appropriate way of creating backups. The most important difference is that xfsdump will back up all XFS attributes as well, whereas this is not the case for other backup utilities like tar, which don't understand XFS metadata. Using xfsdump is not too hard; it backs up files and all their attributes to a storage media, a regular file, or standard output. Once backed up there, you can restore files using the xfsrestore command. For example, use the following command to dump your complete root file system to tape:

```
xfsdump -v trace -f /dev/tape /
```

If you are familiar with using `tar`, you'll notice the similarities between the two commands. As mentioned, if you want to make sure that all XFS-specific attributes are backed up as well, use `xfsdump`.

- `xfs_freeze`: For other file systems, it is rather uncommon to freeze access to the file system, as you can do with the `xfs_freeze` command. Freezing access to a file system is useful if you want to make a snapshot using your volume manager, because it makes sure that nothing is written to the file system for a given time. To "unfreeze" the file system later, use `xfs_freeze` again, which switches on access to the file system again.

What About ReiserFS?

There was a moment in time when ReiserFS was a stable and very fast file system. This file system works particularly well if your server uses applications that work with numerous small files. Unfortunately, ReiserFS is not very stable (and its future is uncertain, as noted earlier), so you should avoid using it. In case you can't avoid using it, this section discusses some ways to make it perform better.

First, ReiserFS can benefit from using an external journal, especially if journal mode is set to `data=journal`. To create a ReiserFS file system that uses an external journal, use `mkreiserfs`:

```
mkreiserfs -j /dev/sda1 /dev/sdb1
```

Some ReiserFS-specific options can be enabled when mounting it. The most important option is `notail`. By default, ReiserFS stores small files and parts at the end of a file directly in its index tree. This makes the file system faster, but also more prone to error. Storing parts of the end of a file directly in the tree may be useful, because it prevents a small piece at the end of a file from using a complete disk block. If you don't want this to happen, use the `notail` option. This is an important mount option, because it will make the file system more stable.

ReiserFS is notorious for being difficult to fix when it encounters problems. If you can no longer mount a particular ReiserFS file system, you need to use `fsck.reiserfs`. This program offers powerful options to check and repair a ReiserFS file system. Table 5-4 lists and describes its most useful options.

Table 5-4. *Most Useful fsck.reiserfs Options*

Option	Description
--check	This is the default option. It will check the file system, but it won't repair errors if they are found.
--fix-fixable	Use this option if the --check option has found an error that it says can be repaired using --fix-fixable. It will help in some situations, but doesn't fix the most serious errors.
--rebuild-tree	This option will rebuild the complete tree on which ReiserFS is based. Only use it if --check tells you that you have to; it is better to avoid it if you can. This option can take a long time to complete, and success is not guaranteed. Therefore, make sure that you have a backup copy of the volume on which you are using this option before you start to use it.
--yes	Use this option to automatically confirm all questions that the program will ask you.

ReiserFS also has a debug utility, debugreiserfs. You can use it to check current settings of your ReiserFS file system. Listing 5-9 gives you an example of its output.

Listing 5-9. *debugreiserfs Gives an Overview of Options Your ReiserFS File System Is Using*

```
root@mel:/# debugreiserfs /dev/system/var
debugreiserfs 3.6.19 (2003 www.namesys.com)


Filesystem state: consistency is not checked after last mounting

Reiserfs super block in block 16 on 0xfe02 of format 3.6 with standard journal
Count of blocks on the device: 26214400
Number of bitmaps: 800
Blocksize: 4096
Free blocks (count of blocks - used [journal, bitmaps, data, reserved]➥
 blocks): 22969500
Root block: 32886
Filesystem is NOT clean
Tree height: 4
Hash function used to sort names: "r5"
Objectid map size 4, max 972
```

```
Journal parameters:
        Device [0x0]
        Magic [0x5ceab519]
        Size 8193 blocks (including 1 for journal header) (first block 18)
        Max transaction length 1024 blocks
        Max batch size 900 blocks
        Max commit age 30
Blocks reserved by journal: 0
Fs state field: 0x0:
sb_version: 2
inode generation number: 47911
UUID: 8ca56b35-eff1-4001-8bfd-ffac01091d1b
LABEL:
Set flags in SB:
        ATTRIBUTES CLEAN
```

In case debugreiserfs shows you an option that you don't like, you can change it for the existing file system by using reiserfstune. This command uses the same options as mkfs.reiserfs; see its man page for more details about these options.

Summary

In this chapter you have learned about file system management. You now know how to tune your file system for optimal performance. You have also learned about some utilities that you can use to fix a file system that is broken. In the next chapter you'll learn how to use Nagios to monitor your Ubuntu Servers from a distance.

CHAPTER 6

■ ■ ■

Network Monitoring
Knowing When It Goes Wrong
Without Watching It

As an administrator, it is your responsibility to know when things are about to go wrong. You can, of course, go sit by your server all day and figure out if everything is going all right, but you probably have better things to do. Nagios offers services to monitor the network for you. In this chapter you'll learn how to install and use Nagios.

Starting with Nagios

Nagios is a network-wide monitoring tool. In this chapter you'll learn how to set it up on your servers. Once it is set up, you can watch the status of servers in your network via a web browser. Don't want to watch a web browser all time? That's fine, because you can configure Nagios to send relevant security alerts to some specified users on the network if something goes wrong. Nagios allows you to monitor local server events, such as running out of disk space, as network events.

Before you install Nagios, make sure that you have a web server configured (you can read more about configuring Apache Web Server in Chapter 11 of my book *Beginning Ubuntu Server Administration*, from Apress) and running. Nagios uses a web interface to show its information, so you can't do without that. Once you have confirmed it is up and running, install the nagios packages:

```
apt-get install nagios2 nagios-plugins nagios-images
```

This command installs about 40 MB of data on your server. Once that is done, you have to complete the installation by setting up authentication. Nagios uses the file

/etc/nagios2/htpasswd.users, but this file is not created automatically. The following command creates it for you, puts a user with the name nagiosadmin in it, and prompts for a password:

```
htpasswd -c /etc/nagios2/htpasswd.users nagiosadmin
```

There are two configuration files related to user authentication. First, /etc/nagios2/apache2.conf contains all settings that allow Nagios to communicate with Apache. Listing 6-1 shows its contents.

Listing 6-1. */etc/nagios2/apache2.conf Sets Up Communication Between Nagios and Apache*

```
root@mel:/etc/nagios2# cat apache2.conf
ScriptAlias /cgi-bin/nagios2 /usr/lib/cgi-bin/nagios2
ScriptAlias /nagios2/cgi-bin /usr/lib/cgi-bin/nagios2
Alias /nagios2/stylesheets /etc/nagios2/stylesheets
Alias /nagios2 /usr/share/nagios2/htdocs
<DirectoryMatch (/usr/share/nagios2/htdocs|/usr/lib/cgi-bin/nagios2)>
        Options FollowSymLinks
        DirectoryIndex index.html
        AllowOverride AuthConfig
        Order Allow,Deny
        Allow From All
        AuthName "Nagios Access"
        AuthType Basic
        AuthUserFile /etc/nagios2/htpasswd.users
        require valid-user
</DirectoryMatch>
```

As you can see, the apache2.conf file contains the authentication settings and some basic paths that Nagios has to use. The other relevant configuration file is /etc/nagios2/cgi.cfg, which contains the name of the admin user that is used for different purposes, as well as other settings that are related to the CGI scripts that Nagios uses. The interesting part of this script is that you can change admin names in it. By default, nagiosadmin is the only user who has administrative permissions to perform different tasks. If, for instance, you want to use another user account for hosts and services-related commands, change it in the cgi.cfg file. Listing 6-2 shows its contents.

Note For better readability, I have removed all comment lines. Consult the configuration file on disk to see the comment lines as well.

Listing 6-2. *cgi.cfg Contains the Authorizations of the admin User*

```
nagios_check_command=/usr/lib/nagios/plugins/check_nagios\
 /var/cache/nagios2/status.dat 5 '/usr/sbin/nagios2'
use_authentication=1
authorized_for_system_information=nagiosadmin
authorized_for_configuration_information=nagiosadmin
authorized_for_system_commands=nagiosadmin
authorized_for_all_services=nagiosadmin
authorized_for_all_hosts=nagiosadmin
authorized_for_all_service_commands=nagiosadmin
authorized_for_all_host_commands=nagiosadmin
default_statusmap_layout=5
default_statuswrl_layout=4
ping_syntax=/bin/ping -n -U -c 5 $HOSTADDRESS$
refresh_rate=90
```

At this point, you have a very basic Nagios server up and running. Before you start to configure it, you need to find out if it works properly. From a workstation, start your browser and connect to the following URL:

```
http://your_nagios_server/nagios2
```

This should give you a login prompt at which you can enter the name and password of the admin user you have just created. After entering these, you should see the Nagios web interface, as shown in Figure 6-1. Don't bother clicking around in it, because you haven't set up anything yet. Therefore, you won't see much for the moment. Read the following sections to find out how to configure Nagios.

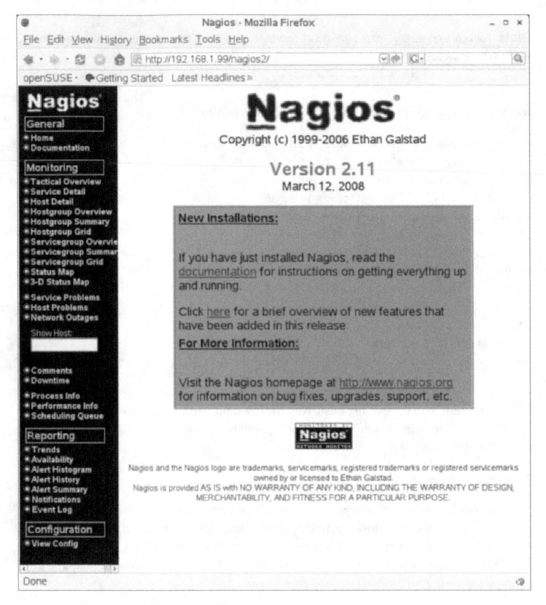

Figure 6-1. *After installing Nagios, connect to it to see if it works.*

■**Note** The Nagios web interface gives access to some documentation that is installed on your server as well. You can use this documentation, but be aware that the paths on Ubuntu Server are different from the pathnames referred to in the documentation.

Configuring Nagios

Nagios uses lots of configuration files. The most difficult part of managing Nagios is to find the right configuration file for a specific purpose. To make it even more difficult, Nagios distinguishes between core configuration files and plug-in configuration files, add-on files that can be used as an extension to the default functionality of Nagios.

Location of the Configuration Files

When you first start working with Nagios, it looks like configuration files are located just about everywhere! To help you pinpoint the locations of these files, the following list identifies the most common directories in which Nagios stores information:

- /etc/nagios2: This is the master configuration directory. It contains the most important configuration files, among which you will find the nagios.cfg configuration file.

- /usr/lib/nagios/plugins: As mentioned, Nagios works with plug-ins. Every plug-in allows you to monitor an additional service. For example, Nagios by itself doesn't know how to monitor Oracle. If, however, the Oracle plug-in has been installed in this directory (which is the case after a default installation), the plug-in can manage Oracle.

- /etc/nagios2/conf.d: This directory contains some of the most important Nagios configuration files. If the file you are looking for is not in here, also check /etc/nagios-plugins/config.

- /etc/nagios-plugins/config: This directory contains the configuration files for the plug-ins that are installed on your server.

- /var/lib/nagios2: Nagios writes its output to this directory. When Nagios has been up and running for some time, you'll find .out files in this directory. These files contain the information that is used by the Nagios web interface.

- /var/log/nagios2: This is the directory where Nagios writes its log files. Use it if anything goes wrong with your Nagios environment.

Before diving deep into the different configuration files, you should also be aware of the /etc/nagios2/commands.cfg file. To do its work, Nagios uses its own command set. The commands.cfg file defines the most important commands. Listing 6-3 gives a partial example.

Listing 6-3. */etc/nagios2/commands.cfg Defines the Most Common Nagios Commands*

```
root@mel:/etc/nagios2# cat commands.cfg
# 'process-host-perfdata' command definition
define command{
        command_name    process-host-perfdata
        command_line    /usr/bin/printf "%b" "$LASTHOSTCHECK$\t$HOSTNAME$➡
\t$HOSTSTATE$\t
$HOSTATTEMPT$\t$HOSTSTATETYPE$\t➡
$HOSTEXECUTIONTIME$\t$HOSTOUTPUT$\t$HOSTPERFDATA$\n" >>➡
 /var/lib/nagios2/host-perfdata.out
        }


# 'process-service-perfdata' command definition
define command{
        command_name    process-service-perfdata
        command_line    /usr/bin/printf "%b" "$LASTSERVICECHECK$\t$HOSTNAME$➡
\t$SERVICEDESC$\t
$SERVICESTATE$\t$SERVICEATTEMPT$\t➡
$SERVICESTATETYPE$\t$SERVICEEXECUTIONTIME$\t$SERVICELATENCY$➡
\t$SERVICEOUTPUT$\t$SERVICEPERFDATA$\n" >> /var/lib/nagios2/service-perfdata.out
        }
```

Nagios commands are well structured. If you feel you are missing any functionality in the default Nagios command set, you can create your own Nagios commands as well. The commands.cfg file contains some hints on how to do that.

The Master Configuration File: nagios.cfg

The master configuration file that Nagios uses is /etc/nagios2/nagios.cfg. This file determines where Nagios should read and write specific information. By using cfg_file statements, it also tells Nagios what additional configuration files to read. For example, these statements can refer to configuration files for specific modules that you want to use. By default, all of these configuration files are disabled, which means that Nagios basically monitors nothing. Of course, it makes sense to enable them, but only after you have modified the configuration file according to your needs. Listing 6-4 shows the part of nagios.cfg that indicates what configuration files to use. Be aware, though, that these are only example files, and in some cases refer to files that don't even exist at the location that is indicated.

Listing 6-4. *From nagios.cfg, Additional Configuration Files Are Included*

```
# Command definitions
cfg_file=/etc/nagios2/commands.cfg

# These other examples are taken from upstream's sample configuration
# files.

# You can split other types of object definitions across several
# config files if you wish (as done here), or keep them all in a
# single config file.

#cfg_file=/etc/nagios2/contactgroups.cfg
#cfg_file=/etc/nagios2/contacts.cfg
#cfg_file=/etc/nagios2/dependencies.cfg
#cfg_file=/etc/nagios2/escalations.cfg
#cfg_file=/etc/nagios2/hostgroups.cfg
#cfg_file=/etc/nagios2/hosts.cfg
#cfg_file=/etc/nagios2/services.cfg
#cfg_file=/etc/nagios2/timeperiods.cfg

# Extended host/service info definitions are now stored along with
# other object definitions:
#cfg_file=/etc/nagios2/hostextinfo.cfg
#cfg_file=/etc/nagios2/serviceextinfo.cfg

# You can also tell Nagios to process all config files (with a .cfg
# extension) in a particular directory by using the cfg_dir
# directive as shown below:

#cfg_dir=/etc/nagios2/servers
#cfg_dir=/etc/nagios2/printers
#cfg_dir=/etc/nagios2/switches
#cfg_dir=/etc/nagios2/routers
```

As a Nagios administrator, it is also useful if you know about the other important lines in the nagios.cfg file. The following list provides an overview of the most important definitions it contains:

- log_file=/var/log/nagios2/nagios.log: This parameter tells Nagios where to log its information.

- cfg_dir=/etc/nagios2/conf.d: This line tells Nagios to include all configuration files in the specified directory.

- cfg_file=/etc/nagios2/commands.cfg: This line tells Nagios to load the configuration file commands.cfg as well. Likewise, other cfg_file lines are used to refer to additional configuration files that Nagios should include.

- status_file=/var/cache/nagios2/status.dat: This file contains current status information about all hosts and services that are monitored. The CGI scripts from the Nagios web server interpret this file and display its contents in a graphical way.

- check_external_command=0: This default line makes sure that no external commands can be executed. If you want to manage Nagios using a web server (which should always be the case), you need to enable this option by giving it the value 1.

- log_rotation_method=d: This line specifies in what way the Nagios log file should be rotated. By default, this will happen daily. Valid values for this parameter follow:

  - n: Don't rotate the log

  - h: Rotate hourly

  - d: Rotate daily

  - w: Rotate weekly

  - m: Rotate monthly

- log_archive_path=/var/log/nagios2/archives: If log rotation is enabled, this parameter describes where the archive of log files should be written to.

Creating Essential Nagios Configuration Files

Nagios needs some minimal configuration files, and they should reside in one of the directories defined in the nagios.cfg file using the cfg_dir directive. The default location to put them would be /etc/nagios2/conf.d. Make sure that you create at least the following configuration files:

- contacts.cfg: This file defines which people should get a message in case of trouble.

- contactgroups.cfg: All contacts specified in contacts.cfg should be a member of at least one contact group. Use this file to define the contact group.

- `templates.cfg`: This file defines templates that can be used by other configuration files.

- `hosts.cfg`: Use this file to define the hosts that Nagios will monitor.

- `hostgroups.cfg`: In large networks, it is useful to subdivide hosts into host groups, such as servers, switches, routers, and so on.

- `services.cfg`: The file defines specific services that you want to monitor for each host.

- `timeperiods.cfg`: This file defines time periods used in all configuration files.

Now it is time to start the real work, which unfortunately involves a lot of typing. In the rest of this chapter, we will work on a small example network in which four Linux servers are used. Three of these are on the internal network, and one of them is on the Internet. Nagios can monitor other operating systems as well, but let's try to set up Linux-based host monitoring first. The following servers are monitored:

- `192.168.1.99`: DHCP, NFS, web, Nagios, SSH

- `192.168.1.100`: Samba, SSH

- `192.168.1.101`: Web, FTP, SSH

- `80.69.93.216`: Web, SSH

Creating a Contacts File

Start with the creation of the `contacts.cfg` file. As specified in `/etc/nagios2/nagios.cfg`, this file should reside in `/etc/nagios2`, so make sure to create it there. Listing 6-5 gives an example of what this file may look like.

Listing 6-5. *Example contacts.cfg File*

```
# contact definition for linda
define contact{
        contact_name                    linda
        alias                           linda thomsen
        service_notification_period     workhours
        host_notification_period        workhours
        service_notification_options    c,r
        host_notification_options       d,r
```

```
    service_notification_commands        notify-by-email
    host_notification_commands           host-notify-by_email
    email                                linda@localhost
}
```

The interesting part of this configuration file is that there are quite a few cross-references. That is, the contacts.cfg file depends on what you do in other configuration files. For instance, the lines service_notification_period and host_notification_period are periods that you will define later in the timeperiods.cfg file.

In the example contacts.cfg file in Listing 6-6, you also see that some service_notification_options and host_notification_options parameters are used. The following service_notification_options parameters can be used:

- n: Do not notify at all

- w: Notify on WARNING states

- u: Notify on UNKNOWN states

- c: Notify on CRITICAL states

- r: Notify when the service recovers and returns to OK state

Likewise, the following host_notification_options parameters can be used:

- n: Do not notify at all

- d: Notify on DOWN host states

- u: Notify if host is unreachable

- r: Notify when host recovers

Defining a Contacts Group

After defining the contacts file, you may want to create a contact group as well. This makes it easier in large implementations to address all contacts at once. Listing 6-6 shows what a contact group may look like.

Listing 6-6. *Example of a Contact Group*

```
# Definition of an admins contact group
define contactgroup{
        contactgroup_name      admins
        alias                  administrators
        members                root,linda
}
```

Defining Hosts and Host Groups

After defining whom to contact if things go wrong, you have to define hosts and, if so required, hostnames. The hosts you define will inherit some of their settings from the host template. On Ubuntu 8.04, you'll find this template in the file /etc/nagios2/conf.d/generic-hosts_nagios2.cfg. Normally you don't need to edit the settings in this file. You just need to refer to it when defining your hosts. This hosts configuration file may look similar to the example shown in Listing 6-7.

Listing 6-7. *Example hosts.cfg File*

```
# definition of Ubuntu Server
define host{
        host_name              mel
        alias                  Ubuntu Server
        address                192.168.1.99
        use                    generic-host
        check_command          check-host-alive
        max_check_attempts     10
        notification_interval  120
        notification_period    24x7
        notification_options   d,u,r
}

#Definition of generic Samba server
define host{
        host_name              syl
        alias                  Samba Server
        address                192.168.1.100
        use                    generic-host
```

```
        check_command            check-host-alive
        max_check_attempts       10
        notification_interval    120
        notification_period      24x7
        notification_options     d,u,r
}

#Definition of internal web server
define host{
        host_name                lin
        alias                    Web Server
        address                  192.168.1.101
        use                      generic-host
        check_command            check-host-alive
        max_check_attempts       10
        notification_interval    120
        notification_period      24x7
        notification_options     d,u,r
}

define host{
        host_name                lor
        alias                    external web server
        address                  80.69.93.216
        use                      generic-host
        check_command            check-host-alive
        max_check_attempts       10
        notification_interval    120
        notification_period      24x7
        notification_options     d,u,r
}
```

In the example hosts.cfg file in Listing 6-7, you can see that some new parameters are used. Of these, the nonobvious parameters are as follows:

- check_command: Refers to the command that Nagios uses to check if the host is up. In all cases, it should refer to the check-hosts-alive command.

- max_check_attempts: Defines how many checks Nagios should run as a maximum. If a host still doesn't reply after reaching this threshold, Nagios will consider it unavailable.

- `notification_interval`: Defines, in minutes, how often you should receive a notification if the problem still exists. Use the value 0 if you want just one notification to be sent after the problem is discovered.

- `notification_period`: Defines during which time period notifications should be sent to the contacts. It is a good idea to use 24x7 here, to make sure that notifications will be sent at all times.

- `notification_options`: Defines in what situations notifications should be sent out. The following options are available:

  - d: Notify if host is down

  - u: Notify if host is unreachable

  - r: Send notification when host recovers

  - n: Do not send notifications

After defining hosts, you must specify the host groups that your hosts belong to. There are many approaches to creating host groups, and a host may be a member of more than one host group. Ultimately, your business needs will dictate which host groups to use. In the example in Listing 6-8, you can see that three different approaches are used to define host groups. First, there is a host group that contains all hosts, and then there are functional host groups, and last there are host groups based on locations that are used.

Listing 6-8. *Host Groups Make Managing Hosts Easier*

```
# All hosts
define hostgroup {
        hostgroup_name    all
        alias             all hosts
        members           *
}

define hostgroup {
        hostgroup_name    internal
        alias             internal hosts
        members           mel, syl, lin
}
```

```
define hostgroup {
        hostgroup_name    webservers
        alias             web servers
        members           mel, lin, lor
}

define hostgroup {
        hostgroup_name    fileservers
        alias             file servers
        members           mel, syl
}
```

Defining Services to Monitor

Now that your hosts and host groups are defined, it's time to work on the services. In the services.cfg file, you define what particular services you want to monitor. Normally, making sure that all relevant services are defined is a lot of work. In Nagios, you can monitor network services as well as local services. For instance, there is a service to check available local disk space, or you can check based on any network protocol as well.

Before you start to work on the services.cfg file, you should understand what it does. In the services file, different services are checked. To do this, Nagios needs plug-ins. You'll find a list of all available plug-ins in the /usr/lib/nagios/plugins directory. I recommend that you have a look at this directory and get an idea of the possibilities that are offered. You can run every plug-in from this directory as an independent executable, which gives you an idea of the plug-in possibilities. Some plug-ins just run and that's all, whereas other plug-ins can have lots of options that enable you to determine what exactly the plug-in should do. Listing 6-9 gives you an example of the help output from the check_disk plug-in. Many plug-ins have complex options like this one, so make sure that you are aware of the options that exist for the plug-ins you want to use before you configure the services.cfg file.

Listing 6-9. *Nagios Plug-ins Often Have Lots of Options to Define What You Want Them to Do*

```
root@mel:/usr/lib/nagios/plugins# ./check_disk --help
check_disk v1848 (nagios-plugins 1.4.11)
Copyright (c) 1999 Ethan Galstad <nagios@nagios.org>
Copyright (c) 1999-2006 Nagios Plugin Development Team
        <nagiosplug-devel@lists.sourceforge.net>
```

This plugin checks the amount of used disk space on a mounted file system and generates an alert if free space is less than one of the threshold values

Usage: check_disk -w limit -c limit [-W limit] [-K limit] {-p path | -x device}
[-C] [-E] [-e] [-g group] [-k] [-l] [-M] [-m] [-R path] [-r path]
[-t timeout] [-u unit] [-v] [-X type]

Options:
 -h, --help
    Print detailed help screen
 -V, --version
    Print version information
 -w, --warning=INTEGER
    Exit with WARNING status if less than INTEGER units of disk are free
 -w, --warning=PERCENT%
    Exit with WARNING status if less than PERCENT of disk space is free
 -c, --critical=INTEGER
    Exit with CRITICAL status if less than INTEGER units of disk are free
 -c, --critical=PERCENT%
    Exit with CRITCAL status if less than PERCENT of disk space is free
 -W, --iwarning=PERCENT%
    Exit with WARNING status if less than PERCENT of inode space is free
 -K, --icritical=PERCENT%
    Exit with CRITICAL status if less than PERCENT of inode space is free
 -p, --path=PATH, --partition=PARTITION
    Path or partition (may be repeated)
 -x, --exclude_device=PATH <STRING>
    Ignore device (only works if -p unspecified)
 -C, --clear
    Clear thresholds
 -E, --exact-match
    For paths or partitions specified with -p, only check for exact paths
 -e, --errors-only
    Display only devices/mountpoints with errors
 -g, --group=NAME
    Group pathes. Thresholds apply to (free-)space of all partitions together
 -k, --kilobytes
    Same as '--units kB'
 -l, --local
    Only check local filesystems

-L, --stat-remote-fs
    Only check local filesystems against thresholds. Yet call stat on➡
remote filesystems
    to test if they are accessible (e.g. to detect Stale NFS Handles)
-M, --mountpoint
    Display the mountpoint instead of the partition
-m, --megabytes
    Same as '--units MB'
-A, --all
    Explicitly select all pathes. This is equivalent to -R '.*'
-R, --eregi-path=PATH, --eregi-partition=PARTITION
    Case insensitive regular expression for path/partition (may be repeated)
-r, --ereg-path=PATH, --ereg-partition=PARTITION
    Regular expression for path or partition (may be repeated)
-I, --ignore-eregi-path=PATH, --ignore-eregi-partition=PARTITION
    Regular expression to ignore selected path/partition (case insensitive)➡
(may be repeated)
-i, --ignore-ereg-path=PATH, --ignore-ereg-partition=PARTITION
    Regular expression to ignore selected path or partition (may be repeated)
-t, --timeout=INTEGER
    Seconds before connection times out (default: 10)
-u, --units=STRING
    Choose bytes, kB, MB, GB, TB (default: MB)
-v, --verbose
    Show details for command-line debugging (Nagios may truncate output)
-X, --exclude-type=TYPE
    Ignore all filesystems of indicated type (may be repeated)

Examples:
 check_disk -w 10% -c 5% -p /tmp -p /var -C -w 100000 -c 50000 -p /
    Checks /tmp and /var at 10% and 5%, and / at 100MB and 50MB
 check_disk -w 100M -c 50M -C -w 1000M -c 500M -g sidDATA -r '^/oracle/SID/data.*$'
    Checks all filesystems not matching -r at 100M and 50M. The fs matching➡
the -r regex are grouped which means the freespace thresholds are➡
applied to all disks together
 check_disk -w 100M -c 50M -C -w 1000M -c 500M -p /foo -C -w 5% -c 3% -p /bar
    Checks /foo for 1000M/500M and /bar for 5/3%. All remaining volumes use 100M/50M

Send email to nagios-users@lists.sourceforge.net if you have questions
regarding use of this software. To submit patches or suggest improvements,
send email to nagiosplug-devel@lists.sourceforge.net

After you have familiarized yourself with the possibilities the plug-ins have to offer, you can start creating the services file. Listing 6-10 shows a very simple example of a services file. In this file, Nagios will monitor whether hosts are available. Next, for web servers, it will monitor whether the web service is still up and running. In this file, Nagios will monitor the availability of hosts, web services, and disk space for host lor.

Like the hosts.cfg file, the services.cfg file also uses a template containing some generic settings. These default settings are read from /etc/nagios2/conf.d/ generic-service_nagios2.cfg. If you want to overwrite settings from the template file, you can include them in the services.cfg file. In Listing 6-10, you can see that that is done for the check on local disk usage for host lor. Consider this not as a complete configuration file, but rather as a starting point to build your own configuration.

Listing 6-10. *services.cfg Defines What Exactly You Want to Monitor*

```
## Check host groups

# Check if all services reply to ping test
define service{
        hostgroup_name          all
        use                     generic-service
        service_description     PING
        check_command           check_ping!100.0,25%!500.0,75%
        notification_interval   0
}

# Check web services availability
define service{
        hostgroup_name          webservers
        use                     generic-service
        service_description     HTTP
        check_command           check_http
        notification_interval   0
}

# Check available disk space
define service{
        host_name               lor
        use                     generic-service
        service_description     Check local disk usage
        is_volatile             0
        check_period            24x7
```

```
        max_check_attempts        3
        normal_check_interva      5
        retry_check_interval      1
        contact_groups            admins
        notification_interval     120
        notification_period       24x7
        notification_options      c,r
        check_command             check_disk!20%!10%!/
}
```

Working with Nagios Commands

Let's first look at the two check commands that are used in this example file:

```
check_ping!100.0,25%!500.0,75%
check_disk!20%!10%!/
```

It may surprise you that the commands are not used exactly as shown in the help output that you see when executing the command with the --help option. If you look closer, you will see that it does work the same way—it is just written in a different way. Look at the check_disk command, for example. This command, as used in the services.cfg script, uses three parameters, separated by exclamation marks. If you look at the help output of /usr/lib/nagios/plugins/check_disk --help, you see the result shown in Listing 6-11.

Listing 6-11. *Partial Output of check_disk Usage Information*

```
root@mel:/usr/lib/nagios/plugins# ./check_disk --help | less
check_disk v1848 (nagios-plugins 1.4.11)
Copyright (c) 1999 Ethan Galstad <nagios@nagios.org>
Copyright (c) 1999-2006 Nagios Plugin Development Team
        <nagiosplug-devel@lists.sourceforge.net>

This plugin checks the amount of used disk space on a mounted file system
and generates an alert if free space is less than one of the threshold values


Usage: check_disk -w limit -c limit [-W limit] [-K limit] {-p path | -x device}
[-C] [-E] [-e] [-g group ] [-k] [-l] [-M] [-m] [-R path ] [-r path ]
[-t timeout] [-u unit] [-v] [-X type]
```

```
Options:
 -h, --help
    Print detailed help screen
 -V, --version
    Print version information
 -w, --warning=INTEGER
    Exit with WARNING status if less than INTEGER units of disk are free
 -w, --warning=PERCENT%
    Exit with WARNING status if less than PERCENT of disk space is free
 -c, --critical=INTEGER
```

As you can see, this command has three options that are required: -w limit, -c limit, and -p path or -x device. -w generates a warning if less than the specified percentage of disk space is free, -c generates a critical event if less than the specified percentage of disk space is free, and -p or -x refers to either the path or the device name that Nagios has to monitor for available disk space. As used in the services.cfg file, these are exactly the three parameters that are used. The same applies to the ping test that is performed from the same script.

Defining Time Periods

The last relevant part of a Nagios configuration is the definition of time periods. In most cases you probably want to see an alert no matter when the event occurs, but in some cases you may choose to forward alerts to specific persons when an event occurs during a given period of the day. Listing 6-5, earlier in the chapter, specified that user linda will get alerts only during work hours. The definition of these time periods comes from the file /etc/nagios2/conf.d/timeperiods_nagios2.cfg. This file contains some useful default definitions of time periods, but can also be modified as required. Listing 6-12 gives an example of its contents.

Listing 6-12. *Using timeperiods_nagios2.cfg to Define During What Times of Day Nagios Has to Act*

```
root@mel:/etc/nagios2/conf.d# cat timeperiods_nagios2.cfg
###########################################################################
# timeperiods.cfg
###########################################################################

# This defines a timeperiod where all times are valid for checks,
# notifications, etc.  The classic "24x7" support nightmare. :-)
```

```
define timeperiod{
        timeperiod_name 24x7
        alias           24 Hours A Day, 7 Days A Week
        sunday          00:00-24:00
        monday          00:00-24:00
        tuesday         00:00-24:00
        wednesday       00:00-24:00
        thursday        00:00-24:00
        friday          00:00-24:00
        saturday        00:00-24:00
        }

# Here is a slightly friendlier period during work hours
define timeperiod{
        timeperiod_name workhours
        alias           Standard Work Hours
        monday          09:00-17:00
        tuesday         09:00-17:00
        wednesday       09:00-17:00
        thursday        09:00-17:00
        friday          09:00-17:00
        }

# The complement of workhours
define timeperiod{
        timeperiod_name nonworkhours
        alias           Non-Work Hours
        sunday          00:00-24:00
        monday          00:00-09:00,17:00-24:00
        tuesday         00:00-09:00,17:00-24:00
        wednesday       00:00-09:00,17:00-24:00
        thursday        00:00-09:00,17:00-24:00
        friday          00:00-09:00,17:00-24:00
        saturday        00:00-24:00
        }

# This one is a favorite: never :)
define timeperiod{
        timeperiod_name never
        alias           Never
        }

# end of file
```

Restarting Nagios with Your Configuration

Your configuration files should now be in place, which means it is time to restart Nagios. To do this, use the command /etc/init.d/nagios2 restart. If you have applied changes to your Apache configuration as well, don't forget to restart the Apache web server also, using /etc/init.d/apache2 restart. When you restart Nagios, watch the console of your server. After all, you did apply lots of changes to the different configuration files, and making one tiny little typing error will cause the restart of Nagios to fail. If there is some serious error that prevents Nagios from restarting, you will see it on the console of your server, as shown in the example in Listing 6-13.

Listing 6-13. *If Nagios Fails to Restart, It Will Tell You Why*

```
root@mel:/etc/init.d# ./nagios restart
 * Restarting nagios2 monitoring daemon nagios2
Nagios 2.11
Copyright (c) 1999-2007 Ethan Galstad (http://www.nagios.org)
Last Modified: 03-12-2008
License: GPL

Reading configuration data...

Error: Unexpected start of object definition in file➥
 '/etc/nagios2/conf.d/services.cfg' on line 12.  Make sure you close➥
 preceding objects before starting a new one.

***> One or more problems was encountered while processing the config files...

     Check your configuration file(s) to ensure that they contain valid
     directives and data defintions.  If you are upgrading from a previous
     version of Nagios, you should be aware that some variables/definitions
     may have been removed or modified in this version.  Make sure to read
     the HTML documentation regarding the config files, as well as the
     'Whats New' section to find out what has changed.

 * errors in config!
```

If an error occurs, fix it and restart Nagios. This part of the configuration requires some patience. You have created lots of configuration files, all by hand, so it's likely that now you have to eliminate lots of errors, also by hand.

█Caution When using `/etc/init.d/nagios2 restart`, the service may falsely report that it is up and running. Don't trust this result. When debugging your Nagios server for configuration errors, first stop it by using `/etc/init.d/nagios2 stop` and then restart it by using `/etc/init.d/nagios2 start`.

Installing NRPE

To monitor some services, you just need Nagios on your server and nothing else. To monitor other parameters on a managed host, you need a local agent on that host as well. The name of the service is NRPE and it exists for different server platforms. Setting up NRPE consists of two parts. The first part happens on the server that you want to monitor, and the second part happens on the Nagios server.

Configuring NRPE on the Monitored Server

Because you may have Linux distributions other than Ubuntu Server in your network, and because these servers may not know `apt-get`, this section covers a more generic way to install the NRPE service on Linux servers. In this method, the `nrpe.tar.gz` file is installed. Of course, you can install NRPE on Ubuntu Server as well. To do this, use `apt-get install nagios-nrpe-plugin`.

█Caution If you want to install NRPE on Ubuntu, don't install and extract the `.tar.gz` file that is offered from the Nagios download site as described in the following procedure. Use the `nagios-nrpe-plugin` package instead. Install it with the command `apt-get install nagios-nrpe-plugin`. If your distribution is not Ubuntu but has a method of installing NRPE from its software repositories, you should always do it that way. Only if that doesn't work can you apply steps 1-4 from the following procedure.

---

1. On the server you want to manage, create a `nagios` user and a `nagios` group and configure `/usr/local/nagios` as the home directory that the user should use:

   ```
   groupadd nagios
   useradd -g nagios -md /usr/local/nagios nagios
   ```

2. Go to `www.nagios.org/download`. From there, click the Go button for Get Addons. Next, select the latest version of NRPE and click Go to continue. In the File Download dialog box that asks you whether you want to save the `nrpe` archive to disk, click Save. Store it somewhere on disk; the `/tmp` directory is a reasonable choice.

3. Assuming that you have just downloaded the `nrpe` package to the `/tmp` directory, use `cd /tmp` to go to that directory, and then use the command `tar zxvf nrpe<version>.tar.gz` to extract it. This creates a subdirectory with the name `nrpe-<version>`.

4. Use `cd` to go into the subdirectory that was just created, and then compile the `nrpe` plug-in using the following commands. If this fails, make sure that you have a C compiler installed on your server.

```
./configure
make all
```

5. Copy the `nrpe` file from the `src` subdirectory to the directory where Nagios would expect its plug-in files to be located. If on your server nothing related to Nagios has been installed so far, use the location `/usr/local/nagios`. If something related to Nagios has already been installed, check whether `/var/lib/nagios` already exists on your server. If it does, copy the `nrpe` file there.

6. In the directory to which you just copied the `nrpe` module, use your editor to create the `nrpe` configuration file. The name of this file must be `nrpe.cfg`, so if you just copied the module to `/var/lib/nagios`, make sure that you create the file `/var/lib/nagios/nrpe.cfg`. Give the file the following contents, while making sure that the `allowed_hosts` line contains the IP address of your Nagios server:

```
server_port=5666
nrpe_user=nagios
nrpe_group=nagios
allowed_hosts=192.168.1.99
```

This basically finishes the NRPE installation. To execute Nagios commands on the host that you are monitoring, you would also need Nagios plug-ins. If nothing was installed yet on your server, download the plug-ins from www.nagios.org (or from your distribution's software repositories) and put them in the default path `/usr/local/nagios/libexec`. If on your server some Nagios components were installed already, check the local server configuration to find the location of the plug-in files. Always check if `/usr/lib/nagios/plugins` exists before putting plug-ins in `/usr/local/nagios/libexec`. Many distributions use this location in `/usr/lib/nagios` to store plug-ins.

Once the plug-ins are installed, you can add to the `nrpe.cfg` configuration file the checks that you want Nagios to perform on this host. For instance, add the following line to check if available disk space on the monitored machine falls below the warning threshold of 20% and the critical threshold of 10%:

```
command[check_disk]=/usr/lib/nagios/plugins/check_disk -w 20 -c 10
```

■**Tip** Before you include the plug-in command in the nrpe.cfg file, make sure it really works. You can verify this by running it from the command line, just as you would include it in the configuration file.

Did it all work? If so, then I recommend that you add the following lines to your nrpe. cfg file as a default. This is information that you would normally be interested in when monitoring a remote host.

```
command[check_users]=/usr/lib/nagios/plugins/check_users -w 5 -c 10
command[check_load]=/usr/lib/nagios/plugins/check_load -w 15,10,5 -c 30,25,20
command[check_zombie_procs]=/usr/lib/nagios/plugins/check_procs -w 5 -c 10 -s Z
command[check_total_procs]=/usr/lib/nagios/plugins/check_procs -w 150 0c 200
```

After you create the NRPE configuration, make sure that the NRPE process is started. Use the options your distribution's runlevels offer to make sure that it will be started automatically when your server reboots.

Configuring the Nagios Server to Use NRPE

The Nagios server should already contain the NRPE plug-in. On Ubuntu Server, it is installed in the directory /usr/lib/nagios/plugins by default. You should now check that you can really use it to contact the managed server. If the managed server has IP address 192.168.1.51, the following command will do the test:

```
/usr/lib/nagios/plugins/check_nrpe -H 192.168.1.51
```

The command should output the version of the NRPE process on the remote server. If that worked, next add the check_nrpe command to the /etc/nagios2/commands.cfg file. This file should contain a section that defines check_nrpe that looks like the following:

```
define command{
    command_name    check_nrpe
    command_line    /usr/lib/nagios/plugins/check_nrpe -H➡
 $HOSTADDRESS$ -c $ARG1$
}
```

Now that you have defined the command, it's time to add a section to the services. cfg file. In this section you will use the generic check_nrpe command, with the particular command you want to execute on the remote host as its argument. For instance, to execute the check_disk command on all remote hosts, define the following section in /etc/nagios2/services.cfg:

```
define service{
    use                     generic-service
    hostgroup_name          all
    service_description     checkspace
    check_command           check_nrpe!check_disk
}
```

You have now finished the configuration of the NRPE plug-in that makes it possible to monitor remote hosts as well. So far, we've talked about Linux hosts only. If you like Nagios, however, you can extend it to other hosts as well. There are NRPE versions available for all major operating systems, including Windows and NetWare. Check the Web for more information on how to configure these.

Managing Nagios

Not that your Nagios server is up and running, you are ready to manage and monitor it using the web interface. In this section, you'll get a quick tour of the web interface. The first window that you should check out is the Tactical Monitoring Overview, shown in Figure 6-2. Especially when managing many nodes with Nagios, this view gives the fastest insight into what is happening on your network. The right part of the window shows you a performance summary, and the bottom part of the window shows you which hosts and services are up and how many problems have been discovered.

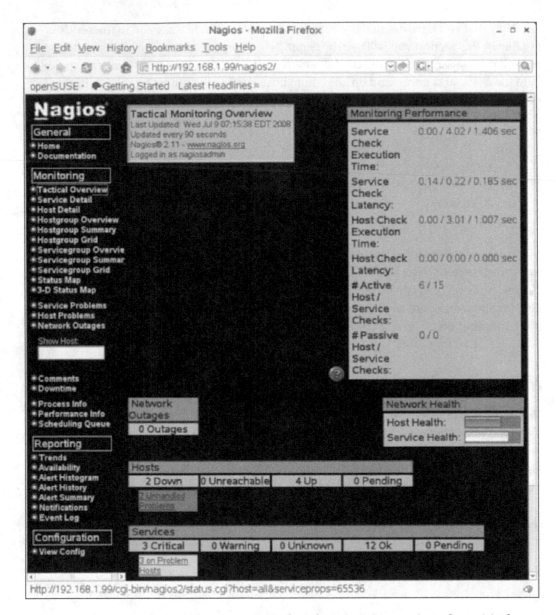

Figure 6-2. *The Tactical Monitor Overview window shows you in one view what critical events have happened on your network recently.*

If you observe that something may be wrong, you'll want to get more details about what is happening. The Monitoring section of Nagios offers different ways of displaying this information. In fact, all options look at the same information, but filter it differently. A very useful window is the Service Detail window, shown in Figure 6-3. From here, you can monitor in detail all the different parameters that are monitored. You can see what is happening both for services that have reached a status of CRITICAL and for services that are still OK. For instance, the disk space module will show you not only that it is OK, but also how much available disk space it has found on monitored nodes. There is just one disadvantage to the Service Detail window: if you monitor many hosts, a lot of information is presented, so it isn't easy to locate the information you need.

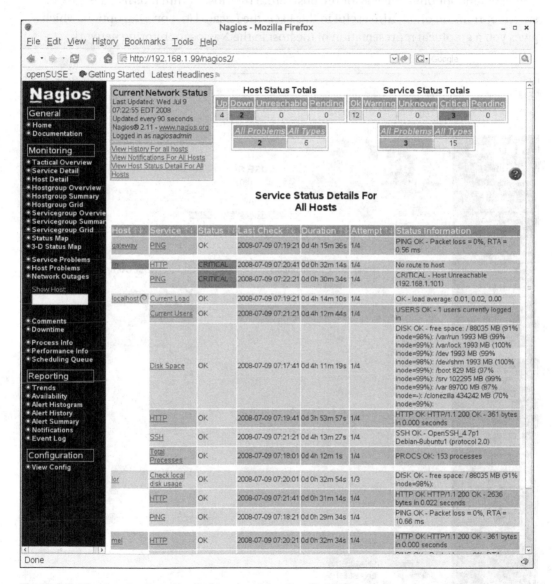

Figure 6-3. *The Service Detail window provides detailed information on service performance parameters.*

Especially if your Nagios environment is set up to monitor lots of hosts, you are going to like the Host Detail window. This window gives an overview of all hosts that Nagios is monitoring, and indicates per host whether or not there are problems. If problems are found, you can easily analyze what exactly is going wrong by clicking the hyperlink next to the host. This brings you to a status screen that shows in-depth information about the host. From this interface, an example of which is shown in Figure 6-4, you can also see all management options available for the host. From the Host Commands list, it is easy to switch options on or off. Also useful in this list is the Locate Host on Map option, which gives you a graphical representation of the host in the Nagios monitoring network.

Figure 6-4. *The individual host view allows you to see exactly what is happening on a host.*

The last options from the Monitoring section that I want to cover here are Service Problems, Host Problems, and Network Outages. Each of these gives you an overview of current problems, sorted by category. This interface helps you in solving critical issues. You can see status information, which attempts to describe what exactly is happening, and, more important, an overview of the duration of a problem. This helps you in solving the longest-existing problem first.

Below the Monitoring section of the Nagios web interface is the Reporting section. The information available here helps you in analyzing historical data. It may not be too shocking that a service has been unavailable for a couple of minutes. As an administrator, you probably want to know how often that has happened; structural problems deserve more attention than occasional problems.

To generate a report from the Reporting section, select Trends. You'll see a simple wizard, the first step of which asks you to indicate if you want to generate a trend report for a service or for a host. Select Service and next click Continue to Step 2. You now see a list of all services that are monitored on the different hosts in your network. For example, if you want to monitor disk space usage on local host, select Localhost;Disk space. Next, continue to step 3 and modify the report options as required. By default, you'll see a report over a period of the last 7 days, but if you want to show a report for the last year, that is equally possible. Next click Create Report and you will see the report displayed in the browser window.

Summary

In this chapter you have learned how to set up a Nagios server for network monitoring. You have learned how Nagios helps you to monitor critical parameters, including both parameters on the individual host that you are monitoring and network parameters. You have also learned how to enable NRPE, which allows you to monitor parameters on a remote host, even a Windows host. When configured the right way, Nagios will notify you when things go wrong. This is useful, but will not automatically restart a service after things go wrong. Heartbeat high availability is needed to do that, as described in the next chapter.

■ ■ ■

## CHAPTER 7

Creating an Open Source SAN
Configuring a DRBD and Heartbeat on Ubuntu Server

In a modern network, a shared storage solution is indispensable. Using shared storage means that you can make your server more redundant. Data is stored on the shared storage, and the servers in the network simply access this shared storage. To prevent the shared storage from becoming a single point of failure, mirroring is normally applied. That means that the shared storage solution is configured on two servers: if one goes down, the other takes over. To implement such a shared storage solution, some people spend thousands of dollars on a proprietary storage area network (SAN) solution. That isn't necessary. In this chapter you will learn how to create a shared storage solution using two server machines and Ubuntu Server software, what I refer to as an open source SAN.

There are three software components that you'll need to create an open source SAN:

- *Distributed Replicated Block Device (DRBD)*: This component allows you to create a replicated disk device over the network. Compare it to RAID 1, which is disk mirroring but with a network in the middle of it (see Chapter 1). The DRBD is the storage component of the open source SAN, because it provides a storage area. If one of the nodes in the open source SAN goes down, the other node will take over and provide seamless storage service without a single bit getting lost, thanks to the DRBD. In the DRBD, one node is used as the primary node. This is the node to which other servers in your data center connect to access the shared storage. The other node is used as backup. The Heartbeat cluster (see the third bullet in this list) determines which node is which. Figure 7-1 summarizes the complete setup.

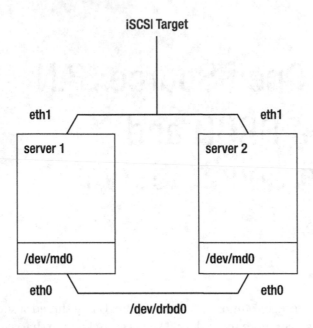

Figure 7-1. *For best performance, make sure your servers have two network interfaces.*

- *iSCSI target*: To access a SAN, there are two main solutions on the market: Fibre Channel and iSCSI. Fibre Channel requires a fiber infrastructure to access the SAN. iSCSI is just SCSI, but over an IP network. There are two parts in an iSCSI solution. The iSCSI target offers access to the shared storage device. All servers that need access use an iSCSI initiator, which is configured to make a connection with the iSCSI target. Once that connection is established, the server that runs the initiator sees an additional storage device that gives it access to the open source SAN.

- *Heartbeat*: Heartbeat is the most important open source high-availability cluster solution. The purpose of such a solution is to make sure that a critical resource keeps on running if a server goes down. Two critical components in the open source SAN are managed by Heartbeat. Heartbeat decides which server acts as the DRBD primary node, and ensures that the iSCSI target is activated on that same server.

Preparing Your Open Source SAN

To prepare your open source SAN, you need to make sure that you have everything necessary to set up the open source SAN. Specifically, you need to make sure that your hardware meets the requirements of a SAN configuration, so that you can install the software needed to create the solution.

Hardware Requirements

The hardware requirements are not extraordinary. Basically, any server that can run Ubuntu Server will do, and because the DRBD needs two servers, you must have two such servers to set this up. You need a storage device to configure as the DRBD, though. For best performance, I recommend using a server that has a dedicated hard disk for operating system installation. This can be a small disk—a basic 36 GB SCSI disk is large enough—and if you prefer, you can use SATA as well.

Apart from that, it is a good idea to have a dedicated device for the DRBD. Ideally, each server has a RAID 5 array to use as the DRBD, but if you can't provide that, a dedicated disk is good as well. If you can't use a dedicated disk, make sure that each of the servers has a dedicated partition to be used in the DRBD setup. The storage devices that you are going to use in the DRBD need to be of equal size.

You also need decent networking. Because you are going to synchronize gigabytes of data, gigabit networking is indispensable. I recommend using a server with at least two network cards, one card to use for synchronization between the two block devices, and the other to access the iSCSI target.

Installing Required Software

Before you start to set up the open source SAN, it's a good idea to install all software that is needed to build this solution. The following procedure describes how to do that:

1. Make sure that the software repositories are up to date, by using the `apt-get update` command.

2. Use `apt-get install drbd8-utils` to install the DRBD software.

3. Use `apt-get install iscsitarget` to install the iSCSI target.

4. Use `apt-get install heartbeat-2` to install the Heartbeat software.

All required software is installed now, so it's time to start creating the DRBD.

Setting Up the Distributed Replicated Block Device

It's time to take the first real step in the SAN configuration and set up the DRBD. Make sure that you have a storage device available on each of the servers involved in setting up the SAN. In this chapter, I'll assume that the name of the storage device is /dev/sdb. To configure the DRBD, you have to create the file /etc/drbd.conf, an example of which is shown in Listing 7-1. You can remove its contents and replace it with your own configuration.

Listing 7-1. *The DRBD Is Configured from /etc/drbd.conf*

```
san1:/etc # cat drbd.conf
# begin resource drbd0
resource drbd0 {
    protocol C;
        startup {degr-wfc-timeout 120;}
        disk {on-io-error detach;}
        net {}
        syncer {
            rate 100m;
            al-extents 257;
        }
    on san1 {
            device /dev/drbd0;
            disk /dev/sdb;
            address 192.168.1.230:7788;
            meta-disk internal;
    }
    on san2 {
            device /dev/drbd0;
            disk /dev/sdb;
            address 192.168.1.240:7788;
            meta-disk internal;
    }
}
# end resource drbd0
```

In this example configuration file, one DRBD is configured, named /dev/drbd0. The configuration file starts with the definition of the resource drbd0. If you would like to add another resource that has the name drbd1, you would add the resource drbd1 { ... }

specification later in the file. Each resource starts with some generic settings, the first of which is always the protocol setting. There are three protocols, A, B, and C, and of the three, protocol C offers the best performance. Next, there are four generic parts in the configuration:

- `startup`: Defines parameters that play a role during the startup phase of the DRBD. As you can see, there is just one parameter here, specifying that a timeout of 120 seconds is used. After this timeout, if a device fails to start, the software assumes that it is not available and tries periodically later to start it.

- `disk`: Specifies what has to happen when a disk error occurs. The current setting `on-io-error detach` makes sure that the disk device is no longer used if there is an error. This is the only parameter that you'll really need in this section of the setup.

- `net`: Contains parameters that are used for tuning network performance. If you really need the best performance, using `max-buffers 2048` makes sense here. This parameter makes sure that the DRBD is capable of handling 2048 simultaneous requests, instead of the default of 32. This allows your DRBD to function well in an environment in which lots of simultaneous requests occur.

- `syncer`: Defines how synchronization between the two nodes will occur. First, the synchronization rate is defined. In the example shown in Listing 7-1, synchronization will happen at 100 MBps (note the setting is in megabytes, not megabits). To get the most out of your gigabit connection, you would set it to `100m` (i.e., almost 1 Gbps), but you should only do this if you have a dedicated network card for synchronization. The parameter `al-extents 257` defines the so-called active group, a collection of storage that the DRBD handles simultaneously. The syncer works on one active group at the same time, and this parameter defines an active group of 257 extents of 4 MB each. This creates an active group that is 1 GB, which is fine in all cases. You shouldn't have to change this parameter.

After the generic settings in `/etc/drbd.conf` comes the part where you define node-specific settings. In the example shown in Listing 7-1, I used two nodes, `san1` and `san2`. Each node has four lines in its definition:

- *The name of the DRBD that will be created*: It should be `/dev/drbd0` in all cases for the first device that you configure.

- *The name of the device that you want to use in the DRBD setup*: This example uses `/dev/sdb`, to make sure that on your server you are using the device that you have dedicated to this purpose.

- *The IP address and port of each of the two servers that participate in the DRBD configuration*: Make sure that you are using a fixed IP address here, to eliminate the risk that the IP address could suddenly change. Every DRBD needs its own port, so if you are defining a /dev/drbd1 resource later in the file, it should have a unique port. Typically, the first DRBD has port 7788, the second device has 7789, and so on.

- *The parameter that defines how to handle metadata* : You should use the parameter meta-disk internal. This parameter does well in most cases, so you don't need to change it.

This completes the configuration of the DRBD. Now you need to copy the /etc/drbd. conf file to the other server. The following command shows you how to copy the drbd.conf file from the current server to the /etc directory on the server san2:

```
scp /etc/drbd.conf san2:/etc/
```

Now that you have configured both servers, it's time to start the DRBD for the first time. This involves the following steps:

1. Make sure that the DRBD resource is stopped on both servers. Do this by entering the following command on both servers:

   ```
   /etc/init.d/drbd stop
   ```

2. Create the device and its associated metadata, on both nodes. To do so, run the drbdadm create-md drbd0 command. Listing 7-2 shows an example of its output.

Listing 7-2. *Creating the DRBD*

```
root@san1:~# drbdadm create-md drbd0
v08 Magic number not found
md_offset 39999528960
al_offset 39999496192
bm_offset 39998271488

Found some data
 ==> This might destroy existing data! <==

Do you want to proceed?
[need to type 'yes' to confirm] yes
```

```
v07 Magic number not found
v07 Magic number not found
v08 Magic number not found
Writing meta data...
initialising activity log
NOT initialized bitmap
New drbd meta data block sucessfully created.
```

```
        --== Creating metadata ==--
As with nodes we count the total number of devices mirrored by DRBD at
at http://usage.drbd.org.
```

```
The counter works completely anonymous. A random number gets created for
this device, and that randomer number and the devices size will be sent.
```

```
http://usage.drbd.org/cgi-bin/insert_usage.pl?nu=2040020564152626401&ru➡
=10893684387669193786&rs=39999536640
```

```
Enter 'no' to opt out, or just press [return] to continue:
success
```

3. Make sure the drbd module is loaded on both nodes, and then associate the DRBD resource with its backing device:

```
modprobe drbd
drbdadm attach drbd0
```

4. Connect the DRBD resource with its counterpart on the other node in the setup:

```
drbdadm connect drbd0
```

5. The DRBD should run properly on both nodes now. You can verify this by using the /proc/drbd file. Listing 7-3 shows an example of what it should look like at this point.

Listing 7-3. *Verifying in /proc/drbd that the DRBD Is Running Properly on Both Nodes*

```
san1:~ # cat /proc/drbd
version: 0.7.22 (api:79/proto:74)
SVN Revision: 2572 build by lmb@dale, 2006-10-25 18:17:21
 0: cs:Connected st:Primary/Secondary ld:Consistent
    ns:0 nr:0 dw:0 dr:0 al:0 bm:0 lo:0 pe:0 ua:0 ap:0
```

6. As you can see, the DRBD is set up now, but both nodes at this stage are configured as secondary in the DRBD setup, and no synchronization is happening yet. To start synchronization and configure one node as primary, use the following command on one of the nodes:

```
drbdadm -- --overwrite-data-of-peer primary drbd0
```

This starts synchronization from the node where you enter this command to the other node.

Caution At this point, you will start erasing all data on the other node, so make sure that this is really what you want to do.

---

7. Now that the DRBD is set up and has started its synchronization, it's a good idea to verify that this is really happening, by looking at /proc/drbd once more. Listing 7-4 shows an example of what it should look like at this point. It will take some time for the device to synchronize completely. Up to that time, the device is marked as inconsistent. That doesn't really matter at this point, as long as it is up and works.

Listing 7-4. *Verify Everything Is Working Properly by Monitoring /proc/drbd*

```
root@san1:~# cat /proc/drbd
version: 8.0.11 (api:86/proto:86)
GIT-hash: b3fe2bdfd3b9f7c2f923186883eb9e2a0d3a5b1b build by phil@mescal,➥
 2008-02-12 11:56:43
 0: cs:SyncSource st:Primary/Secondary ds:UpToDate/Inconsistent C r---
    ns:62144 nr:0 dw:0 dr:62144 al:0 bm:3 lo:0 pe:0 ua:0 ap:0
        [>...................] sync'ed:  0.2% (38084/38145)M
        finish: 18:03:17 speed: 400 (320) K/sec
        resync: used:0/31 hits:3880 misses:4 starving:0 dirty:0 changed:4
        act_log: used:0/257 hits:0 misses:0 starving:0 dirty:0 changed:0
```

In the next section you'll learn how to configure the iSCSI target to provide access to the DRBD from other nodes.

> ■**Tip** At this point it's a good idea to verify that the DRBD starts automatically. Reboot your server to make sure that this happens. Because you haven't configured the cluster yet to make one of the nodes primary automatically, on one of the nodes you have to run the `drbdadm -- --overwrite-data-of-peer primary drbd0` command manually, but only after rebooting. At a later stage, you will omit this step because the cluster software ensures that one of the nodes becomes primary automatically.

Accessing the SAN with iSCSI

You now have your DRBD up and running. It is time to start with the second part of the configuration of your open source SAN, namely the iSCSI target configuration. The iSCSI target is a component that is used on the SAN. It grants other nodes access to the shared storage device. In the iSCSI configuration, you are going to specify that the /dev/drbd0 device is shared with the iSCSI target. After you do this, other servers can use the iSCSI initiator to connect to the iSCSI target. Once a server is connected, it will see a new storage device that refers to the shared storage device. In this section you'll first read how to set up the iSCSI target. The second part of this section explains how to set up the iSCSI initiator.

Configuring the iSCSI Target

You can make access to the iSCSI target as complex as you want. The example configuration file /etc/ietd.conf gives an impression of the possibilities. If, however, you want to create just a basic setup, without any authentication, setting up an iSCSI target is not too hard. The first thing you need is the iSCSI Qualified Name (IQN) of the target. This name is unique on the network and is used as a unique identifier for the iSCSI target. It typically has a name like iqn.2008-08.com.sandervanvugt:drbddisk. This name consists of four different parts. The IQN of all iSCSI targets starts with iqn, followed by the year and month in which the iSCSI target was configured. Next is the inverse DNS domain name, and the last part, just after the colon, is a unique ID for the iSCSI target.

The second part of the configuration file that you will find in each iSCSI target refers to the disk device that is shared. It is a simple line, like Lun 0 Path=/dev/sdc,Type=fileio. This line gives a unique logical unit number (LUN) ID to this device, which in this case is lun 0. Following that is the name of the device that you are sharing. When sharing devices the way I demonstrate in this section, the type will always be fileio. You can configure one LUN, which is what we need in this setup, but if there are more devices that you want to share, you can configure a LUN for each device. Listing 7-5 gives an example of a setup in which two local hard disks are shared with iSCSI (don't use it in your setup of the open source SAN—it's just for demonstration purposes!).

Listing 7-5. *Example of an iSCSI Target that Gives Access to Two Local Disk Devices*

```
Target iqn.2008-08.com.sandervanvugt:mytarget
    Lun 0 Path=/dev/sdb,Type=fileio
    Lun 1 Path=/dev/sdc, Type=fileio
```

The last part of the iSCSI target configuration is optional and may contain parameters for optimization. The example file gives some default values, which you can increase to get a better performance. For most scenarios, however, the default values work fine, so there is probably no need to change them. Listing 7-6 shows the default parameters that are in the example file.

Listing 7-6. *The Example ietd.conf Gives Some Suggestions for Optimization Parameters*

```
#MaxConnections          1
#InitialR2T              Yes
#ImmediateData           No
#MaxRecvDataSegmentLength 8192
#MaxXmitDataSegmentLength 8192
#MaxBurstLength          262144
#FirstBurstLength        65536
#DefaultTime2Wait        2
#DefaultTime2Retain      20
#MaxOutstandingR2T       8
#DataPDUInOrder          Yes
#DataSequenceInOrder     Yes
#ErrorRecoveryLevel      0
#HeaderDigest            CRC32C,None
#DataDigest              CRC32C,None
# various target parameters
#Wthreads                8
```

As the preceding discussion demonstrates, iSCSI setup can be really simple. Just provide an IQN for the iSCSI target and then tell the process to which device it should offer access. In our open source SAN, this is the DRBD. Note, however, that there is one important item that you should be careful with: iSCSI target should always be started on the node that is primary in the DRBD setup. Later you will configure the cluster to do that automatically for you, but at this point, you should just take care that it happens manually. To determine which of the nodes is running as primary, check /proc/drbd. The node that shows the line SyncSource st:Primary/Secondary is the one on which you should start the iSCSI target.

Configuring the iSCSI target at this point is simple:

1. Create the /etc/ietd.conf file. It should exist on both nodes and have exactly the same contents. The example file in Listing 7-7 shows what it should look like.

Listing 7-7. *Use This Configuration to Set Up the ISCSI Target*

```
Target iqn.2008-08.com.sandervanvugt:opensourcesan
       Lun 0 Path=/dev/drbd0,Type=fileio
```

2. On installation, the iSCSI target script was added to your runlevels automatically. You should now stop and restart it. To do this, run the /etc/init.d/iscsitarget stop command. Next run /etc/init.d/iscsitarget start, and it should all work.

Now that your iSCSI target apparently is up and running, you should double-check that indeed it is. To do that, you need to know about the iSCSI target ID. You can get that from the file /proc/net/iet/volume. If at a later stage you want to find out about session IDs, check the /proc/net/iet/session file for those. Listing 7-8 shows what the /proc/net/iet/volume file looks like.

Listing 7-8. *Getting Information About Currently Operational iSCSI Targets from /proc/net/iet/volume*

```
root@san1:~# cat /proc/net/iet/volume
tid:1 name:iqn.2008-08.com.sandervanvugt:opensourcesan
       lun:0 state:0 iotype:fileio iomode:wt path:/dev/drbd0
```

As you can see, the target ID (tid) of the iSCSI target device that you've just configured is 1. Knowing that, you can display status information about that target with the ietadm command. To do that, use ietadm --op show --tid=1. The output of this command will be similar to the output shown in Listing 7-9.

Listing 7-9. *Use ietadm to Get More Details About a Particular iSCSI Target*

```
root@san1:~# ietadm --op show --tid=1
Wthreads=8
Type=0
QueuedCommands=32
```

At a later stage, you can also use `ietadm` to get more information about currently existing sessions.

Before you continue, there is one item that you should take care of. Once the Heartbeat cluster is configured, Heartbeat will decide where the iSCSI target software has started and is running. Therefore, it may not be started automatically from the runlevels. The following procedure shows you how to switch it off using the optional `sysvconfig` tool:

1. Use `apt-get install sysvconfig` to install the `sysvconfig` tool on both nodes.

2. Start `sysvconfig` and, from the main interface, select enable/disable service.

3. As shown in Figure 7-2, browse to the `iscsitarget` service and switch it off by pressing the spacebar on your keyboard.

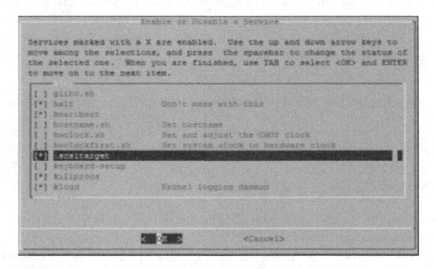

Figure 7-2. *Select the iscsitarget service to switch it off.*

4. Quit the `sysvconfig` editor.

Configuring the iSCSI Initiator

The purpose of an iSCSI initiator is to access shared storage offered by an iSCSI target. This shared storage can be nodes in a high-availability cluster or stand-alone nodes. In this section I'll explain how to configure the iSCSI initiator on a third node, which will allow you to test that everything is working as expected. Once configured properly, the iSCSI initiator will give a new storage device to the server that is accessing the iSCSI SAN. So if your server just had a /dev/sda device before connecting to the iSCSI target, after making connection, it will have a /dev/sdb device as well. Figure 7-3 gives a schematic overview of what you are going to do in this section.

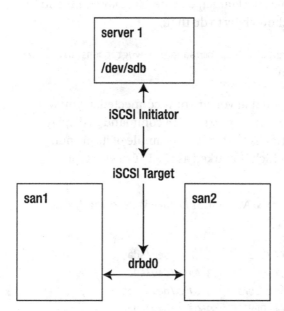

Figure 7-3. *The iSCSI initiator will provide a new SCSI device on the nodes that use it.*

Every operating system has its own solutions to set up an iSCSI initiator. If you want to set it up on Linux, the open-iscsi solution is the most appropriate. First, make sure that it is installed, by running the following command:

```
apt-get install open-iscsi
```

Once installed, you can start its configuration. To do this, use the iscsiadm command. First, you need to discover all available iSCSI targets with this command. After you discover them, you need to use the same command to make a connection. The following procedure shows you how to do this:

1. From the node that needs to access the storage on the SAN, use the `iscsiadm` command as displayed in Listing 7-10. This gives you an overview of all iSCSI targets offered on the IP address that you query.

Listing 7-10. *Use iscsiadm to Discover All Available Targets*

```
root@mel:~# iscsiadm --mode discovery --type sendtargets --portal ➥
192.168.1.230
192.168.1.230:3260,1 iqn.2008-08.com.sandervanvugt:opensourcesan
```

2. Now that you have located an available iSCSI target, use the `iscsiadm` command to log in to it. The following command shows how to do that:

```
iscsiadm --mode node --targetname iqn.2008-08.com.sandervanvugt:opensourcesan➥
 --portal 192.168.1.230:3260 --login
```

3. If it succeeds, this command will tell you that you are now connected. If you want to verify existing connections, use the `iscsiadm -m session` command to display a list of all current iSCSI sessions. Listing 7-11 shows an example of its output; you can now recognize the iSCSI device, which is marked as the IET device type.

Listing 7-11. *Use lsscsi to Check Whether the New iSCSI Device Was Properly Created*

```
root@mel:~# lsscsi
[2:0:0:0]    disk    ATA       ST3500630AS      3.AA    /dev/sda
[3:0:0:0]    disk    ATA       ST3500630AS      3.AA    /dev/sdb
[5:0:0:0]    cd/dvd  LITE-ON   DVDRW LH-20A1S   9L07    /dev/scd0
[6:0:0:0]    disk    Generic   STORAGE DEVICE   9602    /dev/sdc
[6:0:0:1]    disk    Generic   STORAGE DEVICE   9602    /dev/sdd
[6:0:0:2]    disk    Generic   STORAGE DEVICE   9602    /dev/sde
[6:0:0:3]    disk    Generic   STORAGE DEVICE   9602    /dev/sdf
[7:0:0:0]    disk    IET       VIRTUAL-DISK     0       /dev/sdg
```

The advantage of the iSCSI initiator configuration with `iscsiadm` is that the configuration settings are automatically written to configuration files at the moment you apply them. This, however, also has a disadvantage: the same iSCSI connection will always be reestablished. If after a change of configuration you need to change which iSCSI connection is automatically restored, you need to use `iscsiadm` to manually remove your iSCSI connection. If you wanted to do that for the iSCSI connection that was just established, the following command would do the job:

```
iscsiadm --mode node --targetname iqn.2008-08.com.sandervanvugt:opensourcesan➥
 --portal 192.168.1.230:3260 --logout
```

You now have verified your iSCSI configuration and that everything is working fine. The next step is to configure the Heartbeat cluster.

Setting Up Heartbeat

At this stage, you have a DRBD configuration that works, but in which you have to assign the primary server manually. You also have configured the iSCSI target, but it doesn't start automatically. The goal of this section is to install the Heartbeat high-availability clustering software and configure it to automatically assign the primary DRBD node and start the iSCSI target service.

The main goal of Heartbeat is to ensure that vital services are restarted automatically when the node currently hosting such a service goes down. To do this, Heartbeat sends protocol packets (the Heartbeats) to the other nodes in the cluster periodically. If a node seems to be down, the resources are migrated over automatically. In an open source SAN (just as in an expensive proprietary SAN), that doesn't mean the service will be uninterrupted. There will be a short period of interruption, with the advantage that the service automatically restarts. In this section you will learn how to set up Heartbeat so that there will always be a primary DRBD node and an iSCSI target.

Configuring Heartbeat involves three important elements. The first is the `ha.cf` configuration file, which contains a list of all nodes available in the cluster. When Heartbeat starts, it reads this configuration file to determine what exactly it has to start. The second important element is the cluster configuration base itself. This is stored in a file named `cib.xml`. As an administrator, never manually edit this file. Instead, use the `hb_gui` graphical user interface to set it up in a more user-friendly way. Last, you need to configure STONITH, which ensures that no data corruption will occur in your cluster. In the following subsections, you'll learn how to configure all of these.

Setting Up the Base Cluster from /etc/ha.d/ha.cf

In the first part of the cluster setup, you must tell the cluster which nodes it contains. To do that, you use the `/etc/ha.d/ha.cf` configuration file. This can be a very simple configuration file, mentioning not much more than the names of the nodes in the cluster, because the rest of the configuration is stored in an XML file that is maintained by the cluster.

Caution You must set up hostname resolution properly; otherwise, the configuration discussed here is not going to work. The hostnames of all nodes in the cluster as used in DNS or `/etc/hosts` must be the same as the hostnames given by the command `uname -n`.

Listing 7-12 shows an example of a very simple `ha.cf` configuration file.

Listing 7-12. *Example /etc/ha.d/ha.cf Configuration File*

```
udpport 694
autojoin any
crm true
bcast eth0
node san2
node san1
```

In this configuration file, the following options are used:

- `udpport`: This option tells Heartbeat which UDP port to use for its communication. 694 is the default port, and there is no good reason to change it.

- `autojoin`: This parameter enables nodes to join the cluster automatically, without a `node` directive in `ha.cf`. Basically, this practice is bad and unsecure, so disable it by using the `autojoin none` option.

- `crm`: In the old Heartbeat, version 1, all resources in the cluster were created from a configuration file. In the newer Heartbeat, version 2, the cluster resource manager (CRM) is used. The option `crm true` enables the CRM. There is no reason whatsoever to use anything other than `crm true`.

- `bcast eth0`: This line tells Heartbeat to send its protocol packets over network interface `eth0`. For redundancy purposes, it is a good idea to add another network interface as well. For instance, `bcast eth0 eth1` would use both `eth0` and `eth1` to broadcast Heartbeat protocol packets.

After configuring the `ha.cf` file, you need to create a second file, `authkeys`, in the directory `/etc/ha.d`. You use this file to enable or disable authentication between hosts. If you are in a trusted network environment, no authentication is needed. If that's the case, you just use a cyclic redundancy check (CRC) on arriving packets to see if any errors have occurred. Listing 7-13 shows an example of the `authkeys` file.

Listing 7-13. */etc/ha.d/authkeys Tells the Nodes How to Handle Node Authentication*

```
auth 1
1 crc
```

In the last step to create the foundation of the cluster, you need to make sure that the /etc/ha.d/authkeys file has the proper permissions, which is permissions 600. So use chmod 600 /etc/ha.d/authkeys to set them.

Now that you have created the basic configuration, you should copy it to the other node. Heartbeat provides a tool to do that, ha_propagate, which is in the /usr/lib/ heartbeat directory (/usr/lib64/heartbeat if you are using 64-bit Ubuntu Server). Because its directory is not in the search path, you have to run it with its complete path reference:

```
/usr/lib/heartbeat/ha_propagate
```

Now that the configuration is available on both nodes, you can start Heartbeat to see if it's working properly. On both nodes, use the following two commands to start it:

```
/etc/init.d/heartbeat stop
/etc/init.d/heartbeat start
```

This should bring up the Heartbeat software. To verify that it runs, use the crm_mon -i 1 command. This will give you real-time status information about the current state of your Heartbeat cluster. Listing 7-14 gives an example of its output.

Listing 7-14. *Use crm_mon -i 1 to Check Whether the Cluster Is Up and Running*

```
root@san1:~# crm_mon -i 1
Refresh in 1s...


============
Last updated: Wed Jul 30 10:16:14 2008
Current DC: san1 (dac1fb37-fd2c-4fb4-b88d-031cfb8379f4)
2 Nodes configured.
0 Resources configured.
============

Node: san1 (dac1fb37-fd2c-4fb4-b88d-031cfb8379f4): online
Node: san2 (ebc4c600-4c63-49b1-8c4d-26798ae9c75e): online
```

If you see output similar to this, that means the Heartbeat cluster is running and a very basic cib.xml file has been created. For the moment, this cib.xml file contains only information about the nodes that are present in the cluster and their current state. If you're interested in what the configuration currently looks like, use the cibadmin -Q command (see Listing 7-15 for an example).

Listing 7-15. *cibadmin -Q Shows the Current Configuration of the Cluster*

```
root@san1:~# cibadmin -Q
<cib generated="true" admin_epoch="0" epoch="2" num_updates="4" have_quorum="true"➥
ignore_dtd="false" ccm_transition="2" num_peers="2" cib_feature_revision="2.0"➥
dc_uuid="dac1fb37-fd2c-4fb4-b88d-031cfb8379f4">
  <configuration>
    <crm_config>
      <cluster_property_set id="cib-bootstrap-options">
        <attributes>
          <nvpair id="cib-bootstrap-options-dc-version" name="dc-version"➥
value="2.1.3-node: 552305612591183b1628baa5bc6e903e0f1e26a3"/>
        </attributes>
      </cluster_property_set>
    </crm_config>
    <nodes>
      <node id="dac1fb37-fd2c-4fb4-b88d-031cfb8379f4" uname="san1" type="normal"/>
      <node id="ebc4c600-4c63-49b1-8c4d-26798ae9c75e" uname="san2" type="normal"/>
    </nodes>
    <resources/>
    <constraints/>
  </configuration>
  <status>
    <node_state id="dac1fb37-fd2c-4fb4-b88d-031cfb8379f4" uname="san1"➥
crmd="online" crm-debug-origin="do_lrm_query" shutdown="0" in_ccm="true"➥
ha="active" join="member" expected="member">
      <transient_attributes id="dac1fb37-fd2c-4fb4-b88d-031cfb8379f4">
        <instance_attributes id="status-dac1fb37-fd2c-4fb4-b88d-031cfb8379f4">
          <attributes>
            <nvpair id="status-dac1fb37-fd2c-4fb4-b88d-031cfb8379f4-probe➥
_complete"➥
name="probe_complete" value="true"/>
          </attributes>
        </instance_attributes>
      </transient_attributes>
      <lrm id="dac1fb37-fd2c-4fb4-b88d-031cfb8379f4">
        <lrm_resources/>
```

```
      </lrm>
    </node_state>
    <node_state id="ebc4c600-4c63-49b1-8c4d-26798ae9c75e" uname="san2"➡
ha="active" crm-debug-origin="do_lrm_query" crmd="online" shutdown="0" in➡
_ccm="true" join="member" expected="member">
        <lrm id="ebc4c600-4c63-49b1-8c4d-26798ae9c75e">
          <lrm_resources/>
        </lrm>
        <transient_attributes id="ebc4c600-4c63-49b1-8c4d-26798ae9c75e">
          <instance_attributes id="status-ebc4c600-4c63-49b1-8c4d-26798ae9c75e">
            <attributes>
              <nvpair id="status-ebc4c600-4c63-49b1-8c4d-26798ae9c75e-probe➡
_complete" name="probe"_complete" value="true"/>
            </attributes>
          </instance_attributes>
        </transient_attributes>
      </node_state>
    </status>
  </cib>
```

In the `cib.xml` file, you'll find the complete configuration of the cluster. This con-figuration consists of two main parts: `configuration` and `status`. Everything between `<configuration>` and `</configuration>` represents the resources that you have created in the cluster. This is useful information, because you can save it to a file, modify that file, and tune it later on in the process. Everything between the tags `<status>` and `</status>` is current status information about the cluster. This is mainly needed by the cluster itself and you won't normally need to change this information.

The `configuration` section includes the following four parts:

- `crm_config`: Contains generic parameters for your cluster.

- `nodes`: Enables you to see which nodes currently are in the cluster. This should reflect the two `node` lines in `ha.cf`.

- `resources`: Lists resources. This section is still empty in Listing 7-15 because no resources have been configured yet.

- `constraints`: Enables you to create rules to tell the cluster which nodes can service which resources and in what order the resources should be loaded.

Configuring Cluster Resources

The good news is that at this point you are done with the most difficult work. The cluster is operational and ready for the resources you are about to create. Consider the resources to be the services that you want the cluster to manage for you. In this case, we need three resources:

- A resource that automatically configures one of the nodes as the DRBD primary node

- A resource for the iSCSI target

- An IP address that will be used by the iSCSI target

The IP address resource warrants some explanation. This resource is needed because the iSCSI target will roam from one server to another and back from time to time. You do want to configure the iSCSI initiators, however, with an IP address that never changes. For that reason, you are going to configure an IP address resource, and make sure that resource is started whenever the iSCSI target is started. This allows the servers that run an iSCSI initiator simply to connect to the IP address that is offered by the cluster, irrespective of which particular server the iSCSI target is currently served by.

To create cluster resources, Heartbeat provides a graphical user interface named hb_gui. By default, this GUI is not installed, so use apt-get install heartbeat-gui to install it now. If you prefer not to run graphical applications from your server, you can install hb_gui on a graphical desktop. It doesn't really matter where it runs, because you can connect from a client running hb_gui to any server running the Heartbeat cluster software. Assuming that you have installed the heartbeat-gui package on a graphical desktop, the following procedure describes how to configure cluster resources:

1. On the cluster server you want to connect to, you have to give a password to user hacluster, so use passwd hacluster (preferably on both nodes) and give this user a password.

2. From the computer where you have installed hb_gui, open a terminal window and enter the command hb_gui & to start the Heartbeat GUI.

3. From the hb_gui interface, select Connection ➤ Login to open a Login dialog box. Enter the following information:

- *Server(:port)*: The IP address of one of the cluster nodes

- *User Name*: The username `hacluster`

- *Password*: The password that you just assigned to user `hacluster`

Click OK to log in, and wait a few seconds for `hb_gui` to read the configuration from the server. You should then see the Linux HA Management Client window (see Figure 7-4).

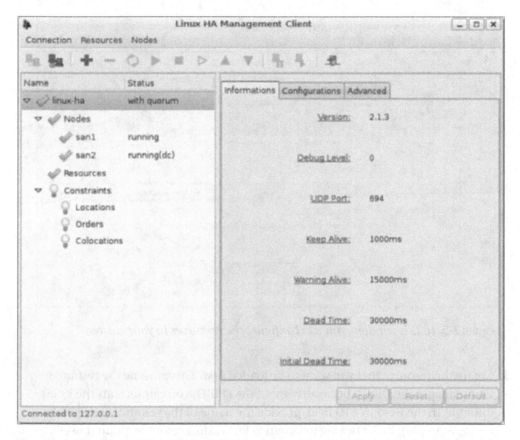

Figure 7-4. *The hb_gui interface shows the current cluster configuration after logging in.*

4. At this point you are ready to create the first resource. Select Resources ➤ Add
   New Item (or just click the + button). In the small dialog box that asks you what
   Item Type you want to create, choose Native and click OK to open the Add Native
   Resource window (see Figure 7-5).

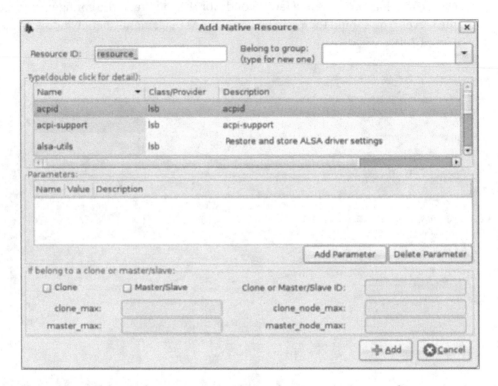

Figure 7-5. *In this window, you can configure the resources in your cluster.*

5. Create the resource that you want to be loaded first. This must be the resource
   that manages the DRBD, because without the DRBD, you cannot start the iSCSI
   initiator. In the Resource ID field, provide the name of the resource (I used drbd
   in this example). In the Belong to Group field, create a resource group (I used
   opensourcesan). The three resources that you are going to create in this example
   depend on each other, and assigning them to a group ensures that they are always
   loaded on the same server and in the order in which they appear in the group.
   Next, in the Type box, select the drbddisk resource type, as shown in the example
   in Figure 7-6.

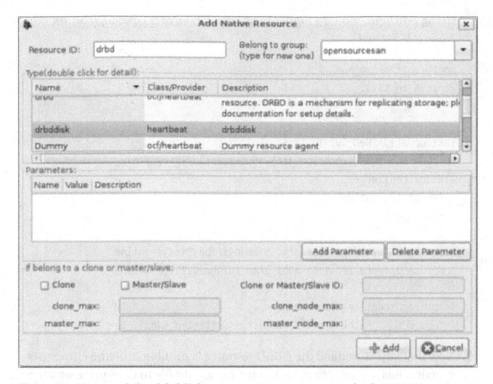

Figure 7-6. *You need the drbddisk resource type to manage which DRBD is going to be the master.*

6. Click Add Parameter. In the Name field, enter the name of the DRBD that you have created. If you've followed the instructions from the beginning of this chapter, this should be set to drbd0, in which case you don't need to enter a value here. Click Add to add the resource. You will see it immediately in the hb_gui interface, added as a part of the group in which you have created it. Its current status is not running. To see if it works, right-click it and select Start. You should see that the hb_gui interface marks it as started and indicates on which node it is running. You can get the same information from the output of the crm_mon -i 1 command, an example of which is shown in Listing 7-16.

Listing 7-16. *crm_mon -i 1 Shows Whether a Resource Is Up and, if So, on Which Node It Is Started*

```
root@san2:~# crm_mon -i 1
Refresh in 1s...


============
Last updated: Wed Jul 30 13:54:58 2008
Current DC: san2 (ebc4c600-4c63-49b1-8c4d-26798ae9c75e)
2 Nodes configured.
1 Resources configured.
============


Node: san1 (dac1fb37-fd2c-4fb4-b88d-031cfb8379f4): online
Node: san2 (ebc4c600-4c63-49b1-8c4d-26798ae9c75e): online


Resource Group: opensourcesan
    drbd        (heartbeat:drbddisk):    Started san1
```

7. Now that you've verified the DRBD resource is running from the cluster perspective, it is a good idea to look at the /proc/drbd file to determine which node currently is the primary DRBD from the DRBD perspective. The output of this command should show you that one of the nodes is running as primary, as you can see in Listing 7-17. If everything is still okay, it's time to go back to the hb_gui interface.

Listing 7-17. */proc/drbd Should Show One Node Is Designated as the Primary DRBD*

```
root@san2:~# cat /proc/drbd
version: 8.0.11 (api:86/proto:86)
GIT-hash: b3fe2bdfd3b9f7c2f923186883eb9e2a0d3a5b1b build by phil@mescal,➡
 2008-02-12 11:56:43
 0: cs:Connected st:Secondary/Primary ds:UpToDate/UpToDate C r---
    ns:0 nr:7587148 dw:7587148 dr:0 al:0 bm:464 lo:0 pe:0 ua:0 ap:0
        resync: used:0/31 hits:473734 misses:464 starving:0 dirty:0 ➡
changed:464
        act_log: used:0/257 hits:0 misses:0 starving:0 dirty:0 changed:0
```

8. Now that the DRBD is working properly, it's time to set up the next resource in the cluster: the IP address that the iSCSI target is going to use. Right-click the resource group you have just created, select Add New Item, choose the Item Type Native, and click OK. This opens the Add Native Resource window, in which you can specify the properties of the resource that you want to add. For the Resource ID, enter **iSCSI_target_IP** and make sure the resource belongs to the group you've just created. Next, in the Type box, select IPaddr2. In the Parameters box, you can see that a parameter with the name ip and the description "IPv4 address" is automatically added. Click in the Value column in that same row to enter an IP address for this resource. This is the unique IP address that will be used to contact the iSCSI target, so make sure to choose an IP address that is not in use already. You'll now see a screen similar to the example shown in Figure 7-7 (but with iSCSI_target_IP in this Resource ID field).

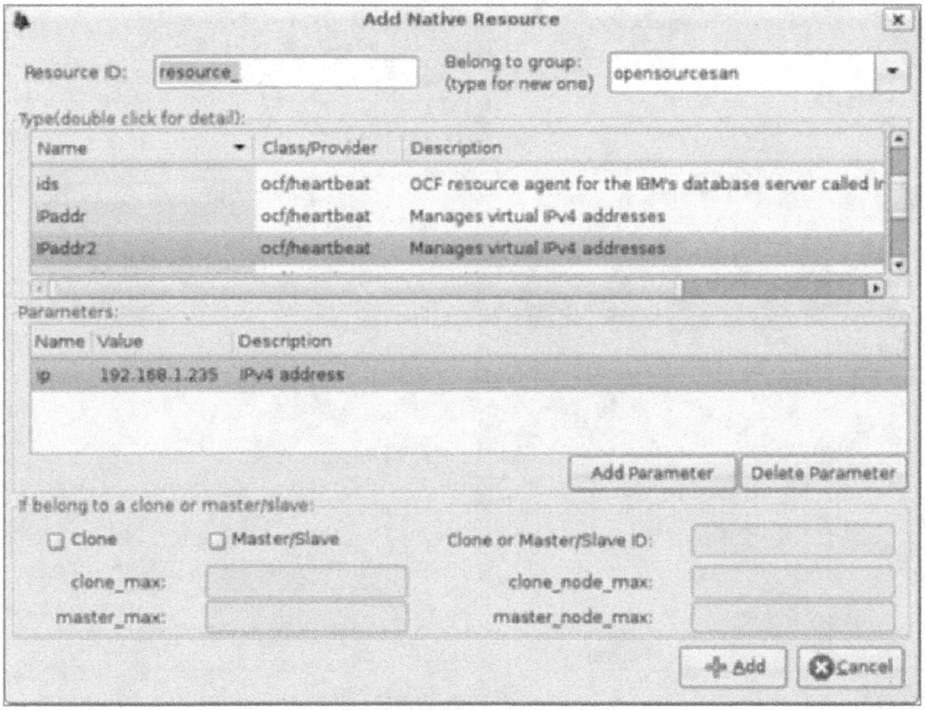

Figure 7-7. *In the Resource ID field, make sure to enter the name of the resource as you want it to appear in the cluster.*

9. With the properties of the IP address resource still visible, click Add Parameter
   and open the Name drop-down list. You'll see a list of preconfigured options
   that you can use to configure the IP address. Typically, you'll want to specify
   cidr_netmask to contain the netmask, and specify nic to identify to which network
   card the IP address should be bound. When specifying the netmask, make sure to
   use the CIDR notation—not 255.255.255.0, but 24, for example. Click Add to add
   the resource to the cluster configuration. You'll see that the resource is added to
   the group, but is not started automatically. To start it from the hb_gui interface,
   right-click it and select Start. The hb_gui interface should now look something like
   Figure 7-8.

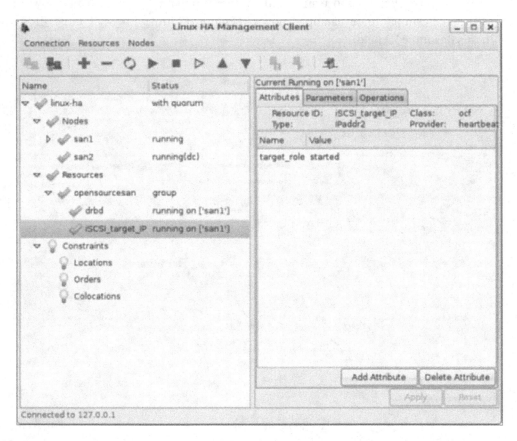

Figure 7-8. *hb_gui now shows the DRBD and the iSCSI_target_IP resources as both started.*

10. You now need to add one more resource, so from the hb_gui interface, right-click the resource group that you created earlier, select Add New Item, select the Native Item Type, and click OK. Give the resource the Resource ID **iSCSItarget** and make sure it belongs to your resource group. Select the iscsitarget resource type in the Type box and click Add. This adds iSCSItarget to the resource group. You can now start the iSCSI target as well, which will activate all the resources in the resource group. Your open source SAN is now fully operational!

Backing Up the Cluster Configuration

Now that you have an operational open source SAN, it is a good idea to make a backup of the configuration that you have so far. You can do this by writing the results of the cibadmin -Q command to a file, which you will learn how to do in this section. You'll also learn how, based on the backup, you can easily remove a resource from the cluster and add it again. In my daily practice as a high-availability consultant, this has saved my skin more than once after a cluster configuration has suddenly disappeared for no apparent reason. To make the backup, run the following command:

cibadmin -Q > /root/cluster.xml

Now that you have created the backup, it's time to open the XML file. In this file, which will be rather large, you'll see lots of information. The information between the <configuration> and </configuration> tags contains the actual cluster configuration as it has been written to the XML file when you configured resources using hb_gui. Using your favorite text editor, remove everything else from the backup file. This should leave you with a result that looks like Listing 7-18.

Listing 7-18. *Backup of the Current Cluster Configuration*

```
root@san2:~# cat cluster.xml
    <configuration>
     <crm_config>
       <cluster_property_set id="cib-bootstrap-options">
         <attributes>
           <nvpair id="cib-bootstrap-options-dc-version" name="dc-version"➥
 value="2.1.3-node: 552305612591183b1628baa5bc6e903e0f1e26a3"/>
         </attributes>
       </cluster_property_set>
     </crm_config>
```

```
        <nodes>
          <node id="dac1fb37-fd2c-4fb4-b88d-031cfb8379f4" uname="san1" type="normal"/>
          <node id="ebc4c600-4c63-49b1-8c4d-26798ae9c75e" uname="san2" type="normal"/>
        </nodes>
        <resources>
          <group id="opensourcesan">
            <meta_attributes id="opensourcesan_meta_attrs">
              <attributes>
                <nvpair id="opensourcesan_metaattr_target_role" name="target_role"➡
 value="stopped"/>
              </attributes>
            </meta_attributes>
            <primitive id="drbd" class="heartbeat" type="drbddisk" ➡
provider="heartbeat">
              <meta_attributes id="drbd_meta_attrs">
                <attributes>
                  <nvpair id="drbd_metaattr_target_role" name="target➡
_role" value="started"/>
                </attributes>
              </meta_attributes>
            </primitive>
            <primitive id="iSCSI_target_IP" class="ocf" type="IPaddr2" ➡
provider="heartbeat">
              <instance_attributes id="iSCSI_target_IP_instance_attrs">
                <attributes>
                  <nvpair id="2018e89e-4ced-4f96-9086-54a4941b2dc7" name="ip"➡
 value="192.168.1.235"/>
                  <nvpair id="8a727863-d06d-4525-8dd6-acbd49cbda3e" name="nic"➡
 value="eth0"/>
                  <nvpair id="7f08b655-0968-4867-b9d4-e20d7b1e9b39" name="cidr➡
_netmask" value="24"/>
                </attributes>
              </instance_attributes>
              <meta_attributes id="iSCSI_target_IP_meta_attrs">
                <attributes>
                  <nvpair id="iSCSI_target_IP_metaattr_target_role" name="target➡
_role" value="started"/>
                </attributes>
              </meta_attributes>
            </primitive>
```

```
        <primitive id="iSCSItarget" class="lsb" type="iscsitarget"➥
provider="heartbeat">
            <meta_attributes id="iSCSItarget_meta_attrs">
              <attributes>
                <nvpair id="iSCSItarget_metaattr_target_role" name="target➥
_role" value="started"/>
              </attributes>
            </meta_attributes>
        </primitive>
      </group>
    </resources>
    <constraints/>
  </configuration>
```

Now it's time to have a closer look at what exactly you have written to the backup file. You will see that in the cluster configuration, there are the following four different parts. Because the output of this command gives you the contents of the cib.xml file, it has the same parts as the cib.xml file in Listing 7-15, discussed earlier in the chapter.

- crm_config: Contains time-out values and other generic settings for your cluster. You haven't configured any yet, so you shouldn't see much here.

- nodes: List the nodes that currently are in the cluster. It should contain both nodes you've added and a unique node ID for each of them.

- resources: Contains the resources that you've just created with hb_gui. This is the most interesting part of the cluster configuration.

- constraints: Contains rules that specify where and how resources can be used. Because you haven't created any constraints yet, this part should be empty as well.

You can manage each of these parts by using the cibadmin command. Have a look at several examples of this command to get a better understanding of what it does. First consider this example:

```
cibadmin -D -o resources -x iscsitarget.xml
```

In this example, cibadmin is used to manage the cluster information base (CIB), which is in the "untouchable" file cib.xml. The option -D indicates that a part of this configuration has to be deleted. The option -o resources tells cibadmin it should work on the resources section of the CIB. Similarly, you could have used -o crm_config, -o nodes, or -o constraints to work on those respective sections. Lastly, -x iscsitarget.xml tells cibadmin what exactly it has to do. In order to do it, cibadmin has to apply the contents of the file `iscsitarget.xml`. This XML file should contain the exact definition of the iSCSI target resources, which are the IP address and the iSCSI target itself. To create this file, you should edit the `cluster.xml` file that you've just created once more. Considering that the definition of each resource starts with `<primitive>` and ends with `</primitive>`, the contents of this file should look as shown in Listing 7-19.

Listing 7-19. *An XML File Containing the Exact Definition of the iSCSI Target Resources*

```
root@san1:~# cat iscsitarget.xml
    <resources>
      <group id="opensourcesan">
        <meta_attributes id="opensourcesan_meta_attrs">
          <attributes>
            <nvpair id="opensourcesan_metaattr_target_role" name="target➥
_role" value="stopped"/>
          </attributes>
        </meta_attributes>
        <primitive id="iSCSItarget" class="lsb" type="iscsitarget"➥
 provider="heartbeat">
          <meta_attributes id="iSCSItarget_meta_attrs">
            <attributes>
              <nvpair id="iSCSItarget_metaattr_target_role" name="target➥
_role" value="started"/>
            </attributes>
          </meta_attributes>
        </primitive>
        <primitive id="iSCSI_target_IP" class="ocf" type="IPaddr2"➥
 provider="heartbeat">
          <instance_attributes id="iSCSI_target_IP_instance_attrs">
            <attributes>
              <nvpair id="1410b6a1-054e-48d7-8c84-810521642f18" name="ip"/>
              <nvpair id="1ae8b7bc-03a1-4f90-b149-5e8aa340aa47" name="nic"➥
value="eth0"/>
              <nvpair id="c5a09c70-be3a-4339-b3ad-daca5f4b4766"➥
name="cidr_netmask" value="24"/>
            </attributes>
          </instance_attributes>
```

```
        <meta_attributes id="iSCSI_target_IP_meta_attrs">
          <attributes>
            <nvpair id="iSCSI_target_IP_metaattr_target_role"➥
name="target_role" value="stopped"/>
          </attributes>
        </meta_attributes>
      </primitive>
    </group>
```

Caution When making an XML file of resources that are part of a group, make sure to include the group information as well, as in Listing 7-19. If you omit this information, the resources will not be placed in the group automatically when you restore them.

Now that you have this XML file, try the second `cibadmin -D` command:

```
cibadmin -D -o resources -x iscsitarget.xml
```

If you still have the `hb_gui` interface open, or look at the result of `crm_mon -i 1`, you'll see that the resources you've created earlier are removed immediately. Want to return them to your cluster configuration? Use the following command:

```
cibadmin -C -o resources -x iscsitarget.xml
```

This will restore the cluster to its original state. I recommend that you always create a backup of your cluster after you are satisfied with the way it functions. Do this by using the following command:

```
cibadmin -Q > ~/clusterbackup.xml
```

This allows you to restore the cluster fast and easily, which you will be happy to know how to do just after you've accidentally removed the complete cluster configuration.

Configuring STONITH

So far so good. The cluster is up and running and the resources are behaving fine. There is one more thing that you need to know how to do to ensure that your cluster continues to function properly. Imagine a situation in which the synchronization link between your two servers gets lost. In that case, each node might think that the other node is dead, decide that it is the only remaining node, and therefore start servicing the cluster resources. Such a situation may lead to severe corruption on the DRBD and must be avoided at all times.

The solution to avoid this situation is STONITH, which stands for "Shoot The Other Node In The Head." On typical servers, STONITH functions by using the management boards that are installed in most modern servers, such as HP Integrated Lights-Out (iLO) or Dell Remote Assistant Card (DRAC). The idea is that you configure a resource in the cluster that talks to such a management board. Only after a server has been "STONITHed" is it safe to migrate resources to another node in the network. You should in all cases create a STONITH configuration for your cluster.

It would take an entire book to describe the configuration of all the STONITH devices. Thus, to enable you to set up STONITH even if you don't have a specialized device, I'll explain how to configure the SSH resource. This resource uses a network link to send an SSH shutdown command to the other server. In real life you would never use this device, because it wouldn't work in many cases in which it is needed (for instance, if the network connection is down), but for testing purposes and to get some STONITH experience, it is good enough.

The following procedure shows you how to create the SSH STONITH device by using the cibadmin command and XML files. Alternatively, you could do the same using the hb_gui interface.

1. Make sure the atd process is installed and running. This is normally the case on Ubuntu Server.

2. To use STONITH, you need to use some generic properties in your cluster. Create a file named cibbootstrap.xml and add the contents shown in Listing 7-20.

Listing 7-20. *To Use STONITH, Your Cluster Needs Some Generic Properties*

```
<cluster_property_set id="cibbootstrap">
<attributes>
<nvpair id="bootstrap-01" name="transition-idle-timeout" value="60"/>
<nvpair id="bootstrap-04" name="stonith-enabled" value="true"/>
<nvpair id="bootstrap-05" name="stonith-action" value="reboot"/>
<nvpair id="bootstrap-06" name="symmetric-cluster" value="true"/>
<nvpair id="bootstrap-07" name="no-quorum-policy" value="stop"/>
<nvpair id="bootstrap-08" name="stop-orphan-resources" value="true"/>
<nvpair id="bootstrap-09" name="stop-orphan-actions" value="true"/>
<nvpair id="bootstrap-10" name="is-managed-default" value="true"/>
<nvpair id="bootstrap-11" name="default-resource-stickiness" ➥
value="INFINITY"/>
</attributes>
</cluster_property_set>
```

3. You need another XML file that defines the STONITH resources. Create a file named `stonithcloneset.xml` and add the contents shown in Listing 7-21.

Listing 7-21. *The XML File that Defines the STONITH Resources*

```
<clone id="stonith_cloneset" globally_unique="false">
<instance_attributes id="stonith_cloneset">
<attributes>
<nvpair id="stonith_cloneset-01" name="clone_node_max" value="1"/>
</attributes>
</instance_attributes>
<primitive id="stonith_clone" class="stonith" type="external/ssh"➥
 provider="heartbeat">
<operations>
<op name="monitor" interval="5s" timeout="20s" prereq="nothing"➥
 id="stonith_clone-op-01"/>
<op name="start" timeout="20s" prereq="nothing" id="stonith_clone-op-02"/>
</operations>
<instance_attributes id="stonith_clone">
<attributes>
<nvpair id="stonith_clone-01" name="hostlist" value=san1,san2"/>
</attributes>
</instance_attributes>
</primitive>
</clone>
```

4. You need to add the contents of these two XML files to the cluster. This causes the configuration to be written to the `cib.xml` file, which is the heart of the cluster and contains the complete configuration. Do this by using the following two commands:

```
cibadmin -C -o crm_config -x bootstrap.xml
cibadmin -C -o resources -x stonithcloneset.xml
```

At this point your cluster is fully operational and well protected. Congratulations, you have successfully created an open source SAN!

Heartbeat Beyond the Open Source SAN

In this chapter you have learned how to set up an open source SAN using Heartbeat and a DRBD. This open source SAN is a good replacement for a SAN appliance. In many enterprise environments, such a SAN is used as the storage back end for a cluster. That means that you can very well end up with another cluster talking to your open source SAN. Such a cluster could, for example, guarantee that your mission-critical Apache Web Servers are always up. Figure 7-9 shows an example of what such a setup could look like.

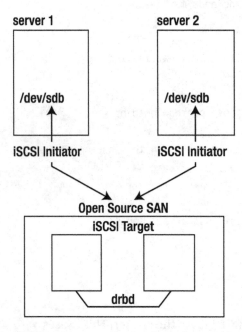

Figure 7-9. *Example of a cluster using the open source SAN*

The following procedure gives you a basic idea of what you need to do to set up such a high-availability solution for your Apache Web Server. Just the general steps that you have to complete are provided here, not the specific details. Based on the information that you have read in this chapter, you should be able to configure such a cluster solution without too many additional details.

1. Configure an iSCSI initiator on all nodes in the Apache cluster. This iSCSI initiator gives each node a new storage device, which, based on the existing configuration that you have, could have the name /dev/sdb. The interesting part is that the devices on both nodes refer to the same storage, so it really is a shared storage environment.

2. From one node, create a partition on the shared storage device and put a file system on it. For a busy Apache Web Server, XFS might be a very good choice (see Chapter 4 of *Beginning Ubuntu Server* for more information on file systems). On the other node, use the partprobe command to make sure that this node can see the new partition also.

3. Create the cluster by creating the /etc/ha.d/ha.cf and /etc/ha.d/authkeys files. Use /usr/lib[64]/heartbeat/ha_propagate to copy the configuration to the other nodes, and start the cluster on both nodes.

4. Start hb_gui and configure a file system resource. You need this file system to be mounted on the directory that contains your Apache document root. The cluster will make sure that the shared file system is mounted only on the server that also runs the Apache resource. Make sure that you specify the device that is used for the shared file system, the mount point as well as the file system type, when configuring this file system resource. You should also put it in a resource group, to ensure that it is bundled with the other resources you need to create for the Apache high-availability solution.

5. Create an IPaddr2 resource, as described earlier in this chapter. This resource should provide an IP address to be used for the Apache cluster resource.

6. On both nodes, make sure that the Apache software is locally installed. You should also make sure that it is not started automatically from your server's runlevel.

7. Make a cluster resource for the Apache Web Server as well. The LSB resource type is easiest to configure, so I recommend using that. Start your cluster, and you will have a high-availability Apache Web Server as well.

Summary

In this chapter you have learned how to use high-availability clustering on Ubuntu Server. This subject merits its own book, but at least you now should be able to set up an open source SAN using a DRBD, iSCSI, and Heartbeat. You should even be able to use this open source SAN for yet another cluster. In the next chapter you'll start to do some advanced networking, by learning how to set up an LDAP server on Ubuntu Server.

CHAPTER 8

■ ■ ■

Configuring OpenLDAP
Centralizing User Management

You can use the Lightweight Directory Access Protocol (LDAP) to manage user, group, and other configuration information in a centralized way. Centralized user management is the purpose for which LDAP is most commonly used. In such a configuration, one server is used as the LDAP server and contains all information that users need to log on to the network. From the client computers, users send their credentials to the LDAP server in order to authenticate.

To set up an LDAP Directory server, you need to configure the LDAP Directory. This Directory contains all information that is required for users to log on to the network. The advantage of the LDAP Directory is that it is compatible with the X.500 standard, which is used by other Directory services as well. Some Directory services that use the X.500 standard are Microsoft Active Directory and Novell eDirectory.

■Note To distinguish between an LDAP Directory and a directory in the file system, I'll refer to an LDAP Directory with an uppercase *D* and to a file system directory with a lowercase *d*.

Using the LDAP Directory

LDAP gives access to the Directory, a hierarchically structured database in which you can store different kinds of configuration data. In an e-mail environment, for example, you can use the LDAP Directory to store usernames and their corresponding e-mail addresses, thus setting up LDAP as a service to look up the e-mail address for a given user. You can also store different configuration information in the LDAP, such as the configuration of your DHCP servers or your DNS database. All this information is stored in a hierarchical structure.

The LDAP hierarchy is created by using container objects, which are comparable to directories used in a computer file system. These containers are also referred to as Directory Components (DCs). These DCs are comparable to the domains in a DNS hierarchy, as in www.sander.fr, except the way you refer to them is a little different in LDAP. Whereas you would refer to www.sander.fr in DNS, you would refer to dc=www,dc=sander,dc=fr in LDAP. You'll learn more about this later in this chapter.

In the Directory, you'll find data about different items. In LDAP terminology, usernames, group names, and printer records are referred to as *entries*, also known as objects or classes. For example, for each user that is created in the Directory, there is a user object. These objects are the building blocks of the LDAP Directory. Each has its own unique name, called the Distinguished Name (DN). This DN consists of the object name (Common Name = cn) and the names of the containers in which the object is stored. If, for example, the container dc=sander,dc=fr includes a user object with the name linda, the DN of this user would be cn=linda,dc=sander,dc=fr.

All objects in LDAP have attributes. Each object has at least one attribute, which is the cn, but in almost all cases, objects have more than one attribute. For a user object, for example, these attributes could be the username, the e-mail address, the telephone number, and a password. To be able to find attributes in LDAP, it is important that each has a correct value. For instance, you would expect an e-mail address to have an at-sign (@) in it, whereas this would not be the case for a telephone number.

Some attributes are mandatory, whereas other attributes are not. For instance, if you want an LDAP user to be able to log in to a Linux server, that user would need all user properties that normally are in /etc/passwd in the LDAP Directory.

All the information about user objects and their attributes is in the LDAP schema. This schema defines the object classes and their associated attributes. In a schema file, every object also gets its place in the ASN.1 structure. This structure, which is also used by the Simple Network Management Protocol (SNMP), gives every object a unique place in management environment, thus making it possible to manage LDAP objects in a uniform way. Listing 8-1 gives a partial example of the schema file that is used to include user information in the LDAP Directory.

Listing 8-1. *In the Schema File, You Can Define Objects and Their Attributes*

```
root@mel:/etc/ldap/schema# cat inetorgperson.schema
# inetorgperson.schema -- InetOrgPerson (RFC2798)
# $OpenLDAP: pkg/ldap/servers/slapd/schema/inetorgperson.schema,v➥
 1.18.2.3 2008/02/11 23:26:49 kurt Exp $
## This work is part of OpenLDAP Software <http://www.openldap.org/>.
##
## Copyright 1998-2008 The OpenLDAP Foundation.
## All rights reserved.
##
```

```
## Redistribution and use in source and binary forms, with or without
## modification, are permitted only as authorized by the OpenLDAP
## Public License.
##
## A copy of this license is available in the file LICENSE in the
## top-level directory of the distribution or, alternatively, at
## <http://www.OpenLDAP.org/license.html>.
#
# InetOrgPerson (RFC2798)
#
# Depends upon
#    Definition of an X.500 Attribute Type and an Object Class to Hold
#    Uniform Resource Identifiers (URIs) [RFC2079]
#        (core.schema)
#
#    A Summary of the X.500(96) User Schema for use with LDAPv3 [RFC2256]
#        (core.schema)
#
#    The COSINE and Internet X.500 Schema [RFC1274] (cosine.schema)


# carLicense
# This multivalued field is used to record the values of the license or
# registration plate associated with an individual.
attributetype ( 2.16.840.1.113730.3.1.1
        NAME 'carLicense'
        DESC 'RFC2798: vehicle license or registration plate'
        EQUALITY caseIgnoreMatch
        SUBSTR caseIgnoreSubstringsMatch
        SYNTAX 1.3.6.1.4.1.1466.115.121.1.15 )


# departmentNumber
# Code for department to which a person belongs.  This can also be
# strictly numeric (e.g., 1234) or alphanumeric (e.g., ABC/123).
attributetype ( 2.16.840.1.113730.3.1.2
        NAME 'departmentNumber'
        DESC 'RFC2798: identifies a department within an organization'
        EQUALITY caseIgnoreMatch
        SUBSTR caseIgnoreSubstringsMatch
        SYNTAX 1.3.6.1.4.1.1466.115.121.1.15 )
```

```
# displayName
# When displaying an entry, especially within a one-line summary list, it
# is useful to be able to identify a name to be used.  Since other attri-
# bute types such as 'cn' are multivalued, an additional attribute type is
# needed.  Display name is defined for this purpose.
attributetype ( 2.16.840.1.113730.3.1.241
        NAME 'displayName'
        DESC 'RFC2798: preferred name to be used when displaying entries'
        EQUALITY caseIgnoreMatch
        SUBSTR caseIgnoreSubstringsMatch
        SYNTAX 1.3.6.1.4.1.1466.115.121.1.15
        SINGLE-VALUE )


# employeeNumber
# Numeric or alphanumeric identifier assigned to a person, typically based
# on order of hire or association with an organization.  Single valued.
attributetype ( 2.16.840.1.113730.3.1.3
        NAME 'employeeNumber'
        DESC 'RFC2798: numerically identifies an employee within an organization'
        EQUALITY caseIgnoreMatch
        SUBSTR caseIgnoreSubstringsMatch
        SYNTAX 1.3.6.1.4.1.1466.115.121.1.15
        SINGLE-VALUE )
...
```

When you install LDAP on Ubuntu Server, the schema is stored in different files. These files are stored in /etc/ldap/schema. After installing a basic LDAP server, you'll have a basic schema. If support for additional objects is required, you can extend this schema by installing additional schema files and loading them in LDAP. Later in this chapter you will learn how to do that. Listing 8-2 shows the schema files that are installed by default.

Listing 8-2. *The Schema Is Stored in Configuration Files Installed in /etc/ldap/schema*

```
root@mel:/etc/ldap/schema# ls
collective.schema    cosine.schema         java.schema    openldap.ldif
corba.schema         duaconf.schema        misc.schema    openldap.schema
core.ldif            dyngroup.schema       nadf.schema    ppolicy.schema
core.schema          inetorgperson.ldif    nis.ldif       README
cosine.ldif          inetorgperson.schema  nis.schema
```

A generic file format is used to work with information in an LDAP environment. This format is known as the LDAP Data Interchange Format (LDIF). As an administrator, you will use LDIF to add information to the LDAP Directory. You'll learn later in this chapter how to use a command as ldapuseradd with an LDIF file as its input to add information to the LDAP Directory.

Introducing OpenLDAP

The LDAP implementation that is used on Ubuntu Server is OpenLDAP (http://www. openldap.org). After you install OpenLDAP, several configuration files, commands, and daemons are copied to your server. Before you perform the actual installation, it's a good idea to have an idea of the different components that are installed.

The most important component of OpenLDAP is the slapd daemon (slapd stands for stand-alone LDAP daemon). You have to start slapd to begin working with LDAP. Basically, slapd is your LDAP server. If more than one LDAP server is used in your network, you can choose to set up one of them as the master server and the other as the slave server. Additionally, you need to set up synchronization between these servers. This synchronization is implemented by using the slurpd daemon. Synchronization in such an environment is initiated by the master server, and the slurpd process makes sure that changes applied on the master server are copied to all slave servers.

To configure LDAP, you need to modify several configuration files located in the directory /etc/ldap. The most important configuration file is slapd.conf. In this file, you define all aspects of the slapd process. Apart from this file, /etc/ldap/schema includes numerous files that comprise the LDAP schema.

Finally, as an administrator, there are various commands that you can use to work with LDAP. As said, all of these use LDIF as the input file format to change information in the Directory. The most important commands and their purpose are listed here (they are explained in more detail later in this chapter):

- ldapadd: Add data to the Directory

- ldapmodify: Change data in the Directory

- ldapdelete: Remove data from the Directory

- ldapsearch: Look for information in the Directory

On a Linux LDAP client, some additional modules are needed as well. First, there is nss_ldap, the module that is installed to make it possible to refer to the LDAP server from the /etc/nsswitch.conf configuration file. Another important module is pam_ldap, which is used by the Pluggable Authentication Modules (PAM) mechanism to refer to the LDAP user. Both modules are required to set up user authentication on LDAP.

Configuring OpenLDAP

Following are the general configuration steps that you must follow to configure Open-LDAP. Each step is described in detail in the subsections that follow.

1. Install the LDAP software.

2. Configure the LDAP server by modifying the /etc/ldap/slapd.conf file.

3. Start slapd.

4. Create an LDIF file and use ldapadd to add information to the LDAP database.

5. Use ldapsearch to verify that your LDAP server is working.

6. (Optional) Set up replication using slurpd (not covered in this book).

Installing OpenLDAP

To install OpenLDAP, you need to install two packages: slapd and ldap-utils. Using root permissions, use the following command to install them:

```
apt-get install slapd ldap-utils
```

After installing the required software packages, this command also asks you to enter a password for the LDAP administrator. If you want to distinguish between local user administration and LDAP administration, make sure to use a different password as the root password (see Figure 8-1).

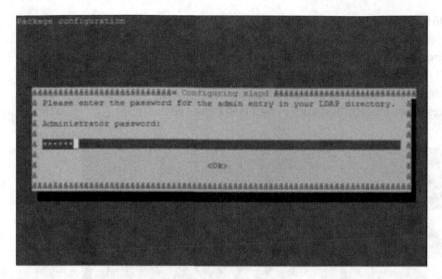

Figure 8-1. *For LDAP administration, you can set up an LDAP administrator with its own password.*

Configuring the Server

On Ubuntu Server, it is easy to create an initial configuration for your LDAP server. If you use the command dpkg-reconfigure slapd, a menu-driven configuration procedure is started automatically. This configuration procedure makes sure that the appropriate configuration is written to /etc/ldap/slapd.conf. This section first covers the configuration as performed with dpkg-reconfigure and then goes into details about the slapd.conf file.

Using dpkg-reconfigure for Initial Configuration

A very convenient way to start the initial OpenLDAP configuration is to use dpkg, as follows:

1. As root, enter the command dpkg-reconfigure slapd to start the menu-driven configuration procedure that helps you to create the /etc/ldap/slapd.conf file in an easy way.

2. The configuration program first asks if you want to omit OpenLDAP configuration. If you choose Yes here, the configuration program stops immediately and nothing will be changed, so choose No.

3. Every LDAP configuration needs a base DN. This base DN typically uses the DNS name of your server and is the starting point of the LDAP configuration. You are not required to use the DNS name of your server here, but if you want integration between LDAP and DNS, entering your server's DNS domain name here makes it a lot easier. By default, the configuration program reads the DNS domain name of your server automatically and applies that (see Figure 8-2).

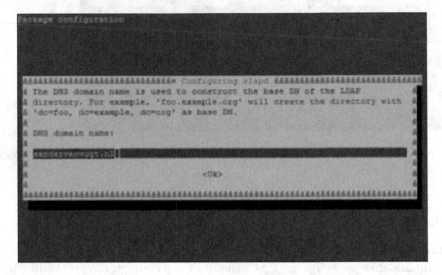

Figure 8-2. *To make LDAP use easier, the LDAP configuration is connected to the DNS configuration.*

4. Next, you need an Organization Name. By default, the DNS domain name from the preceding step is used as the Organization Name, which typically is a good idea. So just press Enter to continue here.

5. Enter the password for the LDAP administrator again. Use the same password that you used before and press Enter to proceed.

6. The configuration utility asks you which database back end you want to use (see Figure 8-3). This is a rather important configuration step. The configuration utility gives you a choice between two advanced databases types: Berkeley Database (BDB) and Hierarchical Database (HDB). Both are transaction-based databases that use write-ahead logging for optimal protection of the data. The only difference between the two is that HDB is a hierarchically structured database, whereas BDB is not. Because LDAP is also created in a hierarchical structure, it is a good idea to use the HDB format here. Both databases use a configuration file named /var/lib/ldap/DB_CONFIG in which you can put database configuration settings. These settings allow you to optimize performance of your database. Listing 8-3 gives the default contents of this file.

Listing 8-3. *Add Configuration Parameters in /var/lib/ldap/DB_CONFIG to Optimize Performance of the LDAP Back-end Database*

```
root@mel:/var/lib/ldap# cat DB_CONFIG
set_cachesize 0 2097152 0
set_lk_max_objects 1500
set_lk_max_locks 1500
set_lk_max_lockers 1500
```

The default settings in this file do well for an LDAP server that doesn't have too many objects. For instance, the basic cache size is 2 MB, and it can cache a maximum number of 1,500 objects. You will never reach these values if you create an LDAP server to handle authentication of 500 users. If, however, your LDAP server is used in an environment in which huge amounts of data have to be managed, you may benefit from increasing these values. See also man (5) slapd-hdb for more information about database optimization.

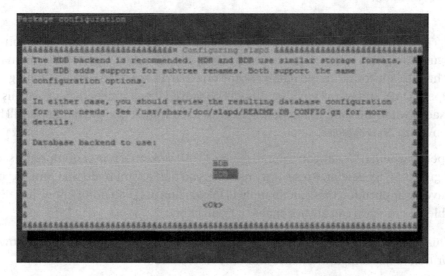

Figure 8-3. *For optimal performance, LDAP uses a hierarchical back-end database.*

7. Next you are asked what you want to do with the LDAP database if you remove the slapd.conf file (see Figure 8-4). Because the database makes sense only if a database configuration refers to it, it is a good idea to purge the database when the slapd.conf file is purged. In order to purge the LDAP configuration from your server, as root use apt-get purge slapd.

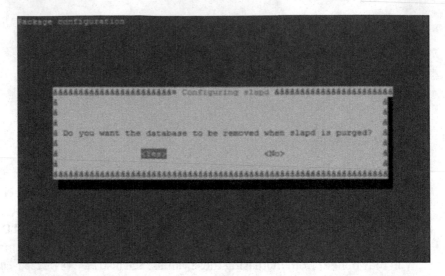

Figure 8-4. *It is a good idea to purge the database when you purge the slapd configuration.*

8. Because you have just specified how to create the new LDAP database, the configuration utility needs to re-create the database. Therefore, it now tells you that it has already found an old database (the one that was created when installing OpenLDAP) and warns you that this will be moved if you proceed. Because this is exactly what you want to happen, select Yes to continue. The old database will be moved to /var/backups.

9. Specify whether or not you want to enable LDAP version 2 protocol support (see Figure 8-5). By default, for security reasons, you don't want to do that, unless you have an application that can't handle LDAP version 3. If you don't know, just disable it here—you can always enable it again later.

10. This completes the configuration of your slapd server. The configuration is now written to its configuration files and LDAP is restarted.

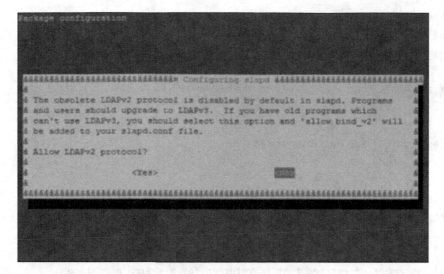

Figure 8-5. *For security reasons, it is a good idea to disable LDAP version 2 support.*

Tuning the slapd.conf Configuration File

You now have a decent `slapd` configuration in place. However, some aspects of the configuration have not been handled yet. Take a look at the configuration file itself, shown in Listing 8-4, to understand all that is happening in it.

Listing 8-4. *The /etc/ldap/slapd.conf Configuration File*

```
root@mel:/etc/ldap# cat slapd.conf
# This is the main slapd configuration file. See slapd.conf(5) for more
# info on the configuration options.

##################################################################
# Global Directives:

# Features to permit
#allow bind_v2

# Schema and objectClass definitions
include         /etc/ldap/schema/core.schema
include         /etc/ldap/schema/cosine.schema
include         /etc/ldap/schema/nis.schema
include         /etc/ldap/schema/inetorgperson.schema
```

```
# Where the pid file is put. The init.d script
# will not stop the server if you change this.
pidfile         /var/run/slapd/slapd.pid

# List of arguments that were passed to the server
argsfile        /var/run/slapd/slapd.args

# Read slapd.conf(5) for possible values
loglevel        none

# Where the dynamically loaded modules are stored
modulepath      /usr/lib/ldap
moduleload      back_hdb

# The maximum number of entries that is returned for a search operation
sizelimit 500

# The tool-threads parameter sets the actual amount of cpu's that is used
# for indexing.
tool-threads 1

#######################################################################
# Specific Backend Directives for hdb:
# Backend specific directives apply to this backend until another
# 'backend' directive occurs
backend         hdb

#######################################################################
# Specific Backend Directives for 'other':
# Backend specific directives apply to this backend until another
# 'backend' directive occurs
#backend                 <other>

#######################################################################
# Specific Directives for database #1, of type hdb:
# Database specific directives apply to this databasse until another
# 'database' directive occurs
database        hdb

# The base of your directory in database #1
suffix          "dc=sandervanvugt,dc=nl"
```

```
# rootdn directive for specifying a superuser on the database. This is needed
# for syncrepl.
# rootdn          "cn=admin,dc=sandervanvugt,dc=nl"

# Where the database file are physically stored for database #1
directory       "/var/lib/ldap"

# The dbconfig settings are used to generate a DB_CONFIG file the first
# time slapd starts.  They do NOT override existing an existing DB_CONFIG
# file.  You should therefore change these settings in DB_CONFIG directly
# or remove DB_CONFIG and restart slapd for changes to take effect.

# For the Debian package we use 2MB as default but be sure to update this
# value if you have plenty of RAM
dbconfig set_cachesize 0 2097152 0

# Sven Hartge reported that he had to set this value incredibly high
# to get slapd running at all. See http://bugs.debian.org/303057 for more
# information.

# Number of objects that can be locked at the same time.
dbconfig set_lk_max_objects 1500
# Number of locks (both requested and granted)
dbconfig set_lk_max_locks 1500
# Number of lockers
dbconfig set_lk_max_lockers 1500

# Indexing options for database #1
index           objectClass eq

# Save the time that the entry gets modified, for database #1
lastmod         on

# Checkpoint the BerkeleyDB database periodically in case of system
# failure and to speed slapd shutdown.
checkpoint      512 30

# Where to store the replica logs for database #1
# replogfile    /var/lib/ldap/replog
```

```
# The userPassword by default can be changed
# by the entry owning it if they are authenticated.
# Others should not be able to see it, except the
# admin entry below
# These access lines apply to database #1 only
access to attrs=userPassword,shadowLastChange
        by dn="cn=admin,dc=sandervanvugt,dc=nl" write
        by anonymous auth
        by self write
        by * none

# Ensure read access to the base for things like
# supportedSASLMechanisms.  Without this you may
# have problems with SASL not knowing what
# mechanisms are available and the like.
# Note that this is covered by the 'access to *'
# ACL below too but if you change that as people
# are wont to do you'll still need this if you
# want SASL (and possible other things) to work
# happily.
access to dn.base="" by * read

# The admin dn has full write access, everyone else
# can read everything.
access to *
        by dn="cn=admin,dc=sandervanvugt,dc=nl" write
        by * read

# For Netscape Roaming support, each user gets a roaming
# profile for which they have write access to
#access to dn=".*,ou=Roaming,o=morsnet"
#        by dn="cn=admin,dc=sandervanvugt,dc=nl" write
#        by dnattr=owner write

#######################################################################
# Specific Directives for database #2, of type 'other' (can be hdb too):
# Database specific directives apply to this databasse until another
# 'database' directive occurs
#database        <other>

# The base of your directory for database #2
#suffix          "dc=debian,dc=org"
```

As you can see, there are many comment lines that explain what happens in the `slapd.conf` file. Let's go through the most important sections of it.

Configuring Schema and Process Files

First, there are four lines that refer to the schema files that your LDAP server is going to use. You may notice that not all the files in /etc/ldap/schema are referred to here. If there are additional files that you want to include in the schema, make sure to create an `include` line for all of them.

Next, there are two lines that refer to status files your LDAP server maintains. Both files are in /var/run/slapd. The `slapd.pid` file maintains the current PID of your `slapd` server, and the `slapd.args` file contains a list of arguments that were passed to the Samba server when it was started. `slapd.args` may be useful for troubleshooting if your `slapd` server doesn't behave the way it should. For example, your `slapd` server might be missing a required argument, in which case you can check `slapd.args` to find out which arguments were used when starting the Samba server. Listing 8-5 shows what the file should look like on a default installation of OpenLDAP.

Listing 8-5. */var/run/slapd/slapd.args Shows with Which Parameters slapd Was Started*

```
root@mel:/var/run/slapd# cat slapd.args
/usr/sbin/slapd -g openldap -u openldap -f /etc/ldap/slapd.conf
```

Modifying Startup Parameters in /etc/init.d/slapd

To know which parameters it should start by default, the /etc/init.d/slapd script, which is executed when your server boots to start the LDAP server, reads the configuration file /etc/default/slapd. As you can see in Listing 8-6, this file contains variables that define with which parameters the `slapd` service should be started.

Listing 8-6. *To Determine Its Startup Parameters, slapd Reads /etc/default/slapd*

```
root@mel:/etc/default# cat slapd
# Default location of the slapd.conf file. If empty, use the compiled-in
# default (/etc/ldap/slapd.conf). If using the cn=config backend to store
# configuration in LDIF, set this variable to the directory containing the
# cn=config data.
SLAPD_CONF=
```

```
# System account to run the slapd server under. If empty the server
# will run as root.
SLAPD_USER="openldap"

# System group to run the slapd server under. If empty the server will
# run in the primary group of its user.
SLAPD_GROUP="openldap"

# Path to the pid file of the slapd server. If not set the init.d script
# will try to figure it out from $SLAPD_CONF (/etc/ldap/slapd.conf by
# default)
SLAPD_PIDFILE=

# slapd normally serves ldap only on all TCP-ports 389. slapd can also
# service requests on TCP-port 636 (ldaps) and requests via unix
# sockets.
# Example usage:
# SLAPD_SERVICES="ldap://127.0.0.1:389/ ldaps:/// ldapi:///"

# If SLAPD_NO_START is set, the init script will not start or restart
# slapd (but stop will still work).  Uncomment this if you are
# starting slapd via some other means or if you don't want slapd normally
# started at boot.
#SLAPD_NO_START=1

# If SLAPD_SENTINEL_FILE is set to path to a file and that file exists,
# the init script will not start or restart slapd (but stop will still
# work).  Use this for temporarily disabling startup of slapd (when doing
# maintenance, for example, or through a configuration management system)
# when you don't want to edit a configuration file.
SLAPD_SENTINEL_FILE=/etc/ldap/noslapd

# For Kerberos authentication (via SASL), slapd by default uses the system
# keytab file (/etc/krb5.keytab).  To use a different keytab file,
# uncomment this line and change the path.
#export KRB5_KTNAME=/etc/krb5.keytab

# Additional options to pass to slapd
SLAPD_OPTIONS=""
```

Configuring Logging

Next in `slapd.conf`, the line `loglevel none` determines how logging should take place. As you can guess, by default, no logging happens at all. This is fine if your LDAP server works well, but if it doesn't, you probably want to configure some more verbose logging. If you do, make sure to enable logging only periodically and switch it off if you don't need it anymore. LDAP logging can be very verbose and eat up available disk space fast. Table 8-1 provides an overview of available options.

Table 8-1. *Available loglevel Options*

Option	Use
trace	Traces function calls.
packets	Debugs packet handling.
args	Enables heavy trace debugging. Also shows arguments of the different functions that are used.
connes	Logs information about connection management.
BER	Prints out all packets sent and received.
filter	Gives information about search filter processing.
config	Displays information about configuration file processing.
ACL	Shows what happens with regard to access control list processing. More information about LDAP ACLs is provided later in this section.
stats	Shows information about connections, LDAP operations, and results. If you want to enable logging, this is the recommended log level.
stats2	Shows what stats log entries were sent.
shell	Prints communication with shell back end.
parse	Gives information about LDAP entry parsing. This is useful if you need to debug why certain information cannot be provided by the LDAP server.
sync	Provides information about LDAP synchronization.
none	Disables logging completely.

Following the log lines in `slapd.conf` are the `modulepath` and `moduleload` lines, which you can use to load additional modules (which I do not cover in this book). The next two lines in `slapd.conf` are of interest with regard to the performance of your LDAP server:

```
sizelimit 500
tool-threads 1
```

sizelimit 500 limits the number of entries returned for a search operation. If you want to export your LDAP database to LDIF files, this limit can be really annoying, because it doesn't allow all the records in your database to be shown. Make sure to increase it as needed to get a complete list of all records. tool-threads 1 tells slapd to run one thread only, in which case you can't benefit from a multicore environment if you have one. On a heavily used LDAP server that runs on a multicore architecture, increase the number of threads to the number of cores that you want to use simultaneously.

After the two lines that specify which database to use, the suffix line specifies the suffix your LDAP server should use. This is the base location in the hierarchical Directory where slapd will expect to see the entries in the database. By default, it has the name of the DNS container your server is in.

Next are a few settings that relate to the database that LDAP maintains. First, dbconfig set_cachesize 0 2097152 0 defines the size of the LDAP cache, with a maximum of 2 MB. This is rather limited, and will cause performance problems if you are using a large LDAP database. If your server has enough RAM, make sure to update it. For instance, use the following to set it to 16 MB: dbconfig set_cachesize 0 16777216 0.

Next, there are three lines that relate to locking:

```
dbconfig set_lk_max_objects 1500
dbconfig set_lk_max_locks 1500
dbconfig set_lk_max_lockers 1500
```

These three lines set the number of objects that can be locked, or opened, simultaneously to a maximum of 1500. If that causes any problems, make sure to increase these parameters to something higher. The exact number you need depends on the use of your LDAP server.

Next in slapd.conf is another important performance-related parameter, index objectClass eq. This option ensures that an index is created based on the object names in use. If you need to find objects based on a specific attribute on a regular basis, make sure to add an index entry for that attribute. For instance, index cn eq would add an index based on the common name of objects.

Configuring ACLs

The last relevant part of the slapd.conf configuration file defines some ACLs. These specify which users can do what on your LDAP database. For instance, the line access to dn.base="" by * read makes sure that anyone can read entries from the LDAP database. This default setting makes your LDAP server usable, but it also poses a potential security risk. To avoid that, make sure to configure your firewall in a way that only authorized users can connect to your LDAP server.

Using ACLs in LDAP is not too hard. Each ACL has the following form:

```
access to what kind and range of data by whoever is allowed access.
```

In this example, first you specify the kind and range of data, which represents the objects you are giving rights to. For example, you can use an asterisk (*) here to allow access to everything, or use something like ou=People,dc=sandervanvugt,dc=nl to limit access. Second, you have to indicate who gets the access. You do this by using the LDAP name of the object you are granting access to. Third, you need to specify what type of access you are granting. The following types of access are available:

- none: No access is allowed.

- auth: The specified user can use the object for authentication only.

- compare: The specified user can compare property values of the object with a specific search string.

- search: The specified user can search for information.

- read: The specified user can read all data.

- write: The specified user can modify all data.

When specifying to which data you want to give access, you can grant object-level access or attribute-level access. For instance, the following example gives user accounts rights to modify some properties of their account:

```
access to dn=".*,dc=sandervanvugt,dc=nl" attrs="cn,sn,description,gecos"
    by self write
```

At this point, make sure that your LDAP server is up and running. Just by installing it, you have already ensured that it is started automatically when you boot your server. To make sure all new settings are used as well, use the following command to restart the slapd server: /etc/init.d/slapd restart.

Adding Information to the LDAP Database

Now that the LDAP server is up and running, it's time to add some information to the database. The way to do that is by creating an LDIF file. In this LDIF file, you define not only the objects that you want to create, but also all the properties these objects should have. Generally, that means a lot of typing to create something like a simple user. Listing 8-7 shows a sample configuration file in which a user is created.

Listing 8-7. *To Add Objects to the Database, Create and Import an LDIF File*

```
root@mel:~# cat example.ldif
dn: ou=people,dc=sandervanvugt,dc=nl
objectClass: organizationalUnit
ou: people

dn: ou=groups,dc=sandervanvugt,dc=nl
objectClass: organizationalUnit
ou: groups

dn: uid=linda,ou=people,dc=sandervanvugt,dc=nl
objectClass: inetOrgPerson
objectClass: posixAccount
objectClass: shadowAccount
uid: linda
sn: thomsen
givenName: linda
cn: linda thomsen
displayName: linda thomsen
uidNumber: 1000
gidNumber: 10000
userPassword: password
gecos:
loginShell: /bin/bash
homeDirectory: /home/linda
shadowExpire: -1
shadowFlag: 0
shadowWarning: 7
shadowMin: 8
shadowMax: 999999
shadowLastChange: 10877
mail: linda.thomsen@sandervanvugt.nl
postalCode: 1234
l: Amsterdam
o: sander
mobile: +31 (0)6 xx xx xx xx
homePhone: +31 (0)2 xx xx xx xx
title: System Administrator
postalAddress:
initials: LT
```

```
dn: cn=example,ou=groups,dc=sandervanvugt,dc=nl
objectClass: posixGroup
cn: example
gidNumber: 10000
```

Because this is the very first LDIF file that you are using, creating only the user account is insufficient. It is a good habit to put users and groups in their own container, so in this LDIF the containers are created first. Creating the containers first is mandatory, because otherwise there is no place in which to put the user and group accounts. You have to do this only in your first LDIF file, because once the containers are created, you can just use them in all upcoming LDIF files.

After you define the LDIF file, you have to define the properties of the user object. The properties in the example LDIF file shown in Listing 8-7 are self-explanatory. In the last part of the LDIF file, you see that a group with the name example is added as well.

Now that the LDIF file is created, it's time to add its contents to the database. This is a simple three-step procedure:

1. Stop slapd: /etc/init.d/slapd stop.

2. Add the content of the LDIF file: slapadd -l example.ldif.

3. Restart the LDAP process: /etc/init.d/slapd start.

The LDIF file is now imported. In the next section you'll read how you can verify whether this worked properly.

Using ldapsearch to Verify Your Configuration

Now that you have added a user to the LDAP Directory, it's time to see if you can retrieve this information via a search. The ldapsearch command from the package ldap-utils will do that for you. In Listing 8-8, ldapsearch is used to get an overview of all information that is currently stored in the LDAP Directory.

Listing 8-8. *Use ldapsearch to Search the LDAP Directory*

```
root@mel:~# ldapsearch -x -b "dc=sandervanvugt,dc=nl"
# extended LDIF
#
# LDAPv3
# base <dc=sandervanvugt,dc=nl> with scope subtree
# filter: (objectclass=*)
# requesting: ALL
#
```

```
# sandervanvugt.nl
dn: dc=sandervanvugt,dc=nl
objectClass: top
objectClass: dcObject
objectClass: organization
o: sandervanvugt.nl
dc: sandervanvugt

# admin, sandervanvugt.nl
dn: cn=admin,dc=sandervanvugt,dc=nl
objectClass: simpleSecurityObject
objectClass: organizationalRole
cn: admin
description: LDAP administrator

# people, sandervanvugt.nl
dn: ou=people,dc=sandervanvugt,dc=nl
objectClass: organizationalUnit
ou: people

# groups, sandervanvugt.nl
dn: ou=groups,dc=sandervanvugt,dc=nl
objectClass: organizationalUnit
ou: groups

# linda, people, sandervanvugt.nl
dn: uid=linda,ou=people,dc=sandervanvugt,dc=nl
objectClass: inetOrgPerson
objectClass: posixAccount
objectClass: shadowAccount
uid: linda
sn: thomsen
givenName: linda
cn: linda thomsen
displayName: linda thomsen
uidNumber: 1000
gidNumber: 10000
gecos:
loginShell: /bin/bash
homeDirectory: /home/linda
shadowExpire: -1
shadowFlag: 0
```

```
shadowWarning: 7
shadowMin: 8
shadowMax: 999999
mail: linda.thomsen@sandervanvugt.nl
postalCode: 1234
l: Amsterdam
o: sander
mobile: +31 (0)6 xx xx xx xx
homePhone: +31 (0)2 xx xx xx xx
title: System Administrator
postalAddress:
initials: LT

# example, groups, sandervanvugt.nl
dn: cn=example,ou=groups,dc=sandervanvugt,dc=nl
objectClass: posixGroup
cn: example
gidNumber: 10000

# search result
search: 2
result: 0 Success

# numResponses: 7
# numEntries: 6
```

As you can see from this example, the ldapsearch command returns not only the user account we've created, but also the name of the administrator, the group, and the containers that exist. The reason so much information is returned is that no filter has been applied. You can use ldapsearch in a more restrictive way by applying a filter. For instance, in the example in Listing 8-9, a filter is used so that only three properties are displayed for user linda.

Listing 8-9. *Use ldapsearch to Display Specific Information Only*

```
root@mel:~# ldapsearch -x -b "dc=sandervanvugt,dc=nl" uid=linda sn givenName cn
# extended LDIF
#
# LDAPv3
# base <dc=sandervanvugt,dc=nl> with scope subtree
# filter: uid=linda
# requesting: sn givenName cn
#
```

```
# linda, people, sandervanvugt.nl
dn: uid=linda,ou=people,dc=sandervanvugt,dc=nl
sn: thomsen
givenName: linda
cn: linda thomsen

# search result
search: 2
result: 0 Success

# numResponses: 2
# numEntries: 1
```

When using ldapsearch, you can use different command-line options. The examples in Listings 8-8 and 8-9 show the most important options:

- -x: Tells ldapsearch not to make a Simple Authentication and Security Layer (SASL) connection, but rather to send information in plain text. I recommend using this option at all times, so that you don't have to apply a complicated SASL configuration.

- -b: Refers to the LDAP search base. This is the name of the container in which you have created all objects.

Other options are not necessary, but, as you can see in the example from Listing 8-9, may be useful anyway. To filter the output provided by ldapsearch, just enter on the command line the names of the properties for which you want to see output.

Using LDAP Management Commands

There are a number of utilities that you can use in an OpenLDAP environment. Table 8-2 lists and describes all the utilities. Following that, you'll find some examples of the most useful utilities (other than slapadd and ldapsearch, which you've already read about).

Table 8-2. *OpenLDAP Utilities*

Utility	Description
slapacl	Tests whether ACLs are working by testing whether certain attributes are available, based on the ACL specifications that are applied in /etc/ldap/slapd.conf.
slapadd	Adds information from an LDIF file to an LDAP database.
slapauth	Tests whether a user can authenticate to LDAP with given authentication credentials.

Utility	Description
slapcat	Converts information from the LDAP database to LDIF format. You can do the same using the ldapsearch tool.
slapdn	Compares the LDAP DNs provided as a command-line argument to see if they comply with the definitions in the LDAP schema.
slapindex	Reindexes the indexes of your LDAP server. This is a very useful utility that you should apply after every major update to the contents of the LDAP database.
slappasswd	Prompts the user for a password and then encrypts that password in such a way that it can be used with the ldapmodify command, or as the rootpw setting in slapd.conf.
slaptest	Checks the sanity of the slapd.conf file.
ldapadd	Adds the contents of an LDIF file to the LDAP database. You can do the same using slapadd.
ldapcompare	Compares an entry in the LDAP database with entry information that is provided on the command line.
ldapdelete	Deletes information from the LDAP database. This command uses LDIF files as input.
ldapmodify	Modifies the contents of an LDAP database, based on LDIF input files.
ldapmodrdn	Changes the relative DN, which normally is merely the object name in the LDAP database.
ldappasswd	Changes the password of an LDAP entry.
ldapsearch	Queries the LDAP database for information.
ldapwhoami	Opens a connection to an LDAP server, binds, and then performs a whoami operation. One of the interesting features of this command is that you *do* need to provide a username to authenticate to the LDAP server, which assumes that you already know who you are.

Modifying Entries in the LDAP Database

This section describes how to modify information in the LDAP database, using ldapmodify. This command needs an LDIF file as its input. This time, however, it refers to an LDIF entry that already exists. It is pretty easy to generate such an LDIF file, using ldapsearch.

Suppose you want to change the password of user linda, created earlier in the chapter. The first step is to get the current definition of linda in LDIF format from the Directory and redirect that to a file. You can do this with the following command:

```
ldapsearch -xLLL -b "dc=sandervanvugt,dc=nl" uid=linda > linda.ldif
```

Next, change the contents you've just created in the LDIF file. Then, use ldapmodify to apply the new information to the LDAP Directory:

```
ldapmodify -x -D "cn=Administrator,dc=sandervanvugt,dc=nl" -W -f linda.ldif
```

The option -x tells LDAP that you don't want to use SASL secured authentication, -D "cn=Administrator,dc=sandervanvugt,dc=nl" tells LDAP what administrator credentials you want to use, -W causes ldapmodify to prompt for a password, and -f linda.ldif makes sure the content of the file linda.ldif is applied to the LDAP database.

Deleting Entries from the LDAP Database

The ldapdelete command allows you to delete information from the LDAP database. The command accepts both LDIF files and command-line arguments to indicate what exactly you want to remove.

Suppose that you want to remove the user john from your LDAP database. That would work with ldapdelete -D "cn=Administrator,dc=sandervanvugt,dc=nl" -x -W "uid=john,ou=people,dc=sandervanvugt,dc=nl". Alternatively, instead of referring to the object you want to remove from the command line, you can create an LDIF file that contains a list of all objects that you want to remove, and then use -f your.ldif to remove them all from the LDAP database.

Changing a Password

Changing a password in an LDAP environment is not as easy as it is in a stand-alone environment, because the password must be stored in an encrypted way and you must tell the LDAP server exactly for whom you want to change the password and what credentials you want to use for that. Listing 8-10 shows how ldappasswd is used to change the password for user linda.

Listing 8-10. *Use ldappasswd to Change a User Password*

```
root@mel:~# ldappasswd -x -D "cn=admin,dc=sandervanvugt,dc=nl"\
 -W -S uid=linda,ou=people,dc=sandervanvugt,dc=nl
New password:
Re-enter new password:
Enter LDAP Password:
```

You can see that several options are used with ldappasswd in this example. First, the option -x is used to tell LDAP you don't want SASL. Next, -D "cn=admin,dc=sandervanvugt,dc=nl" is used to specify the name of the user whose credentials are used to change the password. As you can see, in this case I'm using the admin user for that. Next, -W causes ldappasswd to prompt for the password of user admin, and -S causes ldappasswd to prompt for the password of the user. Following that, you see the complete LDAP name of the user you want to change the password for. A very common mistake is to use the incorrect user

ID, thereby causing an error. You can avoid errors by looking up the user ID you want to use with ldapsearch first.

■Note A user can change their own password as well by using ldappasswd. Just replace the admin name as specified with the -D option with the name of the user account. Every user by default has enough permissions to change their own password.

Logging In to an LDAP Server

You can use LDAP for authentication. To do so, you first set up one LDAP server and populate it with user accounts. Next, you tell all workstations that they have to authenticate with the LDAP server. To do this, you need to configure PAM. To enable other services to search the LDAP server as well when looking for information, you need to configure the /etc/nsswitch.conf file. In this section, you'll first learn how to set up PAM for LDAP authentication, and then learn how to configure nsswitch.conf.

Configuring PAM for LDAP Authentication

When authenticating, PAM is used. This is a system that tells all authentication-related processes where they have to look for user accounts. The only condition is that the process in question has to be linked against the libpam modules, which is the case for most utilities that work with user accounts. Listing 8-11 shows how you can request this information using the ldd command. In this example you can see that /bin/login uses the libpam and libpam_misc libraries. That means that it is PAM enabled, which is good.

Listing 8-11. *Use ldd to Check Whether a Utility Works with PAM*

```
root@mel:~# ldd /bin/login
        linux-gate.so.1 => (0xb7f0c000)
        libcrypt.so.1 => /lib/tls/i686/cmov/libcrypt.so.1 (0xb7ed1000)
        libpam.so.0 => /lib/libpam.so.0 (0xb7ec7000)
        libpam_misc.so.0 => /lib/libpam_misc.so.0 (0xb7ec3000)
        libc.so.6 => /lib/tls/i686/cmov/libc.so.6 (0xb7d74000)
        libdl.so.2 => /lib/tls/i686/cmov/libdl.so.2 (0xb7d70000)
        /lib/ld-linux.so.2 (0xb7f0d000)
```

If a utility is PAM enabled, it typically has a configuration file in /etc/pam.d. In this configuration file, the utility learns where it has to look for authentication-related information. Listing 8-12 gives an overview of all configuration files that are installed on Ubuntu Server.

Listing 8-12. *To Tell PAM Where to Look for Authentication Sources, Each Service Can Have Its Own Configuration File*

```
root@mel:/etc/pam.d# ls
atd    common-account    common-session  login       ppp       sshd
chfn   common-auth       cron                         other     quagga  su
chsh   common-password   hbmgmtd                 passwd  samba   sudo
```

The default configuration file for /bin/login is /etc/pam.d/login, so it is in this configuration file that you have to tell PAM to look for additional authentication sources. Listing 8-13 shows its default contents.

Listing 8-13. *Use /etc/pam.d/login to Tell the Login Program Which Authentication Sources to Use*

```
root@mel:/etc/pam.d# cat login
#
# The PAM configuration file for the Shadow `login' service
#

# Outputs an issue file prior to each login prompt (Replaces the
# ISSUE_FILE option from login.defs). Uncomment for use
# auth       required   pam_issue.so issue=/etc/issue

# Disallows root logins except on tty's listed in /etc/securetty
# (Replaces the `CONSOLE' setting from login.defs)
auth        requisite  pam_securetty.so

# Disallows other than root logins when /etc/nologin exists
# (Replaces the `NOLOGINS_FILE' option from login.defs)
auth        requisite  pam_nologin.so

# SELinux needs to be the first session rule. This ensures that any
# lingering context has been cleared. Without out this it is possible
# that a module could execute code in the wrong domain.  (When SELinux
# is disabled, this returns success.)
session    required   pam_selinux.so close
```

```
# This module parses environment configuration file(s)
# and also allows you to use an extended config
# file /etc/security/pam_env.conf.
#
# parsing /etc/environment needs "readenv=1"
session         required    pam_env.so readenv=1
# locale variables are also kept into /etc/default/locale in etch
# reading this file *in addition to /etc/environment* does not hurt
session         required    pam_env.so readenv=1 envfile=/etc/default/locale

# Standard Un*x authentication.
@include common-auth

# This allows certain extra groups to be granted to a user
# based on things like time of day, tty, service, and user.
# Please edit /etc/security/group.conf to fit your needs
# (Replaces the `CONSOLE_GROUPS' option in login.defs)
auth        optional    pam_group.so

# Uncomment and edit /etc/security/time.conf if you need to set
# time restrainst on logins.
# (Replaces the `PORTTIME_CHECKS_ENAB' option from login.defs
# as well as /etc/porttime)
# account     requisite pam_time.so

# Uncomment and edit /etc/security/access.conf if you need to
# set access limits.
# (Replaces /etc/login.access file)
# account  required       pam_access.so

# Sets up user limits according to /etc/security/limits.conf
# (Replaces the use of /etc/limits in old login)
session    required    pam_limits.so

# Prints the last login info upon succeful login
# (Replaces the `LASTLOG_ENAB' option from login.defs)
session    optional    pam_lastlog.so

# Prints the motd upon succesful login
# (Replaces the `MOTD_FILE' option in login.defs)
session    optional    pam_motd.so
```

```
# Prints the status of the user's mailbox upon succesful login
# (Replaces the `MAIL_CHECK_ENAB' option from login.defs).
#
# This also defines the MAIL environment variable
# However, userdel also needs MAIL_DIR and MAIL_FILE variables
# in /etc/login.defs to make sure that removing a user
# also removes the user's mail spool file.
# See comments in /etc/login.defs
session     optional    pam_mail.so standard

# Standard Un*x account and session
@include common-account
@include common-session
@include common-password

# SELinux needs to intervene at login time to ensure that the process
# starts in the proper default security context. Only sessions which are
# intended to run in the user's context should be run after this.  (When
# SELinux is disabled, this returns success.)
session required pam_selinux.so open
```

In a PAM configuration file, there are four different kinds of modules that you can use:

- auth: Handle validation of user accounts (authentication)

- account: Ensure that when a user tries to access certain resources, PAM checks if the user is authorized to access those resources at that time

- password: Relate to passwords

- session: Used to connect a user to authorized resources once the login procedure has been completed

Each of these module types can be used in four different ways:

- required: Conditions in this module have to be met. If this is not the case, the rest of the PAM file will be processed, but access is denied anyway.

- requisite: Like required, but access is denied immediately.

- sufficient: If conditions in this module are met, the user gets access and other modules from the same module category will be ignored. Therefore, if you're using sufficient in one of the module categories, make sure that you first mention all modules that must be passed in all cases.

- optional: This module is not important for the authentication process. It is used to display the contents of text files.

The last part of a module configuration line refers to the module itself. These modules are in the directory /lib/security and each of them has its own meaning. (In my book *Beginning Ubuntu Server Administration*, I list the most important of these modules and their meaning.) To teach PAM about LDAP, you need to install the libpam-ldap package, using apt-get install libpam-ldap. This enables a short configuration wizard that puts the right options in the file /etc/ldap.conf. This file is used as the default client configuration file for LDAP.

The first screen of the configuration wizard asks you what the URI (Universe Resource Identifier) is for your LDAP server. This URI should look similar to ldap://192.168.1.200 to enable default nonsecure access to the LDAP server. Next, the wizard asks which LDAP protocol version you want to use. Following that, it asks if you want to allow password utilities to talk to LDAP, and if you want to make the local user root the administrator for LDAP as well. It's a good idea to answer Yes to both questions.

Next, the wizard asks if you have to log in to the database (which is LDAP) to get information from it. Because the basic ACLs that are installed by default don't require this, you can safely answer No here. Following that, the wizard asks which LDAP account you want to use for management purposes. By default, this is the account cn=manager,dc=example,dc=net. You have to change this to match the current base DN of your LDAP server, so in the example in this chapter, it would be cn=admin,dc=sandervanvugt,dc=nl. Next, enter the password that you want to use for the root account, to complete the configuration. As a result, the client configuration file /etc/ldap.conf is created to redirect clients to the LDAP server.

Once the client file has been written, you can look at the PAM configuration files. As you may have noticed, PAM uses four files that contain common configuration settings, one for each of the four kinds of modules. The names of these are common-auth, common-account, common-password, and common-session. Basically, these files are pretty simple. Listing 8-14 gives an example of the contents of common-auth, without the comment lines that are added by default.

Listing 8-14. *Contents of the common-auth PAM Configuration File*

```
auth    requisite    pam_unix.so nullok_secure
auth    optional     pam_smbpass.so migrate missingok
```

To have PAM look in LDAP as well, you should include a line that refers to LDAP in all four of the common files. In the files, you want to make sure that PAM first tries to connect to LDAP. If that is successful, PAM doesn't need to look any further; if for some reason LDAP is not available, PAM next should try local authentication mechanisms. So, after modification, the common-auth file would look as shown in Listing 8-15.

Listing 8-15. *Add a Line in All Four of the PAM Common Files to Check LDAP as Well*

```
auth    sufficient   pam_ldap.so
auth    requisite    pam_unix.so nullok_secure
auth    optional     pam_smbpass.so migrate missingok
```

After modifying all four of the PAM common files in /etc/pam.d, all services that use these files will be LDAP aware. An easy test to see if it works is to use su to switch to one of the user accounts that does exist in LDAP, but doesn't exist locally. If that works, your LDAP authentication works as well.

Setting Up nsswitch.conf to Find LDAP Services

The nsswitch.conf file is used in the same specific login-related situations in which PAM is used, but in a more generic way. The nss_ldap package, installed earlier, enables you to include LDAP entries in nsswitch.conf. To make sure that via this mechanism the LDAP database is searched as well, you need to change the passwd, group, and shadow lines as shown in Listing 8-16.

Listing 8-16. *Change nsswitch.conf to Search LDAP*

```
passwd:         compat ldap
group:          compat ldap
shadow:         compat ldap
```

These lines tell the operating system to look in the passwd, group, and shadow files first and then, if the required information is not found there, to check LDAP next. It is common to modify nsswitch to look for user information only in LDAP, but all other search entries from nsswitch can be modified likewise. For example, you can also tell nsswitch to look in LDAP for host-based information.

After setting up `nsswitch`, you need to modify the `/etc/ldap.conf` file to tell the service where in LDAP it should look for the specific kinds of information you are referring to. Listing 8-17 shows the sample lines that you can modify to reflect your specific configuration.

Listing 8-17. *In /etc/ldap.conf, Tell nsswitch Where in LDAP to Find Specific Information*

```
# RFC2307bis naming contexts
# Syntax:
# nss_base_XXX          base?scope?filter
# where scope is {base,one,sub}
# and filter is a filter to be &'d with the
# default filter.
# You can omit the suffix eg:
# nss_base_passwd       ou=People,
# to append the default base DN but this
# may incur a small performance impact.
#nss_base_passwd        ou=People,dc=padl,dc=com?one
#nss_base_shadow        ou=People,dc=padl,dc=com?one
#nss_base_group         ou=Group,dc=padl,dc=com?one
#nss_base_hosts         ou=Hosts,dc=padl,dc=com?one
#nss_base_services      ou=Services,dc=padl,dc=com?one
#nss_base_networks      ou=Networks,dc=padl,dc=com?one
#nss_base_protocols     ou=Protocols,dc=padl,dc=com?one
#nss_base_rpc           ou=Rpc,dc=padl,dc=com?one
#nss_base_ethers        ou=Ethers,dc=padl,dc=com?one
#nss_base_netmasks      ou=Networks,dc=padl,dc=com?ne
#nss_base_bootparams    ou=Ethers,dc=padl,dc=com?one
#nss_base_aliases       ou=Aliases,dc=padl,dc=com?one
#nss_base_netgroup      ou=Netgroup,dc=padl,dc=com?one
```

Note There are two `ldap.conf` files: `/etc/ldap.conf` is used by `nsswitch.conf`, and `/etc/ldap/ldap.conf` is used by PAM. By default, these two files do not have the same content. To avoid problems, I recommend putting all required settings in one of these files and creating in the other file a symbolic link to refer to that file.

Testing LDAP Client Connectivity

Now that your LDAP client is set up properly, you can test whether it's working. To do this, you can use the getent command. By using this command, you can get information from a specific database source. For instance, if you use the command getent passwd, the command shows you user accounts from all passwd sources. Because you have just set up nsswitch to look in /etc/passwd as well as LDAP, the command displays user accounts from both sources. Comparing the output from the getent command carefully with the output from /etc/passwd, you will see that more is listed than just the contents of the /etc/passwd file (provided that you have added user accounts to LDAP successfully).

Summary

In this chapter you have learned how to set up OpenLDAP. This service provides useful functionality, because it is a centralized solution for management of user accounts and other configuration. You have also learned how to set up OpenLDAP to enable LDAP user authentication. In the next chapter you'll learn about Samba, another service that you can hook up to LDAP.

■ ■ ■

## CHAPTER 9

Integrating Samba
Making It Work with Windows

You may already have a Samba server up and running in your network. Many people do, because it's such an easy and convenient solution to offer file sharing to Windows clients. Few people, however, have a Samba server that is integrated with other operating systems used in their environment. Achieving such integration is the focus of this chapter. In this chapter you'll first read a short section on how to quickly and easily set up a simple Samba server that offers file sharing and nothing more. In that section you will use the smbpasswd command to add individual user accounts. Sure, that works, but it's not a very sophisticated solution if you have many users to manage, because you need to create every user account twice.

Following the short introduction, there are three sections that explain how to truly integrate Samba in your network. The first section explains how to integrate Samba with LDAP, which is useful because it provides one centralized location from which you can manage user accounts. Next, you'll read how to set up your Samba server as a Windows NT 4–style Primary Domain Controller (PDC). This solution explains how you can replace a current Windows NT 4 server with Samba without your users even noticing the change. The last section explains how to integrate Samba in Active Directory. It teaches you how to set up Samba as a member server in Active Directory. Currently, making it more than a member server still isn't possible, because Samba version 4, which is supposed to make that possible, is not in a stable state yet.

Setting Up Samba the Easy Way

In this section you'll learn the easy way to set up Samba. It explains how you can define a share and create a Samba user that has access to this share. At the end of this section, you'll learn how to test whether this share is working properly.

Setting up Samba the easy way involves the following general steps, each of which is explained in detail in the sections that follow:

1. Create a local directory to share.

2. Set permissions on this directory.

3. Configure `smb.conf` to define the share.

4. Create a Samba user account.

5. Test access to the share.

Creating a Local Directory to Share

So what exactly is a share? Basically, it is a directory on the local Linux file system that is accessible over the network. To create such a share, the first step is to create a local directory. This is as easy as applying the `mkdir` command. So, assuming you want to share a local directory with the name `/share`, simply use `mkdir /share` to create the local directory.

Applying Permissions to the Local Directory

When working with Samba, you need to make sure that the appropriate permissions are applied to the share. These permissions are granted to a local user account. You can grant permissions the easy way, by just entering the command `chmod 777 /share`, but I don't recommend doing that. It is much better to create a dedicated group in Linux and make members of that group all users to whom you want to give access to the share. Assuming that the name of this group is `sambagroup`, you use `chgrp sambagroup /share` to make that group the share owner. Once that is done, apply the permissions, granting full permissions to the user owner and group owner and no permissions to others: `chmod 770 /share`. This creates a situation that is much more secure, because it ensures that other users cannot access the share.

Defining the Share

Now that you have set up everything that is necessary on the local file system, you need to define the share in Samba. Before you can start setting it up, you must install it first. There are several packages that relate to the Samba file server. You can get a list of them by using the `aptitude search samba` command. Listing 9-1 shows the result of this command when applied to my test server.

Listing 9-1. *aptitude search samba Provides an Overview of Available Samba Packages*

```
root@mel:~# aptitude search samba

p   dpsyco-samba              - Automate administration of access to samba
p   ebox-samba                - ebox - File sharing
p   egroupware-sambaadmin     - eGroupWare Samba administration applicatio
p   gsambad                   - GTK+ configuration tool for samba
i   samba                     - a LanManager-like file and printer server
v   samba-client              -
i A samba-common              - Samba common files used by both the server
p   samba-dbg                 - Samba debugging symbols
p   samba-doc                 - Samba documentation
p   samba-doc-pdf             - Samba documentation (PDF format)
p   system-config-samba       - GUI for managing samba shares and users
```

To make sure that all packages are installed, use the following command:

```
apt-get install samba dpsyco-samba ebox-samba egroupware-sambaadmin gsambad➥
 smbclient samba-common samba-dbg samba-doc samba-doc-pdf system-config-samba
```

■**Note** The preceding command is not appropriate for my server, because the base packages samba and samba-common are already installed. However, it will install, in all situations, everything that is needed to operate a Samba server. I have also replaced the samba-client package with smbclient, because otherwise the installer would tell me that two Samba client packages are available and ask which one I want to install.

Now that all Samba packages have been installed, you can edit the general Samba configuration file /etc/samba/smb.conf to define the share. In smb.conf, there are two types of sections. The first type is the section [global], which contains global settings for your server. The second type consists of the different sections in which the individual shares are defined. You can recognize them by the name of the share, written between square brackets. For instance, to define a share for your directory /share, the section header would be [share]. The definition of this share can be really simple, as shown in Listing 9-2.

Listing 9-2. *Defining a Share Isn't Complicated*

```
[share]
    comment = shared directory
    read only = no
    path = /share
```

Of course, there are lots of other options that you can add to the share to make it fancier, but basically, if you define the share in this fashion it will work. So save your settings, and the share will be accessible. It takes a maximum of one minute before the share will automatically appear.

You've now set up basic access to the share. Before continuing, it's a good idea to check if it really works. You can do that by using the smbclient -L localhost command, which shows a list of all available shares on the local machine. It prompts for a user password as well, but because no user credentials are needed to display a list of shares, you can just press Enter to proceed. Listing 9-3 shows the output of this command.

Listing 9-3. *Use smbclient -L localhost to Get an Overview of All Available Shares*

```
root@mel:~# smbclient -L localhost
Password:
Domain=[MEL] OS=[Unix] Server=[Samba 3.0.28a]

        Sharename       Type        Comment
        ---------       ----        -------
        print$          Disk        Printer Drivers
        share           Disk        shared directory
        IPC$            IPC         IPC Service (mel server (Samba, Ubuntu))
Domain=[MEL] OS=[Unix] Server=[Samba 3.0.28a]

        Server                  Comment
        ---------               -------


        Workgroup               Master
        ---------               -------
        WORKGROUP
```

At this point, your share is up and running and available, so it's time to proceed to the next step and create a Samba user account.

Creating a Samba User Account

So why does a user need a Samba user account if they already have a Linux user account? To access a share, the user, who typically works on a Windows machine, needs to enter his credentials. When doing this from a Windows machine, the password that he enters is encrypted in the Windows way. The problem is that the Linux authentication mechanism doesn't know how to handle this encryption. For that reason, the user needs a Samba user account that has a password that is encrypted the Windows way.

The Samba user account must match an existing Linux user account. That means that you first have to create the Linux account and then create the Samba account. Yes, that means creating the same user twice. If you don't like that solution, you need one of the advanced solutions, such as Samba integration with LDAP, described later in this chapter.

To create a Samba account, you need to use the smbpasswd command. For instance, to create a user with the name linda, use smbpasswd -a linda. The command will ask you to enter the Samba password twice, after which the Samba user account is created.

Testing Access to the Share

Now that you have created the Samba user account, it's time for a small test. Sure, you can do the test from Windows and make a connection to the share by entering the share name in the //servername/sharename format, but by doing that, you are introducing other factors that may fail as well. For instance, the Windows test may fail because of a mis-configured firewall. At this point, we just want to know whether the Samba server is functioning the right way. Test it by using the mount command:

```
mount -t smbfs -o username=linda //localhost/share /mnt
```

If this command succeeds in mounting the Samba share on the /mnt directory, you have established that the Samba server is working.

As an alternative way to test access to your share, you may use the smbclient command. This command offers an interface that is pretty similar to the FTP client command-line interface; you can use put and get to transfer files from and to the Samba shared directory from the smbclient shell interface. To perform the same test on //localhost/share, use smbclient --user=linda //localhost/share. If successful, this command opens a shell interface to the directory. Try for example the ls command to get a list of all files in the share. Listing 9-4 shows an example of a short smbclient session. In this example, user linda authenticates, uses ls to show a list of existing files, uses get to download the file to her current directory, and finally uses quit to close the smbclient interface.

Listing 9-4. *The smbclient Tool Is Similar to the FTP Client Interface*

```
root@mel:~# smbclient --user=linda //localhost/share
Password:
Domain=[MEL] OS=[Unix] Server=[Samba 3.0.28a]
smb: \> ls
  .                              D        0  Wed Aug 13 04:39:36 2008
  ..                             D        0  Wed Aug 13 04:15:33 2008
  file1                                   0  Wed Aug 13 04:39:34 2008
  file2                                   0  Wed Aug 13 04:39:36 2008

                50796 blocks of size 2097152. 43939 blocks available
smb: \> get file1
getting file \file1 of size 0 as file1 (0.0 kb/s) (average nan kb/s)
smb: \> quit
```

With your Samba server up and running, now it's time to integrate it with LDAP.

Integrating Samba with LDAP

There are three tasks to accomplish if you want to integrate Samba with LDAP. First, you need to prepare Samba to talk to LDAP. Next, you have to prepare LDAP as well. Finally, you can tell Samba to use LDAP.

Preparing Samba to Talk to LDAP

The major difference between the Samba configuration just discussed and integration with LDAP is in one line in the [global] section of smb.conf. The following line defines that, by default, passwords are stored in the Trivial Database (TDB) that Samba uses by default:

```
passdb backend = tdbsam
```

This method works fine if you are using only one Samba server or if you are using Samba as a domain controller in an environment in which no backup domain controllers are available. If you are using Samba in a larger-scale environment, you can write user account information to an LDAP database. To do that, you need to change the passdb backend parameter to refer to an LDAP server. The following example would do that:

```
passdb backend = ldapsam
```

You have now prepared Samba to talk to LDAP. In the next section you'll learn how to configure LDAP to talk to Samba as well.

Preparing LDAP to Work with Samba

To store Samba user information in the LDAP Directory, you have to prepare the LDAP Directory first. LDAP needs to know about the new Samba object classes that you are going to store in it, and you can teach OpenLDAP that by including the `samba.schema` file. After installing the Samba packages as explained in the preceding section, you will find this file in the directory `/usr/share/ebox-samba/samba.schema`. Follow these steps to add this file to the LDAP environment:

1. Use `cp /usr/share/ebox-samba/samba.schema /etc/ldap/schema` to copy the schema file to the directory in which LDAP expects it to be.

2. Open `/etc/ldap/slapd.conf` with an editor and make sure the following schema files are included:

```
# Schema and objectClass definitions
include          /etc/ldap/schema/core.schema
include          /etc/ldap/schema/cosine.schema
include          /etc/ldap/schema/nis.schema
include          /etc/ldap/schema/inetorgperson.schema
include          /etc/ldap/schema/samba.schema
```

3. Restart the LDAP service, using `/etc/init.d/slapd restart`.

At this point, you have extended the LDAP schema. By doing that, three different classes have been added:

- `sambaDomain`: Used to store information that is used between Samba domain controllers. You only need this class when setting up an environment with several domain controllers (see the section "Using Samba as a Primary Domain Controller" later in the chapter).

- `sambaSamAccount`: Used to extend the user properties in LDAP to include Samba properties as well.

- `sambaGroupMapping`: Used to add properties that are necessary to make a normal Linux group a Samba group as well.

By default, the Samba user has two password hashes that are stored in LDAP. If you do nothing, both of them are readable as plain text passwords. Therefore, when using

LDAP as the password back end for Samba, you should make sure that only the Samba service has access to these passwords, by adding an ACL to LDAP. You can accomplish this by including the following code in /etc/ldap/slapd.conf:

```
access to attr=sambaNTPassword,SambaLMPassword
   by cn=admin,dc=sandervanvugt,dc=nl write
   by * none
```

Also, to increase performance, you should add some indexes to LDAP. This allows LDAP to find required information much faster. Make sure that the following indexes are added in /etc/ldap/slapd.conf:

```
index    uid,cn,displayName,memberUid    eq
index    uidNumber,gidNumber             eq
index    sambaSID                        eq,sub
```

Finally, restart the LDAP service, using /etc/init.d/slapd restart.

Telling Samba to Use LDAP

Now that the LDAP service is all prepared, you have to apply some modifications to /etc/samba/smb.conf to tell it that it has to use LDAP. You need to explain where it can find the LDAP server, and you need to secure communications.

Connecting Samba to LDAP

First and foremost, you need to use the passd backend global parameter to tell Samba where to go for password information. This option takes a URI as an argument, telling Samba where it can find LDAP. For example, if the LDAP server is available at IP address 192.168.1.200, the parameter looks as follows:

```
passdb backend = ldapsam:ldap://192.168.1.200/
```

This option tells Samba to go to the specified IP address to get password information, but what happens if this LDAP server goes down? There are two approaches to provide more redundancy:

- Configure LDAP as a resource in a Heartbeat cluster (see Chapter 7 for more details on Heartbeat). In such a configuration, you still have one LDAP server only, but Heartbeat will manage where it runs and will make sure that it is highly available. If the server that currently hosts LDAP goes down, Heartbeat will start LDAP somewhere else. The only implementation requirement is that you have to put the LDAP Directory and its configuration files on a shared storage device, so that another server, when it takes over the LDAP service, can still access the database and configuration. This is the solution that I prefer.

- Implement LDAP replication, using the slurpd process. When doing this, changes that are applied to the master LDAP server are replicated to the replica LDAP servers automatically. This could work also, but there is a disadvantage: the replica LDAP server is read-only and therefore of limited use. If you choose this solution, you can refer to both LDAP servers using the passdb backend definition in smb.conf:

```
passdb backend = ldapsam:"ldap://192.168.1.200 ldap://192.168.1.210"
```

Configuring Secure Connections

Basically, your Samba server is now capable of connecting to LDAP, but there is a problem still: connections from Samba to LDAP are all in plain text. So if the LDAP Directory is not on the same server as the Samba daemon, you should apply security. The preferred method to do that is by including the ldap ssl parameter in smb.conf:

```
ldap ssl = start_tls
```

Next, you need to tell Samba the identity of the administrator who has write permissions in LDAP. To do this, use the ldap admin dn parameter in smb.conf. You already created an ACL in LDAP to give the appropriate rights to manage user passwords to a user with the name admin, so it makes sense to tell Samba as well that this admin user is the administrator for all LDAP-related stuff:

```
ldap admin dn = cn=admin,dc=sandervanvugt,dc=nl
```

At this point you must make sure that Samba knows what password to use for this LDAP administrator. To create a password, first restart Samba to enforce all changes so far, and then use smbpasswd -W to write the password. As this is the Samba password that is needed to connect to the LDAP server, the password is not written to LDAP, but rather to the /etc/samba/secrets.tdb file. Make sure this file is not readable by normal users; the password is stored in a readable way in this file. In Listing 9-5 you can see what happens when writing this password.

Listing 9-5. *Use smbpasswd -W to Write the Password of the LDAP Administrator*

```
root@mel:~# smbpasswd -W
Setting stored password for "cn=admin,dc=sandervanvugt,dc=nl" in secrets.tdb
New SMB password:
Retype new SMB password:
```

Specifying Where to Put the Objects in LDAP

At this point, Samba knows all it has to know to get to LDAP for administration tasks. It's time to proceed to the next part, in which you specify where in the LDAP Directory you want to create Samba-related objects. Four parameters are required and the last is optional:

- ldap suffix: The base container in LDAP that you are working from.

- ldap user suffix: The base container for user accounts. Like all following parameters, the name of this container is written as a name that is relative to the container specified with ldap suffix.

- ldap machine suffix: The base container for machine accounts.

- ldap group suffix: The base container for group accounts.

- ldap idmap suffix: Required if you want to use Winbind to get user information from a Windows environment. Winbind creates SIDs, which in an LDAP-integrated environment are stored in the container specified here.

At this point, you should have in the [global] section of smb.conf the information shown in Listing 9-6.

Listing 9-6. *Summary of Parameters Required in smb.conf for LDAP Integration*

```
passdb backend = ldap
ldap admin dn = "cn=admin,dc=sandervanvugt,dc=nl"
ldap suffix = "dc=sandervanvugt,dc=nl"
ldap user suffix = "ou=people"
ldap machine suffix = "ou=machines"
ldap group suffix = "ou=group"
ldap idmap suffix = "ou=idmap"
```

At this point you can restart your Samba server. It is now integrated with LDAP.

Using Samba As a Primary Domain Controller

In a Windows environment, a domain is used to manage users for a group of computers. The only option to do this in a centralized way in NT 4 is to use domains. Since Windows 2000, Active Directory has been introduced as a system that sits above domains. Samba cannot be configured as an Active Directory environment yet, so the best thing you can do if you want to work with a domain-like environment is to configure Samba as an NT 4–style domain controller. This section gives some tips on how to do that. Be aware that setting up a well-tuned, scalable domain environment requires extensive knowledge of the working of Microsoft networks. This goes far beyond the scope of this book, so in this section you'll learn just about the basic requirements needed to set up a Samba domain. Consider this section an introduction to the subject matter only; for more information consult the man pages or the documentation at http://www.samba.org.

Changing the Samba Configuration File

The first step in setting up a domain environment is to change the Samba configuration file properly. Listing 9-7 shows the settings required in the /etc/samba/smb.conf [global] section.

Listing 9-7. *Samba Domain Controller Settings*

```
[global]
    netbios name = STN
    workgroup = UK
    security = user
    passdb backend = ldapsam:ldap://192.168.1.200
    logon script = %U.bat
    domain master = yes
    os level = 50
    local master = yes
    preferred master = yes
    domain logons = yes
    logon path = \\%N\profiles\%U
    logon drive = H:
    logon home = \\%N\%U
    login script = logon.cmd
```

```
[netlogon]
     comment = Network Logon Service
     path = /home/samba/netlogon
     guest ok = yes
     read only = yes
     share modes = no
[profiles]
     comment = User profiles
     path = /home/samba/profiles
     guest ok = no
     browseable = no
     create mask = 600
     directory mask = 0700
```

Table 9-1 summarizes the relevant parameters from the [global] section of Listing 9-7. Make sure to include the parameters from the [netlogon] and [profiles] sections as they appear in Listing 9-7, because you need them to make your Samba server function as a PDC.

Table 9-1. *Parameters Specific for Domain Configuration*

Parameter	Description
netbios name	This parameter is the name that your server will have in the Microsoft network.
security	This parameter specifies how security should be handled. If you want to configure your server as a domain controller, set it to security = user.
passdb backend	Use this parameter to specify in what kind of database you want to store user and group information. The most common values for this parameter are smbpasswd, tdbsam, and ldapsam. The easiest way to configure your server is to use the tdbsam option, which creates a local database on your Samba server. The most flexible way to configure it is to use the ldapsam option, although this does require the configuration of an LDAP server and makes things more complicated. If you want to set up your Samba environment with PDCs as well as BDCs, make sure to use the ldapsam option.
logon script	For Windows users, you can create a Windows logon script in Samba. This parameter refers to the logon script, which is a batch file that is executed automatically when the user logs in. In this example, the Samba server checks if there is a script for your user that has the name of the user account, followed by .bat. This script should be placed in the directory specified with the path parameter in the [netlogon] share.
domain master	This parameter tells the nmbd naming process that this server must be responsible for maintaining browse lists in the complete network. These browse lists allow others in the network to view a complete list of all members of the Windows network. A domain controller should always be the domain master for your network.

Parameter	Description
local master	This parameter defines which server is used as the local master browser. A domain master browser communicates with local master browsers, which are servers that are responsible for maintaining browse lists on local network segments. Apart from being the domain master, your Samba servers should be local master browsers as well.
os level	Even if you specify that your server should be local master and domain master, this doesn't really guarantee that it also will be the master browser. In a Windows network, the master browser is selected by election. To increase the chances that your server will be the master browser, make sure to you use a value higher than 32 for the os level parameter. The highest value is the most likely to win the browser elections.
preferred master	Normally, browser elections happen only occasionally. Use this parameter to force a new browser election immediately when the Samba server comes up.
domain logins	Set this parameter to yes to make this server a domain controller.
login path	This parameter specifies where the user's profile directory is found. To make this work, make sure that the [profiles] share is properly set up. In this parameter, the variable %N is used to refer to the local server name, and %U is used to refer to the home directory of the current user.
logon drive	This parameter provides for the user a drive letter that can be used as the logon drive.
logon home	Use this parameter to specify where the home directory is located.

As you can see, you need to use many parameters to make sure that the Samba server is elected to be the master browser for your network. To configure a master browser, you need the nmbd service, which handles Windows naming to be started as well. This service is started automatically when you start Samba.

Creating Workstation Accounts

Now that you have your domain environment, you should add workstations to it. For every workstation that is going to be a member of a domain, you need a workstation account on the Samba server. Setting up a workstation account is similar to setting up a user account. First you need to add the account to the local user database on your server, and then you need to add the workstation account as a workstation to the Samba user database. Notice that the name of the workstation should end with a $ sign, to indicate that it is a workstation. To create a workstation with the name ws10, for example, first use useradd ws10$ to create it in /etc/passwd. Next, add the workstation to the smbpasswd file by using the smbpasswd -a -m ws10 command. Notice that in the smbpasswd command, there is no need to use the $ to specify that it is a workstation; this is handled automatically by the -m option.

Integrating Samba in Active Directory

In its current version, you can't make a Samba server an Active Directory domain controller. Although the people in the Samba project team are working very hard to make this possible, they haven't been successful yet. You can, however, make Samba a member server in an Active Directory (AD) domain. That means you still need Windows 200*x* servers to fulfill the role of domain controllers.

The advantage of making Samba a member server in an AD domain is that users can log on to Active Directory and get access to all resources that are offered by the Samba server. There are two methods to connect Samba to Active Directory. The first method is to make Samba a member of the Active Directory domain, using simple passwords; the second method is to make Samba a member server in AD, using Kerberos authentication.

Making Samba a Member of the Active Directory Domain

To integrate Samba with Active Directory, the first step is to make it a member of the domain. This is a relatively easy procedure that you have to accomplish partly on a Windows server and partly on the Samba server:

1. Create user accounts for your users in Active Directory. Samba offers the resources, but in this setup, authentication is handled by Active Directory. So make sure that all users exist in Active Directory.

2. Create the Samba user as a Linux user and apply permissions for this user. So, you need one general Samba user on Linux, and you need to grant this user access permissions to the shared resources. You can grant these by using chmod 770 on the directory you want to share.

3. Modify the smb.conf configuration file. The following options are required in the [global] section to connect Samba to Active Directory:

```
[global]
    workgroup = NAME_OF_AD_DOMAIN
    password server = IP_ADDRESS_OF_A_200X_SERVER
    security = ADS
```

4. Add the Samba server to Active Directory. To do this, you need a computer account in Active Directory. Use the net command on the Samba server to create this user account in Active Directory: net ads join -U Administrator%password will do the job for you (replace password with the actual password of the Active Directory administrator). The Samba account now appears in Active Directory.

Using Kerberos to Make Samba a Member of Active Directory

In recent Windows versions, Microsoft has been focusing more on Kerberos authentication. Therefore, it is a good idea to use Kerberos on Samba as well. For more information about Kerberos, read Chapter 13. The advantage of using Kerberos is that it is never necessary to send passwords over the wire; instead, authentication tickets are used, which is a much more secure method. Follow this procedure to set up Kerberos authentication:

1. Tell Samba that it should use Kerberos, by modifying the `smb.conf` configuration file as follows:

```
[global]
    workgroup = YOUR_AD_DOMAIN
    realm = YOUR_AD_DOMAIN.MSFT
    ads server = YOUR_AD_SERVER
    security = ads
```

2. Get the initial Kerberos tickets. Use the `kinit` command, followed by the name of the Kerberos realm in the Active Directory environment: `kinit administrator@YOUR_AD_DOMAIN.MSFT`.

3. Add the Samba server to Active Directory. Use `net ads join -U Administrator%password`. This adds your server to Active Directory, and because your server now knows how to use Kerberos, Kerberos will be used for secure communications.

Authenticating Linux Users on Windows with Winbind

Up to now, I have assumed that your Linux users are defined in the Linux environment. This is not the most practical solution if you run a mainly Windows environment with some Linux users. In such an environment, it would be useful to maintain user accounts in Windows and redirect Linux users to Windows for authentication. Winbind helps you to do exactly that. The following procedure shows you how to set up a Winbind environment:

1. Install the `winbind` package by using `apt-get install winbind`.

2. Create in Active Directory the user accounts you want to be able to authenticate on Linux.

3. On Linux, modify the /etc/nsswitch.conf configuration file. In this file, you have to tell Linux that it should use Winbind before trying to authenticate locally on Linux. The following two lines will do that for you:

```
passwd:    winbind compat
group:     winbind compat
```

4. Modify the PAM configuration. You should make sure that before getting to normal Linux-based authentication, the user tries to authenticate on Windows. To make this happen, make sure that the line auth sufficient pam_winbind.so is inserted as the first line in the files common-auth, common-account, common-password, and common-session in /etc/pam.d.

5. Modify the smb.conf configuration file. Because Winbind is related to Samba, it gets its configuration from smb.conf. The code in Listing 9-8 makes sure that a complete environment is created for users that come in through Winbind.

Listing 9-8. *Winbind Parameters in /etc/samba/smb.conf*

```
[global]
    winbind separator = +
    winbind cache time = 15
    template shell = /bin/bash
    idmap uid = 10000-20000
    idmap gid = 10000-20000
    template homedir = /home/%U
    winbind uid = 10000-20000
    winbind gid = 10000-20000
    workgroup = YOUR_AD_DOMAIN
```

6. Restart Winbind by running /etc/init.d/winbind restart.

7. Winbind should do its work now. To test if it works well, you can log in at the Linux prompt with a Windows user account. To do this, at the login prompt, use the full username, including the name of the Windows Domain. That means that you would log in with a username such as DOMWIN+linda (which is what user linda would use to log in to the domain DOMWIN). To separate the domain name and username, you must use a + sign between the two.

Summary

In this chapter you learned how to integrate Samba with Windows. After a short introduction on generic Samba basics, you read how to integrate Samba with LDAP. Basically, this offers a very nice solution in which Samba uses a hierarchical replicated database as its user configuration back end. Next, you read how Samba can offer PDC functionality to replace a Windows NT 4–style domain controller. In the last part of this chapter, you read more about the integration between Samba and Active Directory. You read how to make Samba a member server in Active Directory, and how to set up Winbind, which allows you to manage Linux users from Active Directory. In the next chapter you'll learn how to set up Ubuntu Server as a mail server.

■ ■ ■

## CHAPTER 10

Configuring Ubuntu Server As a Mail Server

Sending and Receiving Mail Easily

One of the most common functions of a Linux system is to serve mail. Several Linux-based mail server programs are available for this purpose. Several programs are available to accomplish this task. In this chapter you will learn what is necessary to build a solution to send and receive e-mail on a network. Because Ubuntu Server uses the Postfix mail server by default to send mail to other networks, this chapter covers Postfix. Different solutions are available to allow users to connect to their mailboxes to fetch mail. One of the easiest to use of these solutions is Qpopper, so that is the solution of choice in this chapter.

Understanding the Components of a Mail Solution

If you want to understand what is needed to build a mail server that can handle e-mail for a complete network, you need to understand the three different agents that are used to process Internet e-mail:

- *Mail transfer agent (MTA)*: This is the software that sends e-mail. This e-mail is sent by the client that the user has used to compose and send the message. This recipient MTA sends the e-mail to an MDA (defined next). Some well-known MTAs are Postfix, Sendmail, and qmail. SMTP is an example of a protocol that can be used by an MTA to deliver e-mail.

- *Mail delivery agent (MDA)*: The MDA works together with the MTA on the server that is used by the recipient. The MDA makes sure the e-mail is stored in a location in which the user can access it. Postfix comes with an integrated MDA as well.

- *Mail user agent (MUA)*: After the mail is stored by the MDA, the MUA is the program that the user uses to read the mail. The MUA can retrieve mail in several ways: by using a protocol such as IMAP or POP, remotely by using a file access protocol, or through access to local files. When the MUA uses IMAP or POP, there always is a server component (for example, Qpopper) and a client component that is used by the client.

The core component of a mail solution is the MTA. This component makes sure that mail can be exchanged by hosts on the Internet. When sending mail on the Internet, the MTA analyzes the mail address of the recipient. This mail address includes a reference to the DNS domain used by the client. The MTA then contacts the authoritative DNS server of the recipient to find out which server is used as the MTA ("mail exchanger") in that domain. When the MTA knows which server to contact, it sends the mail over to the MTA of the recipient's domain. Once it arrives there, the MTA of the recipient checks whether the recipient is a user that exists on the local machine. If so, the mail is handed over to the MDA, which stores the mail in the mailbox of that user. If not, the MTA sends it to another MTA that helps to deliver the message to the mailbox of the recipient.

When the mail has been stored by the MDA in the mailbox of a local user, the user can access it in one of several ways, the most common of which is to use POP or IMAP. If the user uses POP, the mail is transferred to the user, but the user can choose to keep the message on the server instead. If IMAP is used, all messages are stored on the server and are not transferred to the client computer. When setting up a mailbox for a user, an administrator can choose to make it either a POP mailbox or an IMAP mailbox. In the following section you'll read how to configure the Postfix MTA. After that, you'll learn how to set up Qpopper and Cyrus IMAPd to receive mail messages.

Configuring the Postfix MTA

Postfix is a very modular mail server, comprising several programs that work together to make the Postfix mail server function. This is in contrast to Sendmail, an alternative UNIX MTA. The advantage of Postfix being a modular mail server is that it is easier for the administrator to manage all individual programs that comprise the Postfix mail server. The disadvantage is that, as an administrator, you need to know how all these separate programs function. Wietse Venema originally developed Postfix as a mail server that would be easier to administer and more secure than Sendmail. Because it is monolithic, Sendmail is in general much harder to secure properly. Postfix also is a very rich mail server that has many features.

■**Tip** You can find a complete list of all Postfix features and instructions on how to configure them at http://www.postfix.org/documentation.html.

How Postfix works as a modular mail server becomes clearer from a discussion of how mail traffic is handled by Postfix, so that is presented first. After that, you will learn how to install and configure Postfix.

Handling Inbound and Outbound Mail

Generally speaking, Postfix can handle two kinds of mail: inbound mail and outbound mail. The inbound mail that Postfix handles may be messages sent from a local user to another local user or messages sent over the network to a local user. The outbound mail that Postfix handles may be messages intended for a recipient on the same server as the sender, messages intended for a recipient on a remote server, or undeliverable messages.

Processing Inbound Mail from a Local User to Another Local User

The following list explains how Postfix processes inbound mail, a graphical representation of which is shown in Figure 10-1:

1. When Postfix receives mail that is sent by another local user, Postfix uses the postdrop command to place the mail in the maildrop queue, to ensure that the mail stays on the same machine.

2. The pickup daemon picks up the mail from the maildrop queue and checks whether the mail matches given rules regarding such things as the content, size, and other factors.

3. The pickup daemon passes the e-mail to the cleanup daemon, which makes sure the mail is formatted in the proper way, by doing the following:

- Replaces missing header lines in the e-mail if the mail program of the end user didn't do that already

- Deletes double recipient addresses

- Uses the `trivial-rewrite` daemon to convert the e-mail address in the header into a name in the proper `user@somedomain` format, using the lookup tables found at `/etc/postfix/canonical` and `/etc/postfix/virtual` (as covered in "Tuning Postfix with Lookup Tables" later in this chapter)

- Reformats data in the header according to all rules that apply

4. The `cleanup` daemon copies the e-mail to the incoming queue and sends a message to the queue manager (`qmgr`) to notify it that this mail has arrived.

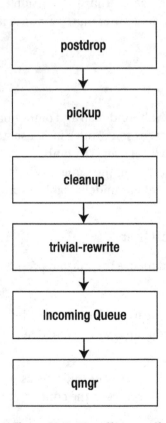

Figure 10-1. *Handling mail sent by a local user to another local user*

Processing Inbound Mail Sent over the Network to a Local User

If incoming mail was received over the network, the process is slightly different from that presented in the preceding section, mainly because Postfix doesn't need to use the postdrop and pickup daemons to handle mail sent over the network to a local user. The procedure is as follows (see Figure 10-2):

1. Postfix first uses the smtpd process to handle mail coming in over the network. This process performs some basic checks on the e-mail before handing it over to the cleanup daemon.

2. The cleanup daemon performs the same tasks as when processing local mail (see the bulleted list in step 3 in the preceding section).

3. After the trivial-rewrite daemon has done its work, the mail is placed in the incoming queue, where the queue manager takes further care of it.

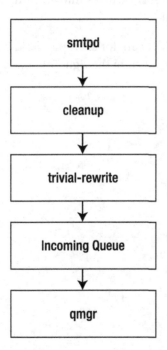

Figure 10-2. *Handling inbound mail coming from the same network*

Processing Outbound Mail Intended for a Local User

Being the MTA, Postfix is responsible as well for processing outbound mail. Basically, all outbound messages are placed in the incoming queue first. From there, the procedure is as follows for outbound mail intended for a local user (see Figure 10-3):

1. The queue manager (qmgr) picks up the mail from the incoming queue and places it in the active queue as soon as no other mail is in that queue.

2. The trivial-rewrite daemon determines where the mail should go: to a local user (the case here), to a user over the Internet, or to a UNIX user that uses UUCP to retrieve the mail (the latter method is somewhat primitive, so I don't discuss it here).

3. The trivial-rewrite daemon kicks the mail back to the queue manager, which orders the local delivery service /usr/lib/postfix/local to put it in the mailbox of the local user. Before doing that, the local delivery service takes into account all aliases and forwarding rules that apply to the mail.

4. The local daemon decides where to send the mail. It can, for example, send it to the procmail system, which analyzes the mail and puts it in the right folder.

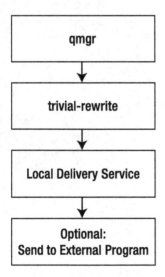

Figure 10-3. *Processing mail for a local user*

Processing Outbound Mail Intended for a User on a Remote System

When the mail is intended for a user on a remote system, the procedure is as follows (see Figure 10-4):

1. Again, the queue manager fetches the mail from the incoming queue and copies it to the active queue as soon as it is empty.

2. The `trivial-rewrite` daemon checks whether the mail is for a local user (see the previous section) or a remote user (as in this example). If the mail is intended for a remote user, all lookup tables that apply to that user are checked and then the mail is passed to the queue manager.

3. The queue manager activates the SMTP service that delivers the e-mail to the other server.

4. The `smtpd` process uses DNS to find the MTA for the target host and delivers it that MTA.

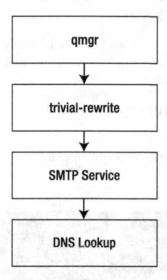

Figure 10-4. *Delivering mail to remote users*

Processing Undeliverable Mail

Finally, there is always a possibility that an e-mail cannot be delivered by the queue manager to either a local or a remote user. If that's the case, `qmgr` puts the mail in the deferred queue. When it is in there, the queue manager copies it back to the active queue at regular intervals and tries again to deliver it, until either a defined threshold is reached or the mail is delivered successfully.

Installing Postfix and Configuring the Initial Settings

To install Postfix, use `apt-get install postfix`. This command also launches a configuration program in which you can enter the most important settings for your mail server. The following procedure describes the steps that this configuration program guides you through:

1. Specify what kind of mail server you want to configure. The following choices are available (see Figure 10-5):

   - *No configuration*: This option makes sure your current configuration is not touched.

   - *Internet Site*: Use this option if your mail server is directly connected to the Internet and no intermediate mail servers are used.

   - *Internet with smarthost*: Use this option if you don't send out mail directly to the Internet, but rather use an intermediate host to do that. Receiving mail can happen directly via SMTP or by using fetchmail.

   - *Satellite system*: With this option, all mail goes through a smarthost, which handles the Internet connection for you.

   - *Local only*: Use this option if there is no network connection and mail is handled for local users only.

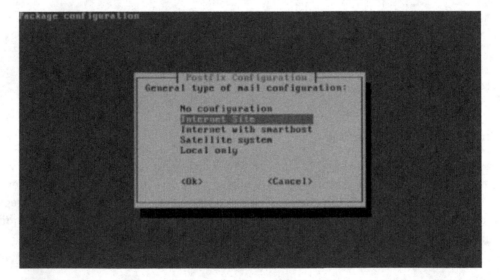

Figure 10-5. *To make configuring Postfix easier, the configuration program asks you what kind of mail server you are configuring.*

2. Enter the DNS domain name that should be used in the mail addresses of your users (see Figure 10-6). For example, if you want the mail address of some user to be linda@example.com, the name you enter here should be **example.com**.

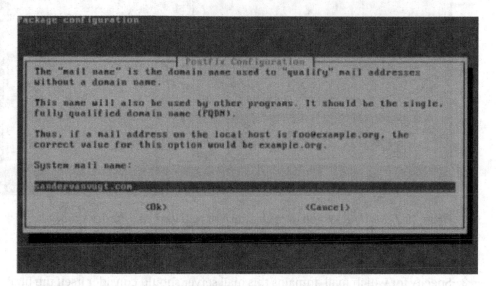

Figure 10-6. *Enter the DNS domain name for your mail server.*

3. The Postfix files are copied to your server and the basic configuration is written. Once completed, your Postfix mail server is ready for further configuration.

Configuring Postfix Further

The initial configuration that you set up when installing Postfix works fine, but it isn't very comprehensive. Therefore, right after you finish the initial configuration, I recommend continuing the configuration by running dpkg-reconfigure postfix. The following procedure describes how to configure Postfix from that interface:

1. The first two steps are exactly the same as the first two steps of the installation program. Accept the values that you entered earlier.

2. The third screen asks you what to do with mail for the user's postmaster, root, and other system accounts (see Figure 10-7). It is a good idea to forward this mail, and you have to do that to an existing user. So enter the name of a user account here.

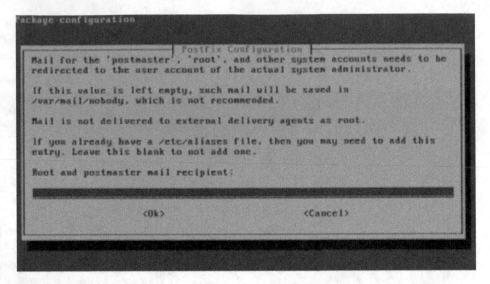

Figure 10-7. *Mail for system accounts such as root and postmaster should be forwarded to an existing user account.*

3. Specify for which mail domains this mail server should consider itself the final destination (see Figure 10-8). Only domain names entered here will be accepted in user mail addresses. If your server is responsible for several domain names, you should enter all of them here. Also make sure to list localhost, because you need it to handle mail between local users.

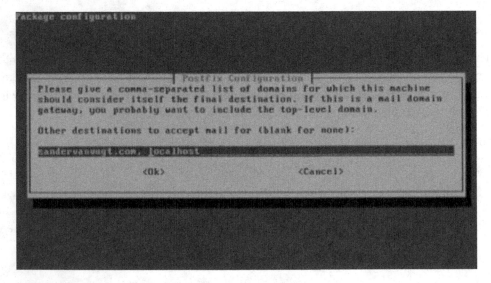

Figure 10-8. *Enter the DNS domain names of all domains your mail server is responsible for.*

4. If you are on a slow Internet connection, it is a good idea to force synchronous mail updates. Mail takes longer to come through, but less bandwidth is wasted. If mail is not processed synchronously and you are not using a journaling file system, there is a chance you will lose mail. If you have a fast Internet connection and your server is using a journaling file system (which is true in almost all cases), select No, as shown in Figure 10-9.

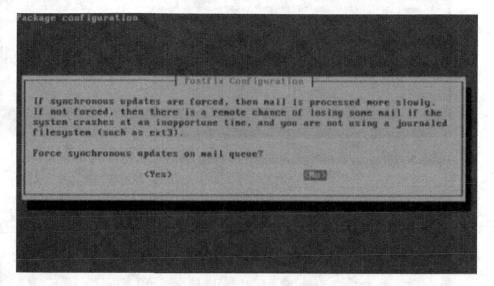

Figure 10-9. *If you are using a journaling file system on your server, choose No.*

5. Tell Postfix for which networks it is allowed to forward (relay) e-mail. By default, it does so only for its own IP address. If you are configuring this server as the local mail server for your network, make sure that you enter the IP address and subnet mask for that network in the screen shown in Figure 10-10. So, for example, if you are on the local network 192.168.1.0, enter **192.168.1.0/24** here, to allow relaying for every IP address that starts with 192.168.1.

6. If you want to put a limit on the maximum size of local mailboxes, enter that limit, in bytes, in the screen shown in Figure 10-11. If you don't need a limit, keep the default value of 0.

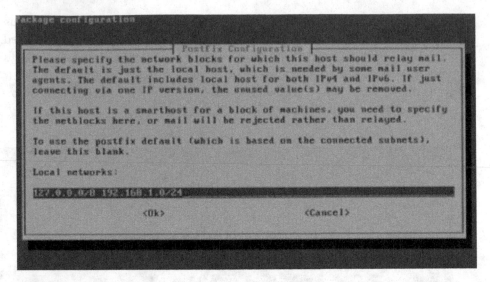

Figure 10-10. *Enter the IP address of your local network here to allow relaying.*

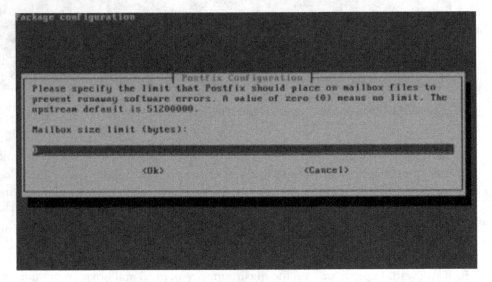

Figure 10-11. *If you want to limit mailboxes to a maximum size, enter that limit here, specifying it in bytes.*

7. If you want to add an extension to the name of local recipients, add that extension in the screen shown in Figure 10-12. By default, a + sign is added. If you don't need such an extension, you can leave this field blank.

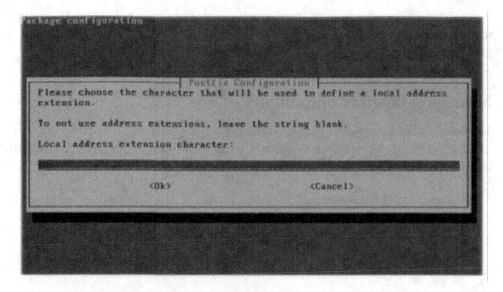

Figure 10-12. *If you don't need to use local address extensions, leave this field blank.*

8. Specify which Internet protocols you want to use in Postfix (see Figure 10-13). By default, it takes all protocols that are enabled on your server. If you just want to use IPv4, select only that protocol.

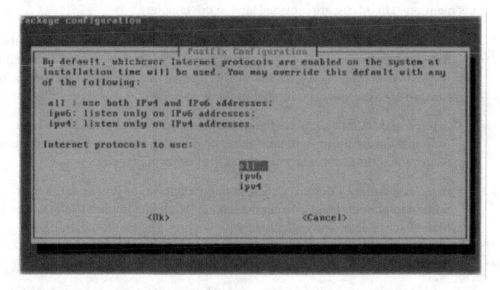

Figure 10-13. *By default, Postfix will use all enabled Internet protocols.*

9. The settings you've specified are written to the Postfix configuration files and Postfix is restarted.

You now have a functioning Postfix mail server. However, there are many options that you can still configure. In the following sections you'll learn which options are available and which configuration file to change to modify these options.

Managing Postfix Components

The Postfix mail server consists of several components. First, on Ubuntu Server, you find the init script in /etc/init.d, which you can use to start to the server, among other things. This script listens to all common arguments that can be used on most init scripts:

- start: Starts the server

- status: Displays the current status of the server

- reload: Tells Postfix to reread its configuration files after changes have been applied

- restart: Stops and then restarts Postfix

- stop: Stops the server

To troubleshoot a Postfix server, you must be aware of all the different components that are written to your server when Postfix is installed. Following is a list of all files and default directories that are created when installing Postfix (more details on the components mentioned in this list are provided later in this chapter):

- /etc/aliases: Contains aliases for local mail addresses. These aliases can be used to redirect to some other address mail that comes in on a given address. The initial configuration program has made sure that all mail that comes in for user root is forwarded to the user account that you have specified.

- /etc/postfix/: Contains all configuration files used by the Postfix mail server. Among them are the most important files, main.cf and master.cf, which contain all generic settings necessary to operate the Postfix mail server.

- /usr/lib/postfix/: Contains all binary components of the Postfix mail server. Some components mentioned in the section "Handling Inbound and Outbound Mail," such as local and qmgr, are in this directory. The binaries in this directory are started when needed; there is no need for an administrator to start them manually.

- /usr/sbin/: Contains all programs needed by the administrator to manage the Postfix mail server.

- /usr/bin/: Contains two symbolic links, mailq and newaliases. Both refer to the /sbin/exim4 program. They allow an administrator who is used to managing the Exim MTA to manage Postfix in an Exim-like style.

- /var/spool/postfix/: Contains all queues used by Postfix. Also, if Postfix runs in a chroot-jail, this directory contains the subdirectories etc and lib that contain necessary configuration files.

- /usr/share/doc/postfix/: Contains some documentation for Postfix.

Configuring the Master Daemon

Postfix is a modular service. In this modular service, one daemon is used to manage all other components of the Postfix server: the master daemon /usr/lib/postfix/master. This is the first process that is started when you activate the Postfix script from /etc/init.d. To do its work, the master daemon reads its configuration file /etc/postfix/master.cf, which includes for every Postfix process an entry that specifies how it should be managed. Listing 10-1 provides an example of the top lines from this configuration file.

Listing 10-1. *Example Lines from /etc/postfix/master.cf*

```
#
====================================================================
# service type private unpriv chroot wakeup maxproc command+args
#              (yes)   (yes)  (yes)  (never) (100)
#
====================================================================
smtp            inet n     -      n      -       -     smtpd
#submission inet n         -      n      -       -     smtpd
#       -o smtpd_etrn_restrictions=reject
#       -o smtpd_client_restrictions=permit_sasl_authenticated
...
pickup          fifo n     -      n      60      1     qmqpd
cleanup         unix n     -      n      -       0     pickup
qmgr            fifo n     -      n      300     1     qmgr
...
rewrite         unix -     -      n      -       -     trivial-rewrite
```

In the master.cf file, all services that are a part of Postfix are specified by using some predefined fields. Following is a list of all fields and a summary of the values that you can use for these fields. Note that not all field options can be chosen randomly for the Postfix components; if you are not absolutely sure of what you are doing, changing them is not recommended. The default values ensure that the processes will normally work just fine.

- service: Specifies the name of the process. Normally, just the name of the service is mentioned.

- type: Specifies the connection type. The possible values are inet if a TCP/UDP socket is used, unix if a local UNIX domain socket is used for communication within the system, or fifo if it is a named pipe.

- private: Specifies how the service can be accessed. Use y if the service must be accessible only from within the mail system; use n if you want to allow external access as well. Choosing n is required if the service is of the type inet, because otherwise you wouldn't be able to access it.

- unpriv: Specifies whether or not the service will run with root privileges. Use y to tell the component it should run with the privileges of the Postfix user account; use n to let the service run as root.

- chroot: Specifies whether or not the service should run in a chroot environment. If set to y, the root path is normally set to /var/spool/postfix/, but an alternative root path can be set from /etc/postfix/main.cf.

- wakeup: This option is relevant for only the pickup daemon and the queue manager, because they have to become active at regular intervals. For these daemons, provide a number. All other processes have the value 0, which disables the wakeup feature.

- maxproc: Gets its value from the default_process_limit value in /etc/postfix/main.cf and determines the maximum number of instances of this process that can run simultaneously. The default is normally set to 100.

- command +args: Defines what command must be activated with what arguments to run this component. The name of this command is relative to the directory in which the Postfix binaries are installed (/usr/lib/postfix). If you want the command to be verbose, make sure to include the -v option.

Configuring Global Settings

Most of the settings that determine how Postfix does its work are set in the file /etc/postfix/main.cf. Listing 10-2 provides an example of its contents.

Listing 10-2. *main.cf Defines How Postfix Should Do Its Work*

```
root@ubuntu:/etc/postfix# cat main.cf
# See /usr/share/postfix/main.cf.dist for a commented, more complete version


# Debian specific:  Specifying a file name will cause the first
# line of that file to be used as the name.  The Debian default
# is /etc/mailname.
#myorigin = /etc/mailname

smtpd_banner = $myhostname ESMTP $mail_name (Ubuntu)
biff = no

# appending .domain is the MUA's job.
append_dot_mydomain = no

# Uncomment the next line to generate "delayed mail" warnings
#delay_warning_time = 4h


readme_directory = no

# TLS parameters
smtpd_tls_cert_file=/etc/ssl/certs/ssl-cert-snakeoil.pem
smtpd_tls_key_file=/etc/ssl/private/ssl-cert-snakeoil.key
smtpd_use_tls=yes
smtpd_tls_session_cache_database = btree:${data_directory}/smtpd_scache
smtp_tls_session_cache_database = btree:${data_directory}/smtp_scache

# See /usr/share/doc/postfix/TLS_README.gz in the postfix-doc package for
# information on enabling SSL in the smtp client.

myhostname = ubuntu.home.nl
alias_maps = hash:/etc/aliases
alias_database = hash:/etc/aliases
myorigin = /etc/mailname
mydestination = sandervanvugt.com, localhost
relayhost =
mynetworks = 127.0.0.0/8 192.168.1.0/24
```

```
mailbox_size_limit = 0
recipient_delimiter =
inet_interfaces = all
inet_protocols = all
```

You can use many parameters in `main.cf`. Some of the most useful parameters are listed and described here:

- `command_directory`: Specifies the directory in which the Postfix Administration tools are located. The default value is `/usr/sbin`.

- `daemon_directory`: Specifies the directory in which the Postfix daemon is located.

- `inet_interfaces`: Specifies where Postfix listens for incoming mail. The default value for this setting is the loopback UP address. If you want Postfix to listen on external interfaces as well, you must specify either the IP address to listen on or `all`, the latter of which makes sure Postfix listens on all interfaces for incoming mail.

- `mail_owner`: Specifies the user who is owner of the mail queue. By default, this is the user `postfix`.

- `mydestination`: Specifies a list of domains for which the server accepts incoming mail. If incoming mail is sent to a domain not listed here, it will be rejected.

- `mynetworks`: Specifies which network is used as the local network. This setting is important, because other parameters (such as `smtpd_recipient_restrictions`) rely on it.

- `mydomain`: Specifies the DNS domain of the computer that runs Postfix.

- `myorigin`: Specifies the domain that appears as sender for e-mails sent locally. By default, the fully qualified domain name (FQDN) of the host sending the mail is used.

- `queue_directory`: Specifies the location of the directory in which the mail queues are held. The default location is `/var/spool/postfix`.

- `smtpd_recipient_restrictions`: Specifies which is the trusted network. Normally, the networks defined with the `mynetworks` variable are considered trusted networks. Mail clients from this network are allowed to relay mail through your Postfix mail server, whereas other clients are not.

- `smtpd_sender_restrictions`: Specifies which senders should always be ignored, to prevent your server from accepting spam. The default value for this parameter is `reject_maps_rbl`, which contains a default list of senders to reject.

Configuring a Simple Postfix Mail Server

Enough settings, parameters, and variables for now. The interesting question is, what work do you really need to do to enable a simple Postfix mail server? We've already gone through the configuration module, so let's see now if we can configure the mail server from the configuration files as well. In the scenario presented in this section, the simple mail server needs to send mail to the Internet for local users only. It also needs to be able to receive mail from the Internet, destined for users on the local domain.

Sending Mail to Other Servers on the Internet

To make this procedure as easy as possible, the following instructions show how to forward mail to the mail server of the Internet provider, which is a very common scenario:

1. Stop the Postfix server by using /etc/init.d/postfix stop.

2. Open /etc/postfix/main.cf in an editor and edit the following settings. Make sure to use the settings that are appropriate for your network.

    - inet_interfaces = all: This line allows Postfix to work on all network interfaces of your server.

    - mynetworks = 192.168.1.0/24: This line is an important security measure, because it tells Postfix which networks it should service.

    - smtp_recipient_restrictions = permit_mynetworks,reject: This line tells Postfix to accept recipients only from the networks specified in the mynetworks line.

    - masquerade_domains = yourdomain.com: This line is used to make sure that all the names of all subdomains in your mail domain are linked to your DNS domain name.

    - relayhost = host.internetprovider.com: If you want to forward mail to the mail host of an Internet provider, this line identifies the host that is used for this purpose.

3. Save the file, close the editor, and restart Postfix by using the /etc/init.d/postfix start command.

Accepting Mail from Other Servers on the Internet

Often, your mail server also needs to accept mail coming from the Internet that is sent to local users on your network. In such a configuration, it is very important that you set up some basic protection. You want to prevent your mail server from being misused as an open relay by spammers. Also, the DNS system must know that your mail server is the responsible mail server for your domain. You can do this by adding an MX record in the DNS database. After you make the required modifications to DNS, you have to configure your mail server for (at least) three extra tasks:

- Accept incoming mail that is addressed to your domain

- Reject incoming mail that is not addressed to your domain

- Reject mail from known spam sources

To configure your mail server to receive mail from the Internet, follow this procedure:

1. Stop the Postfix server by using `/etc/init.d/postfix stop`.

2. Open `/etc/postfix/main.cf` with your favorite editor and edit the following settings. Make sure to use the proper settings for your environment.

   - `inet_interfaces = all`: Allows Postfix to receive and send mail on all network interfaces.

   - `mynetworks = 192.168.1.0/24, 127.0.0.0/8`: Specifies the IP addresses of the network(s) you are on.

   - `myhostname = myserver.mydomain.com`: Specifies the fully distinguished DNS name of your host.

   - `mydomain = mydomain.com`: Specifies the name of the DNS domain that your Postfix server is servicing.

   - `mydestination = $myhostname, localhost.$mydomain, $mydomain`: Identifies the hosts that should be handled by the MTA as its destinations. All other destinations will be rejected.

   - `maps_rbl_domains = rbl-domains.mydomain.com`: Works as very primitive spam protection to identify unauthorized servers.

   - `smtpd_sender_restrictions = reject_maps_rbl`: Allows you to work with black lists, which are lists of servers that always should be denied use of this MTA for mail transfer.

   - `smtpd_recipient_restrictions = permit_mynetworks, reject_unauth_destination`: Makes sure that only mail going to trusted networks, and to no other networks, is handled by your MTA.

3. Save the modifications you have made to the `main.cf` file and start the Postfix process again by using `/etc/init.d/postfix start`. Your mail server is now ready to receive mail from the Internet.

Tuning Postfix with Lookup Tables

The main task of the Postfix mail server is to process mail. Based on the configuration you have created so far, your Postfix mail server is capable of doing so. You can also enhance the functionality of Postfix by applying rules. For this purpose, you can configure Postfix to use lookup tables. Many lookup tables are available, but none are created by default. For every lookup table that you want to use, you have to define it as a separate file in the directory /etc/postfix and activate it from variables in the file /etc/postfix/main.cf. After defining the lookup table, you need to convert it to the proper format by using the postmap command. In general, applying settings from a lookup table is a three-step procedure:

1. Refer to the lookup table in /etc/postfix/main.cf. For example, to indicate what file should be used for the sender_canonical lookup table, in /etc/postfix/main.cf, you would create the following line:

   ```
   sender_canonical_maps = hash:/etc/postfix/sender_canonical
   ```

2. Edit the lookup table file (for example, /etc/postfix/sender_canonical) with an editor and make all required modifications.

3. Use the postmap command to write the lookup table in the appropriate format; for example, postmap hash:/etc/postfix/sender_canonical.

All lookup tables are created according to the same syntax rules. It may not surprise you that a line starting with a # is not interpreted as a command line. Less obvious is that a line that begins with a space is regarded as a continuation of the previous line. You should therefore be very careful not to include any spaces in a line by accident. You can use the following lookup tables:

- access: Use to deny or accept mail from given hosts.

- canonical: Use to specify an address mapping for local and nonlocal addresses.

- recipient_canonical: Use to specify address mappings for the address of the recipient of a message.

- relocated: Use to provide information about a new location a user has moved to.

- sender_canonical: Use to specify address mappings for the address of the sender of an outgoing or incoming mail message.

- transport: Use to specify a mapping from a mail address to a message delivery or relay host.

- virtual: Use to rewrite recipient addresses for all local, virtual, and remote mail destinations. This is not like the aliases table, described next, which is used for local destinations only.

The `aliases` lookup table is the only lookup table that does not have a configuration file in `/etc/postfix`; it is in the `/etc` directory instead. The purpose of the `aliases` lookup table is to rewrite recipient addresses for local destinations.

The following sections provide more information on the use of all these lookup tables.

The access Lookup Table

You can use the `access` lookup table to reject or allow messages from a list of defined senders. This table is evaluated by the `smtpd` daemon for all incoming messages. To activate this table, add the line `smtpd_sender_restrictions` = `hash:/etc/postfix/access` to `main.cf`. Then, in the `/etc/postfix/access` file, you specify a list of mail addresses (in the first column) and an action for each mail address (in the second column). You can specify the e-mail addresses as patterns. You can refer to an actual e-mail address (`some-one@somewhere.com`), but you also can refer to complete or partial IP addresses or domain names. The following are the possible actions that you can specify for each mail address:

- `nnn message`: The e-mail is rejected with a numerical code (`nnn`) as defined in RFC 821, followed by the text message specified here.

- `REJECT`: The e-mail is rejected with a generic error message.

- `OK`: The message is accepted.

- `DISCARD`: The message is discarded and no information is sent to the sender.

An example of the contents of the `access` lookup table follows:

```
mydomain.co         OK
spam@drugs.com  550 No Spam allowed on this server
19.145.0.10         REJECT
1.2.3               REJECT
1.2.3.4             OK
```

The canonical Lookup Table

The `canonical` lookup table is very powerful: it rewrites both sender and recipient addresses of both incoming and outgoing mail. These addresses are rewritten not only in the header of your message, but also in the envelope. The `canonical` lookup table is processed by the `cleanup` daemon. To activate this table, add the following line to `/etc/postfix/main.cf`:

```
canonical_maps = hash:/etc/postfix/canonical
```

In the first column of the canonical table, you specify addresses or domain names that should be rewritten. The second column of the canonical table specifies the e-mail address to which the mail has to be routed. An example of the contents of the canonical table follows:

```
sales@mydomain.com        jdoe@mydomain.com
@west.mydomain.com        someone@mydomain.com
```

You should be aware that the canonical lookup table works on both e-mail recipients and senders. If you want to rewrite only recipient addresses or only sender addresses, use the recipient_canonical or sender_canonical lookup table, respectively, instead.

The recipient_canonical Lookup Table

The recipient_canonical table is used in the same way as the canonical table to rewrite e-mail addresses. Whereas the canonical table works on both recipient and sender addresses, the recipient_canonical table is used just on recipient addresses of incoming and outgoing mail. The syntax of this table is exactly the same as the syntax of the canonical table. To activate it, use the following entry in /etc/postfix/main.cf:

```
recipient_canonical_maps = hash:/etc/postfix/recipient_canonical
```

The sender_canonical Lookup Table

Whereas the recipient_canonical table is used to rewrite recipient addresses, the sender_canonical table is used to rewrite sender addresses of incoming and outgoing mail. This table is read as well by the cleanup daemon, and you can activate the table by including the following in main.cf:

```
sender_canonical_maps = hash:/etc/postfix/sender_canonical
```

The relocated Lookup Table

When a user is no longer valid on your mail system, you can choose to just let the mail messages to that user bounce. As an alternative, you can send a reply to the sender of an incoming mail to that user, informing the sender where the user currently can be found. To activate the relocated lookup table, add the following to main.cf:

```
relocated_maps = hash:/etc/postfix/relocated
```

When processing mail, the smtpd daemon checks the relocated file to see if there is a matching line. The first column in this file contains a reference to the e-mail address of the former user. This may be the plain mail address of this user, or it may be a regular expression that makes sure that a series of mail addresses is matched. In the second column, there is an informational message. This can be just the new e-mail address, but it can also include other information on how to contact the user. An example of the contents of the `relocated` table follows:

```
rmills@somewhere.com       rmills@nowhere.sh
 @nowhere.com               This company doesn't exist anymore
lthomassen@somewhere.com   Doesn't work here anymore
```

The transport Lookup Table

The main purpose of the `transport` table is to route e-mail messages. It makes a decision on incoming mail: is this message going to be processed by the local mail server, or by another mail server? To use this table, add the following to `main.cf`:

```
transport_maps = hash:/etc/postfix/transport
```

The first column provides a description of the recipient address in the message. This can be a user (`someone@somedomain.com`) or a domain. If a domain is used, there is a difference between `somedomain` and `.somedomain`. The former is for messages that are sent just to that domain, whereas the latter includes its subdomains as well. Including information on subdomains is the default behavior, so it is normally not necessary to include them. The second column indicates how the message should be handled, using the notation `transport:nexthop`. For `transport`, possible values are `local`, `smtp`, or `uucp`, specifying the method to use to contact the next hop. `nexthop` refers to the machine that should be contacted to process this message. An example of the `transport` table follows:

```
awesomedomain.com       smtp:mx1.awesomedomain.com
nodomain                uucp:mx10
```

The virtual Lookup Table

To make sending messages to the right person easier to understand, the administrator can choose to use virtual domains. These can be considered subdomains of a real DNS domain. The virtual domain is a domain that does not really exist in DNS; it only exists on the MTA. When mail comes in for a user in the virtual domain, the `virtual` table makes sure it is delivered to the correct user in the real domain. To activate the `virtual` domain table, add the following to `main.cf`:

```
virtual_maps = hash:/etc/postfix/virtual
```

The first line of the virtual domain file can be considered a header for the rest of the file. The first column of the first line lists the name of the virtual domain itself. In the second column, you can put a random description. In the subsequent lines, users in the virtual domain are specified in the first column. The second column mentions the name of the real user to whom the mail has to be forwarded. An example of the contents of a virtual domain table follows:

```
virtualdomain.com        some text
john@virtualdomain.com   john
user1@virtualdomain.com  kylie
user2@virtualdomain.com  julie
```

The aliases Lookup Table

The aliases lookup table is used to define aliases in the file /etc/aliases; it is the only table that is not in /etc/postfix, probably to maintain compatibility with the Sendmail mail server, which can use the same file. To activate this table, add the following to main.cf:

```
alias_maps = hash:/etc/aliases
```

The following is an example of the contents of the /etc/aliases file. The use of \ in front of the name of the user root ensures that the mail is delivered to a local user, whereas all other names can exist on a network system like NIS or LDAP as well. Also note that the use of multiple aliases in the same aliases file is possible, which allows you to make the system more flexible.

```
root:           \root, franck
mailer-daemon:  root
postmaster:     root
webmaster:      root
sales:          jim@somedomain.com
wwwrun:         webmaster
```

If changes are made to the aliases file, make sure these changes are processed. You can use either of two commands to do that: postalias /etc/aliases, to process the changes in the Postfix style, or newaliases, to process the changes in the Sendmail style.

Using Postfix Management Tools

Managing Postfix is not only about creating the configuration files with the correct syntax. Some management tools are available as well. These administration tools all run from the command line. The following is an overview of the most important tools:

- `newaliases`: Used to generate the database file `/etc/aliases.db` from the file `/etc/aliases`.

- `mailq`: Lists all e-mail in the mail queue that has not yet been sent.

- `postalias`: Same as `newaliases`.

- `postcat`: Displays in a readable form the contents of a file in the queue directories.

- `postconf`: Used to change the content of Postfix variable. If you run it without arguments, an overview is provided of the current configuration of all variables.

- `postfix`: Used as a troubleshooting command. Use `postfix check` to find any configuration errors. Use `postfix flush` to force all e-mail from the deferred queue to be sent immediately. After making changes to the Postfix configuration files, use `postfix reload` to reload configuration files.

- `postmap`: Used to convert the lookup tables in the `/etc/postfix` directory to hash files.

- `postsuper`: An important maintenance command. `postsuper -s` removes all unneeded files and directories; running this command before starting the Postfix server is always recommended. If after a system crash old files still remain, `postsuper -p` removes all unneeded old files.

Receiving E-mail Using IMAP or POP3

Postfix is the MTA that makes sure that mail is sent over the Internet. When this mail arrives at the destination server, a mechanism is needed to retrieve the e-mail and deliver it to the computer of the end user. Basically, two methods are available: If using IMAP, the user establishes a connection to the server and interacts with their mail directly on the server. This is a good solution if the end user always has a connection to the mail server. If that isn't the case, it is more useful to use POP3, which transfers all mail to the computer of the client. Be aware, however, that a client using POP3 has the option to keep the mail messages on the mail server, and that most IMAP mail clients offer an option to store mail offline.

Ubuntu Server offers different solutions to receive e-mail. In this chapter we'll cover the following:

- *Cyrus IMAPd*: A complete solution that allows users to access mail by using either IMAP or POP3

- *Procmail*: A solution that allows you to filter incoming mail.

- *Qpopper*: An easy solution that offers POP3 functionality only

Fetching E-mail Using Cyrus IMAPd

Cyrus IMAPd is a very flexible service that can be used to get incoming mail. In this section, you will learn how to install and configure this MDA.

Installing Cyrus IMAPd

The first step is to install Cyrus IMAPd. For this purpose, you need the `cyrus-imapd` package; use `apt-get install cyrus22-imapd` to install it. To install the management utilities as well, use `apt-get install cyrus22-admin`. Once the package is installed, you have to configure Postfix to provide e-mail through Cyrus IMAPd. Include the following in the Postfix `master.cf` file:

```
cyrus  unix - n n - - pipe
  user=cyrus argv=/usr/lib/cyrus/bin/deliver -e -r ${sender} -m
  ${extension} ${user}
```

From `master.cf`, Postfix calls the `deliver` program, which delivers all e-mail to recipients on the system. This program replaces the Postfix `local` program. In order for Cyrus IMAPd to do this, all recipients must exist as local users in `/etc/passwd` on the server where Postfix is used. Another task you need to perform to make Cyrus IMAPd responsible for all incoming mail is to modify `/etc/postfix/transport`. In the `transport` lookup table, you enter a line in which specify your domain and specify that `cyrus` is the responsible handler for incoming mail:

```
somedomain.com     cyrus:
```

After you make this modification, generate the corresponding lookup table with the command `postmap hash:/etc/postfix/transport`.

Understanding Cyrus IMAPd

To implement Cyrus IMAPd successfully, you first need to understand all the components that are written to your system when installing Cyrus IMAPd:

- `/etc/cyrus.conf`: This is the basic configuration file Cyrus works with. The file contains generic settings that define how Cyrus will work. Normally, it is not necessary to make changes to this file.

- `/etc/imapd.conf`: In this file, the working of the IMAP protocol is defined. Some important settings are made in this file, as you can read later in this chapter.

- `/var/lib/cyrus/`: In this directory, you find several important files that Cyrus works with. These include log files, database files, and files that contain information about mailboxes of users on your system.

- `/var/lib/cyrus/mailboxes.db`: This file includes all mailboxes. Make sure you back it up on a regular basis.

- `/var/lib/cyrus/log/`: If you are using the Cyrus mechanism for logging, its log files are stored here. In this directory, a file is created that has a name that is equivalent to the PID of the Cyrus IMAPd process.

- `/var/lib/cyrus/quota/`: In this directory, you can add quotas for the accounts on your server.

- `/var/lib/cyrus/shutdown`: If you need to shut down the system, create this file. In the file, you can include a line that will be sent to connected clients. Normally this line would be a warning telling the clients to disconnect. Also, when this file exists, no new connections can be made, thus allowing you to shut down the system for maintenance.

- `/var/lib/cyrus/msg/motd`: Use this file to send a message to clients when they connect. The first line in this file will be displayed to connecting clients.

Configuring /etc/imapd.conf

The main configuration file for the Cyrus server is `/etc/imapd.conf`. This file contains several settings that define how the server is to be used. Some of the most important settings are listed and described next:

- `configdirectory`: Specifies the directory that contains the working environment and important configuration files for your server. By default, it is set to `/var/lib/imap`.

- `partition-default`: Specifies the location in which the mailboxes are stored. By default, it is set to `/var/spool/imap`.

- `admins`: Lists users with administrative permissions for the Cyrus IMAPd server. By default, only the user `cyrus` has administrative permissions.

- `allowanonymouslogin`: Specifies whether a user is allowed to connect without providing a username and password. This is very bad practice with regard to security, so always make sure this is set to `no`.

- autocreatequota: Specifies the maximum amount of e-mail data that can be stored in a user's mailbox. By default, it is set to 10000, which equals 10 MB; you probably want to increase that. If set to 0, the user is not allowed to create new mail folders, and if set to -1, no quota is applied.

- quotawarn: Specifies when the user should get a warning that he is running out of available disk space. By default, this parameter is set to 90%.

- timeout: Specifies the number of minutes after which an inactive client is disconnected automatically.

- sasl_pwcheck_method: Specifies the authentication method that should be used. By default, saslauthd is used for this purpose. This makes sure that passwords are transmitted over the network with some basic encryption applied to them.

After making modifications to the imapd.conf file, you should restart the IMAPd server. If saslauthd is used for secure transmission of authentication data over the network, two processes are needed: first start saslauthd, and then use /etc/init.d/cyrus start to start the Cyrus mail server as well. To make sure that saslauthd is started, edit the configuration file /etc/default/saslauthd and set the parameter START=yes.

Managing User Mailboxes

The first step in managing user mailboxes is to add users to the system. These users are normal Linux users that you add to /etc/passwd. These users don't need a home directory, because all they use is their mailboxes that are stored in /var/lib/cyrus. Also, no shell is needed. However, the users do need the ability to reset their passwords. Therefore, make sure /usr/bin/passwd is specified as the default shell.

After you install the mail server and add users to your system, you can start administration. To perform administration tasks, you need the user account cyrus. Be aware that no default password is added for this user, so you need to set it manually. After setting it, you can use the cyradm command for administration of the Cyrus server. This command opens an interactive shell in which you can use several administration commands. To activate this shell, use the cyradm -user cyrus -auth login localhost command. Next, you can start administration tasks. A summary of the most important commands that you can use follows:

- listmailbox: Lists the names of all mailboxes.

- createmailbox: Creates a mailbox. The user for whom you are creating the mailbox must have a valid account in /etc/passwd.

- deletemailbox: Deletes a mailbox.

- `renamemailbox`: Renames a mailbox.

- `setquota`: Sets a quota on a mailbox.

- `listquota`: Gives an overview of quotas that are applied currently.

If, for example, you want to create a mailbox for user `alex`, follow these steps:

1. Make sure that user `alex` exists in `/etc/passwd`.

2. Open the `cyradm` tool using `cyradm -user cyrus -auth login localhost`.

3. From the `cyradm` interactive shell, use `createmailbox user.alex` to create a mailbox for your user. Make sure the username is specified as `user.alex`. This also sets default permissions to the mailbox, which allows the user to use his own mailbox.

4. Use `listmailbox` to check that the mailbox has been created successfully.

5. Close the interactive interface, using the `exit` command.

Basically, this is everything you need to create a mailbox for users. Of course, many more options are available from the `cyradm` interface. You can get an overview of all options by using the `help` command from within the administration interface.

Filtering Incoming E-mail with procmail

When mail is coming in to your server, you can filter this mail and determine where the mail needs to be stored by using the `procmail` MDA. Use `apt-get install procmail` to install it. `procmail` can sort e-mail automatically, forward it to other recipients, or delete it automatically according to some criteria the user has specified. This can be useful as a kind of primitive spam filter.

To use `procmail`, you have to call it from the `/etc/postfix/main.cf` file. This is normally done with the following line, so make sure it exists:

```
mailbox_command = /usr/bin/procmail
```

When it is activated, you can use `procmail` to set up automatic e-mail filtering and redistribution. By default, e-mail is delivered to the user mailboxes in `/var/spool/mail/`. You can change this default behavior by creating a `.procmail` file in the home directory of the individual user. Listing 10-3 provides an example of automatic mail filtering performed by `procmail`.

Listing 10-3. *Example of .procmail Mail Filtering File*

```
PATH=/bin:/usr/bin
MAILDIR=$HOME/Mail
LOGFILE=$MAILDIR/mail.log

:0
* ^From.*somedomain
$MAILDIR/Somedomain

:0 ^Subject.*viagra
$MAILDIR/spam

:0
*
$MAILDIR/Inbox
```

In this example, after some specific variables have been set that specify where mail binaries can be found, three rules are applied. The first rule specifies that data in the From field will be compared to *somedomain. If there is a match, the mail is automatically forwarded to the Somedomain folder in the mailbox of the user. The second rule specifies that all messages that have "viagra" in the message subject line are forwarded automatically to the spam folder. This is a very primitive way of handling spam. The third rule specifies that all other mail (matching the * criterion) is placed in the folder Inbox.

Getting E-mail with POP3 Using Qpopper

Qpopper is an excellent choice if you want to set up a simple POP3 server. To install it, use apt-get install qpopper. This adds a line to /etc/inetd.conf to start it automatically. Since using inetd is not a recommended method, I suggest starting Qpopper through xinetd. To do this, use apt-get install xinetd first to install it, and then create a file with the name /etc/xinetd.d/qpopper that has the same contents as the example file in Listing 10-4.

■**Note** Running Qpopper through xinetd is a viable solution if the mail server is not too busy. If it is, you should make sure that it is started as a real daemon that is available at all times. If not, Qpopper will suffer from bad performance.

Listing 10-4. *Example of the /etc/xinetd.d/qpopper Configuration File*

```
#
# qpopper - pop3 mail daemon
#
service pop3
{
#
        disable          = no
        socket_type      = stream
        protocol         = tcp
        wait             = no
        user             = root
        server           = /usr/sbin/qpopper
        server_args      = -s
        flags            = IPv4
}
```

In this example, the most important line is `disable = no`. This line makes sure the Qpopper service is started automatically when a POP request is incoming. After you make the required modifications to this file, make sure to (re)start `xinetd` by using `/etc/init.d/xinetd [re]start`. After you make sure that Qpopper is started, just one task remains. As an end user, you have to configure your favorite POP client and connect to the POP3 server. You will see that e-mail automatically starts coming in to your mailbox.

Summary

This chapter explained the basics of how to set up Ubuntu Server as a mail server. You learned how to configure Postfix as an easy-to-maintain MTA that exchanges mail with other servers on the Internet and makes sure users in your network can be reached from everywhere. You also learned how to set up Cyrus IMAPd as an IMAP mail server and how to use Qpopper as a very easily configured POP mail client. This chapter didn't cover every aspect of setting up a successful mail server, only the basics. You should be aware that setting up a mail server involves more than just making the processes work. For example, you should configure spam and virus protection, which goes beyond the scope of this chapter.

CHAPTER 11

■ ■ ■

Managing Ubuntu Server Security

Configuring Cryptography and AppArmor

Ubuntu Server offers some powerful security options. In this chapter you'll learn how to set up two important security solutions. First, you'll learn how to create and manage a PKI environment and certificate authority, using OpenSSL cryptography. Next, you'll be introduced to AppArmor, a new feature in Ubuntu Server 8.04 that helps you to secure individual applications.

Managing Cryptography

In the age of the Internet, cryptography has become increasingly important. When data is sent across insecure networks, you need to make sure the data is protected. When communicating with a host on the other side of the world, you need to make sure that the host really is the host you think it is (authentication). To do this, cryptography can help. In this section you will learn how to use OpenSSL to implement a secure cryptographic infrastructure. The following subjects are discussed:

- Introduction to SSL

- Public and private keys

- The need for a certificate authority

- Creating a certificate authority and server certificates

Introduction to SSL

Before Netscape invented the Secure Sockets Layer (SSL) protocol in 1994, there was no good way to protect data against the eyes of interceptors when the data traveled across the Internet. With SSL, data can be encrypted and clients and servers can be authenticated using digital certificates. These digital certificates are based on the X.509 standard and contain not only the public key of any party on the Internet, but also a digital signature that guarantees the authenticity of that public key.

Netscape wanted SSL to become an Internet standard, so it released enough information to enable others to create SSL libraries as well. The OpenSSL suite that is used in Linux environments is a direct result of that. In 1999, SSL's successor was introduced, Transport Layer Security (TLS). The only fundamental difference between SSL and TLS is that TLS is standardized by the Internet Engineering Task Force (IETF).

Public and Private Keys

SSL works with public/private key pairs. These can be used for two purposes: to prove identity and to encrypt messages. In an SSL environment, every host must have its own public/private key pair.

As an example of how SSL works, imagine that Linda wants to send an encrypted e-mail message to Kylie. To send an encrypted message, a user always needs the public key of the user to whom they want to send the encrypted message, so Linda first needs to get Kylie's public key. To make sure that everyone has easy access to a copy of her public key, Kylie can, for example, publish her public key on a web site, put it in an LDAP Directory server, or attach it to every e-mail she sends out. After Linda has obtained Kylie's public key, she can use it to encrypt the e-mail message that she subsequently sends to Kylie. Because Kylie's public key is directly related to the private key that only Kylie has access to, only Kylie, using her private key, is able to decrypt the message.

Public/private key pairs can also be used to establish identity. An example of this is Secure Shell (SSH) key-based authentication. (SSH is covered in my book *Beginning Ubuntu LTS Server Administration*, Second Edition, also published by Apress in 2008.) In such a scenario, the user who wants to authenticate makes sure that a copy of his public key is stored on the server on which he wants to authenticate. Next, on authentication, the server sends a random message to the user asking him to sign it with his private key. The client then sends the signed data to the sever and the server decrypts the data with the client's public key. If the decrypted data matches the previously sent data, the client is authenticated, because he has proven his identity.

The Need for a Certificate Authority

The scenario described in the preceding section is realistic and works well, but there is one problem: when Linda receives Kylie's public key, how can she be sure that it is Kylie's public key and not the public key of someone pretending to be Kylie? That's where the certificate authority (CA) comes in. A CA guarantees the authenticity of public keys of users and servers. It does so by signing this public key with its own private key. The result of this is a public key certificate in which the public key of the user is present, together with the signature of the CA. The user application, which should have a copy of the public key of the CA, can verify automatically that the signature is valid, and therefore can use this guaranteed public key certificate without consulting the user. If on the other hand a certificate is signed by a CA of which the public key is unknown on the local host, the user application notifies the user about the issue and allows the user to decide what to do with that certificate. Of course, the user can decide to trust that the public key in the certificate is authentic, but there is no way to guarantee that.

The main purpose of a CA is to guarantee the authenticity of a public key, but who in this case is there to guarantee the authenticity of the CA? This is where the trusted root comes in. Generally speaking, there are two different kinds of CAs:

- *Local CAs*: CAs that run within a company and are used to create certificates for keys of individual servers.

- *Trusted root CAs*: CAs that are trusted by everyone and used to create keys for other CAs. In other words, the trusted root is a CA that guarantees the authenticity of other CAs.

The reason the trusted root is trusted is that most applications already have the public key of such a trusted root CA by default. Therefore, the applications will automatically accept the certificate signed by such a trusted root. It is, however, not necessary for every user to go to the trusted root directly; within a company, you can create your own CA and choose whether or not to create a certificate for that CA. If you want a certificate that guarantees the authenticity of the public key in your certificate, you need to get it signed by a trusted root instance. VeriSign is a well-known example of a company that can do that for you. By using a trusted root, a chain of trust is created.

In a chain of trust, the certificate of the end user is signed by your own in-company CA. The certificate of this CA in turn is signed by a trusted root such as VeriSign or, if the certificate is for use within your company only, by a trusted root that you have created for your company. When a user receives this certificate, she will not be able to verify the certificate of the CA that signed the certificate, but because this certificate in turn is signed by a trusted root that is well known, an encrypted session can be established without problems. The bottom line is that when a certificate is signed by a trusted root, it is safe.

As a company, you can choose to sign every certificate that is used by an external CA, but this is expensive. A cheaper solution is to create your own CA, which in turn has its certificate signed by an external CA. That way, you have a certificate that is trusted by all external parties. If trust with external parties is not a requirement, as an alternative, you can choose to create a CA with a self-signed certificate. Of course, this solution is not as good as a solution in which trust is guaranteed by an external party, but if you have the option to manage within your network all workstations that work with this certificate, the guarantee of an external party isn't necessary. Just copy the public key certificate of your CA to all these workstations and it will work anyway. In the next section you will learn how to set up your own CA and then create certificates.

Tip If someone is able to steal the private key from your CA, all keys signed by that CA are compromised. Therefore, you should make sure the private key cannot be stolen. A good method to ensure that does not happen is to create a dedicated CA and isolate it from the network. The CA only needs to sign public keys, and it doesn't need a network connection to do so.

Creating a Certificate Authority and Server Certificates

To create a CA and certificates on Ubuntu Server, you can use the openssl command. In this section you'll learn how to use the openssl command to create a certificate and a self-signed CA. Because the self-signed CA is the highest level in the CA hierarchy in this example, it will be a root CA.

The following steps explain how to proceed:

1. Decide where you want to create the directory structure in which you want to put the CA. This should be a directory structure that can't be accessed by other users. The home directory of the user root, for example, might be a good location, because no ordinary users have access to this directory. From the directory of your choice, start with mkdir root-CA to create a subdirectory in which the CA will store its files.

2. Next, some subdirectories must be created in this root-CA directory. The names of these subdirectories are predefined in the configuration file /etc/ssl/openssl.cnf, so don't try anything creative unless you are willing to change all settings in this configuration file as well. The command mkdir certs newcerts private crl creates these subdirectories for you. The following list describes the purpose of each of these subdirectories:

- **certs**: Stores all signed public key certificates. This directory can be publicly accessible.

- **newcerts**: Stores all new certificates that haven't been signed yet.

- **private**: Stores the private key of your server. Protect it like the crown jewels! The least you should do is give this directory permission mode 700 (chmod 700 private).

- **crl**: Stores Certificate Revocation Lists, if any are needed in your environment.

3. To make creating the certificate for the root CA a bit easier, open the configuration file /etc/ssl/openssl.cnf. In this file you will find some default settings that are used when you create new certificates. Read the file and modify all settings as required. You at least need to make sure that all directory paths are accurate, by modifying the HOME and dir variables. Also, it is a good idea to set the names of the certificates to the correct value. Listing 11-1 shows an example of what this should look like. All nonessential parameters have been omitted from the listing.

Listing 11-1. *Some Important Settings from openssl.cnf*

```
HOME                       = /root/root-CA
dir                        = /root/root-CA
...
certificate                = $dir/cacert.pem
...
private_key                = $dir/private/privkey.pem
...
```

4. Now that you have properly tuned the configuration file, you can create a self-signed certificate for the root CA. The following command creates the certificate with a 1024-bit RSA key that is valid for 10 years:

```
openssl req -newkey rsa:1024 -x509 -days 3650 -keyout➥
 private/privkey.pem -out cacert.pem
```

The main command used here is openssl. This command has several parameters that can be used as if they were independent commands. The parameter req is used to create the self-signed certificate (check its man page to see everything it can be used for). To make clear where these keys should be created, -keyout is used to specify where to put the private key, and -out is used to define the location of the public key. All the other options are used to specify with what parameters the key must be created.

5. Creating the key starts an interface in which several questions are asked (see Listing 11-2). The most important is the prompt for a pass phrase. Using a pass phrase is mandatory, especially in this example, because we are creating a root CA; without a pass phrase, it would be possible for anyone accessing your machine to create public key certificates signed by this CA, which would make this CA worthless. You will also be prompted to enter a Distinguished Name, which is the complete name of the server using the key. Often it is similar to the fully qualified DNS domain name.

Listing 11-2. *Creating the Public/Private Key Pair for the CA*

```
root@mel:~/root-CA# openssl req -newkey rsa:1024 -x509 -days 3650 -out➥
 cacert.pem -keyout private/privkey.pem
Generating a 1024 bit RSA private key
....++++++
....................++++++
writing new private key to 'private/privkey.pem'
Enter PEM pass phrase:
Verifying - Enter PEM pass phrase:
-----
You are about to be asked to enter information that will be incorporated
into your certificate request.
What you are about to enter is what is called a Distinguished Name or a DN.
There are quite a few fields but you can leave some blank
For some fields there will be a default value,
If you enter '.', the field will be left blank.
-----
Country Name (2 letter code) [AU]:NL
State or Province Name (full name) [Some-State]:
Locality Name (eg, city) []:
Organization Name (eg, company) [Internet Widgits Pty Ltd]:
Organizational Unit Name (eg, section) []:
Common Name (eg, YOUR name) []:Myself
Email Address []:myself@example.com
```

Note You should always check the output of the openssl commands carefully. It's not easy to see errors, but it is easy to make them through small typing mistakes. You should fix all errors before proceeding to the next step.

6. You now have your own root CA, which means you can create your own certificates, used for any purpose. For example, you can create server certificates for secure e-mail or create client certificates to connect a notebook to a VPN gateway. Before you can start creating your own certificates, you need to create the OpenSSL database. This database consists of two files in which OpenSSL keeps track of all the certificates that it has issued; you need to create these two files manually before you start. To create this simple database, change to the home directory of your root CA, use touch index.txt, and then use echo 01 > serial.

7. Now that you have the database index files, you need to create the key pair and the associated key signing request. To do this, first use cd /root/root-CA to go to the root directory that is used by your CA. Next, enter the command

```
openssl req -new -keyout private/mailserverkey.pem➡
 -out certs/mailserver_req.pem -days 365
```

This example uses the name mailserverkey, which makes it easy to identify what the key is used for; you can use any name you like here. With this command, you have created a new key pair, of which the private key is stored in /root/root-CA/private, and the public key is dropped in /root/root-CA/certs. Listing 11-3 shows the process of creating these keys.

Listing 11-3. *Creating a Public/Private Key Pair for Your Server*

```
root@mel:~/root-CA# openssl req -new -keyout private/mailserverkey.pem➡
 -out certs/mailserver_req.pem -days 365
Generating a 1024 bit RSA private key
.................++++++
.............++++++
writing new private key to 'private/mailserverkey.pem'
Enter PEM pass phrase:
Verifying - Enter PEM pass phrase:
-----
You are about to be asked to enter information that will be incorporated
into your certificate request.
What you are about to enter is what is called a Distinguished Name or a DN.
There are quite a few fields but you can leave some blank
For some fields there will be a default value,
If you enter '.', the field will be left blank.
-----
```

```
Country Name (2 letter code) [AU]:NL
State or Province Name (full name) [Some-State]:NB
Locality Name (eg, city) []:Amsterdam
Organization Name (eg, company) [Internet Widgits Pty Ltd]:SomeCompany
Organizational Unit Name (eg, section) []:somewhere
Common Name (eg, YOUR name) []:Me
Email Address []:me@somecompany.com

Please enter the following 'extra' attributes
to be sent with your certificate request
A challenge password []:
An optional company name []:
```

8. You now have created the CA and a key pair that you want to get signed. If, unlike in this simple example setup, the CA that needs to sign the key does not run on your own server, you would now copy it to the server that does the signing. In this simple setup, because the CA is on the same server, you can sign the CA using the following command:

```
openssl ca -policy policy_anything -notext -out certs/mailservercert.pem➥
 -infiles certs/mailserver_req.pem
```

Make sure that you run this command from the root directory of the CA as well. In this command, for signing the key, the default policy is used, policy_anything, which is defined as the default setting in the openssl.cnf configuration file. The option -notext is used to limit the amount of output produced by this command. Then the name of the resulting certificate is given: certs/mailservercert.pem. This certificate can be created only because earlier you created a signing request with the name mailserver_req.pem. This mailserver_req.pem request is in the certs directory. In a situation in which you need to sign a public key that is generated on another server, you only have to make sure that this public key is copied to this directory; the signing request would find it and the public key certificate would be created without any problem. Listing 11-4 shows the output that is generated when signing this certificate.

Listing 11-4. *Signing the Certificate Just Created*

```
root@mel:~/root-CA# openssl ca -policy policy_anything -notext -out➥
 certs/mailservercert.pem -infiles certs/mailserver_req.pem
Using configuration from /usr/lib/ssl/openssl.cnf
Enter pass phrase for /root/root-CA/private/privkey.pem:
```

```
Check that the request matches the signature
Signature ok
Certificate Details:
        Serial Number: 1 (0x1)
        Validity
            Not Before: Aug 15 09:32:12 2008 GMT
            Not After : Aug 15 09:32:12 2009 GMT
        Subject:
            countryName               = NL
            stateOrProvinceName       = Some-State
            localityName              = Roosendaal
            organizationName          = MyComp
            commonName                = MyName
            emailAddress              = myname@mycomp.com
        X509v3 extensions:
            X509v3 Basic Constraints:
                CA:FALSE
            Netscape Comment:
                OpenSSL Generated Certificate
            X509v3 Subject Key Identifier:
                BD:17:8C:D3:BD:39:E8:59:B6:47:4A:A4:FF:A1:40:8C:30:73:CD:B2
            X509v3 Authority Key Identifier:
                keyid:83:B5:79:F1:73:23:56:42:F1:17:B8:8A:AD:CA:B6:C9:E6:79:DC
:5E

Certificate is to be certified until Aug 15 09:32:12 2009 GMT (365 days)
Sign the certificate? [y/n]:y


1 out of 1 certificate requests certified, commit? [y/n]y
Write out database with 1 new entries
Data Base Updated
```

You now have created the public/private key pair for your mail server and you have signed it with your own self-signed root CA. For more details on how to use the openssl command, check man openssl(1). Also note that each option, such as req and ca, has its own man page.

Securing Applications with AppArmor

Installing a firewall is one important element in ensuring the security of servers and networks. A firewall, however, won't protect you if there is a security hole in your application. For example, a buffer-overflow problem could give an intruder root access to your system without any limitation. Therefore, you need a solution to secure applications on a per-application basis. AppArmor is such a solution and it is integrated in Ubuntu Server. AppArmor uses the security framework in the Linux kernel to make sure that an application can only perform tasks defined in an AppArmor profile, no matter what the name is of the user account that the application is started with. In this section you'll learn how to configure AppArmor.

Note An alternative to AppArmor is SELinux, which is used by other Linux distributions, such as Red Hat. On Ubuntu Server, AppArmor is used because it is much easier to configure and offers the same level of protection.

AppArmor Components

Before you start to install and use AppArmor, it is useful to understand how it works. The core component of AppArmor is the profile. You can create a profile for every application, and in that profile you can define exactly what the application can and cannot do. The functionality of AppArmor profiles is based on two Linux kernel modules, apparmor and aamatch_pcre, that hook in directly to the Linux Security Modules (LSM) framework of the kernel. These modules, which load as soon as you start working with AppArmor, work together to make it possible to use POSIX capabilities to define exactly what an application can and cannot do.

You can consider the set of POSIX capabilities to be an addition to the Linux permissions system. Whereas a permission defines what a user can do to a file, a capability defines what actions the user can perform on the system as a whole, including files. For example, the CAP_AUDIT_WRITE capability allows users to write to the audit log, and the CAP_CHOWN capability allows users to change UIDs and GIDs. Normal users by default have limited capabilities, whereas user root has all of them. That is also why user root is all-powerful on your Linux server and has no real limitations.

Note The POSIX standard defines common standards for Linux and UNIX operating systems. POSIX capabilities include all actions that can happen on a Linux (and UNIX) system.

Basically, if an application is started as root and has an AppArmor profile as well, the AppArmor profile determines what the application can do, regardless of the fact that the user is logged in as root. That means that with AppArmor, you can even create limitations for root.

An AppArmor profile defines an application's capabilities and file-access permissions. Listing 11-5 gives an example of how these capabilities and permissions are applied in the default profile for ntpd. You can find this example profile in /etc/apparmor.d/usr.sbin.ntpd.

Listing 11-5. *Example Profile for ntpd*

```
root@mel:/etc/apparmor.d# cat usr.sbin.ntpd
# Last Modified: Thu Aug  2 14:37:03 2007
# $Id: usr.sbin.ntpd 915 2007-08-15 18:31:26Z seth_arnold $
# --------------------------------------------------------------------
#
#    Copyright (C) 2002-2005 Novell/SUSE
#
#    This program is free software; you can redistribute it and/or
#    modify it under the terms of version 2 of the GNU General Public
#    License published by the Free Software Foundation.
#
# --------------------------------------------------------------------

#include <tunables/global>
/usr/sbin/ntpd flags=(complain) {
  #include <abstractions/base>
  #include <abstractions/nameservice>
  #include <abstractions/xad>

  capability ipc_lock,
  capability net_bind_service,
  capability setgid,
  capability setuid,
  capability sys_chroot,
  capability sys_resource,
  capability sys_time,
```

```
    network inet dgram,
    network inet stream,
    network inet6 stream,

    /drift/ntp.drift rwl,
    /drift/ntp.drift.TEMP rwl,
    /etc/ntp.conf r,
    /etc/ntp/drift* rwl,
    /etc/ntp/keys r,
    /etc/ntp/step-tickers r,
    /etc/ntpd.conf r,
    /etc/ntpd.conf.tmp r,
    /tmp/ntp* rwl,
    /usr/sbin/ntpd rmix,
    /var/lib/ntp/drift rwl,
    /var/lib/ntp/drift.TEMP rwl,
    /var/lib/ntp/drift/ntp.drift rw,
    /var/lib/ntp/drift/ntp.drift.TEMP rw,
    /var/lib/ntp/etc/* r,
    /var/lib/ntp/ntp.drift rw,
    /var/lib/ntp/ntp.drift.TEMP rw,
    /var/lib/ntp/var/run/ntp/ntpd.pid w,
    /var/log/ntp w,
    /var/log/ntp.log w,
    /var/log/ntpstats/loopstats* lrw,
    /var/log/ntpstats/peerstats* lrw,
    /var/opt/novell/xad/rpc/xadsd rw,
    /var/run/nscd/services r,
    /var/run/ntpd.pid w,
    /var/tmp/ntp* rwl,
    @{PROC}/net/if_inet6 r,
}
```

■Note The reason that SUSE and Novell are referenced in this example AppArmor profile is that AppArmor is open source technology owned by Novell. Some elements, such as the profiles that are used, are applied on Ubuntu without any modifications.

Listing 11-5 first includes some additional configuration files. Next, the POSIX capabilities that are needed for this program are defined. If the program would run as root, it would have access to all 31 capabilities defined in the POSIX standard. Together, these capabilities allow for complete access to the system. In this case, you can see that the number of capabilities is limited to seven. For a complete list of all capabilities, consult man 7 capabilities. Following the capabilities, a list of files and directories is provided, and for each of these files and directories, the profile defines the permissions that the process has. Table 11-1 gives an overview of all permissions that you can use in AppArmor.

Table 11-1. *Overview of AppArmor Permissions*

Permission	Use
r	Gives read access to the resource.
w	Gives write access to the file. This also allows the program to remove the file.
l	Gives link access to a file. This allows a process to create or remove links.
m	Allows executable files to be loaded in memory (known as executable mapping).
ix	Sets the mode to inherit execute, which allows a program that is executed by this program to inherit the current profile settings for execution.
px	Sets the mode to discrete profile execute, which indicates that a program needs its own AppArmor profile.
Px	Indicates that the program needs its own profile, but is allowed to load its environment variables without that.
ux	Allows the program to run without any AppArmor profile restrictions being applied to it. Don't use this permission, because it is insecure.
Ux	Allows the program to run without any AppArmor profile restrictions being applied to it in its own environment. Don't use this permission, because it is insecure.

Installing and Starting AppArmor

Installing AppArmor is easy: it is installed by default. Also, many applications that have an AppArmor profile will automatically install this profile. I recommend installing the available additional profiles as well, by using the following command:

```
apt-get install apparmor-profiles
```

To start AppArmor, some services are needed. You can start these services manually with the /etc/init.d/apparmor start command. To stop AppArmor, use /etc/init.d/apparmor stop, or use /etc/init.d/apparmor kill if you want to unload the AppArmor kernel modules also. If AppArmor is installed, you don't need to include AppArmor services in the startup procedure, because AppArmor will load automatically when your server boots. AppArmor also has a restart/reload option, which you activate with /etc/init.d/apparmor restart or /etc/init.d/apparmor reload. There is no difference between these two commands; both force AppArmor to reread its configuration. Be aware, however, that if you reload the AppArmor configuration, all applications that are confined by AppArmor should be reloaded as well. Therefore, it may be a better idea just to restart your complete server, using the reboot command as root.

Creating and Managing AppArmor Profiles

To create and manage profiles, several command-line tools are available. The most useful command is genprof, short for generate profile. This section shows you how use this command to create an AppArmor profile for the w3m application.

Note w3m is a text-based web browser. It doesn't offer the same functionality as a full-scale graphical browser, but it is useful anyway. Use apt-get install w3m to install it on your server if necessary.

The following steps show how to create a profile for w3m with genprof:

1. From a terminal window, use the genprof command, followed by the name of the application that you want to profile. For example, use genprof w3m to create a profile for the w3m browser. If no current profile for this program exists on your server and this is the first time you have started the profiling application for this program, genprof asks whether you want to access the online profile repository to see if a profile for your application exists in there. In general, it is a good idea to download profiles from the online profile repository, but to teach you how you can create a profile yourself, do not select this option in this procedure. Instead, press D to tell genprof that you don't want to go to the online profile directory. Listing 11-6 shows the output produced by genprof at this stage.

Listing 11-6. *Use genprof to Tell AppArmor You Want to Create Another Profile*

```
root@mel:~# genprof w3m

Please start the application to be profiled in
another window and exercise its functionality now.

Once completed, select the "Scan" button below in
order to scan the system logs for AppArmor events.

For each AppArmor event, you will be given the
opportunity to choose whether the access should be
allowed or denied.

Profiling: /usr/bin/w3m

[(S)can system log for SubDomain events] / (F)inish
```

■**Note** You could use a plain text console as well to run `genprof`, but for multitasking reasons, it is much more convenient to run it from a terminal window in a graphical session. If you don't have a graphical environment available, you can use virtual consoles, which are activated with the Alt+<Function key> keystroke.

---

2. Leave the `genprof` command running in a console and start the program for which you want to create the profile (see Listing 11-7). Make sure that you use as much as possible of its functionality. For a web browser like w3m, that means you have to visit several web pages (make sure to visit some that start scripts as well), open a file, and so on.

Listing 11-7. *To Create a Reliable Profile, Use As Much of the Program Functionality As Possible*

```
root@MYL:~# w3m www.fsf.org
Free Software Foundation
```

â¢ About
â¢ Campaigns
â¢ Volunteer
â¢ Donate
â¢ Join
â¢ Shop

Since 1985 we've been fighting for essential freedoms for computer users

Freedom Fry

Stephen Fry

Mr. Stephen Fry introduces you to free software, and reminds you of a very
special birthday.

Take action: France plans to adopt a law, which would punish people who fail
to
'respect' copyright on the Internet.

   â¢ Find out more about our campaigns, activism and latest news
   â¢ GNU - a complete free software operating system
âª â â Viewing <Welcome! - Free Software Foundation>

3. When you are finished using the application, press S in the terminal where genprof
    is running, to start scanning the log file to analyze what exactly the application
    needs to do its work. The genprof command next asks you what to do for each
    event it has detected for your application (see Listing 11-8 for some examples).

Listing 11-8. *When Creating the Profile, Authorize Every Part of Your Application*

```
root@mel:~# genprof w3m
Writing updated profile for /usr/bin/w3m.
Setting /usr/bin/w3m to complain mode.

Please start the application to be profiled in
another window and exercise its functionality now.

Once completed, select the "Scan" button below in
order to scan the system logs for AppArmor events.
```

For each AppArmor event, you will be given the
opportunity to choose whether the access should be
allowed or denied.

```
Profiling: /usr/bin/w3m

[(S)can system log for SubDomain events] / (F)inish
Reading log entries from /var/log/messages.
Updating AppArmor profiles in /etc/apparmor.d.

Profile:  /usr/bin/w3m
Execute:  /bin/dash
Severity: unknown

[(I)nherit] / (P)rofile / (U)nconfined / (D)eny / Abo(r)t / (F)inish
Complain-mode changes:

Profile:  /usr/bin/w3m
Path:     /dev/pts/1
Mode:     rw
Severity: 9

 1 - #include <abstractions/consoles>
 [2 - /dev/pts/1]

[(A)llow] / (D)eny / (G)lob / Glob w/(E)xt / (N)ew / Abo(r)t / (F)inish
Adding /dev/pts/1 rw to profile.

Profile:  /usr/bin/w3m
Path:     /etc/hosts
Mode:     r
Severity: unknown

 1 - #include <abstractions/nameservice>
 [2 - /etc/hosts]

[(A)llow] / (D)eny / (G)lob / Glob w/(E)xt / (N)ew / Abo(r)t / (F)inish
```

```
Profile:  /usr/bin/w3m
Path:     /etc/hosts
Mode:     r
Severity: unknown

  1 - #include <abstractions/nameservice>
  2 - /etc/hosts
 [3 - /etc/*]
```

```
[(A)llow] / (D)eny / (G)lob / Glob w/(E)xt / (N)ew / Abo(r)t / (F)inish
Adding /etc/* r to profile.
```

```
Profile:  /usr/bin/w3m
Path:     /etc/w3m/config
Mode:     r
Severity: unknown

 [1 - /etc/w3m/config]
```

```
[(A)llow] / (D)eny / (G)lob / Glob w/(E)xt / (N)ew / Abo(r)t / (F)inish
```

To create the profile, genprof calls the logprof command in the background; logprof is specially designed to analyze the AppArmor log file /var/log/audit/ audit.log. If the profiled application needs to access a program, genprof gives you the following possibilities:

- *Inherit*: The executed program inherits the permissions of its parent program.

- *Profile*: Requires that a previously defined profile already exist for the executed program.

- *Unconfined*: Allows the program to run without a security profile.

- *Deny*: Denies access to the program that is called by the program you are creating the profile for. For instance, in Listing 11-8 you can see that w3m calls the dash shell. If at this point you deny access, that would mean that your program would never be able to start this subshell. This would probably break the functionality of your program.

In the profiled application needs to access a file, you have the following options:

- *Allow*: Gives access to the file.

- *Deny*: Prevents the program from accessing this file.

- *Glob*: Selecting Glob once replaces the filename with an asterisk, including all files in the directory. Selecting Glob a second time allows your application to access files in the parent directory of the directory in which the file is located.

- *Glob w/Ext*: Selecting this option once gives the program access to all files that have the same extension as the selected file. Selecting this option a second time gives the program access to all files with the same extension in the parent directory of the directory in which the file is located.

4. After you have indicated for each event what you want to do with it, from the genprof window, press the F key. This terminates genprof activity and creates the profile.

5. Restart your application to enable AppArmor to protect it. When it starts, it will behave according to the rules that you have just created in the profile in /etc/apparmor.d/profiles.

Updating a Profile

If a profile already exists for your application, you can update it using a specific procedure. In this procedure, you first have to put your application in complain mode, by using the aa-complain command. By doing this, you activate learning mode for the program that is specified. To activate this mode for the program w3m, you could use aa-complain w3m. You can also refer directly to its profile file: aa-complain /etc/apparmor.d/usr.bin.w3m. It's even possible to apply a generic update on all profiles that currently exist, by using aa-complain /etc/apparmor.d/*. Once the programs are in complain mode, you can start using them. If you have used enough functionality to update the program, you can now update the profile. Use aa-logprof -d /etc/apparmor.d to update all profiles, or aa-logprof -f /etc/apparmor.d/your.program to update the profile of a specific application.

Monitoring AppArmor's Status

This section introduces several commands that you can use to monitor AppArmor's status from the command line.

The /etc/init.d/apparmor status command gives you a generic overview of current AppArmor activity, as shown in the example in Listing 11-9.

Listing 11-9. *apparmor status Displays Current AppArmor Activity*

```
root@mel:/etc/init.d# ./apparmor status
apparmor module is loaded.
14 profiles are loaded.
3 profiles are in enforce mode.
   /usr/sbin/mysqld
   /usr/sbin/slapd
   /usr/sbin/avahi-daemon
11 profiles are in complain mode.
   /usr/sbin/ntpd
   /usr/sbin/identd
   /usr/sbin/nmbd
   /sbin/klogd
   /sbin/syslogd
   /usr/sbin/smbd
   /sbin/syslog-ng
   /usr/sbin/traceroute
   /usr/sbin/nscd
   /usr/sbin/mdnsd
   /bin/ping
6 processes have profiles defined.
2 processes are in enforce mode :
   /usr/sbin/mysqld (8818)
   /usr/sbin/slapd (5389)
0 processes are in complain mode.
4 processes are unconfined but have a profile defined.
   /sbin/syslogd (5202)
   /sbin/klogd (5246)
   /usr/sbin/nmbd (6083)
   /usr/sbin/ntpd (6204)
```

When you see that AppArmor is protecting some processes (as indicated in the lines that specify processes are in enforce mode), you probably want to find out what processes these are. To do this, have a look at the /sys/kernel/security/apparmor/pro-files file. This shows a complete list of all process files that currently are protected by AppArmor. For an example of its contents, see Listing 11-10.

Listing 11-10. */sys/kernel/security/apparmor/profiles Lists All Process Files Currently Protected by AppArmor*

```
root@mel:/# cat /sys/kernel/security/apparmor/profiles
/usr/sbin/traceroute (complain)
/usr/sbin/smbd (complain)
/usr/sbin/slapd (enforce)
/usr/sbin/ntpd (complain)
/usr/sbin/nscd (complain)
/usr/sbin/nmbd (complain)
/usr/sbin/mysqld (enforce)
/usr/sbin/mdnsd (complain)
/usr/sbin/identd (complain)
/usr/sbin/avahi-daemon (enforce)
/sbin/syslogd (complain)
/sbin/syslog-ng (complain)
/sbin/klogd (complain)
/bin/ping (complain)
```

A third command that is pretty useful to monitor the current status of AppArmor is unconfined. This command shows you a list of all processes that currently are active but do not have an AppArmor profile loaded. In other words, these are the unprotected commands for which you should consider creating and loading a profile as well. See Listing 11-11 for an example.

Listing 11-11. *unconfined Generates a List of All Running Programs Not Protected by AppArmor*

```
root@mel:/# cat /sys/kernel/security/apparmor/profiles
/usr/sbin/traceroute (complain)
/usr/sbin/smbd (complain)
/usr/sbin/slapd (enforce)
/usr/sbin/ntpd (complain)
/usr/sbin/nscd (complain)
/usr/sbin/nmbd (complain)
/usr/sbin/mysqld (enforce)
/usr/sbin/mdnsd (complain)
/usr/sbin/identd (complain)
/usr/sbin/avahi-daemon (enforce)
```

```
/sbin/syslogd (complain)
/sbin/syslog-ng (complain)
/sbin/klogd (complain)
/bin/ping (complain)
```

Summary

Security is an important feature on every server. In this chapter you learned about two important security-related items. First, you learned how to use openssl to create a certificate authority and sign your own public key certificates. In the second part of this chapter, you learned how to use AppArmor to add an additional layer of security to your applications. In the next chapter, you will learn how to configure Ubuntu Server as a VPN server.

■ ■ ■

## CHAPTER 12

Configuring Ubuntu Server As a VPN Server

Networking Securely over the Internet

If you need to connect securely to a server that is not on your site, one option is to purchase a dedicated line. Unfortunately, dedicated lines are expensive. A cheap and very common alternative is to configure a Virtual Private Network (VPN), a connection between two sites or two computers that goes over the Internet. VPNs are available as hardware appliances, but it is relatively easy to configure Linux as a VPN server.

Because the Internet by nature is an unsecured network, you have to implement security measures when setting up a VPN. These security measures are applied by using encryption. Several solutions are available to create a VPN. You are probably already familiar with one of them: when you establish an SSH session with your server and start a program on your server that displays its output on the local workstation, basically you are using a VPN. However, an SSH VPN is not the most versatile VPN solution. A very popular and versatile Linux VPN solution is OpenVPN, which uses functionality from the OpenSSL package to ensure its security. In this chapter you'll learn how to set up a VPN that is based on OpenVPN.

Installing and Configuring OpenVPN

As with most software on Ubuntu Server, installing OpenVPN is not too hard: just run `apt-get install openvpn` to download and install the software. The installation process installs all software and also starts the openvpn daemon. You can manipulate the process from its init scripts as well. For example, you can start it with /etc/init.d/openvpn start and stop it with /etc/init.d/openvpn stop. Unfortunately, the init script doesn't provide an option to get the current status of the openvpn software.

Before you set up the VPN itself, as covered later in this section, you need a clear understanding of the way in which a VPN normally is configured, as described next.

VPN Networking

In most VPN solutions, a dedicated network interface is created and maintained by the VPN. In OpenVPN, this is the tun interface, instead of the eth0 interface you normally see for an Ethernet network card. Working with two interfaces makes configuring the VPN slightly complex. The node on which the VPN is configured has to distinguish between traffic that must be sent through the VPN to the other site and traffic that can be sent straight to the Internet or to other nodes in the same local network. Figure 12-1 gives an overview of this situation. To make sure the node does this, you have to configure routing.

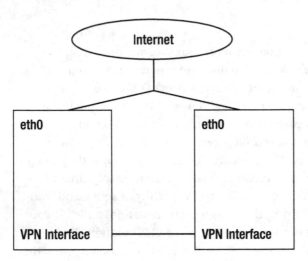

Figure 12-1. *Schematic overview of a VPN configuration*

Before going any further, you should determine if you want to use a routed VPN or a bridged VPN. OpenVPN offers both options. However, in most situations you will use routing. Routing is easier to set up and offers better flexibility with regard to access control. Bridging is useful only if you need to use very specific features of your VPN, such as in the following cases:

- The VPN needs to handle protocols other than IP, such as IPX.

- You are running applications that rely on LAN broadcasts over the VPN.

- You want to browse to Windows shares without setting up a Samba or WINS naming server.

Generating Certificates

OpenVPN heavily relies on the use of certificates, so before you start to configure the VPN, you should set up a public key infrastructure (PKI). Before the mutual trust that is required on the VPN can be established, the server and client must exchange their PKI certificates.

■**Note** Although this chapter refers to a client/server VPN setup, a VPN can also be established between sites, in which case one site is configured as the client and the other is configured as the server.

In Chapter 11 you learned how to set up a certificate authority (CA). Because OpenVPN has its own scripts to set up the complete PKI infrastructure, this chapter also covers setting up the CA. If you already have a CA, you can skip this configuration and proceed to creating certificates for the client and the server.

Configuring the Certificate Authority

By default, you'll find the OpenVPN scripts that help you to build the CA and its keys in the directory /usr/share/doc/openvpn/examples/easy-rsa/2.0. Copy these scripts to /etc/openvpn/easy-rsa to prevent them from being overwritten when you're updating software on your server.

When setting up a CA and associated certificates, you need to specify what country, province, and city you are in. You also need to enter other personal parameters, such as the name of your organization and the administrator e-mail address. In OpenVPN, you enter these details in the file /etc/openvpn/easy-rsa/vars. Listing 12-1 provides an example of this file. Most of the lines in this example file can be used as displayed. You need to modify only the last four lines, which refer to your specific information.

Listing 12-1. *vars Makes Passing the Appropriate Parameters Easier when Generating the CA*

```
root@mel:/etc/openvpn/easy-rsa# cat vars
# easy-rsa parameter settings

# NOTE: If you installed from an RPM,
# don't edit this file in place in
# /usr/share/openvpn/easy-rsa --
# instead, you should copy the whole
# easy-rsa directory to another location
# (such as /etc/openvpn) so that your
# edits will not be wiped out by a future
# OpenVPN package upgrade.

# This variable should point to
# the top level of the easy-rsa
# tree.
export EASY_RSA="`pwd`"

#
# This variable should point to
# the requested executables
#
export OPENSSL="openssl"
export PKCS11TOOL="pkcs11-tool"
export GREP="grep"



# This variable should point to
# the openssl.cnf file included
# with easy-rsa.
export KEY_CONFIG=`$EASY_RSA/whichopensslcnf $EASY_RSA`

# Edit this variable to point to
# your soon-to-be-created key
# directory.
#
```

```
# WARNING: clean-all will do
# a rm -rf on this directory
# so make sure you define
# it correctly!
export KEY_DIR="$EASY_RSA/keys"

# Issue rm -rf warning
echo NOTE: If you run ./clean-all, I will be doing a rm -rf on $KEY_DIR

# Increase this to 2048 if you
# are paranoid.  This will slow
# down TLS negotiation performance
# as well as the one-time DH parms
# generation process.
export KEY_SIZE=1024

# In how many days should the root CA key expire?
export CA_EXPIRE=3650

# In how many days should certificates expire?
export KEY_EXPIRE=3650

# These are the default values for fields
# which will be placed in the certificate.
# Don't leave any of these fields blank.
export KEY_COUNTRY="US"
export KEY_PROVINCE="CA"
export KEY_CITY="SanFrancisco"
export KEY_ORG="Fort-Funston"
export KEY_EMAIL="me@myhost.mydomain"
```

After making sure that the vars file contains the appropriate parameters, you can create the CA. You do this by executing three scripts from the /etc/openvpn/easy-rsa directory:

```
source ./vars
./clean-all
./build-ca
```

Of these commands, the first two just clean up the current configuration and pass to your current environment the variables you've set in /etc/openvpn/easy-rsa/vars. The latter command generates the CA for you. Listing 12-2 gives an example of the output of these commands.

Listing 12-2. *Generating the Certificate Authority with the easy-rsa Scripts*

```
root@mel:/etc/openvpn/easy-rsa# source ./vars
NOTE: If you run ./clean-all, I will be doing a rm -rf on /etc/openvpn/easy-rsa/keys
root@mel:/etc/openvpn/easy-rsa# ./clean-all
root@mel:/etc/openvpn/easy-rsa# ./build-ca
Generating a 1024 bit RSA private key
.....................................++++++
.......................................++++++
writing new private key to 'ca.key'
-----
You are about to be asked to enter information that will be incorporated
into your certificate request.
What you are about to enter is what is called a Distinguished Name or a DN.
There are quite a few fields but you can leave some blank
For some fields there will be a default value,
If you enter '.', the field will be left blank.
-----
Country Name (2 letter code) [NL]:
State or Province Name (full name) [NB]:
Locality Name (eg, city) [Roosendaal]:
Organization Name (eg, company) [sander]:
Organizational Unit Name (eg, section) []:
Common Name (eg, your name or your server's hostname) [sander CA]:
Email Address [mail@sander.fr]:
```

Creating Server Keys

At this point the CA is available and you can generate keys. The following command creates the keys for the server (replace yourserver with the actual name of your server):

```
./build-key-server yourserver
```

Executing this command starts an interactive command sequence. When it asks if you want to sign the keys as well, enter yes. This makes sure that you can start using the keys immediately. Listing 12-3 shows the output of the build-key-server command.

Listing 12-3. *Use build-key-server to Create Keys for Your Server*

```
root@mel:/etc/openvpn/easy-rsa# ./build-key-server mel
Generating a 1024 bit RSA private key
.....++++++
.................................................++++++
writing new private key to 'mel.key'
-----
You are about to be asked to enter information that will be incorporated
into your certificate request.
What you are about to enter is what is called a Distinguished Name or a DN.
There are quite a few fields but you can leave some blank
For some fields there will be a default value,
If you enter '.', the field will be left blank.
-----
Country Name (2 letter code) [NL]:
State or Province Name (full name) [NB]:
Locality Name (eg, city) [Roosendaal]:
Organization Name (eg, company) [sander]:
Organizational Unit Name (eg, section) []:
Common Name (eg, your name or your server's hostname) [mel]:
Email Address [mail@sander.fr]:

Please enter the following 'extra' attributes
to be sent with your certificate request
A challenge password []:
An optional company name []:
Using configuration from /etc/openvpn/easy-rsa/openssl.cnf
Check that the request matches the signature
Signature ok
The Subject's Distinguished Name is as follows
countryName           :PRINTABLE:'NL'
stateOrProvinceName   :PRINTABLE:'NB'
localityName          :PRINTABLE:'Roosendaal'
organizationName      :PRINTABLE:'sander'
commonName            :PRINTABLE:'mel'
emailAddress          :IA5STRING:'mail@sander.fr'
Certificate is to be certified until Aug 24 07:46:42 2018 GMT (3650 days)
Sign the certificate? [y/n]:y
```

```
1 out of 1 certificate requests certified, commit? [y/n]y
Write out database with 1 new entries
Data Base Updated
```

Creating Client Keys

Now that the server keys have been created, you can create keys for your client as well. Creating client keys is almost the same procedure as creating the server keys, but you use ./build-key client, still from the /etc/openvpn/easy-rsa directory. Replace client with the actual name of the client you are creating the keys for. Listing 12-4 shows the output of this command. When you run this command, answer yes to the questions that are asked.

Listing 12-4. *Use build-key to Create Keys for Your Clients*

```
root@mel:/etc/openvpn/easy-rsa# ./build-key myl
Generating a 1024 bit RSA private key
..++++++
...................................++++++
writing new private key to 'myl.key'
-----
You are about to be asked to enter information that will be incorporated
into your certificate request.
What you are about to enter is what is called a Distinguished Name or a DN.
There are quite a few fields but you can leave some blank
For some fields there will be a default value,
If you enter '.', the field will be left blank.
-----
Country Name (2 letter code) [NL]:
State or Province Name (full name) [NB]:
Locality Name (eg, city) [Roosendaal]:
Organization Name (eg, company) [sander]:
Organizational Unit Name (eg, section) []:
Common Name (eg, your name or your server's hostname) [myl]:
Email Address [mail@sander.fr]:

Please enter the following 'extra' attributes
to be sent with your certificate request
A challenge password []:
An optional company name []:
Using configuration from /etc/openvpn/easy-rsa/openssl.cnf
```

```
Check that the request matches the signature
Signature ok
The Subject's Distinguished Name is as follows
countryName           :PRINTABLE:'NL'
stateOrProvinceName   :PRINTABLE:'NB'
localityName          :PRINTABLE:'Roosendaal'
organizationName      :PRINTABLE:'sander'
commonName            :PRINTABLE:'myl'
emailAddress          :IA5STRING:'mail@sander.fr'
Certificate is to be certified until Aug 24 08:13:05 2018 GMT (3650 days)
Sign the certificate? [y/n]:y


1 out of 1 certificate requests certified, commit? [y/n]y
Write out database with 1 new entries
Data Base Updated
```

Generating Diffie-Hellman Parameters

You now have a public/private key pair for your server and for your client. Next, you need to generate the Diffie-Hellman parameters that are required for the key exchange between client and server. Use the ./build-dh command from /etc/openvpn/easy-rsa to generate these parameters. Listing 12-5 shows the output of this command.

■**Note** The Diffie-Hellman key exchange is a cryptographic protocol that is needed to exchange two symmetric keys over a unsecured channel. You need these keys to establish a secure channel over which you can continue building the VPN.

Listing 12-5. *Use build-dh to Generate the Diffie-Hellman Parameters*

```
root@mel:/etc/openvpn/easy-rsa# ./build-dh
Generating DH parameters, 1024 bit long safe prime, generator 2
This is going to take a long time
.................................................................
.................................................................
.................................................................
.....+..........................................................
```

```
..............................................................
..............................................................
..............................................................
.+..............................................+................+..
.............................................+.+.............................
..............................................................
...........+.....+...........................................
...........................+...+..............................
...........++*++*++*
```

At this point, a set of keys is created in the directory /etc/openvpn/easy-rsa/keys. Table 12-1 gives an overview of the keys and their use.

Table 12-1. *Overview of Keys Generated*

Filename	Needed By	Purpose
ca.crt	Server and all clients	Root CA certificate
ca.key	Server	Root CA key
dh.pem	Server	Diffie-Hellman parameters
server.crt	Server	Server certificate
server.key	Server	Server key
client.crt	Client	Client certificate
client.key	Client	Client key

Copying the Keys to the Client

Now that you have created all the keys, it is time to copy the client keys to the client. The following procedure summarizes how to do this:

1. Use ssh to open a session to your client, and then create a directory in which you can store the keys, using mkdir /etc/openvpn/keys.

2. Close the SSH session to your client, using the exit command.

3. From your server, use scp to copy the client keys to the client. The name of the client key should reflect the name of the client, so if your client's name is my1, the keys should be named my1.crt and my1.key. The following command (when used from the /etc/openvpn/easy-rsa/keys directory) copies the keys to the proper location on the client:

```
scp my1* root@client-ip-or-name:/etc/openvpn/keys
```

4. The client should have the certificate of your in-company CA as well. You created this certificate earlier in this procedure, and it is stored in the file /etc/openvpn/easy-rsa/key/ca.crt. Copy this as well, using the following command:

```
scp ca.crt root@client-ip-or-name:/etc/openvpn/keys
```

Configuring the VPN Server

Now that you have created the public and private keys, you can create the configuration files. Both the server and the client need a configuration file. (The next section covers the client configuration.) You can copy the sample files from /usr/share/doc/openvpn/examples/sample-config-files, which is recommended, because the sample configuration files already contain everything that you need to set up the VPN.

By default, the sample server.conf file creates a VPN in which a network interface with the name tun is used for routing. This interface listens to client connections coming in on UDP port 1194 and distributes IP addresses from the 10.8.0.0/24 subnet. In most situations, this configuration works fine. There is one piece of information you have to change, though: the sample server.conf file does not use the keys that you've just generated, so change the ca, cert, key, and dh parameters to reflect the proper keys. Listing 12-6 shows the most important lines from the lengthy sample configuration file.

Listing 12-6. *Critical Parameters from server.conf*

```
root@mel:/etc/openvpn# cat server.conf
port 1194
proto udp
dev tun
ca /etc/openvpn/keys/ca.crt
cert /etc/openvpn/keys/server.crt
key /etc/openvpn/keys/server.key
```

```
dh /etc/openvpn/keys/dh1024.pem
server 10.8.0.0 255.255.255.0
ifconfig-pool-persist ipp.txt
keepalive 10 120
comp-lzo
persist-key
persist-tun
status /var/log/openvpn-status.log
verb 3
```

Now that you have created the configuration file for the server, it is time to start the OpenVPN service. You would normally do that by executing the init script /etc/init.d/ openvpn start, but because this is the first time you are starting it, you may want to see some more output. Therefore, run the following command:

```
openvpn --config /etc/openvpn/server.conf
```

If anything is wrong in your configuration, this command identifies it in its output. An example of such an error message is provided in Listing 12-7.

Listing 12-7. *Starting openvpn from the Command Line Outputs Any Error Messages*

```
root@mel:/etc/openvpn/easy-rsa/keys# openvpn --config /etc/openvpn/server.conf
Tue Aug 26 04:53:15 2008 OpenVPN 2.1_rc7 i486-pc-linux-gnu [SSL] ➡
[LZO2] [EPOLL] built on Jun 11 2008
Tue Aug 26 04:53:15 2008 Diffie-Hellman initialized with 1024 bit key
Tue Aug 26 04:53:15 2008 Cannot load certificate file ➡
/etc/openvpn/easy-rsa/keys/server.crt: error:02001002:system ➡
library:fopen:No such file or directory: error:20074002:BIO ➡
routines:FILE_CTRL:system lib: error:140AD002:SSL ➡
routines:SSL_CTX_use_certificate_file:system lib
Tue Aug 26 04:53:15 2008 Exiting
```

As you can see in Listing 12-7, the openvpn program complains that it can't find the server.crt file that the configuration file refers to. This complaint is valid, because the files of my server keys have the name of the server itself. So, in my case, I have to replace server.* in the server.conf file with mel.*. As Listing 12-8 shows, the next attempt is more successful.

Listing 12-8. *The Server Console Indicates a Successful Start of openvpn*

```
root@mel:/etc/openvpn# openvpn --config /etc/openvpn/server.conf
Tue Aug 26 04:58:48 2008 OpenVPN 2.1_rc7 i486-pc-linux-gnu [SSL] ➥
[LZO2] [EPOLL] built on Jun 11 2008
Tue Aug 26 04:58:48 2008 Diffie-Hellman initialized with 1024 bit key
Tue Aug 26 04:58:48 2008 /usr/bin/openssl-vulnkey -q -b 1024 -m <modulus omitted>
Tue Aug 26 04:58:48 2008 TLS-Auth MTU parms [ L:1542 D:138 EF:38 EB:0 ET:0 EL:0 ]
Tue Aug 26 04:58:48 2008 TUN/TAP device tun0 opened
Tue Aug 26 04:58:48 2008 TUN/TAP TX queue length set to 100
Tue Aug 26 04:58:48 2008 ifconfig tun0 10.8.0.1 pointopoint 10.8.0.2 mtu 1500
Tue Aug 26 04:58:48 2008 route add -net 10.8.0.0 netmask 255.255.255.0 gw 10.8.0.2
Tue Aug 26 04:58:48 2008 Data Channel MTU parms [ L:1542 D:1450 EF:42➥
 EB:135 ET:0 EL:0 AF:3/1 ]
Tue Aug 26 04:58:48 2008 Socket Buffers: R=[1048576->131072] S=[1048576->131072]
Tue Aug 26 04:58:48 2008 UDPv4 link local (bound): [undef]:1194
Tue Aug 26 04:58:48 2008 UDPv4 link remote: [undef]
Tue Aug 26 04:58:48 2008 MULTI: multi_init called, r=256 v=256
Tue Aug 26 04:58:48 2008 IFCONFIG POOL: base=10.8.0.4 size=62
Tue Aug 26 04:58:48 2008 IFCONFIG POOL LIST
Tue Aug 26 04:58:48 2008 Initialization Sequence Completed
```

You now can use Ctrl+C to interrupt the openvpn service, and then restart it, but using the init script this time: /etc/init.d/openvpn start. As you can see, no comments are output to your computer monitor, but when you use ifconfig, you can see that a new device is added to your server. The VPN uses the tun device to route all VPN traffic to the other side. Listing 12-9 shows what it looks like.

Listing 12-9. *After a Successful Start of the VPN, a tun Device Is Added to the Server*

```
root@mel:/etc/openvpn# ifconfig tun0
tun0      Link encap:UNSPEC  HWaddr 00-00-00-00-00-00-00-00-00-00-00-00-00-00-00-00
          inet addr:10.8.0.1  P-t-P:10.8.0.2  Mask:255.255.255.255
          UP POINTOPOINT RUNNING NOARP MULTICAST  MTU:1500  Metric:1
          RX packets:0 errors:0 dropped:0 overruns:0 frame:0
          TX packets:0 errors:0 dropped:0 overruns:0 carrier:0
          collisions:0 txqueuelen:100
          RX bytes:0 (0.0 B)  TX bytes:0 (0.0 B)
```

Configuring a Linux VPN Client

Now that the server is configured successfully, it's time to create the client configuration. Let's start with a Ubuntu desktop client first. Before you configure it, make sure that the required software is installed. Install the OpenVPN package just as you have done on the server. For instance, you can use sudo apt-get install openvpn to install it from the command line. There is no need to do anything with the keys, because you have already copied them to the client.

Note In this procedure, you have created the client keys on the server. An alternative method is to create them on the client and then issue a certificate signing request from the client to the server. This requires more work, but because the private key is created on the client computer and never leaves the client computer, it is also considered a more secure method. Consult Chapter 11 for more information about this procedure.

As on the server, you can use the sample client.conf file from /usr/share/doc/openvpn/examples/sample-config-files. In this sample file, you must change the names of the key files you are referring to. Also, you should include the correct address of the VPN server. Normally, this is a public IP address that can be reached on the Internet. Before the client sets up the VPN connection, the client must contact this public address to set up the connection. Figure 12-2 gives an overview of how the public IP address is used to set up the VPN connection.

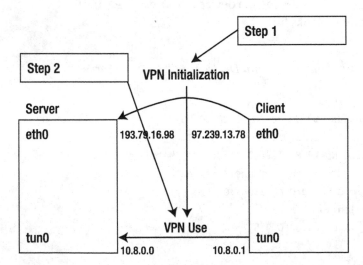

Figure 12-2. *To initialize the VPN connection, the client first contacts the public IP address of the server.*

Listing 12-10 shows an example of what the client configuration file looks like. In this file, I used an IP address from the private address range to contact the server. I did this because, in my test environment, I created the VPN connection over my private network. This can be useful if for some reason you don't completely trust the private network. Normally, however, this would be the public IP address of the server.

Listing 12-10. *Example Client Configuration File*

```
root@MYL:/etc/openvpn# cat client.conf
client
remote 192.168.1.99
port 1194
proto udp
dev tun
resolv-retry infinite
nobind
ca /etc/openvpn/keys/ca.crt
cert /etc/openvpn/keys/myl.crt
key /etc/openvpn/keys/myl.key
keepalive 10 120
user nobody
group nogroup
persist-key
persist-tun
status /var/log/openvpn-status.log
verb 3
mute 20
comp-lzo
```

Now use the openvpn command to test the connection:

```
openvpn --config /etc/openvpn/client.conf
```

In its verbose output, this command shows whether it has been successful. An example is provided in Listing 12-11.

Listing 12-11. *Starting the Client Manually on the First Attempt Shows Whether It Was Successful*

```
root@MYL:/etc/openvpn/keys# openvpn --config /etc/openvpn/client.conf
Tue Aug 26 11:32:43 2008 OpenVPN 2.1_rc7 i486-pc-linux-gnu [SSL] ➡
[LZO2] [EPOLL] built on Jun 11 2008
Tue Aug 26 11:32:43 2008 WARNING: No server certificate verification ➡
method has been enabled.  See http://openvpn.net/howto.html#mitm for more info.
Tue Aug 26 11:32:43 2008 /usr/bin/openssl-vulnkey -q -b 1024 -m <modulus omitted>
Tue Aug 26 11:32:43 2008 LZO compression initialized
Tue Aug 26 11:32:43 2008 Control Channel MTU parms [ L:1542 D:138 ➡
EF:38 EB:0 ET:0 EL:0 ]
Tue Aug 26 11:32:43 2008 Data Channel MTU parms [ L:1542 D:1450 EF:42 ➡
EB:135 ET:0 EL:0 AF:3/1 ]
Tue Aug 26 11:32:43 2008 Local Options hash (VER=V4): '41690919'
Tue Aug 26 11:32:43 2008 Expected Remote Options hash (VER=V4): '530fdded'
Tue Aug 26 11:32:43 2008 NOTE: UID/GID downgrade will be delayed ➡
because of --client, --pull, or --up-delay
Tue Aug 26 11:32:43 2008 Socket Buffers: R=[110592->131072] S=[110592->131072]
Tue Aug 26 11:32:43 2008 UDPv4 link local: [undef]
Tue Aug 26 11:32:43 2008 UDPv4 link remote: 192.168.1.99:1194
Tue Aug 26 11:32:43 2008 TLS: Initial packet from 192.168.1.99:1194,➡
 sid=a2338f7c 329dacc8
Tue Aug 26 11:32:43 2008 VERIFY OK: depth=1,➡
/C=NL/ST=NB/L=Roosendaal/O=sander/CN=sander_CA/emailAddress=mail@sander.fr
Tue Aug 26 11:32:43 2008 VERIFY OK: depth=0, ➡
/C=NL/ST=NB/L=Roosendaal/O=sander/CN=mel/emailAddress=mail@sander.fr
Tue Aug 26 11:32:43 2008 Data Channel Encrypt: Cipher 'BF-CBC' ➡
initialized with 128 bit key
Tue Aug 26 11:32:43 2008 Data Channel Encrypt: Using 160 bit message ➡
hash 'SHA1' for HMAC authentication
Tue Aug 26 11:32:43 2008 Data Channel Decrypt: Cipher 'BF-CBC' ➡
initialized with 128 bit key
Tue Aug 26 11:32:43 2008 Data Channel Decrypt: Using 160 bit message ➡
hash 'SHA1' for HMAC authentication
Tue Aug 26 11:32:43 2008 Control Channel: TLSv1, cipher TLSv1/SSLv3 ➡
DHE-RSA-AES256-SHA, 1024 bit RSA
Tue Aug 26 11:32:43 2008 [mel] Peer Connection Initiated with 192.168.1.99:1194
Tue Aug 26 11:32:44 2008 SENT CONTROL [mel]: 'PUSH_REQUEST' (status=1)
```

```
Tue Aug 26 11:32:44 2008 PUSH: Received control message:➥
 'PUSH_REPLY,route 10.8.0.1,topology net30,ping 10,ping-restart➥
 120,ifconfig 10.8.0.6 10.8.0.5'
Tue Aug 26 11:32:44 2008 OPTIONS IMPORT: timers and/or timeouts modified
Tue Aug 26 11:32:44 2008 OPTIONS IMPORT: --ifconfig/up options modified
Tue Aug 26 11:32:44 2008 OPTIONS IMPORT: route options modified
Tue Aug 26 11:32:44 2008 TUN/TAP device tun0 opened
Tue Aug 26 11:32:44 2008 TUN/TAP TX queue length set to 100
Tue Aug 26 11:32:44 2008 ifconfig tun0 10.8.0.6 pointopoint 10.8.0.5 mtu 1500
Tue Aug 26 11:32:44 2008 route add -net 10.8.0.1 netmask 255.255.255.255 gw 10.8.0.5
Tue Aug 26 11:32:44 2008 GID set to nogroup
Tue Aug 26 11:32:44 2008 UID set to nobody
Tue Aug 26 11:32:44 2008 Initialization Sequence Completed
```

If the client has started successfully, use Ctrl+C to stop it again. Next, you can start it using its init script: /etc/init.d/openvpn start. After a successful start, you now have a tun0 interface at the client as well. By monitoring this interface, you can get more details about the VPN connection, such as the IP address of the server and the number of packets sent over the VPN connection (see Listing 12-12).

Listing 12-12. *The tun0 Interface on the Client Shows Status Information About the VPN Connection*

```
root@MYL:/etc/openvpn/keys# ifconfig tun0
tun0      Link encap:UNSPEC  HWaddr 00-00-00-00-00-00-00-00-00-00-00-00-00-00-00-00
          inet addr:10.8.0.6  P-t-P:10.8.0.5  Mask:255.255.255.255
          UP POINTOPOINT RUNNING NOARP MULTICAST  MTU:1500  Metric:1
          RX packets:0 errors:0 dropped:0 overruns:0 frame:0
          TX packets:0 errors:0 dropped:0 overruns:0 carrier:0
          collisions:0 txqueuelen:100
          RX bytes:0 (0.0 B)  TX bytes:0 (0.0 B)
```

By initializing the VPN connection, your routing configuration has also been changed. Changing the routing configuration makes sure that all packets destined for the VPN host are sent to the VPN host, whereas packets destined for the Internet or other networks follow the default route to your normal gateway. Listing 12-13 shows what routing looks like after initializing a VPN connection on the client.

Listing 12-13. *By Initializing the VPN, Routing Is Modified Automatically*

```
root@MYL:/etc/openvpn/keys# route -n
Kernel IP routing table
Destination     Gateway         Genmask         Flags Metric Ref    Use Iface
10.8.0.5        0.0.0.0         255.255.255.255 UH    0      0        0 tun0
10.8.0.1        10.8.0.5        255.255.255.255 UGH   0      0        0 tun0
192.168.1.0     0.0.0.0         255.255.255.0   U     0      0        0 eth0
169.254.0.0     0.0.0.0         255.255.0.0     U     1000   0        0 eth0
0.0.0.0         192.168.1.254   0.0.0.0         UG    0      0        0 eth0
```

Configuring Windows Clients

OpenVPN is available for Windows clients as well. First, you need to create keys for this client as well. To do this, follow the procedure described earlier in this chapter in the section "Generating Certificates." To get the Windows client, download the graphical installer from http://openvpn.se. Install the program and then copy keys and certificates to the directory c:\program files\OpenVPN\keys. In this directory, you should also create the client configuration file for your Windows machine. The name client.opvn is fine. You can see an example of its contents in Listing 12-14.

Note On Windows, some of the extensions that OpenVPN uses are different.

Listing 12-14. *Example Contents for client.opvn on Windows*

```
ca v:\\Program\ Files\\openvpn\keys\\ca.crt
cert c:\\Program\ Files\\openvpn\keys\\client.crt
key c:\\Program\ Files\\openvpn\\keys\\client.key
ns-cert-type server
tls-auth c:\\Program\ Files\\openvpn\\keys\\ta.key 1
comp-lzo
verb 3
```

After you create the configuration file on Windows, right-click the OpenVPN icon in the taskbar (the red icon depicting two computers).

Summary

In this chapter you have learned how to set up a VPN connection, using the popular OpenVPN package. In the next chapter, you will learn how to set up Kerberos and NTP.

■■■

## CHAPTER 13

Configuring Kerberos and NTP on Ubuntu Server
Using an Alternative Method to Handle Authentication

The preceding two chapters explained how to use a public key infrastructure (PKI) to secure services. A PKI protects network traffic very well and can also be used for authentication. Kerberos was developed purely as an authentication service and not to protect network traffic. Kerberos has become an increasingly popular choice for authentication, particularly because Microsoft uses it in Active Directory environments, including in Linux implementations of Active Directory. In this chapter, you'll read how to set up Kerberos version 5 on Ubuntu Server. Because Kerberos heavily depends on proper time synchronization, I'll first explain how to set up an NTP time server.

Configuring an NTP Time Server

To use Kerberos for authentication, the nodes involved must agree on the time that is used. If there is too much time difference between the Kerberos server and the Kerberos client, authentication will be refused. Therefore, it is a good idea to set up an NTP time server first. Once you have done that, you need to choose between the two Kerberos versions that are available: MIT Kerberos, which is the original Kerberos that was developed by the Massachusetts Institute of Technology, and Heimdal Kerberos, which was meant to be an improvement on MIT Kerberos but has never become very popular on Linux. For that reason, this chapter covers how to set up MIT Kerberos, version 5 in particular, which is the current version. Version 4 has some major security problems, so you should not use that version; use version 5 only.

For many networked applications (Heartbeat clustering, for example, introduced in Chapter 7), knowing the correct time is essential for proper operation. On the Internet, the Network Time Protocol (NTP) is the de facto standard for time synchronization. In this section, you'll learn how to configure your server as an NTP time server as well as an NTP client. This section covers the following subjects:

- How NTP works

- Configuring a stand-alone NTP time server

- Configuring your server to fetch its time from a time-reference source

- Tuning NTP operation

How NTP Works

The basic idea of NTP is that all servers on the Internet can synchronize time with one another. In this way, a global time can be established so that only minimal differences exist in the time setting on different servers. To reach this goal, all servers agree upon the same time, no matter what time zone they are in. This time is known as Universal Time Coordinated (UTC): a server receives its time in UTC and then calculates its local time from that by using its time zone setting.

Synchronizing time with other servers in an NTP hierarchy relies on the concept of stratums. Every server in the NTP hierarchy has a stratum setting between 1 and 15, inclusive, or 16 if the clock is not currently synchronized at all. The highest stratum level that a clock can use is 1. Typically, this is a server that's connected directly to an atomic clock that has a very high degree of accuracy. The stratum level that is assigned to a server that's directly connected to an external clock depends on the type of clock that's used. In general, though, the more reliable the clock is, the higher the stratum level will be.

A server can get its time in two different ways: by synchronizing with another NTP time server or by using a reference clock. If a server synchronizes with an NTP time server, the stratum used on that server will be determined by the server it's synchronizing with: if a server synchronizes with a stratum 3 time server, it automatically becomes a stratum 4 time server.

To specify what time your server is using, you have to edit the /etc/default/rcS configuration file, in which you'll find the UTC= setting. To use UTC on your server, make sure its value is set to yes; if you don't want to use UTC, set it to UTC=no. The latter choice is reasonable only in an environment in which all servers are in the same local time zone.

The local time zone setting is maintained in the /etc/localtime binary file, which is created upon installation and contains information about your local time zone. To change it afterward, you need to create a link to the configuration file that contains information on your local time zone. You can find these configuration files in /usr/share/

zoneinfo. Next, link the appropriate file to the /etc/localtime file. For example, sudo ln -sf /usr/share/zoneinfo/MET /etc/localtime changes your local time zone setting to Middle European Time (MET).

If, on the other hand, a reference clock is used, a server does not get its time from a server on the Internet but instead determines its own time. Again, the default stratum used is determined by the type and brand of reference clock that's used. If it's a very reliable clock, such as one synchronized via GPS, the default stratum setting will be high. If a less reliable clock (such as the local clock in a computer) is used, the default stratum will be lower.

If a server gets its time from the Internet, it makes sense to use Internet time and use a very trustworthy time server. If no Internet connection is available, use an internal clock and set the stratum accordingly (which means lower). If you're using your computer's internal clock, for example, it makes sense to use a low stratum level, such as 5.

Configuring a Stand-Alone NTP Time Server

Just two elements are needed to make your own NTP time server: the configuration file and the daemon process. First, make sure that all required software is installed, by running apt-get install ntp-server as root. Next, start the daemon process, ntpd, by using the /etc/init.d/ntpd startup script. After you change the settings in the daemon's configuration file, /etc/ntp.conf, to make the daemon work properly in your environment, you can start the daemon process manually by using /etc/init.d/ntp start.

The content of the NTP configuration file /etc/ntp.conf really doesn't have to be very complex. Basically, you just need three lines to create an NTP time server, as shown in Listing 13-1.

Listing 13-1. *Example ntp.conf Configuration*

```
server 127.127.1.0
fudge 127.127.1.0      stratum 10
server ntp.yourprovider.somewhere
```

The first line in Listing 13-1 specifies what server the NTP daemon should use if the connection with the NTP time server is lost for a long period of time (specified in advanced settings); this line makes sure that the local clock in your server will not drift too much, by making a reference to a local clock. Every type of local clock has its own IP address from the range of loopback IP addresses. The format of this address is 127.127.<t>.<i>, where the third byte refers to the type of local clock that is used and the fourth byte refers to the instance of the clock your server is connected to. The default address to use to refer to the local computer clock is 127.127.1.0. Notice that all clocks that can be used as an external reference clock connected locally to your server have their own IP address. The documentation for your clock tells you what address to use.

Tip Even if your server is connected to an NTP server that's directly on the Internet, it makes sense to use at least one local external reference clock on your network as well, to ensure that time synchronization continues if the Internet connection fails for a long period of time.

The second line in Listing 13-1 defines what should happen if the server falls back to the local external reference clock specified in the first line. This line starts with the keyword fudge to indicate an abnormal situation. Here, the local clock should be used, and the server sets its stratum level to 10. By using this stratum, the server indicates that it's not very trustworthy but that it can be used as a time source if necessary.

The last line in Listing 13-1 shows what should happen under normal circumstances. This line normally refers to an IP address or a server name on the network of the Internet service provider. As long as the connection with the NTP time server is fine, this line specifies the default behavior.

Pulling or Pushing the Time

An NTP time server can perform its work in two different ways: by pushing (broadcasting) time across the network, or by allowing other servers to pull the time from it. In the default setting, the NTP server that gets its time from somewhere else regularly asks this server what time is used. When both nodes have their times synchronized, this setting will be incremented to a default value of 1,024 seconds. As an administrator, you can specify how often time needs to be synchronized by using the minpoll and maxpoll arguments on the line in /etc/ntp.conf that refers to the NTP time server, as shown in the example in Listing 13-2.

Listing 13-2. *Configuring the Synchronization Interval*

```
server 127.127.1.0
fudge 127.127.1.0 stratum 10
server ntp.provider.somewhere minpoll 4 maxpoll 15
```

The minpoll setting determines how often a client should try to synchronize its time if time is not properly synchronized, and the maxpoll value indicates how often synchronization should occur if time is properly synchronized. The values for the minpoll and maxpoll parameters are kind of weird logarithmically: they refer to the power of 2 that should be used. Therefore, minpoll 4 is actually 2^4 (which equals 16 seconds), and the default value of 1,024 seconds can be noted as minpoll 10 (2^{10}). Any value between 4 and 17, inclusive, can be used.

If you are configuring an NTP node as a server, you can use the broadcast mechanism as well. This makes sense if your server is used as the NTP time server for local computers that are on the same network (because broadcast packets are not forwarded by routers). If you want to do this, make sure the line broadcast 192.168.0.255 (use the broadcast address for your network) is included in the ntp.conf file on your server and that the broadcastclient setting is used on the client computer.

If you want to configure a secure NTP time server, you should think twice before configuring the broadcast setting. Typically, a broadcast client takes its time from any server in the network, as long as it broadcasts NTP packets on the default NTP port 123. Therefore, to change the time on all computers in your network, someone could introduce a bogus NTP time server with a very high stratum configured.

Configuring an NTP Client

The first thing to do when configuring a server to act as an NTP client is to make sure that the time is more or less accurate. If the difference is greater than 1,024 seconds, NTP considers the time source to be bogus and refuses to synchronize with it. Therefore, it's recommended that you synchronize time on the NTP client manually before continuing. To manually synchronize the time, the ntpdate command is very useful: use it to get time only once from another server that offers NTP services. To use it, specify the name or IP address of the server you want to synchronize with as its argument:

```
ntpdate ntp.yourprovider.somewhere
```

By using this command, you'll make a once-only time adjustment on the client computer. After that, you can set up ntpd for automatic synchronization on the client computer.

Caution   Too often, ntpdate is used only for troubleshooting purposes, after the administrator finds out that ntpd isn't synchronizing properly. In this case, the administrator is likely to see a "socket already in use" error message. This happens because ntpd has already claimed port 123 for NTP time synchronization. You can verify this with the netstat -platune | grep 123 command, which displays the application currently using port 123. Before ntpdate can be used successfully in this scenario, the administrator should make sure that ntpd is shut down on the client by using /etc/init.d/ntp stop.

If the time difference between server and client is not greater than 1,000 seconds, ntp.conf can be configured on the NTP client. A typical NTP client configuration is very simple—you just need to specify the server you want to get the time from, as in the following example:

```
server 192.168.0.10
```

You may also prefer to set a backup option by using the fudge option, but this is optional. Normally, I recommend that you don't set this option on every single server in the network that's using NTP. As an administrator, you might prefer to set this on one server in your network only and let all other NTP clients in your network get the time from that server. So, to create an NTP hierarchy, I recommend letting one or two servers in the network get their time from a reliable time source on the Internet, such as pool.ntp.org. Next, to ensure that an NTP time source is still available when the Internet connection goes down, use the fudge option on the same servers. Doing so ensures that they will still be the servers with the highest stratum level in your network, and time services will not be interrupted.

Checking NTP Synchronization Status

After you've started the NTP service on all computers in your network, you probably want to know whether it's working correctly. The first tool to use is the ntptrace command, which provides an overview of the current synchronization status. When using ntptrace, you should be aware that it will always take some time to establish NTP synchronization. The delay occurs because an NTP client normally synchronizes only every 16 seconds, and it may fail to establish correct synchronization the first time it tries. Normally, however, it should take no longer than a few minutes to establish NTP time synchronization.

Another tool to tune the working of NTP is the ntpq command, which offers its own interactive interface from which the status of any NTP service can be requested. As when using the FTP client, you can use a couple of commands to "remotely control" the NTP server. In this interface, you can use the help command to see a list of available commands.

As an alternative, you can run ntpq with some command-line options. For example, the ntpq -p command gives an overview of current synchronization status. Listing 13-3 provides an example of the result, in which several parameters are displayed:

- remote: The name of the other server

- refid: The IP address of the server you are synchronizing with

- st: The stratum used by the other server

- t: The type of clock used on the other server (L stands for local clock; u for an Internet clock)

- when: The number of seconds since the last poll

- poll: The number of seconds used between two polls

- reach: The number of times the other server has been contacted successfully

- delay: The time between an NTP request and the answer

- offset: The difference, in seconds, between the time on your local computer and that on the NTP server

- jitter: The error rate in your local clock, expressed in seconds

Listing 13-3. *Use ntpq -p to Slow the Current Synchronization Status on Your Server*

```
root@RNA:~# ntpq -p
     remote           refid      st t when poll reach   delay   offset  jitter
==============================================================================
 fiordland.ubunt 192.36.133.17    2 u   10   64    1    2.247  -357489   0.002
```

Customizing Your NTP Server

Thus far, I have explained the basic NTP time configuration, but you can also fine-tune the configuration to guarantee a higher degree of precision. There are several files that you can use for this purpose. First are the files that are created automatically by the NTP daemon. Next, there are some security settings in ntp.conf that you can use to limit which servers are allowed to get time from your server. In this section, you'll read about fine-tuning the NTP drift file and NTP log file and applying NTP security.

Configuring the NTP Drift File

No matter how secure the local clock on your computer is, it's always going to be slightly off: either too fast or too slow. For example, a clock might lag behind NTP time by 2 seconds every hour. This difference is referred to as the clock's drift factor, and it's calculated by comparing the local clock with the clock on the server that provides NTP time to the local machine. Because NTP is designed also to synchronize time when the connection to the NTP time server is lost, the NTP process on your local computer must know what this drift factor is. So, to calculate the right setting for the drift factor, it's very important that an accurate time is being used on the server with which you are synchronizing.

Once NTP time synchronization has been established, a drift file is created automatically. On Ubuntu Server, this file is created in /var/lib/ntp/ntp.drift, and the local NTP process uses it to calculate the exact drifting of your local clock, which thus allows it to compensate for the drift. Because the drift file is created automatically, you don't need to worry about it. However, you can choose where the file is created by using the `driftfile` parameter in `ntp.conf`:

```
driftfile /var/lib/ntp/ntp.drift
```

Note Remember that NTP is a daemon. Like most daemons, it reads its configuration file only when it's first started. So, after all modifications, use `/etc/init.d/ntpd restart` to make sure that the modifications are applied to your current configuration.

Configuring the NTP Log File

The NTP log file is another file that's created automatically for you. Like all other log files, this file is very important because it allows you to see exactly what has happened when something goes awry. If time is synchronized properly, it's not the most interesting log file on your system: it just tells you that synchronization has been established and what server is used for synchronization. After installation, Ubuntu Server is not set up to create an individual log file for time services, but you can change that by using the `logfile` statement in `/etc/ntp.conf`. This may be a good idea if you want to change the messages generated by the time server from the generic messages in `/var/log/messages`.

```
logfile  /var/log/ntp
```

Applying NTP Security

If your NTP server is connected to the Internet, you may want to restrict access to it. If no restrictions are applied, the entire world can access your NTP server. If you don't like that idea, add some lines to `ntp.conf`, as shown in Listing 13-4.

Listing 13-4. *Applying Security Restrictions to Your NTP Time Server*

```
restrict default noquery notrust nomodify
restrict 127.0.0.1
restrict 192.168.0.0 mask 255.255.255.0
```

Note Some Linux distributions configure their NTP service in such a way that no one can access it. Having problems getting time from a server? Make sure that at least some minimal restrictions are in place that allow other servers to use the server in question as an NTP server.

The restrict settings prevent inappropriate conduct of clients. The first line of Listing 13-4 specifies what exactly is considered inappropriate. First, it allows the default settings for accessing the server. Next, it disallows three types of packets, using noquery, notrust, and nomodify. Disallowing these packets ensures that no contact whatsoever is allowed for NTP clients. In the second and third lines of Listing 13-4, exceptions to these settings are created for the local NTP service and all computers in the network 192.168.0.0. Add a similar restrict line for every IP address or range of IP addresses that has to be allowed to use your NTP server.

Understanding Kerberos

Before you start to configure Kerberos, you need to know more about how it functions. Too many people try to configure it without understanding what they are doing, and that simply doesn't work. When MIT developed Kerberos, it had three design goals in mind:

- Find an alternative for passwords circulating on the network

- Manage access rights to services

- Deal with user databases

Kerberos version 5 fulfills all three design goals. Of these, the most interesting is how Kerberos deals with passwords. No passwords are ever stored locally on a machine, no matter whether that machine is a server or a workstation. This greatly reduces your risks when your machine gets hacked, and that is also the most important reason why many Linux services currently are available in a Kerberized version, which is a version that uses Kerberos instead of the normal authentication mechanism.

In a Kerberos environment, three parties play a role:

- Client

- Service

- Key Distribution Center (KDC)

These three parties mutually trust one another, because they are in the same *realm*, a trusted environment set up by an administrator. A Kerberos session always begins with the user logging in to the KDC. The KDC has a database with password hashes (so it doesn't know the actual user passwords). When authenticating, the user creates a hash that is based on his password. By comparing the hashes, the KDC can verify that the user has entered the correct password. If this is the case, the KDC gives the user a Ticket Granting Ticket (TGT).

Next, the user uses the TGT to get access to services. The KDC again plays an important role, because it grants a session ticket for each of the services the user wants to connect to. Once this session ticket is obtained, the user can access related services for as long as he remains logged in.

Note The goal of this chapter is to help you configure Kerberos, not to make you an expert in Kerberos cryptography. Therefore, I have simplified this section a bit to make it easier to understand what is happening. You can find a good detailed explanation of Kerberos cryptography at `http://en.wikipedia.org/wiki/Kerberos_protocol`.

Installing and Configuring Kerberos

To install Kerberos on Ubuntu Server, you have to install several packages. Use `apt-get install` to install the packages `krb5-admin-server`, `krb5-kdc`, `krb5-config`, `krb5-user`, and `krb5-clients`. When you install the packages using `apt-get install krb5-admin-server krb5-kdc krb5-config krb5-user krb5-clients`, the installation program automatically starts a configuration program to create a realm and add servers to it. (Again, the Kerberos realm is the trusted environment shared by the different users and servers involved in Kerberos.) As the name of the realm, the installer takes your DNS suffix. If you don't like that choice, no problem, because you can change it later. The installer next asks you to list the servers you want to add to the realm (see Figure 13-1). You just need to enter the names of servers that you want to be KDC servers in this interface. You probably just want one server name here. Enter the name of this server and then proceed to the next screen.

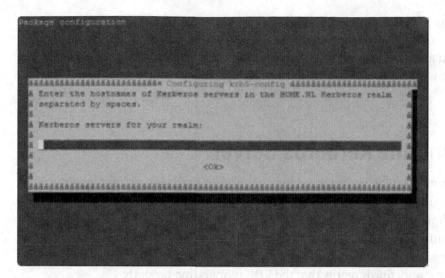

Figure 13-1. *The installation program helps you to set up a Kerberos realm.*

In the realm, you will have one server that is used as the administrative server. Enter the name of the server that you want to use for that purpose (see Figure 13-2) and then proceed to the next screen.

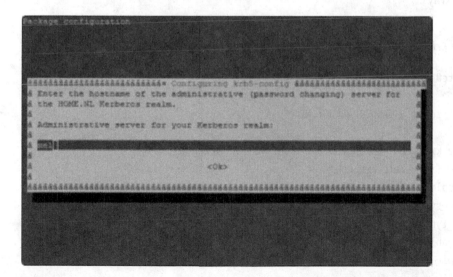

Figure 13-2. *One of the servers in the realm is used as the administrative server.*

While the installer is finishing the software installation, you may see an error generated by kadmind, complaining that it is missing a file. For now, ignore this error; you will fix it later when you are setting up Kerberos. The software installation is now completed and you have a basic working configuration. In the next section you'll read how to tune this configuration.

Configuring the Kerberos Server

There are two configuration files involved in configuring a Kerberos server: /etc/krb5. conf, which contains generic Kerberos configuration settings, and /etc/krb5kdc/kdc.conf, in which you'll find the configuration of the KDC. In this section, you'll first tune these two Kerberos configuration files. After that, you'll create the Kerberos database and the stash file; set up a Kerberos administrative user account for authentication purposes; add user accounts; and, finally, verify that the KDC is operating properly.

Configuring Generic Kerberos Settings

Listing 13-5 shows the contents of /etc/krb5.conf after installation of the Kerberos packages (for readability, I have removed some of the default sections that you probably don't need to see anyway).

Listing 13-5. *The krb5.conf Configuration File Just After Kerberos Installation*

```
root@ubuntu:/etc# cat krb5.conf
[libdefaults]
        default_realm = SANDERVANVUGT.NL

# The following krb5.conf variables are only for MIT Kerberos.
        krb4_config = /etc/krb.conf
        krb4_realms = /etc/krb.realms
        kdc_timesync = 1
        ccache_type = 4
        forwardable = true
        proxiable = true

# The following encryption type specification will be used by MIT Kerberos
# if uncommented.  In general, the defaults in the MIT Kerberos code are
# correct and overriding these specifications only serves to disable new
# encryption types as they are added, creating interoperability problems.
```

```
# default_tgs_enctypes = aes256-cts arcfour-hmac-md5 des3-hmac-sha1\
 des-cbc-crc des-cbc-md5
# default_tkt_enctypes = aes256-cts arcfour-hmac-md5 des3-hmac-sha1\
 des-cbc-crc des-cbc-md5
# permitted_enctypes = aes256-cts arcfour-hmac-md5 des3-hmac-sha1\
 des-cbc-crc des-cbc-md5


# The following libdefaults parameters are only for Heimdal Kerberos.
        v4_instance_resolve = false
        v4_name_convert = {
                host = {
                        rcmd = host
                        ftp = ftp
                }
                plain = {
                        something = something-else
                }
        }
        fcc-mit-ticketflags = true


[realms]
        SANDERVANVUGT.NL = {
                kdc = mel
                kdc = myl
                kdc = ubuntu
                admin_server = mel
        }
        ATHENA.MIT.EDU = {
                kdc = kerberos.mit.edu:88
                kdc = kerberos-1.mit.edu:88
                kdc = kerberos-2.mit.edu:88
                admin_server = kerberos.mit.edu
                default_domain = mit.edu
        }
        MEDIA-LAB.MIT.EDU = {
...
        CS.CMU.EDU = {
                kdc = kerberos.cs.cmu.edu
                kdc = kerberos-2.srv.cs.cmu.edu
                admin_server = kerberos.cs.cmu.edu
        }
```

```
        DEMENTIA.ORG = {
                kdc = kerberos.dementia.org
                kdc = kerberos2.dementia.org
                admin_server = kerberos.dementia.org
        }
        stanford.edu = {
                kdc = krb5auth1.stanford.edu
                kdc = krb5auth2.stanford.edu
                kdc = krb5auth3.stanford.edu
                admin_server = krb5-admin.stanford.edu
                default_domain = stanford.edu
        }

[domain_realm]
        .mit.edu = ATHENA.MIT.EDU
        mit.edu = ATHENA.MIT.EDU
        .media.mit.edu = MEDIA-LAB.MIT.EDU
        media.mit.edu = MEDIA-LAB.MIT.EDU
        .csail.mit.edu = CSAIL.MIT.EDU
        csail.mit.edu = CSAIL.MIT.EDU
        .whoi.edu = ATHENA.MIT.EDU
        whoi.edu = ATHENA.MIT.EDU
        .stanford.edu = stanford.edu

[login]
        krb4_convert = true
        krb4_get_tickets = false
```

The following are the sections that you might want to edit in the default configuration file shown in Listing 13-5:

- [libdefaults]: Defines the name of your realm. If you want to change the name, change it here.

- [realms]: Defines the realm itself, based on the name that is used in [libdefaults]. By default, you'll find two different kinds of lines: the kdc lines are used to define the servers that can be used as KDC servers, and the admin_server line defines which of the servers has administrative privileges. If you need to add new servers to your Kerberos configuration, do it here. As you can see, some default realms are included as well. You don't need them, so you can remove them if you prefer.

- [domain_realm]: Contains a list of DNS domains and their corresponding Kerberos realms. This section is useful to connect realms that are not in your own company. As you see, your current realm is not added here automatically. You should fix that, by adding two lines to the bottom of this section. In my case, I added the following two lines to make a mapping between DNS and the Kerberos realm:

```
sandervanvugt.nl = SANDERVANVUGT.NL
.sandervanvugt.nl = SANDERVANVUGT.NL
```

• [login]: Contains some default settings that are used in the authentication procedure. Of all these parameters, normally you don't need to change many. Just make sure that the realm name is the name you want to use and that all KDC servers are listed.

Configuring the KDC Settings

The second configuration file, /etc/krb5kdc/kdc.conf, contains default settings for the KDC. Listing 13-6 shows its default configuration right after installation of the Kerberos packages on Ubuntu Server.

Listing 13-6. *kdc.conf Contains Default Settings for the KDC*

```
root@ubuntu:/etc/krb5kdc# cat kdc.conf
[kdcdefaults]
    kdc_ports = 750,88

[realms]
    SANDERVANVUGT.NL = {
        database_name = /var/lib/krb5kdc/principal
        admin_keytab = FILE:/etc/krb5kdc/kadm5.keytab
        acl_file = /etc/krb5kdc/kadm5.acl
        key_stash_file = /etc/krb5kdc/stash
        kdc_ports = 750,88
        max_life = 10h 0m 0s
        max_renewable_life = 7d 0h 0m 0s
        master_key_type = des3-hmac-sha1
        supported_enctypes = des3-hmac-sha1:normal des-cbc-crc:normal➥
des:normal des:v4 des:norealm des:onlyrealm des:afs3
        default_principal_flags = +preauth
    }
```

In the kdc.conf file, the [realms] section defines settings for each of your realms, with the name of your realm in all uppercase letters. All particular settings for that realm are listed between curly brackets. As you can see in Listing 13-6, basically they are just lists of where to find certain files. In this file also, you normally don't have to change much to get a working Kerberos server.

Creating the Kerberos Database and the Stash File

After you have set up the configuration files properly, it's time to create the Kerberos database and the stash file. The stash file contains a local encrypted copy of the master key and is used to automatically authenticate the KDC when your server boots. To protect the stash file, you need to enter a password twice when creating it.

Listing 13-7 shows an example of creating the configuration using the kdb5_util create -s command. If you want to create the configuration files for a different realm, use -r realm to specify the name of the realm you want to create them for. For instance, kdb5_util -r myrealm -s would initialize the configuration for a realm with the name myrealm.

Listing 13-7. *To Initialize the Kerberos Configuration, Use krdb5_util create -s*

```
root@ubuntu:~# kdb5_util create -s
Loading random data
Initializing database '/var/lib/krb5kdc/principal' for realm 'SANDERVANVUGT.NL',
master key name 'K/M@SANDERVANVUGT.NL'
You will be prompted for the database Master Password.
It is important that you NOT FORGET this password.
Enter KDC database master key:
Re-enter KDC database master key to verify:
```

As the result of this command, various files are created in the directory /var/lib/krb5kdc: the Kerberos database in the files principal.db and principal.ok, the administrative database in principal.kadm5, the database lock file in principal.kadm5.lock, and the stash file in .k5stash. One file is not created automatically, kdadm.acl, which contains access control lists for your Kerberos configuration. Create it in /etc/krb5kdc and give it the following contents:

```
*/admin#YOURREALM.WHATEVER
```

For instance, in my case, this would be */admin#SANDERVANVUGT.NL.

Starting Kerberos and Creating an Administrative User Account

Now that you have set up Kerberos, make sure that it is started. On Ubuntu Server, Kerberos is managed with two scripts in /etc/init.d: krb5-admin-server and krb5-kdc. If your server is both a KDC server and the administrative server, restart both of these services, as follows. If your server is just a KDC server, you only need the last of these two lines.

```
/etc/init.d/krb5-admin-server restart
/etc/init.d/krb5-kdc restart
```

One of the first things you need to configure is a Kerberos administrative user account that you can use for authentication purposes. To create this account, you'll use the addprinc command from the kadmin.local interface. So at this point, first enter the command kadmin.local. Make sure that the user you create is added to the admin group. You can do that by using a slash between the user and the group name when creating it; addprinc sander/admin would create a user with the name sander and put that user in the admin group. Listing 13-8 shows all commands that are required to set up such an administrative user account.

Note In Kerberos, you don't create "user accounts," you create "principals." A principal is something that can log in. Principals can be users or workstations. In this discussion, I prefer to stick with the traditional Linux terminology, "user accounts."

Listing 13-8. *Setting Up an Administrative User Account*

```
root@ubuntu:/etc/init.d# kadmin.local
Authenticating as principal root/admin@SANDERVANVUGT.NL with password.
kadmin.local:  addprinc sander/admin
WARNING: no policy specified for sander/admin@SANDERVANVUGT.NL; ➥
 defaulting to no policy
Enter password for principal "sander/admin@SANDERVANVUGT.NL":
Re-enter password for principal "sander/admin@SANDERVANVUGT.NL":
Principal "sander/admin@SANDERVANVUGT.NL" created.
kadmin.local: quit
```

Adding User Accounts

Now that the Kerberos server is configured and operational, it's time to add user accounts. This is something that you must do for all users you want to be capable of using Kerberos. To do this, you can use the kadmin.local command. Listing 13-9 shows how this command is used to add an account for user sander. This account must be added in order to use the administrative user sander (created in Listing 13-8) for administration purposes.

Listing 13-9. *Use kadmin.local to Add User Accounts to Your Kerberos Configuration*

```
root@ubuntu:/etc/krb5kdc# kadmin.local
Authenticating as principal root/admin@SANDERVANVUGT.NL with password.
kadmin.local:  addprinc sander
WARNING: no policy specified for sander@SANDERVANVUGT.NL; defaulting to no policy
Enter password for principal "sander@SANDERVANVUGT.NL":
Re-enter password for principal "sander@SANDERVANVUGT.NL":
Principal "sander@SANDERVANVUGT.NL" created.
kadmin.local:  q
```

Verifying that the KDC Is Operational

So far, you have set up your Kerberos server, but you haven't tested whether it really works. That's going to change now. First, you are going to use the kinit command, followed by your username, to get a Ticket Granting Ticket from the KDC. Next, you are going to use the klist command to see if you have obtained this TGT. Listing 13-10 shows the result of these two commands.

Listing 13-10. *Use kinit and klist to Verify Your KDC Is Operational*

```
root@mel:~# kinit sander
Password for sander@SANDERVANVUGT.NL:
root@mel:~# klist
Ticket cache: FILE:/tmp/krb5cc_0
Default principal: sander@SANDERVANVUGT.NL

Valid starting     Expires            Service principal
09/01/08 07:35:20  09/01/08 17:35:20  krbtgt/SANDERVANVUGT.NL@SANDERVANVUGT.NL
        renew until 09/02/08 07:35:18


Kerberos 4 ticket cache: /tmp/tkt0
klist: You have no tickets cached
```

Configuring the Kerberos Client

Now that you've set up the Kerberos server, it is time to configure the client. A "client" in this context is a service that uses Kerberos services. Basically, that means that the Kerberos client uses some application that talks to the KDC to handle authentication. First, I explain how to configure the `rsh` and `rlogin` services as Kerberos clients. Because I intend simply to demonstrate how configuring a Kerberos client works, I've chosen two easy-to-configure applications. After that, you'll read how to handle authentication with a Kerberos server.

Configuring Simple Kerberos Applications

Setting up a simple Kerberos application requires the following steps:

1. Make sure that each client has a `krb5.conf` configuration file that contains valid settings and shows the client where to find the realm and its associated KDC servers. Normally, this is the same file as the `krb5.conf` file on the KDC, so you can just copy and use that.

2. Install the Kerberos packages on the client. Use the package manager on your client to set this up. On Ubuntu Desktop Edition, it is a good start to install the `krb5-user` and `krb5-client` packages.

Tip For an initial Kerberos test, it is a good idea to use the Remote Shell (`rsh`) service. This service is easy to configure and completely Kerberized (and therefore secure). Make sure that on your server the package `krb5-rsh-server` is installed, and install `krb5-user` on the client to configure this service.

---

3. To start the Kerberized versions of your software (`rsh` and `rlogin` in this example), start them with `xinetd`.

4. On the server, you need to add an account for your server. Assuming the name of your server is `blah.example.com`, use the following command from the `kadmin.local` interface on your KDC server:

   ```
   addprinc -randkey host/blah.example.com
   ```

5. Start all services on your server that use Kerberos. They will use the Kerberos configuration automatically.

Logging In with Kerberos

Okay, you likely haven't set up Kerberos to use a Kerberized version of rsh, have you? Let's talk about the real work now and see what you need to do to enable a workstation to log in using Kerberos. Because I can't possibly provide a generic login procedure that works on all Linux distributions, you may encounter differences with regard to the names of files and services as you work through the following procedure, which describes how to use Kerberos for login authentication on Ubuntu Desktop Edition. The steps in this section assume that you have already performed a basic Kerberos configuration on the client computer, as described in the preceding section.

1. Make a connection between the PAM login service and Kerberos, by including in /etc/krb5.conf an [appdefaults] section that defines how to use PAM. Listing 13-11 shows an example.

   Listing 13-11. *PAM Settings in krb5.conf*

   ```
   [appdefaults]
           pam = {
                   debug = false
                   ticket_lifetime = 36000
                   renew_lifetime = 36000
                   forwardable = true
                   hosts = mel.sandervanvugt.nl
                   max_timeout = 30
                   timeout_shift = 2
                   initial_timeout = 1
           }
   ```

2. Install the PAM modules for Kerberos support if they not already installed. On Ubuntu Desktop Edition, the name of the module is libpam-krb5. Use your favorite package manager to install it (for instance, apt-get install libpam-krb5).

3. To make sure that Kerberos handles authentication for all PAM-enabled services, add a line to each of the four PAM files that are used by almost all authentication processes, as follows:

   - common-auth: Add the following line:

     ```
     auth            sufficient          /lib/security/pam_krb5.so
     ```

   - common-account: Add the following line:

     ```
     account     sufficient          /lib/security/pam_krb5.so
     ```

- common-session: Add the following line:

  ```
  session        optional           /lib/security/pam_krb5.so
  ```

- common-password: Add the following line:

  ```
  password    sufficient           /lib/security/pam_krb5.so use_authtok
  ```

These changes make sure that Kerberos is always tried first in all steps of the authentication process. If authentication using Kerberos fails, your server will fail back to normal passwd-based authentication.

4. At this point, your workstation can authenticate against the Kerberos KDC. You should now first try to authenticate without logging out (that makes troubleshooting easier if it fails). For instance, you could use the ssh localhost command for a quick and easy test. Use the Kerberos accounts that you created earlier on your server.

5. Did it work? Good! At this point, you have to create Kerberos accounts for all user accounts. Unfortunately, there is no good automated method to do this yet. On the Kerberos administrative server, use kadmin.local, and from there use addprinc to add your Kerberos user accounts.

Summary

Kerberos is an important technology that you can use for authentication purposes. In this chapter you read how to set up NTP (which is a requirement for Kerberos to work properly) and the Kerberos server. You also learned how to configure a Kerberos client and use some basic services that are Kerberos enabled. In the final and last chapter of this book, you'll learn how to troubleshoot Ubuntu Linux.

■ ■ ■

## CHAPTER 14

Ubuntu Server Troubleshooting
Fixing the Most Common Problems

Although Ubuntu Server is an extremely stable server operating system, you might encounter problems occasionally, ranging from a Linux-related issue to a simple hardware failure. In this chapter you'll learn how to troubleshoot some of the most common problems.

Some say troubleshooting is difficult and requires years of experience. Experience indeed helps, but a good analytical mind is the most important troubleshooting tool. In day-to-day troubleshooting, you first have to determine where exactly a given problem has occurred. If, for example, you have a problem with a kernel module, it doesn't make much sense to troubleshoot your web server.

After determining the location and scope of the problem as well as you can, you can apply your skills to fix the problem. This requires that you have a good understanding of how the erratic system component is supposed to function and can choose the correct tool to repair it. This chapter first explains how to determine where exactly a problem has occurred. Next, it introduces you to some of the best troubleshooting tools to use. Finally, this chapter identifies some of the most common problems and explains how to fix them.

Note This chapter assumes that you are familiar with basic principles of Ubuntu system administration. If you want to refresh your knowledge, try *Beginning Ubuntu LTS Server Administration, Second Edition*, in which I explain essential concepts such as the boot procedure and kernel management.

Identifying the Problem

The most common first step when trying to identify a problem is to reboot your server and wait until the problem occurs. Most problems reveal themselves as your server boots, because most services are activated during the boot process. Therefore, knowing the different stages of the boot process is very important. If you succeed in determining the stage in which a problem occurs, you have made a good start in troubleshooting the problem. The following list summarizes the different phases in the boot process:

1. *Hardware initialization*: Hardware initialization occurs during the Power On Self Test (POST). During this phase, your computer reads the BIOSes of the different hardware components and performs a check to see if all devices can initialize properly. If any of them can't initialize properly, you will not see the Grub prompt appear on your server and your server will warn you with clear error messages or beeps. If that happens, consult the documentation of your server to find out how to fix the hardware issue.

2. *Grub loading*: After initializing the hardware, the server accesses the boot device and reads the boot loader in the master boot record (MBR), which is the first sector of 512 bytes at the beginning of the bootable hard drive. The MBR includes two important components. First is the Grub boot loader. This system component is installed in the first 446 bytes of the MBR and makes sure that the operating system on your server can load. To do this, Grub accesses its configuration in the directory /boot/grub. Second in the MBR is the partition table. This component is essential for accessing all files on your server. If in this stage there is an error, you typically get a Grub error and, most important, the kernel will not start to load. If there is no error, you can access the Grub menu, displayed in Figure 14-1. So if you see that the kernel has started to load (see Figure 14-2), you know that your server has passed stages 1 and 2 successfully.

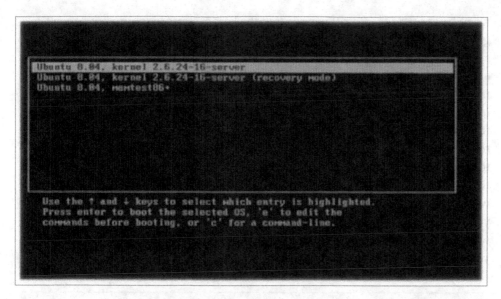

Figure 14-1. *If you see the Grub menu, the first 446 bytes of the MBR have been read.*

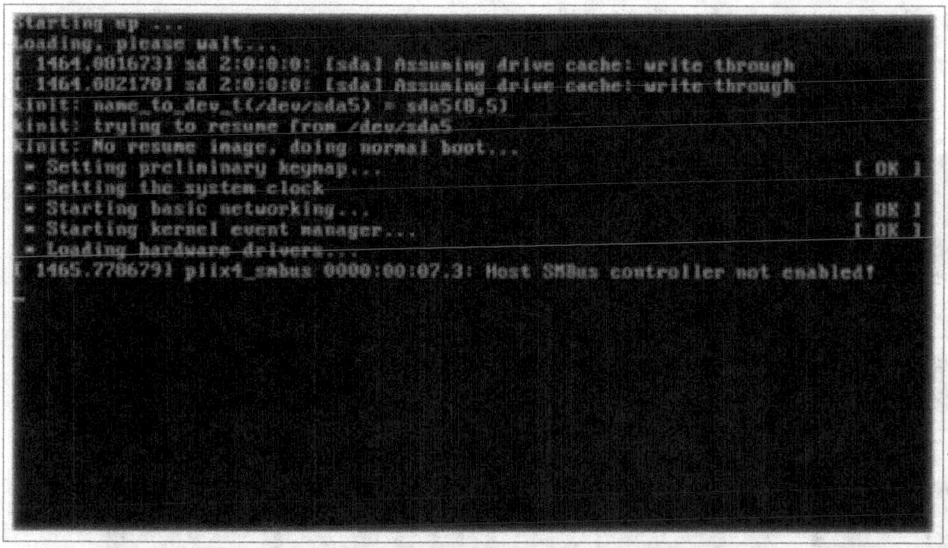

Figure 14-2. *The kernel has started to load, which indicates the first two stages of your server's boot procedure have completed successfully.*

3. *Kernel and initrd loading*: If you see that the kernel starts loading, that doesn't guarantee success with regard to the kernel and the ramfs image that contains some required drivers. It's possible that either the kernel itself or some of the drivers associated with the kernel still may not load. If that is the case, you will see the message "kernel panic" in most cases, or sometimes the kernel just stops loading, as in the example shown in Figure 14-3. Either way, you know for sure that the error is related to the kernel. You might get a kernel panic if you have tried to recompile the kernel and failed, or if one of the parameters that you have passed to Grub is wrong. A kernel panic can also be caused by a failing kernel module, but this is rare. So, if you've just recompiled your kernel and then get a kernel panic when you attempt to reboot, you know what is wrong (you did keep a copy of your old kernel, didn't you?). If you didn't recently recompile your kernel, check whether something has changed recently with regard to Grub parameters. If not, you may have a failing driver, or initrd.

■**Tip** Grub by default is configured not to show information about the kernel initialization. To make trouble-shooting easier, I recommend removing the line that reads `quiet` from the `/boot/grub/menu.lst` file. If you see a `splash=` statement, remove that as well.

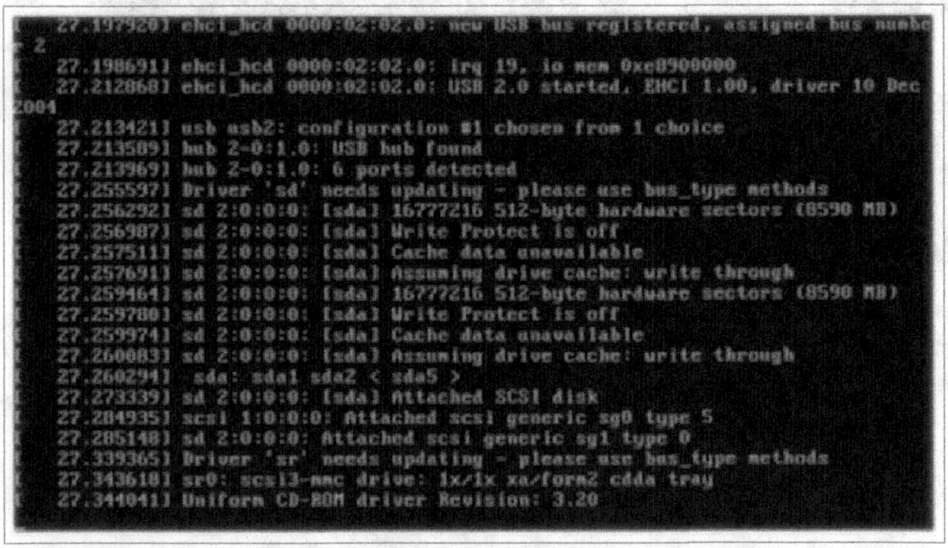

Figure 14-3. *If the kernel just stops loading, the problem is definitely in phase 3 of the boot procedure.*

4. *Upstart*: On Ubuntu Server, Upstart is responsible for starting the init process and associated essential services. To do this, Upstart executes all scripts it finds in the directory /etc/event.d (see Listing 14-1). You will rarely see messages that are related to Upstart itself, because it is just the service that is responsible for loading other services. If, however, none of the services on your server can initialize, or you get an error related to init (such as you can see in Figure 14-2), something may be wrong with Upstart. Make sure that its configuration directory, /etc/event.d, is readable.

Listing 14-1. *To Start Important System Services, Upstart Reads the Configuration Files in /etc/event.d*

```
root@MYL:/etc/event.d# ls
control-alt-delete   rc1    rc4    rc-default    sulogin        tty3    tty6
logd                 rc2    rc5    rcS           tty1    tty4
rc0                  rc3    rc6    rcS-sulogin   tty2    tty5
```

5. *Essential services*: Once Upstart has loaded, it starts executing the scripts it finds in /etc/event.d. Basically, these scripts don't execute anything, but just redirect you to other scripts that are in the directory /etc/init.d and executed from the directory that corresponds to the current runlevel. For example, if you are currently in runlevel 3, the services that are started are started from the directory /etc/rc3.d (see Listing 14-2).

There is such a directory for every runlevel between 0 and 6, inclusive, determining exactly what should be started when entering a runlevel. As you can see in Listing 14-2, the runlevel directories don't contain real files, but instead contain symbolic links to files that are located in the directory /etc/init.d. Here the system finds the real services that it should start. If one of these script fails, you typically see an error. Because these are essential services, such as the service that loads file systems, your system will most likely stop, giving you a clear indication of what is wrong. If the problem is obvious, you can just fix the problem. In some cases, the problem might not be obvious, in which case you should look at the order in which the scripts are started and try to deduce from that order which script failed. For instance, if you notice that the SSH process never gets loaded, it is obvious that the problem is in one of the scripts executed just before that.

Listing 14-2. *The Order of the Runlevel Scripts May Help You to Find Which Script Failed*

```
root@mel:/etc/rc3.d# ls -l
total 4
-rw-r--r-- 1 root root 556 2008-04-19 01:05 README
lrwxrwxrwx 1 root root  18 2008-04-29 14:52 S10sysklogd -> ../init.d/sysklogd
lrwxrwxrwx 1 root root  34 2008-05-01 06:15 S10xserver-xorg-input-wacom ->➡
../init.d/xserver-xorg-input-wacom
lrwxrwxrwx 1 root root  15 2008-04-29 14:52 S11klogd -> ../init.d/klogd
lrwxrwxrwx 1 root root  14 2008-06-22 14:48 S12dbus -> ../init.d/dbus
lrwxrwxrwx 1 root root  17 2008-08-25 14:42 S16openvpn -> ../init.d/openvpn
lrwxrwxrwx 1 root root  14 2008-04-30 14:55 S16ssh -> ../init.d/ssh
lrwxrwxrwx 1 root root  23 2008-08-15 05:57 S17mysql-ndb-mgm ->➡
../init.d/mysql-ndb-mgm
lrwxrwxrwx 1 root root  17 2008-05-17 11:34 S17portmap -> ../init.d/portmap
lrwxrwxrwx 1 root root  19 2008-08-15 05:57 S18mysql-ndb -> ../init.d/mysql-ndb
lrwxrwxrwx 1 root root  14 2008-05-17 11:34 S18nis -> ../init.d/nis
lrwxrwxrwx 1 root root  15 2008-08-15 05:57 S19mysql -> ../init.d/mysql
lrwxrwxrwx 1 root root  24 2008-05-01 14:52 S19postgresql-8.3 ->➡
../init.d/postgresql-8.3
lrwxrwxrwx 1 root root  15 2008-08-11 02:53 S19slapd -> ../init.d/slapd
lrwxrwxrwx 1 root root  21 2008-06-11 09:22 S20dhcp3-relay -> ../init.d/dhcp3-relay
lrwxrwxrwx 1 root root  14 2008-05-01 14:52 S20ebox -> ../init.d/ebox
lrwxrwxrwx 1 root root  15 2008-07-09 03:05 S20exim4 -> ../init.d/exim4
lrwxrwxrwx 1 root root  17 2008-05-27 15:35 S20ifplugd -> ../init.d/ifplugd
lrwxrwxrwx 1 root root  21 2008-07-30 04:09 S20iscsitarget -> ../init.d/iscsitarget
lrwxrwxrwx 1 root root  14 2008-06-20 15:02 S20kvm -> ../init.d/kvm
lrwxrwxrwx 1 root root  21 2008-08-11 10:46 S20libnss-ldap -> ../init.d/libnss-ldap
lrwxrwxrwx 1 root root  21 2008-06-20 15:02 S20libvirt-bin -> ../init.d/libvirt-bin
lrwxrwxrwx 1 root root  20 2008-05-17 11:34 S20nfs-common -> ../init.d/nfs-common
lrwxrwxrwx 1 root root  27 2008-05-17 11:34 S20nfs-kernel-server -> ➡
../init.d/nfs-kernel-server
lrwxrwxrwx 1 root root  23 2008-05-17 11:34 S20openbsd-inetd ->➡
../init.d/openbsd-inetd
lrwxrwxrwx 1 root root  16 2008-06-23 09:12 S20quagga -> ../init.d/quagga
lrwxrwxrwx 1 root root  15 2008-04-29 14:01 S20rsync -> ../init.d/rsync
lrwxrwxrwx 1 root root  15 2008-04-30 16:58 S20samba -> ../init.d/samba
lrwxrwxrwx 1 root root  17 2008-05-17 18:29 S20sysstat -> ../init.d/sysstat
lrwxrwxrwx 1 root root  19 2008-05-17 11:34 S20tftpd-hpa -> ../init.d/tftpd-hpa
```

```
lrwxrwxrwx 1 root root  17 2008-08-14 09:36 S20winbind -> ../init.d/winbind
lrwxrwxrwx 1 root root  16 2008-06-11 09:40 S20xinetd -> ../init.d/xinetd
lrwxrwxrwx 1 root root  18 2008-08-14 04:08 S21quotarpc -> ../init.d/quotarpc
lrwxrwxrwx 1 root root  14 2008-05-17 11:34 S23ntp -> ../init.d/ntp
lrwxrwxrwx 1 root root  15 2008-04-29 14:52 S25mdadm -> ../init.d/mdadm
lrwxrwxrwx 1 root root  17 2008-07-09 03:05 S30nagios2 -> ../init.d/nagios2
lrwxrwxrwx 1 root root  15 2008-06-25 14:28 S30squid -> ../init.d/squid
lrwxrwxrwx 1 root root  22 2008-05-17 11:34 S40dhcp3-server -> ➡
../init.d/dhcp3-server
lrwxrwxrwx 1 root root  26 2008-05-17 16:51 S40drbl-clients-nat -> ➡
../init.d/drbl-clients-nat
lrwxrwxrwx 1 root root  14 2008-07-30 04:02 S70drbd -> ../init.d/drbd
lrwxrwxrwx 1 root root  19 2008-07-30 04:02 S75heartbeat -> ../init.d/heartbeat
lrwxrwxrwx 1 root root  14 2008-04-29 14:00 S89atd -> ../init.d/atd
lrwxrwxrwx 1 root root  14 2008-04-29 14:00 S89cron -> ../init.d/cron
lrwxrwxrwx 1 root root  17 2008-05-01 14:51 S91apache2 -> ../init.d/apache2
lrwxrwxrwx 1 root root  18 2008-04-29 14:52 S99rc.local -> ../init.d/rc.local
lrwxrwxrwx 1 root root  19 2008-04-29 14:52 S99rmnologin -> ../init.d/rmnologin
```

6. *Networking*: Among the most important of the nonessential services is networking. If networking fails, many other services will fail as well. So if you see that many services that depend on networking fail, check your network configuration. The network is started from the script /etc/init.d/networking. This script reads in /etc/network/interfaces which network configuration it should start (see Listing 14-3). If something is wrong with your network, the most likely problem is an error in this script. Test network connectivity after you think you have fixed a network problem; ping is still the best utility to perform such tests.

Listing 14-3. *The /etc/init.d/networking Script Learns from /etc/network/interfaces Which Configuration to Initialize*

```
root@mel:/etc/network# cat interfaces
# This file describes the network interfaces available on your system
# and how to activate them. For more information, see interfaces(5).

# The loopback network interface
auto lo
iface lo inet loopback
```

```
        # The primary network interface
        #auto eth0
        #iface eth0 inet static
        #        address 192.168.1.99
        #        netmask 255.255.255.0
        #        network 192.168.1.0
        #        broadcast 192.168.1.255
        #        gateway 192.168.1.254
        #        # dns-* options are implemented by the resolvconf package, if ➥
        installed
        #        dns-nameservers 193.79.237.39
        #        dns-search sandervanvugt.nl
        auto br0
        iface br0 inet static
                address 192.168.1.99
                network 192.168.1.0
                netmask 255.255.255.0
                broadcast 192.168.1.255
                gateway 192.168.1.254
                bridge_ports eth0
                bridge_fd 0
                bridge_hello 2
                bridge_maxage 12
                bridge_stop off
        auto eth1
        iface eth1 inet static
                address 10.0.0.10
                netmask 255.255.255.0
                network 10.0.0.0
                broadcast 10.0.0.255
```

7. *Nonessential services*: If you have made it this far, basically, your server is operational. You still might have a service fail, though. If one of your services fails, the most likely problem is a configuration error in the service script. Check the documentation about your service and try to repair the script. Once you have arrived at this stage, at least you know for sure that the problem exists in a particular service, so you can start troubleshooting at the right location.

Troubleshooting Tools

There are some very useful tools that you must have available before you start a trouble-shooting session:

- `init=/bin/bash`: This Grub option enables you to load a shell immediately after the kernel has loaded successfully.

- *Rescue a Broken System option*: This option on the Ubuntu Server installation CD takes you to an environment in which you can apply your troubleshooting techniques.

- *A Linux live CD*: One of my personal favorites, and thus covered in this section, is Knoppix (`http://www.knoppix.com`), a live CD that contains lots of useful utilities that help you to troubleshoot a failing server. If you choose a different live CD, find one that doesn't have restrictions and takes you to an unlimited root shell as fast as possible.

Working with init=/bin/bash

The tool that is easiest to use is the option `init=/bin/bash` that you can pass to Grub when booting. It takes you to the end of the third stage of the boot procedure, right after the kernel and initrd have been loaded. This option is useful in cases where you have found that the kernel can load successfully, but there is an essential problem later in the boot procedure. Here is how you can activate it:

1. Reboot your server. During the three seconds that Ubuntu Server by default shows the Grub prompt, press Escape to access the options available in the Grub menu, an example of which is shown in Figure 14-4.

2. Select the line that has the kernel image you want to start (typically, this is the first line) and press e to edit the commands that are in this boot loader menu option. This shows you the lines in the `/boot/grub/menu.lst` file that are defined for this section (see Figure 14-5).

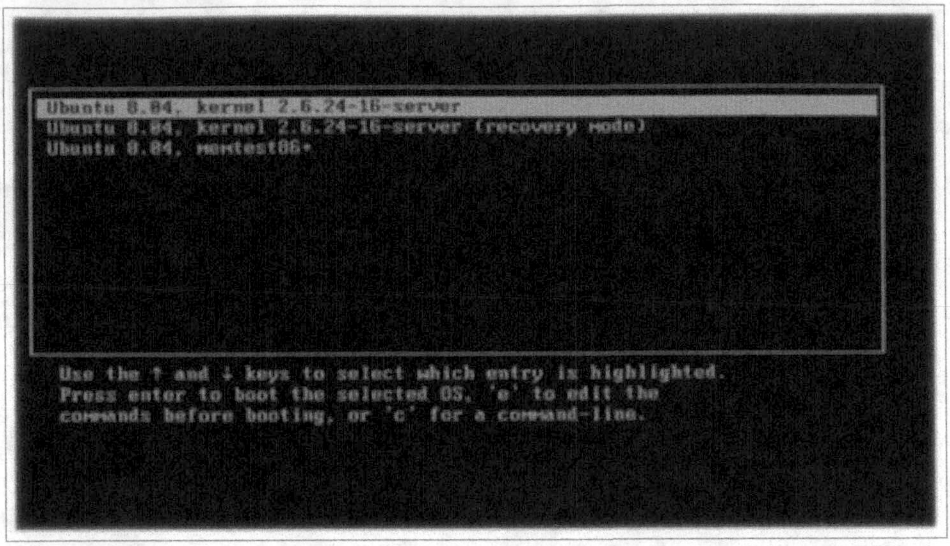

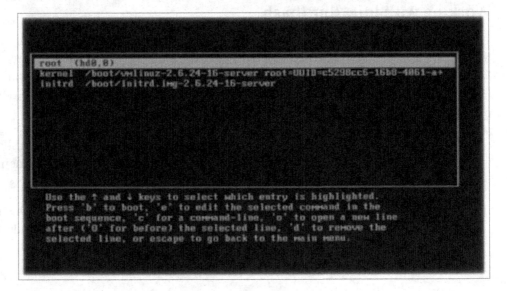

Figure 14-4. *From the Grub menu, you can pass options to the boot loader.*

Figure 14-5. *By selecting the section you want to start, you see the different lines that comprise that section.*

3. Select the line that starts with `kernel` and press e to edit this line. You'll now see a new window in which you can edit this line. Go to the end of its text and add the option `init=/bin/bash`. Next, press Enter, followed by b to boot the kernel with this option. This takes you to a bash shell prompt from which you can start your troubleshooting session (see Figure 14-6).

4. You are now in a bash shell, without anything being mounted or started for you. This offers you an excellent starting point for troubleshooting. Mount your file systems and execute all services that you want to test by hand.

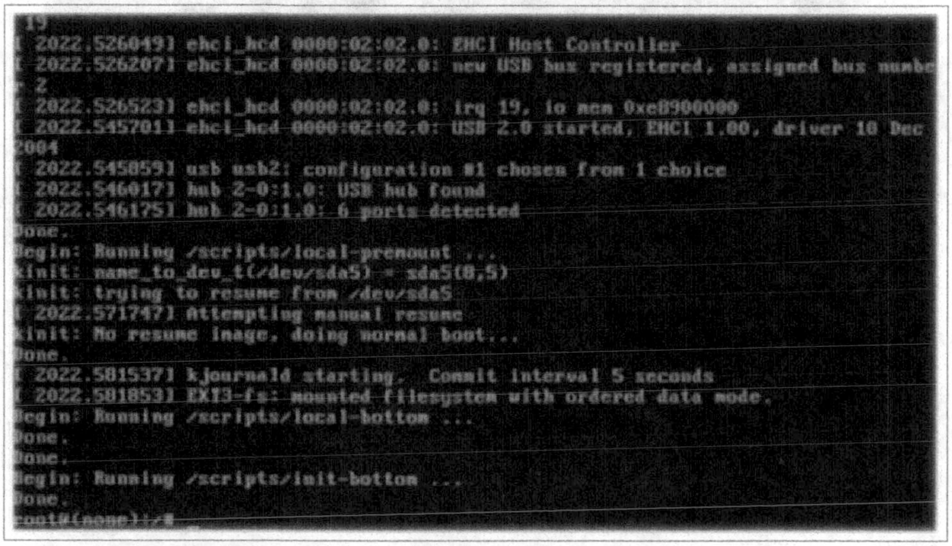

Figure 14-6. *Using the option init=/bin/bash is the quickest way to access a troubleshooting shell.*

Rescue a Broken System

The Ubuntu Server installation CD includes an option named Rescue a Broken System. This option is useful if you find that you can no longer boot your normal kernel image. Its main advantage is that it has its own kernel. Therefore, if for whatever reason `init=/bin/bash` doesn't work for you, use this option. The following procedure describes how it works:

1. Put the Ubuntu Server installation CD in your server's optical drive and reboot your server. Make sure it boots from the optical drive.

2. When you see the installation interface shown in Figure 14-7, select Rescue a Broken System and press Enter.

Figure 14-7. *On the Ubuntu Server installation CD, you'll find an option to rescue a broken system.*

3. You now see a few screens asking for your language and related settings. Enter the required information to make sure that your server loads the correct code table and keyboard settings.

4. After loading the appropriate keyboard settings, if your server has multiple network cards, you have to specify which network card you want to use. Your server then tries to get an IP address from the DHCP server on your network. Next, enter a temporary hostname. It doesn't really matter what you choose here, so the default hostname Ubuntu is fine (see Figure 14-8).

5. After asking you for time zone information, the rescue system tries to detect your hard disk layout. If it succeeds, it gives you a list of partitions (see Figure 14-9) and you have to tell it which partition you want to use as the root file system. It doesn't matter if you don't know which one to use; if you make an error here, you can just try another partition.

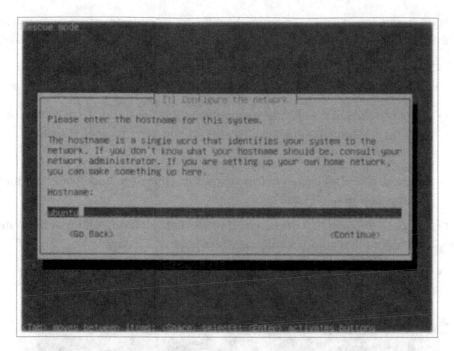

Figure 14-8. *Using the option Rescue, a Broken System gives you a temporary hostname and network configuration.*

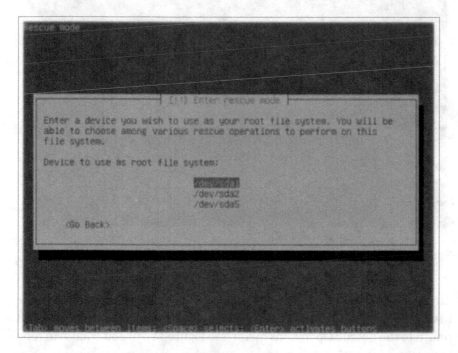

Figure 14-9. *To initialize the root file system, you have to tell the rescue system which partition it should use to mount it.*

6. At this point, you get an overview of the different rescue operations that are available (see Figure 14-10). You can choose from the following options:

- *Execute a shell in* /dev/yourrootdevice: Use this option to launch a shell in which your root file system is mounted already.

- *Execute a shell in the installer environment*: Use this option to launch a shell without anything mounted yet. This allows you to perform all mounts manually.

- *Reinstall GRUB boot loader*: If you know that your Grub boot loader is faulty, use this option to reinstall it.

- *Choose a different root file system*: If you want to try a different root file system and mount that automatically, use this option.

- *Reboot the system*: Select this option to reboot your server.

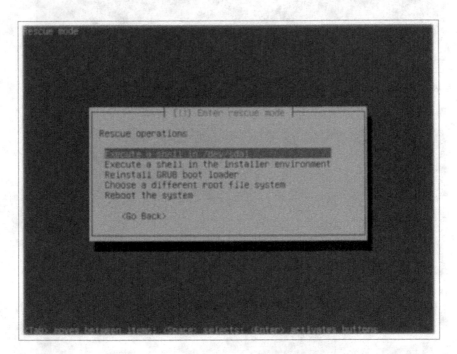

Figure 14-10. *In rescue mode you have five different options.*

7. After you select the rescue option that you want to use, you are dropped in a shell in which you can repair your system. Once you are done with that, press Exit to return to the Rescue Operations menu (see Figure 14-10) and choose to reboot your server.

■Note When I wrote this, there was a bug that takes you back to the main installation menu, in which the next step allows you to partition your disks. When you see this menu, you can select the option Finish the Installation or just hard reset your server. Both options restart your server.

Working with a Knoppix Rescue CD

If you choose to work from a generic rescue disk, Knoppix is a good choice that offers you complete flexibility in repairing your server. You can download Knoppix from http:// www.knoppix.com. In this section you'll read how to boot from Knoppix and how to enter a chroot environment in which you can troubleshoot your Linux server.

Troubleshooting goes much better from a chroot environment because you don't work with your Ubuntu Server file system from a mounted directory; instead, you actually change the root of the rescue disk to this directory. The advantage of this is that all utilities will work with their native paths. For instance, if a command like grub-install expects its menu.lst file to be in /boot/grub/menu.lst, the utility is not going to work if, due to the fact that you have mounted your server disks somewhere else, the path to this file has become /mnt/boot/grub/menu.lst. By using chroot, you can change root to the /mnt directory, with the advantage that your commands will find all configuration files at the right location.

The following procedure describes how to activate such a chroot environment from the Knoppix live CD:

1. Boot your server from the Knoppix CD. You'll see the Knoppix welcome screen (see Figure 14-11). Press Enter to start loading Knoppix.

2. During the load procedure, Knoppix prompts you to choose the language that you want to use. (In this procedure, I assume that you have started in English.) You next see the Knoppix desktop from which you start your work.

3. Click the terminal screen icon in the icon bar. This opens the Shell Konsole, with a prompt at which you have only user permissions. Enter sudo su to get root permissions.

4. Enter the mount command. The output of this command shows that you don't yet have any file system mounted on your server and that you are working completely from RAM file systems that have been initialized from the Knoppix CD (see Figure 14-12).

Figure 14-11. *From the Knoppix desktop, you can start repairing your server.*

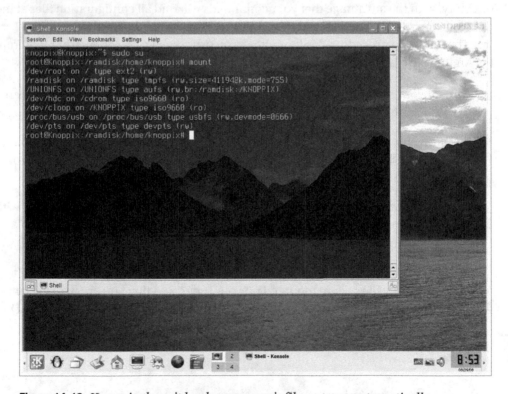

Figure 14-12. *Knoppix doesn't load your server's file systems automatically.*

5. Identify which partition is the root partition. You may not know exactly how your
   server is organized, so a good command to start with is `fdisk -l`. This shows you
   a list of all partitions that exist on your server. There are two possibilities here. You
   may see disk devices only, or you may also see dm devices (which refer to LVM
   logical volumes). If the latter is true, you are using LVM and need to take some
   extra steps; the section "Problems with LVM Logical Volumes," later in this chapter, explains how to initialize logical volumes manually. The present procedure
   assumes that you are working with local disk devices only, in which case `fdisk -l`
   may give you a result similar to the output shown in Listing 14-4.

Listing 14-4. *fdisk -l Enables You to Check the Partition Layout of Your Server*

```
root@Knoppix:~# fdisk -l

Disk /dev/sda: 8589 MB, 8589934592 bytes
255 heads, 63 sectors/track, 1044 cylinders
Units = cylinders of 16065 * 512 = 8225280 bytes

   Device Boot    Start     End    Blocks   Id  System
/dev/sda1    *        1     993   7976241   83  Linux
/dev/sda2            994    1044   409657+    5  Extended
/dev/sda5            994    1044   409626   82  Linux swap / Solaris
```

In the example in Listing 14-4, there isn't much doubt about which is the root partition. The `/dev/sda1` partition is the only one that has Id 83, so it is the only one
that contains a Linux file system. If you have more than one Linux partition, you
just have to try to mount all of them one by one to find out which contains the root
file system.

6. Mount the partition that you think is the root partition. Use the `/mnt` directory in
   the Knoppix file system as the temporary mount point:

```
mount /dev/sda1 /mnt
```

7. Before you go into the `chroot` environment, it is a good idea to make sure your
   `/proc` and `/dev` directories are working. These directories are generated dynami-
   cally and will be needed by many of the tools you use. To make sure these
   tools still work, you should mount both directories, by using the following two
   commands:

```
mount -o bind /dev /mnt/dev
mount -t proc proc /mnt/proc
```

8. Go to the /mnt directory using cd /mnt. At this point, you still see the prompt root@Knoppix: /mnt#. Enter chroot . to change the current directory to be presented as the root directory. You are in the chroot environment now, as shown in Listing 14-5, and can start troubleshooting.

Listing 14-5. *Use chroot for Troubleshooting*

```
root@Knoppix:/mnt# chroot .
root@Knoppix:/#
```

At this point you are ready to use your troubleshooting environment. In the next section you will read about some scenarios in which a rescue environment like the Knoppix Live CD is useful.

■**Note**   There is no fundamental difference between using the Knoppix Live CD and using the Ubuntu Server Installation CD for your rescue operations. I prefer Knoppix, though, because the Knoppix CD offers many useful utilities. In the next section, use whichever solution you prefer.

Common Problems and How to Fix Them

Although Ubuntu Server is a fairly stable server platform, you may encounter some problems. This section gives you some hints for troubleshooting the following common problems:

- Grub errors

- No master boot record

- Partition problems

- LVM logical volume problems

- Kernel problems

- File system problems

- Lost administrator password

Grub Errors

The very first thing that happens on your computer is Grub initialization. In some situations you may find that Grub simply tells you that it cannot load. You may encounter different results from Grub errors:

- Grub is completely wiped

- Grub gives a Grub error message

- Grub gives a missing-file error

The following sections explain how you can reinstall Grub if it is completely wiped, and how you can manually load Grub if you see a Grub error or a missing file error message.

Reinstalling Grub

If Grub is completely wiped, you will see nothing but a blinking cursor when your server boots; no Grub message is displayed. If this happens, it is likely that you have lost the complete MBR of your server, so there is no way that you can boot it. Take a rescue CD and boot your server from there. Then, activate a chroot environment and enter grub-install, followed by the name of the device on which you want to install Grub (for instance, grub-install /dev/sda, as shown in Listing 14-6). This will read /boot/grub/menu.lst (make sure that you have mounted it if boot is on a separate partition!) and reinstall Grub for you.

Listing 14-6. *grub-install Offers an Easy Solution to Reinstall Grub*

```
root@Knoppix:/# grub-install /dev/sda
You shouldn't call /sbin/grub-install. Please call /usr/sbin/grub-install instead!

Searching for GRUB installation directory ... found: /boot/grub
Installation finished. No error reported.
This is the contents of the device map /boot/grub/device.map.
Check if this is correct or not. If any of the lines is incorrect,
fix it and re-run the script `grub-install'.

(hd0)    /dev/sda
```

Loading Grub Manually

grub-install offers a good solution if the Grub code in the MBR doesn't work anymore. It may also fix some of the cases in which Grub gives you an error message and refuses to load any further. In some situations, you may encounter a problem in the Grub configuration file. If that happens, troubleshooting from the Grub prompt is useful, because you can manually load all lines that normally are loaded automatically from menu.lst. The advantage? You will see exactly where the problem occurs and thus be able to fix it easily.

The following procedure shows how to load the Grub configuration from the Grub prompt:

1. Restart your server. When it shows you that Grub is loading, press Escape to display the Grub menu, listing all available boot options from /boot/grub/menu.lst.

2. From the menu, press c to get to the Grub command-line interface, shown in Figure 14-13.

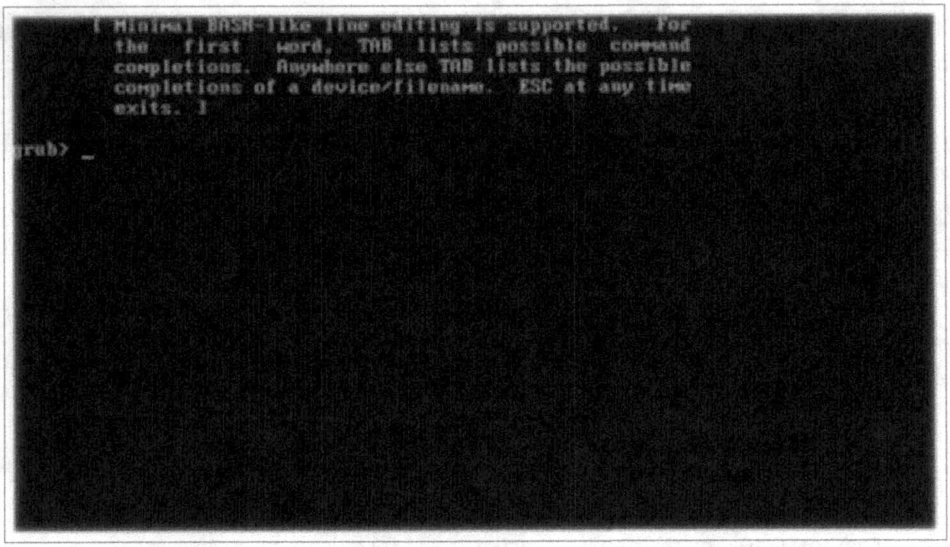

Figure 14-13. *The Grub command-line interface enables you to manually load the complete Grub configuration.*

3. At this point, it is a good idea to type **help** at the command prompt, just to get an idea of the commands that are available from within the Grub command line (see Figure 14-14 for an example).

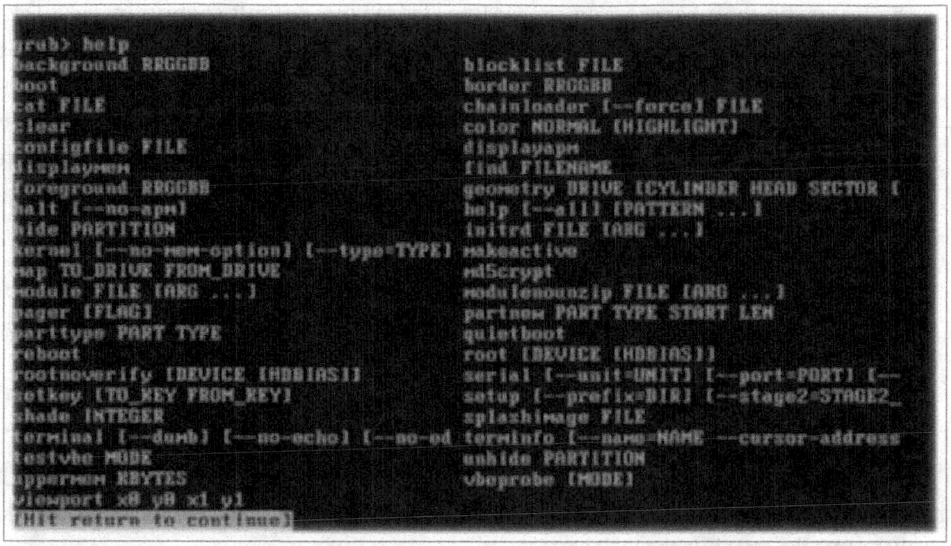

Figure 14-14. *The Grub command-line interface offers its own commands to troubleshoot Grub.*

4. To load Grub manually, you now have to execute all lines from the menu.1st file. Fortunately, you don't have to remember them, but instead can display the menu. 1st file by using cat /boot/grub/menu.1st. Normally, at the end of the file you can read the boot information that your server uses (see Figure 14-15 for an example).

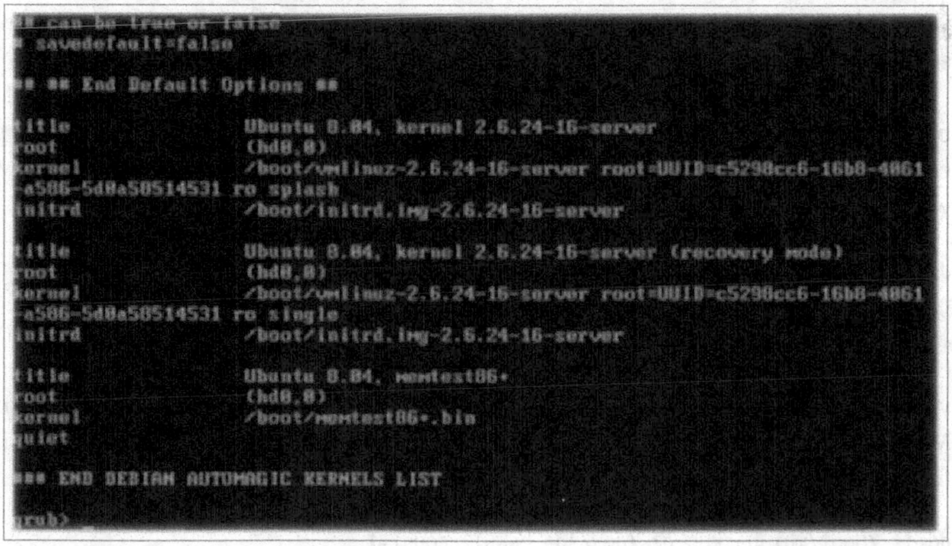

Figure 14-15. *Read the menu.lst file for an example of the options your server normally uses when booting.*

5. Enter the root, kernel, and initrd lines from your default section in menu.lst. Then, type **boot** to start booting your server. Observe your server at the same time to make sure that no error messages are displayed. Because your server didn't start automatically from this configuration, there is probably an error in the configuration it uses. If there is, read the error code and fix the problem. This may require that you mount your server's file system from a rescue CD first to see the exact filenames and device names you are using.

6. Found the error? Then your server will boot completely. If you fixed the wrong part, it will stop while loading the kernel. In the latter case, try again until you have found and fixed the error.

Tip Ubuntu Server uses the UUID of your root partition to boot. If that doesn't work, replace the UUID with the normal device name (for example, /dev/sda1). It is a lot easier to type and will show you immediately whether or not the error is in the UUID part.

No Master Boot Record

If you don't have a backup of the MBR, restoring it requires that you first fix your partition table and then restore Grub. These procedures are covered elsewhere in this chapter, so I won't repeat them here. The next section explains how to fix your partition table. After restoring the partition table, you'll be able to access your disk partitions and logical volumes again, enabling you to restore Grub. You learned how to do that in the previous section.

Of course, you can avoid going through the complex process of restoring your MBR by creating a backup MBR before you encounter trouble. This is a relatively simple procedure. As root, from the command line enter the following command (replace /dev/sda with the actual name of your server's boot device):

```
dd if=/dev/sda of=/boot/mbr_backup bs=512 count=1
```

This command makes a copy of the first 512 bytes on your hard drive (the MBR) and copies that to a file named mbr_backup in /boot. Repeat this command after every change you make to the partition table or Grub code. If some day you run into troubles with your MBR, you just have to boot your server from the rescue CD and restore the MBR using the following command:

```
dd if=/boot/mbr_backup of=/dev/sda bs=512 count=1
```

Partition Problems

Generally speaking, you may encounter two different kinds of partition problems. You may have lost the complete partition table, or you may have a problem with the file system on a partition. If the latter is the case, read the section "File System Problems" later in this chapter. If you have lost all partitions, you need a rescue CD and gpart to find the exact information about the beginning and end of the partitions on your server's hard disk. Once you've found that, use fdisk to re-create the partitions, as follows:

1. Start your server from the rescue CD and make sure that you open a console in which you have root permissions.

2. Type **gpart /dev/sda** to scan your hard drive for all partitions. This may take quite some time (count on anything from 5 seconds to an hour). Once the scan is finished, you will see your partition information, as in the example in Listing 14-7.

Listing 14-7. *Use gpart to Help Find Lost Partitions*

```
root@Knoppix:~# gpart /dev/sda

Begin scan...
Possible partition(Linux ext2), size(7789mb), offset(0mb)
Possible extended partition at offset(7789mb)
   Possible partition(Linux swap), size(400mb), offset(7789mb)
End scan.

Checking partitions...
Partition(Linux ext2 filesystem): primary
Partition(Linux swap or Solaris/x86): primary
Ok.

Guessed primary partition table:
Primary partition(1)
    type: 141(0x83)(Linux ext2 filesystem)
    size: 7789mb #s(15952480) s(63-15952542)
    chs:  (0/1/1)-(992/254/61)d (0/1/1)-(992/254/61)r

Primary partition(2)
    type: 140(0x82)(Linux swap or Solaris/x86)
    size: 400mb #s(819248) s(15952608-16771855)
    chs:  (993/1/1)-(1023/254/63)d (993/1/1)-(1043/254/59)r
```

```
Primary partition(3)
   type: 000(0x00)(unused)
   size: 0mb #s(0) s(0-0)
   chs:  (0/0/0)-(0/0/0)d (0/0/0)-(0/0/0)r

Primary partition(4)
   type: 000(0x00)(unused)
   size: 0mb #s(0) s(0-0)
   chs:  (0/0/0)-(0/0/0)d (0/0/0)-(0/0/0)r
```

Evaluate the information that gpart gives you carefully; after all, gpart stands for
Guess Partition. It guesses—nothing more, nothing less. For instance, on my
example server I have swap in a logical partition /dev/sda5. As you can see, gpart
did find the swap partition with its correct size, beginning, and end on disk, but
it couldn't determine that it is a logical partition. Based on this information,
you would try to re-create the swap partition on /dev/sda2. Your server would
boot with that, but would give errors as well. That doesn't really matter, though,
because once your server has booted, you can check system files like /etc/fstab to
find on what partition your swap originally was, and then repair the partitions.

3. Now that you have found the original partition boundaries, write them down and
   start fdisk using fdisk /dev/sda. Ignore the message about your disk's size and
   press n to start the interface to create a new partition. Next, press p to create the
   first primary partition. When it asks what partition number you want to assign,
   press 1.

4. Next comes the important part: you have to specify where the partition originally
   started and ended. To find this information, you need the chs (cylinder, heads,
   sector) line in the gpart output for this partition. Consider the following line:

```
chs:  (0/1/1)-(992/254/61)d (0/1/1)-(992/254/61)r
```

In this line, the first number between brackets indicates the original starting cylinder, which in this example is cylinder 0. The second series of numbers between
brackets tells you where the partition originally ended, in this case on cylinder 992.
There is one catch, though: in fdisk the first cylinder is cylinder 1. That means that
all other cylinders as displayed with gpart need to be incremented by 1. So, you
have to create a partition now that starts at cylinder 1 and ends on cylinder 993.
Repeat steps 3 and 4 to re-create your other partitions as well and then close fdisk
by pressing w. You'll probably see a message stating that the new partition table
can be used only after a reboot. Listing 14-8 shows you what has happened so far.

Listing 14-8. *Re-creating a Partition Using fdisk*

```
root@Knoppix:~# fdisk /dev/sda

The number of cylinders for this disk is set to 1044.
There is nothing wrong with that, but this is larger than 1024,
and could in certain setups cause problems with:
1) software that runs at boot time (e.g., old versions of LILO)
2) booting and partitioning software from other OSs
   (e.g., DOS FDISK, OS/2 FDISK)

Command (m for help): n
Command action
   e   extended
   p   primary partition (1-4)
p
Partition number (1-4): 1
First cylinder (1-1044, default 1): 1
Last cylinder or +size or +sizeM or +sizeK (1-1044, default 1044): 993

Command (m for help): n
Command action
   e   extended
   p   primary partition (1-4)
p
Partition number (1-4): 2
First cylinder (994-1044, default 994):
Using default value 994
Last cylinder or +size or +sizeM or +sizeK (994-1044, default 1044):
Using default value 1044

Command (m for help): w
The partition table has been altered!

Calling ioctl() to re-read partition table.

WARNING: Re-reading the partition table failed with error 16: Device or ➥
resource busy.
The kernel still uses the old table.
The new table will be used at the next reboot.
Syncing disks.
```

5. Reboot your server to activate the changes.

You now have recovered your partitions. It may work, it may not. If it doesn't work, I recommend starting by re-creating the first partition first. Try to mount it from the rescue CD, and if that works, continue from there, re-creating all other partitions you need. Once you have successfully reconstructed the root partition, read /etc/fstab, because it gives you invaluable information about the original device names that you've used.

Tip LVM, extended, and swap partitions use another partition type. In fdisk, press l to get an overview of available partition types, and press t to change the type of a partition. Don't forget to reboot after changing your partition table.

LVM Logical Volume Problems

If your server is configured with LVM, troubleshooting is slightly more difficult. You may encounter the following problems with LVM volumes:

- On bootup, the server doesn't find LVM logical volumes.

- Scanning a device for LVM problems causes problems on that device.

- A device is not activated automatically.

Fixing LVM Boot Problems

When your server boots, it scans for LVM volumes. It does this by executing the pvscan command from the startup scripts. If something is wrong, the pvscan process will fail and, as a result, you'll have to initialize LVM yourself. This is not too hard if you understand how LVM works. The bottom layer in LVM consists of physical devices. These are storage devices that have an LVM signature added to them (they can also be partitions). Not every storage device is a physical device. You need to initialize these storage devices by using the pvcreate command before you can use them.

The second layer in LVM consists of volume groups. A volume group is a collection of storage devices (or only one storage device) from which logical volumes can be created. During your configuration of LVM, you created one or more volume groups, using the vgcreate command. Your server uses vgscan to activate the volume groups when booting.

Logical volumes are the storage devices that you will create a file system on and mount on your server. You use lvcreate to create them, and lvscan to scan them. Figure 14-16 gives an overview of the LVM setup.

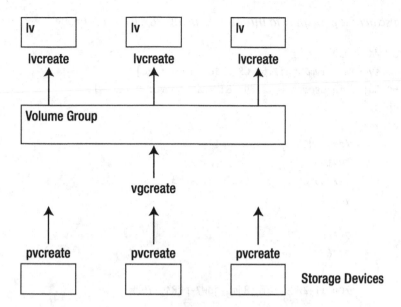

Figure 14-16. *Overview of the LVM structure*

The following procedure explains how to troubleshoot LVM logical volumes:

1. Before you start to troubleshoot, it is good to get an overview of your logical volumes. The best way to do that is by using lvdisplay. If it encounters a problem, it will tell you "No volume groups found," in which case you need to check the LVM chain to see if everything is set up right.

2. If your LVM structure has never worked, start by checking the storage devices themselves. If you've added partitions to the LVM setup, the partition should be marked as partition type 8e. Use fdisk -l /dev/sda to confirm this. If it isn't set to type 8e, use fdisk /dev/sda to open fdisk on your server's hard drive, press t, and then enter the number of the partition whose type you want to change. Next enter **8e**, save the settings, and reboot. It might work now.

3. If your LVM structure still doesn't work, use pvdisplay to check whether the storage devices are marked as LVM devices. If they are not, but you are sure that you have set them up as LVM devices earlier, use pvscan /dev/sda. If this also doesn't work, use pvcreate /dev/sda to set up your storage device as an LVM device. Listing 14-9 shows the result that pvdisplay and pvscan would normally give you.

Listing 14-9. *Use pvscan and pvdisplay to Initialize Existing Physical Volumes*

```
root@mel:~# pvscan /dev/md0
  PV /dev/md0    VG system    lvm2 [912.69 GB / 10.69 GB free]
  Total: 1 [912.69 GB] / in use: 1 [912.69 GB] / in no VG: 0 [0    ]
root@mel:~# pvdisplay
  --- Physical volume ---
  PV Name                /dev/md0
  VG Name                system
  PV Size                912.69 GB / not usable 1.69 MB
  Allocatable            yes
  PE Size (KByte)        4096
  Total PE               233648
  Free PE                2736
  Allocated PE           230912
  PV UUID                ZOqNiT-ZWH3-Yqfh-8jmi-jdW7-pNR4-IY6JW1
```

4. Repeat the preceding steps, but this time for the volume groups on your server. So, first use vgdisplay to see your current volume groups. If that doesn't give you a result, use vgscan to tell your server to scan for volume groups on your storage devices. Listing 14-10 shows the result of these commands.

Listing 14-10. *vgscan and vgdisplay Can Be Very Helpful When Fixing Volume Group Problems*

```
root@mel:~# vgscan
  Reading all physical volumes.  This may take a while...
  Found volume group "system" using metadata type lvm2
root@mel:~# vgdisplay
  --- Volume group ---
  VG Name                system
  System ID
  Format                 lvm2
  Metadata Areas         1
  Metadata Sequence No   6
  VG Access              read/write
  VG Status              resizable
  MAX LV                 0
  Cur LV                 5
  Open LV                5
```

```
Max PV                  0
Cur PV                  1
Act PV                  1
VG Size                 912.69 GB
PE Size                 4.00 MB
Total PE                233648
Alloc PE / Size         230912 / 902.00 GB
Free  PE / Size         2736 / 10.69 GB
VG UUID                 9VeHJR-nkCX-20fg-3BUq-152H-WqFW-3B2Sw7
```

5. Now that both your physical volumes and your volume groups are available, you may still have to scan your logical volumes (use lvdisplay first to see if they were activated automatically). The command sequence repeats itself: first use lvscan to scan for available volumes and then use lvdisplay to see whether the volumes came up successfully. Listing 14-11 shows you the result of these two commands.

Listing 14-11. *Use lvscan and lvdisplay to Initialize Your Logical Volumes*

```
root@mel:~# lvscan
  ACTIVE              '/dev/system/root' [100.00 GB] inherit
  ACTIVE              '/dev/system/swap' [2.00 GB] inherit
  ACTIVE              '/dev/system/var' [100.00 GB] inherit
  ACTIVE              '/dev/system/srv' [100.00 GB] inherit
  ACTIVE              '/dev/system/clonezilla' [600.00 GB] inherit
root@mel:~# lvdisplay
  --- Logical volume ---
  LV Name                /dev/system/root
  VG Name                system
  LV UUID                C2QCPB-vtTJ-E3QN-hoZE-dfZE-cBiZ-zz06mN
  LV Write Access        read/write
  LV Status              available
  # open                 1
  LV Size                100.00 GB
  Current LE             25600
  Segments               1
  Allocation             inherit
  Read ahead sectors     0
  Block device           254:0
```

```
--- Logical volume ---
LV Name                /dev/system/swap
VG Name                system
LV UUID                1NY8gw-TZgt-9Xxp-6FnA-2HEa-HUmv-tnqnI5
LV Write Access        read/write
LV Status              available
# open                 2
LV Size                2.00 GB
Current LE             512
Segments               1
Allocation             inherit
Read ahead sectors     0
Block device           254:1

--- Logical volume ---
LV Name                /dev/system/var
VG Name                system
LV UUID                OyzvpN-U1uC-3Hra-7iOn-Sljz-pweh-1J8FsO
LV Write Access        read/write
LV Status              available
# open                 2
LV Size                100.00 GB
Current LE             25600
Segments               1
Allocation             inherit
Read ahead sectors     0
Block device           254:2

--- Logical volume ---
LV Name                /dev/system/srv
VG Name                system
LV UUID                zUwbXR-7T1T-2yAJ-34Ri-FiFf-Wruc-ql5QtS
LV Write Access        read/write
LV Status              available
# open                 1
LV Size                100.00 GB
Current LE             25600
Segments               1
Allocation             inherit
Read ahead sectors     0
Block device           254:3
```

```
--- Logical volume ---
LV Name                 /dev/system/clonezilla
VG Name                 system
LV UUID                 zh1jLm-k3ut-UjwD-fBkh-GArt-HxII-i5342d
LV Write Access         read/write
LV Status               available
# open                  1
LV Size                 600.00 GB
Current LE              153600
Segments                1
Allocation              inherit
Read ahead sectors      0
Block device            254:4
```

6. Make sure that all LVM logical volumes are marked as available. You can see this in the LV Status line of the output of lvdisplay. If the status is anything other than available, read the upcoming subsection "A Device Is Not Activated Automatically."

Excluding Devices for LVM

Imagine a situation in which you are working with virtualization. Your host server uses LVM, and you decide that your virtual servers should each get an LVM logical volume as the storage back end. In the virtual servers, you want to use LVM as well. When your virtual machine boots, it can't initialize LVM volumes. It complains that the devices are already being used.

The problem in the preceding scenario occurs if you don't exclude your LVM devices from being scanned for LVM volumes on bootup of the host server. Therefore, the host server will find LVM volumes within the LVM devices and just activate them. The result is that the virtual server that is supposed to use these volumes finds that they are already in use and concludes that it can't use them. The solution is to exclude the LVM devices from being scanned for LVM volumes when the host server boots.

To exclude LVM devices, you have to modify the LVM configuration file /etc/lvm/lvm. conf. Listing 14-12 provides some example lines that you can use to exclude devices.

Listing 14-12. *Some Example Lines to Exclude Devices from lvm.conf*

```
# By default we accept every block device:
filter = [ "a/.*/" ]

# Exclude the cdrom drive
# filter = [ "r|/dev/cdrom|" ]

# When testing I like to work with just loopback devices:
# filter = [ "a/loop/", "r/.*/" ]

# Or maybe all loops and ide drives except hdc:
# filter =[ "a|loop|", "r|/dev/hdc|", "a|/dev/ide|", "r|.*|" ]
```

As you can see, the `filter` statement uses regular expressions both to include and exclude devices. All devices that you want to include start with a| and all devices that you want to exclude start with r|. So, for example, if you want to make sure that while booting your /dev/drbd0 device is not scanned by pvscan, vgscan, or lvscan, include the following line somewhere in the configuration file:

```
filter = [ "r|/dev/drbd0" ]
```

Next, restart your server to activate the new configuration. The newly designated devices should now be excluded.

Tip Personally, I don't like all the comments in the /etc/lvm/lvm.conf file, because I want to see very clearly which devices I'm including and which devices I'm excluding in the LVM setup. Thus, I recommend removing all comment lines so that you have a configuration file that is easy to read and in which it is easy to identify any mistakes that you've accidentally made.

A Device Is Not Activated Automatically

Another problem that you might encounter is that LVM volumes are all discovered fine but their status remains inactive. If that happens, you can use lvchange to change their state to active. Consider the following example line:

```
lvchange -a y /dev/system/srv
```

This command changes the state of the volume from inactive to active. This normally works, but in some particular cases, it doesn't. I have seen a situation in which a snapshot volume was linked to the original volume, but the snapshot volume was completely filled up and therefore deactivated automatically. That's good, you would think, because it can't do any harm that way, but it also deactivates the original volume. If the original volume is deactivated because of a failing snapshot, there is no way to get it up again with lvchange. In that case, you would first have to remove the snapshot, using a command like

```
lvremove /dev/system/snapshot
```

Once the snapshot volume has been removed properly, you can change the state of the original volume back to active.

Tip Always remember that a snapshot is for temporary use only. Remove it immediately if you don't need it anymore.

Kernel Problems

Fortunately, serious kernel problems are relatively rare, but they do occur. Typically, when the kernel has a problem on a machine that has been functional for quite some time, the machine will just hang. If this happens, the first thing to do is to find out what kind of "hang" it is. There are interruptible hangs and noninterruptible hangs. To find out which kind of hang your server is experiencing, press the Caps Lock key. If the Caps Lock light switches on or off, you have an interruptible hang. If it doesn't, you have a noninterruptible hang.

Interruptible Hang

The best thing to do when you have an interruptible hang is to dump a stack trace of the responsible process. To do this, you must have Magic SysRq enabled. Check if this is the case in the file /proc/sys/kernel/sysrq. If it is not enabled, use zcat /proc/config.gz | grep SYSRQ to see whether or not this feature is compiled. If it is enabled, it has the value 1; if it's not, it has the value 0. On Ubuntu Server, it is enabled by default. If on your server it is not enabled for some reason, put the following line in /etc/sysctl.conf and reboot your server to make sure that sysrq is enabled by default (see Chapter 4 for more information on sysctl):

```
kernel.sysrq=1
```

Now when the server hangs, press Alt+Print Screen+t to tell your system to dump a stack trace to the console. Next, use the dmesg command to dump the stack trace on your server's screen. You can also reboot, and after the reboot read /var/log/messages, because the stack trace is dumped there as well. Listing 14-13 shows partial output of the stack trace.

Listing 14-13. *A Stack Trace Can Help Troubleshoot Interruptible Hangs*

```
[ 1451.314592]  [<c01a6918>] do_ioctl+0x78/0x90
[ 1451.314596]  [<c01a6b5e>] vfs_ioctl+0x22e/0x2b0
[ 1451.314599]  [<c02230ed>] rwsem_wake+0x4d/0x110
[ 1451.314603]  [<c01a6c36>] sys_ioctl+0x56/0x70
[ 1451.314607]  [<c010839a>] sysenter_past_esp+0x6b/0xa1
[ 1451.314616]  =========================
[ 1451.314617] console-kit-d S f3ddbde8     0  6784       1
[ 1451.314619]        f3d64b80 00000086 00000002 f3ddbde8 f3ddbde0 00000000➥
 c04980e0 c049b480
[ 1451.314623]        c049b480 c049b480 f3ddbdec f3d64cc4 c35a3480 ffffd253➥
 00000000 000000ff
[ 1451.314626]        00000000 00000000 00000000 0000003a 00000001 c35aa000➥
 00005607 c027858a
[ 1451.314630] Call Trace:
[ 1451.314640]  [<c027858a>] vt_waitactive+0x5a/0xb0
[ 1451.314643]  [<c012b0c0>] default_wake_function+0x0/0x10
...
[ 1451.314123]   .jiffies                    : 114039
[ 1451.314124]   .next_balance               : 0.114020
[ 1451.314126]   .curr->pid                  : 0
[ 1451.314127]   .clock                      : 247950.082330
[ 1451.314128]   .idle_clock                 : 0.000000
[ 1451.314140]   .prev_clock_raw             : 1451264.185399
[ 1451.314141]   .clock_warps                : 0
[ 1451.314142]   .clock_overflows            : 92068
[ 1451.314143]   .clock_deep_idle_events     : 0
[ 1451.314145]   .clock_max_delta            : 9.999478
[ 1451.314146]   .cpu_load[0]                : 0
[ 1451.314147]   .cpu_load[1]                : 0
[ 1451.314148]   .cpu_load[2]                : 0
[ 1451.314149]   .cpu_load[3]                : 0
[ 1451.314140]   .cpu_load[4]                : 0
[ 1451.314141]
```

```
[ 1451.314141] cfs_rq
[ 1451.314142]     .exec_clock                    : 0.000000
[ 1451.314143]     .MIN_vruntime                  : 0.000001
[ 1451.314145]     .min_vruntime                  : 9571.283382
[ 1451.314146]     .max_vruntime                  : 0.000001
[ 1451.314147]    .spread                         : 0.000000
[ 1451.314149]     .spread0                       : -3276.906118
[ 1451.314150]     .nr_running                    : 0
[ 1451.314151]     .load                          : 0
[ 1451.314152]     .nr_spread_over                : 0
[ 1451.314153]
[ 1451.314153] cfs_rq
[ 1451.314154]     .exec_clock                    : 0.000000
[ 1451.314156]     .MIN_vruntime                  : 0.000001
[ 1451.314157]     .min_vruntime                  : 9571.283382
[ 1451.314158]     .max_vruntime                  : 0.000001
[ 1451.314160]     .spread                        : 0.000000
[ 1451.314161]     .spread0                       : -3276.906118
[ 1451.314162]     .nr_running                    : 0
[ 1451.314163]     .load                          : 0
[ 1451.314164]     .nr_spread_over                : 0
[ 1451.314166]
[ 1451.314166] runnable tasks:
[ 1451.314167]             task   PID       tree-key  switches  prio
exec-runtime ➡
        sum-exec      sum-sleep
[ 1451.314168] -------------------------------------------------------------------
----------------------
[ 1451.314172]
```

The best thing to do with this stack trace is to have it reviewed by someone who specializes in this kind of troubleshooting. Doing it yourself requires extensive knowledge of the C programming language and goes far beyond the scope of this book. If you have purchased support with Canonical, send the stack trace to them for analysis. They will be able to find the offending process and tell you why it caused a system to hang.

■**Tip** In many cases, system hangs are caused by tainted (unsupported) kernel modules. It is easy to find out whether your kernel is tainted: `cat /proc/sys/kernel/tainted` gives the value 1 if your kernel is tainted. Basically, all kernel modules that come from commercial organizations and do not fall under the GPL license are considered tainted modules. Try to avoid such modules as much as possible.

Noninterruptible Hang

If you have an interruptible hang, consider yourself lucky. At least you can make a stack trace dump and send that to your support organization. If you have a hang and your server doesn't reply to anything anymore (noninterruptible), that is a much worse situation, because it is hard to get debugging information.

If your system experiences noninterruptible hangs often, you can force your kernel to generate an Oops (which is an error message that it generates when it stops) and dump its stack trace to STDOUT. To obtain this information, you need to pass the boot option nmi_ watchdog to the kernel when booting the kernel with Grub. This will poll your CPU every 5 seconds. If the CPU responds, nothing happens. If it doesn't respond, the NMI handler kernel component generates an Oops and dumps information to STDOUT. To obtain this information, it is useful to connect a serial console to your server (you don't want to write down all this information manually, do you?).

Tip If a noninterruptible hang has never occurred but suddenly occurs after you've added a new piece of hardware, the new hardware likely is causing the hang. Try to configure your server without this piece of hardware to avoid the problems.

File System Problems

Normally, you won't encounter too many problems with your server's file systems. However, in some cases, if things do go wrong, you may end up with a damaged file system. In this section you'll learn how to still access a damaged Ext3 file system and how to repair a ReiserFS file system that has problems.

Accessing a Damaged Ext3 File System

If after an error you apparently can no longer access your Ext2 or Ext3 file system, you still might be able to access it. This section presents advanced mount options that allow you to access data that you might have considered lost.

In order to access a file system, you need the superblock, a 1 KB block that contains all metadata about the file system. This data is needed to mount the file system. It normally is the second 1 KB block on an Ext3 file system. Listing 14-14 shows part of the contents of the superblock as displayed with the debugfs utility.

Listing 14-14. *A Superblock As Displayed with debugfs*

```
Filesystem volume name:      <none>
Last mounted on:             <not available>
Filesystem UUID:             09979101-96e0-4533-a7f3-0a2db9b07a03
Filesystem magic number:     0xEF53
Filesystem revision #:       1 (dynamic)
Filesystem features: has_journal ext_attr filetype needs_recovery sparse_super large_
file
Default mount options:       (none)
Filesystem state:            clean
Errors behavior:             Continue
Filesystem OS type:          Linux
Inode count:                 5248992
Block count:                 10486428
Reserved block count:        524321
Free blocks:                 3888202
Free inodes:                 4825214
First block:                 0
Block size:                  4096
Fragment size:               4096
Blocks per group:            32768
Fragments per group:         32768
Inodes per group:            16352
Inode blocks per group:      511
```

Problems with your file system arise if, due to some error, the superblock isn't accessible anymore. Fortunately, some backup copies of the superblock are written on the Ext2 and Ext3 file systems by default. You can use these backup copies to mount a file system that you may have considered lost.

The actual position on disk of the first backup of the superblock depends on the size of the file system. On modern, large file systems, you will always find it at block 32768. To access it, you can use the mount option -o sb. The issue, however, is that mount expects you to specify the position of the superblock in 1024-byte blocks, whereas the default block size for a modern Ext3 volume or partition is 4096 bytes. Therefore, to tell the mount command where it can find the superblock, you have to multiply the position of the superblock by 4, which would result in the block value 141072 in most cases. For example, if your /dev/sda5 file system has a problem, you can try mounting it with the command mount -o sb=141072 /dev/hda5 /somewhere.

Now that you have mounted the problematic file system and thus limited the scope of the problem to the superblock, it is time to fix the problem. You can do so by copying the backup superblock to the location of the old superblock, using `dd if=/dev/hda5 of=/dev/hda5 bs=1024 skip=141072 count=1 seek=1`. Once finished, your file system should be accessible again just as it was before the problem occurred.

Repairing ReiserFS

The best and at the same time worst thing about ReiserFS is the database it uses to store files. The database makes ReiserFS a very fast file system that deals with lots of small files especially well, but when it breaks, it seriously breaks and you risk losing all your data. Fortunately, the Ubuntu Server version of `reiserfsck` does a decent job of repairing database problems.

At the moment the database seriously goes wrong and a normal `fsck` can't save you anymore, you need its power options. Before using them, you should always try `reiserfsck --fix-fixable`. This is a nondestructive option in which you don't risk losing your data. If that doesn't help, there are two advanced options. If you suspect that the problem is in the superblock, use `reiserfsck --rebuild-sb`. This option analyzes information in the file system and tries to rebuild the superblock. In some situations, just using this option is not enough, and you need to use `reiserfsck --rebuild-tree` after that. This option completely rebuilds the database tree based on information in the file system. Note, however, that this may seriously go wrong; I have started this option on a damaged file system that had thousands of files in hundreds of directories, only to end up with one large directory named `/lost+found`. If that happens to you, you really do need your backup tape, but anyway, it is worth a try.

Caution Before using `reiserfsck --rebuild-tree`, make sure that you have a decent backup of your file system.

Lost Administrator Password

To administer your server, you need administrative privileges. If you didn't change any defaults, the first user you created while installing the server has permissions to use the `sudo` command to perform administration tasks. (This isn't true for any of the subsequent users you created.) If you delete this user account by accident, you have a problem. In this section you'll learn how to fix it.

If you subsequently lose the password for the user account that can use the sudo command, just log in as root and grant this user a new password. If you can't log in as root, the following procedure explains how to log in as root using a rescue CD and then re-create a user that has administrative permissions on your server:

1. Boot from a rescue CD as described in the section "Working with a Knoppix Rescue CD" earlier in this chapter. Make sure to mount the /dev and /proc directories and establish a chroot environment that points to your server's root directory.

2. You are now root on your server's file system. Use the passwd command to reset the password for the user root. You have reestablished access to the root account.

3. Reboot your server without the Knoppix CD and verify that you can log in as root, using the password that you've just set.

4. Re-create an administrative user account that is not root. If, for example, the name of this user account is linda, use useradd -m linda. To be able to use sudo to execute commands as root, you must make sure that this user account is a member of the group adm. To make user linda a member of the group adm, use usermod -G adm linda.

5. Use passwd linda to give the user you've just created a password. You have now reestablished a user account that can be used to perform administration tasks on your server.

Tip A good precautionary measure to take *before* you lose the administrator password it to give the user root a password (by default, this user doesn't have a password). Use sudo su to become root, and then use the passwd command to set a password for root. Use a complex password, but one that you will be sure to remember.

Summary

In this chapter you learned how to troubleshoot Ubuntu Server. You have read how to fix some common issues that may arise when working with Ubuntu Server. Of course, covering all possible problems in one chapter is impossible, but the knowledge that you have acquired from this chapter should help you to fix quite a few common problems.

This is the last chapter in this book. I certainly hope you have enjoyed it!

Index

Symbols

64-bit version of Ubuntu Server, 7

A

aa-complain command, 299

accepting mail from servers on Internet, 267–268

accessing damaged Ext3 file system, 378–380

access lookup table, configuring Postfix to use, 270

ACLs, slapd.conf file, 214–215

Active Directory and Samba
Kerberos authentication, setting up, 245
making Samba member of domain, 244
overview of, 241, 244

active memory, 58

administrative user account for Kerberos server, creating, 337–338

administrator password, lost, dealing with, 380–381

aliases lookup table, configuring Postfix to use, 273

allocating files in file systems, 111

allocation groups, 112, 125

allocsize option (XFS), 126

analyzing Ext2/Ext3 file system
debugfs utility, 122–124
dumpe2fs and tune2fs utilities, 120–122
e2fsck utility, 120

Anticipatory scheduler (I/O scheduler), 97

Apache Web Server, high-availability solution for, 194

AppArmor
components of, 290–291
creating and managing profiles, 294–299
installing and starting, 293–294
monitoring status of, 299–302
overview of, 290
permissions, 293
updating profiles, 299

apparmor status command, 299

apt command, 31

apt-get command, 163

apt-get install drbl command, 31

apt-get purge slapd command, 205

apt-get update command, 163

aptitude search samba command, 232

assigning directory for Clonezilla, 35–36

attributes of LDAP objects, 198

authentication
See also Kerberos
for enterprise network installation, 3
of Linux users, 245–246
using LDAP for
nsswitch.conf file, 228–229
PAM, configuring, 223–228
testing client connectivity, 230

authkeys file, 176

B

backing up
cluster configuration, 187–191
files, snapshot technology for, 5

balanced trees (b-trees), 115

barrier option (XFS), 127

barriers, to avoid reordering in journal file systems, 114

Beginning Ubuntu Server Administration (van Vugt), 131

bitmaps, inode and block, 112–113

blocked process, 51

boot partition, creating, 12

boot problems of LVM logical volumes, 368–373

boot process, phases in, 344–350
/boot/grub/menu.lst file, 351

■ C

caching, types of, 91
canonical lookup table, configuring Postfix to use, 270
certificate authority (CA)
    creating, 284–289
    need for, 283–284
    OpenVPN, configuring, 305–308
cfg_file statements (Nagios), 136
changing password in LDAP environment,
    223
check command (Nagios), 148–149
check_disk plug-in (Nagios), output from,
    144–147
checking NTP synchronization status,
    326–327
check_nrpe command (Nagios), 154
chroot environment
    activating from Knoppix Rescue CD,
        357
    listing, 360
    troubleshooting and, 357
cibadmin command, 189–191
cibadmin -Q command, 177, 179, 187
cib.xml file, 177–179
cleanup daemon, 251
client keys (OpenVPN)
    copying, 312
    creating, 310–311
clients
    See also Kerberos client
    cloning, 39–43
    configuring for cloning, 36–38
    NTP, configuring, 325–326
Clonezilla imaging server
    assigning directory for, 35
    cloning clients, 39–43
    configuring, 36
    configuring for cloning, 36–38
    Diskless Remote Boot in Linux
        configuring software, 32–33
        DHCP server, setting up, 33–35
    installing software, 31–32
        setting up, 30
    setting up, 29
cluster configuration, backing up, 187–191
cluster resources, configuring, 180–187
commands
    aa-complain, 299
    apparmor status, 299
    apt, 31
    apt-get, 163
    apt-get install drbl, 31
    apt-get update, 163
    aptitude search samba, 232
    check, 148–149
    check-nrpe, 154
    cibadmin, 189–191
    cibadmin -Q, 177, 179, 187
    crm_mon -i 1, 177, 183
    debugfs utility
        help, 124
        ls, 122
        lsdel, 123
    dpkg-reconfigure postfix, 257–262
    fdisk, 366–367
    fdisk -l, 359
    free -m, 57
    gpart, 365–366
    help, 326
    ietadm, 171
    ifconfig, 73–74
    ipcs -m, 95
    iscsiadm, 173
    iscsiadm -m session, 174
    kadmin.local, 337, 338
    kinit, 338
    klist, 338
    LDAP
        apt-get purge slapd, 205
        dpkg-reconfigure slapd, 203–206
        for management, 220–221
        getent, 230
        ldapadd, 201
        ldapdelete, 201, 222
        ldapmodify, 201, 221
        ldappasswd, 223
        ldapsearch, 201, 217–220
        ldd, 223

ls -i, 110
lsof, 71
lsscsi, 174
lvchange, 374
lvdisplay, 369–373
lvscan, 371–373
mkdir /share, 232
mount, 235
Nagios tool, 135, 148–149, 154
netstat -tulpn, 78
nice, adjusting process priority with, 89–90
ntpdate, 325
ntpq, 326
ntpq -p, 326
ntptrace, 326
OpenLDAP, 201
openssl, 284
openvpn, 314
/opt/drbl/sbin/drbl-client-switch, 37–38
/opt/drbl/sbin/drblpush -i, 32
/opt/drbl/sbin/select-in-client, 38
pmap, 63, 65
ps aux, 62
postdrop, 251
pvdisplay, 369
pvscan, 368
reiserfsck, 380
smbclient, 235
smbclient -L localhost, 234
smbpasswd, 231, 235
smbpasswd -W, 239
stat, 110
stats, 112
sysctl, 84, 85
taskset, 90, 91
time, 80
unconfined, 301
vgdisplay, 370
vgscan, 370
vmstat -d, 67
vmstat -s
    CPU performance and, 52, 58
    memory performance and, 59
xfsdump, 127
xfs_freeze, 128

xfs_growfs, 125–127
xfs_info, 125
xfs_repair, 127
xfs_rtcp, 127
common-auth configuration file (PAM)
    contents of, 227
    modified, 228
Complete Fair Queueing (I/O scheduler), 97
components
    Cyrus IMAPd, 275–276
    Postfix MTA, 262–263
configuration file
    storing settings in, 84
configuration files
    for Nagios tool
        contacts.cfg, 139
        contacts group, defining, 140
        creating, 138–139
        hosts and host groups, defining, 141–143
        services.cfg, 144–148
        timeperiods_nagios2.cfg, 149–151
    OpenLDAP, 201
configuring
    See also configuration files
    clients for cloning in Clonezilla imaging server, 36–38
    Clonezilla imaging server, 35–36
    cluster resources, 180–187
    Cyrus IMAPd, 276–277
    Diskless Remote Boot in Linux software, 32–33
    DRBD, 164–165
    Heartbeat, 175–179
    huge pages, 92–93
    iSCSI initiator, 173–175
    iSCSI target, 169–172
    Kerberos, 330–332
    Kerberos client, 339
    Kerberos server
        administrative user account, 337–338
        database and stash file, 336
        generic settings, 332–335
        KDC settings, 335–336
        user accounts, adding, 338
        verifying KDC is operational, 338–339

Nagios server to use NRPE, 154–155
Nagios tool
    location of configuration files,
        135–136
    master configuration file, 136–138
    restarting with configuration, 151
NRPE on monitored server, 152–154
nsswitch.conf file to find LDAP services,
    228–229
NTP client, 325–326
NTP time server
    drift file, 327
    log file, 328
    security restrictions, applying,
        328–329
OpenLDAP
    database, adding information to,
        215–217
    overview of, 202
    server, 203–215
    slapd server, 203–206
    verifying configuration with
        ldapsearch command, 217–220
OpenVPN
    certificate authority, 305–308
    client keys, 310–311
    copying keys to client, 312
    Diffie-Hellman parameters, 311–312
    server keys, 308–310
PAM for LDAP authentication, 223–228
Postfix MTA
    components, 262–263
    dpkg-reconfigure command, 257–262
    global settings, 264–266
    initial settings, 256–257
    master daemon, 263–264
    overview of, 250–251
    simple mail server, 267–268
    to handle inbound and outbound
        mail, 251–255
    to use lookup tables, 269–273
Samba servers
    applying permissions to local direc-
        tory, 232
    defining share, 232–234
    local directory to share, creating, 232

    as primary domain controllers,
        241–243
    testing access to share, 235–236
    user account, creating, 235
    workstation accounts, creating, 243
stand-alone NTP time server, 323–324
STONITH, 191–193
Ubuntu Server as mail server, 249
VPN server
    Linux VPN client, 316–319
    overview of, 313–316
    Windows VPN client, 320
connection to SAN for enterprise network
    installation, 2–3
contacts file for Nagios tool, creating, 139
contacts group for Nagios tool, defining,
    140
container objects, 198
contents of inodes, showing, 110–111
context switches, performance and, 52
copying keys to client (OpenVPN), 312
CPU
    analyzing performance of, 51– 57
    monitoring with top utility, 46– 49
    tuning
        adjusting process priority using nice
            command, 89–90
        overview of, 87– 89
        SMP environments, 90–91
        thread scheduler, 87–88
crm_mon -i 1 command, 177, 183–184
cryptography
    certificate authority
        creating, 284–289
        need for, 283–284
    key pairs, 282
    overview of, 281
    SSL and, 282
Cyrus IMAPd
    components, 275–276
    installing, 275
    main configuration file, 276–277
    managing user mailboxes, 277–278

■ D

database
    for Kerberos server, creating, 336
    LDAP
        adding information to, 215–217
        deleting entries from, 222
        modifying entries in, 221
Deadline scheduler (I/O scheduler), 97
debugfs utility
    Ext2/Ext3 file system, 122–124
    overview of, 378
    showing contents of inodes with,
        110–111
debugreiserfs tool, 129–130
default page size, in memory, 57
default schema files of LDAP, 200–201
deleting entries from LDAP database, 222
device-device option (Clonezilla), 39
device-image option (Clonezilla), 39
devices for LVM logical volumes, 374–375
DHCP server, setting up, 33–35
Diffie-Hellman parameters, generating,
        311–312
digital certificates, 282
directory
    See also LDAP Directory
    assigning for Clonezilla, 35–36
    description of, 111–112
    /etc/event.d, 347
    /etc/init.d, 347
Directory Components (LDAP), 198
disabling LDAP version 2 support, 206
disk activity, and storage performance, 66
disk layout
    blueprint of, 6–7
    file system, choosing, 5–6
    RAID, setting up, 4–5
Diskless Remote Boot in Linux (DRBL),
        setting up
    configuring software, 32–33
    DHCP server, 33–35
    installing software, 31–32
    overview of, 30
disk mirroring (RAID method), 4
disk striping (RAID method), 4
Distinguished Name (LDAP), 198

Distributed Replicated Block Device
        (DRBD)
    monitoring, 168–169
    SAN and, 161
    setting up, 164–165
    starting, 166–167
dpkg-reconfigure postfix command,
        257–262
dpkg-reconfigure slapd command,
        203–206
drbddisk resource type, 182
DRBL (Diskless Remote Boot in Linux),
        setting up
    configuring software, 32–33
    DHCP server, 33–35
    installing software, 31–32
    overview of, 30
drift file, NTP, configuring, 327
dual-core server, monitoring performance
        on, 47
dumpe2fs utility, 120–122

■ E

e2fsck utility, 120
easy-rsa scripts, generating certificate
        authority with, 308
editing Samba configuration file, 233
e-mail, receiving
    Cyrus IMAPd, using, 275–278
    overview of, 274
    procmail, using, 278–279
    Qpopper, using, 279–280
e-mail, sending. See Postfix MTA
enterprise network installation
    64-bit version of, 7
    authentication handling, 3
    completing, 22–23
    connection to SAN, 2–3
    file system, choosing, 5–7
    LVM logical volumes, creating, 16–22
    overview of, 1
    post-installation tasks
        multipathing, setting up, 26–27
        NIC bonding, setting up, 24–26
    preparing for, 3–4
    RAID, setting up, 4–5
    server hardware, 2

software-based RAID, setting up, 9–16
starting, 8
entries in LDAP, 198
using, 25
/etc/defaults/slapd file, 211–213
/etc/event.d directory, 347
/etc/ha.d/authkeys file, 176
/etc/ha.d/ha.cf file, 175–179
/etc/ietd.conf file, 169
/etc/imapd.conf file, 276–277
/etc/init.d directory, 347
/etc/init.d/networking script, 349–350
/etc/lvm/lvm.conf file, 373
/etc/mke2fs.conf configuration file
contents of, 116
options, 117–119
/etc/modprobe.d/aliases, loading correct
kernal modules using, 25
/etc/modprobe.d/arch/i386 file, containing correct bonding options
/etc/nagios2/apache2.conf file, contents
of, 132
/etc/nagios2/cgi.cfg file, contents of, 132
/etc/nagios2/commands.cfg file, contents
of, 135
/etc/network/interfaces, creating bond()
devices using, 26
/etc/pam.d/login file contents, 224
/etc/postfix/main.cf file, parameters, 266
/etc/postfix/master.cf file
listing, 263
predefined fields and default values,
264
/etc/ssl/openssl.cnf file, 285
/etc/xinetd.d/qpopper configuration file,
279
ethtool utility, 74, 75
Ext2/Ext3 file system
accessing damaged, 378–380
analyzing and repairing
debugfs utility, 122–124
dumpe2fs and tune2fs utilities,
120–122
e2fsck utility, 120
creating, 116–119

description of, 6, 116
mounting, 119
extents, description of, 112

■F
fdisk command, 366–367
fdisk -l command, 359
Fibre Channel, 162
files, backing up, snapshot technology for,
5
file systems
accessing damaged Ext3, 378–380
analyzing Ext2/Ext3, 119–124
choosing at installation, 5–7
description of, 6, 109
indexing, 115
inodes and directories, 110–112
journaling, 114–115
mounting, 112–113, 119
optimizing
Ext2/Ext3, 116–119
ReiserFS, 128–130
XFS, 124–128
repairing
Ext2/Ext3, 119–124
ReiserFS, 380
superblocks, inode bitmaps, and block
bitmaps, 112–113
troubleshooting, 378
filtering incoming e-mail, 278–279
fork() system call, 91
forwarding mail to servers on Internet, 267
free -m command, 57
measuring performance, 86
fsck.reiserfs tool, 128–129

■G
generic network performance optimization, 106–107
getent command, 230
global settings for Postfix, configuring,
264–266
gpart command, 365
Grub
boot loader, 344
configuring huge pages with, 92
command-line interface, 362

loading, 362–364
reinstalling, 361
troubleshooting, 361
Grub menu, 344, 351

■H

ha.cf file, 175–179
hardware initialization, 344
hardware interrupts, performance and, 52
hardware requirements for SAN, 163
hb_gui interface (Heartbeat), 180–183
Heartbeat
    configuring ha.cf file, 175–179
    hb_gui interface, 180–183
    SAN and, 162
Heimdal Kerberos, 321
help command, 326
help command (debugfs utility), 124
hierarchical structure of LDAP, 197
high-availability solution for Apache Web
        Server, 194
high memory, 59
hi performance category (top utility), 49
Host Detail window (Nagios), 157
hosts and host groups for Nagios tool,
        defining, 141–143
huge pages, configuring, 92–93

■I

id performance category (top utility), 48
identifying problem for troubleshooting,
        344–350
ietadm command, 171
ifconfig command, 73–74
imaging network, schematic overview of,
    32
imaging server (Clonezilla)
    assigning directory for, 35
    clients for cloning, configuring, 36–38
    cloning client, 39–43
    configuring, 36
    Diskless Remote Boot in Linux
        configuring software, 32–33
        DHCP server, setting up, 33–35
        installing software, 31–32
        setting up, 30
    setting up, 29

inactive memory, 58
inbound mail
    from local user to local user, processing,
        251–252
    Postfix and, 251
    sent over network to local user, process-
        ing, 253
indexing, description of, 115
init=/bin/bash tool, 351–353
initrd loading, 346
init script (Postfix), 262
inode bitmaps, 112–113
inodes, 110–112
installation
    See also installing
    64-bit version of Ubuntu Server, 7
    completing, 22–23
    LVM logical volumes, creating, 16–22
    on enterprise network
        authentication handling, 3
        connection to SAN, 2–3
        file system, choosing, 5–7
        overview of, 1
        preparing for, 3–4
        RAID, setting up, 4–5
        server hardware, 2
    post-installation tasks
        multipathing, setting up, 26–27
        NIC bonding, setting up, 24–26
    software-based RAID, setting up, 9–16
    starting, 8
installing
    See also installation
    AppArmor, 293
    Cyrus IMAPd, 275
    Diskless Remote Boot in Linux software,
        31–32
    Kerberos, 330–332
    Nagios tool, 131
    NRPE service on Linux servers, 152–153
    OpenLDAP, 202
    OpenVPN, 303
    Postfix, 256
    software for SAN, 163
integrating Samba server
    in Active Directory

Kerberos authentication, setting up, 245

making Samba member of domain, 244

with LDAP

configuring secure connections, 239

connecting Samba to LDAP, 238–239

preparing LDAP, 237–238

preparing Samba, 236–237

specifying where to put objects, 240

Internet time, 323

inter-process communication, optimizing, 94–96

interrupt counter, 53

interruptible hang, 375–377

I/O scheduler

description of, 96

optimizing, 97–98

iostat utility

disk performance and, 69

-x option, 70, 71

ipcs -lm command, 94

IPTraf tool

Additional Ports option, 75

description of, 75

interface, 77

LAN station monitor, 77

IQN (iSCSI Qualified Name) of target, 169

iscsiadm command, 173

iscsiadm -m session command, 174

iSCSI initiator, configuring, 173–175

iSCSI Qualified Name (IQN) of target, 169

iSCSI target

configuring, 169–172

SAN and, 162

iscsitarget resource type, 187

J

Journaled File System (JFS), 6

journaling

modes of, 114–115

ReiserFS and, 128

K

kadmin.local command, 337, 338

kdc.conf file listing, 335–336

KDC (Kerberos Distribution Center), 330, 338–339

Kerberos

See also Kerberos server; NTP time server

authentication, setting up for Samba servers, 245

client

configuring, 339

logging in with, 340–341

description of, 321

design goals for, 329

installing and configuring, 330–332

versions of, 321

Kerberos Distribution Center (KDC), 330, 338–339

Kerberos server

configuring

database and stash file, 336

generic settings, 332–335

KDC settings, 335–336

starting and creating administrative user account, 337–338

user accounts, adding, 338

verifying KDC is operational, 338–339

kernel panic, 346

kernel

interruptible hang, 375–377

loading, 346

noninterruptible hang, 378

parameters, tuning, 98–100

symmetric multiprocessing, 88

troubleshooting, 375

kinit command, 338

klist command, 338

Knoppix Rescue CD, 357–360

krb5.conf file

after installation, 332–335

PAM settings, 340

L

ldapadd command (LDAP), 201

ldap.conf files, 229

ldapdelete command (LDAP), 201, 222

LDAP (Lightweight Directory Access Protocol)

See also OpenLDAP

back-end database, 205

Data Interchange Format, 201

default schema files, 200–201

hierarchical structure of, 197
integrating Samba with
  configuring secure connections, 239
  connecting Samba to LDAP, 238–239
  preparing LDAP, 237–238
  preparing Samba, 236–237
  specifying where to put objects, 240
object attributes, 198
schema, 198–200
using for authentication
  nsswitch.conf file, 228–229
  PAM, configuring, 223–228
  testing client connectivity, 230
LDAP Directory
  default schema files, 200–201
  schema file, 198–200
  using, 197
ldapmodify command, 201, 221
ldappasswd command, 223
ldapsearch command, 201, 217–220
ldap-utils package, 217
ldd command, 223
libpam-ldap package, 227
Lightweight Directory Access Protocol. *See*
  LDAP
Linux
  open-iscsi solution, 173
  servers, installing NRPE service on,
    152–153
  users, authenticating, 245–246
  VPN client, configuring, 316–319
load average for system, 46
load balancing, 88
local certificate authority, 283
local time zone setting, 322
log file, NTP, configuring, 328
logging in with Kerberos client, 340–341
logging slapd.conf file, 213–214
logical blocks, and file systems, 109
logical partitions for RAID setup, 5
lookup tables, configuring Postfix to use
  access, 270
  aliases, 273
  canonical, 270
  overview of, 269–270
  recipient_canonical, 271
  relocated, 271

  sender_canonical, 271
  transport, 272
  virtual, 272
lost administrator password, dealing with,
  380–381
low memory, 59
ls command (debugfs utility), 122
lsdel command (debugfs utility), 123
ls -i command, 110
lsof command, 71, 73
lsscsi command, 174
lvchange command, 374
lvdisplay command, 369–373
LVM logical volumes
  boot problems, fixing, 368–373
  creating on top of software RAID device,
    16–22
  device not activated automatically,
    374–375
  excluding devices for, 374
  troubleshooting, 368
lvscan command, 371–373

■ M

mail delivery agent (MDA)
  description of, 250
  procmail, 278–279
mail server
  configuring simple, 267–268
  configuring Ubuntu Server as, 249
mail solution
  components of, 249–250
  receiving e-mail
    Cyrus IMAPd, using, 275–278
    overview of, 274
    procmail, using, 278–279
    Qpopper, using, 279–280
mail transfer agent (MTA)
  description of, 250
  Postfix, configuring
    components, 262–263
    dpkg-reconfigure command, 257–262
    global settings, 264–266
    initial settings, 256–257
    master daemon, 263–264
    overview of, 250–251
    simple mail server, 267–268

to handle inbound and outbound
mail, 251–255
to use lookup tables, 269–273
Postfix management tools, 273–274
mail user agent (MUA), 250
management tools, Postfix MTA, 273–274
managing
AppArmor profiles, 294–299
Nagios tool, 155–159
user mailboxes, 277–278
XFS file system, 126
man -k xfs utility (XFS), 127
master boot record (MBR)
in boot process, 344
troubleshooting, 364
master daemon, 263–264
MDA (mail delivery agent)
description of, 250
procmail, 278–279
memory
analyzing performance of, 57– 65
configuring huge pages, 92–93
inter-process communication, optimizing, 94–96
optimizing usage of, 92–96
overview of, 91
write cache, optimizing, 93–94
memory monitoring with top utility, 49–50
mirroring, and shared storage, 161
MIT Kerberos, 321
mkdir /share command, 232
modifying entries in LDAP database, 221
modules (OpenLDAP), 201
monitoring
AppArmor status, 299–302
DRBD, 168–169
monitoring network. See Nagios tool
mount command, 235
mounting
Ext2/Ext3 file system, 119
file systems, 112–113
moving processes to other CPU cores, 88
MTA (mail transfer agent)
description of, 250
Postfix, configuring
components, 262–263
dpkg-reconfigure command, 257–262

global settings, 264–266
initial settings, 256–257
master daemon, 263–264
overview of, 250–251
simple mail server, 267–268
to handle inbound and outbound
mail, 251–255
to use lookup tables, 269–273
Postfix management tools, 273–274
MUA (mail user agent), 250
multi core environment
benefits of, 88
symmetric multiprocessing kernel, 88
Multidisk utility, 15
multipathing, setting up, 26–27
multitasking system, performance in, 52

■N

Nagios tool
check_disk plug-in, output from,
144–147
commands, 148–149
configuration files, creating
contacts.cfg, 139
contacts group, defining, 140
hosts and host groups, defining,
141–143
overview of, 138–139
services.cfg, 144–148
timeperiods_nagios2.cfg, 149–151
configuring
location of configuration files,
135–136
master configuration file, 136–138
Nagios server to use NRPE, 154–155
installing, 131
managing
Host Detail window, 157
Reporting section, 159
Service Detail window, 156
Tactical Monitor Overview window,
155
restarting with configuration, 151
user authentication, 132–134
netstat tool
options, 80
-tulpn option, 78

network
  monitoring performance of, 73–80
  optimizing performance
    generic network, 106
    kernel parameters, tuning, 98, 100
    overview of, 98
    Samba and NFS, 105–106
    TCP acknowledgements, 102–103
    TCP read and write buffers, 101–102
    TCP Syn queue, 103–105
    TCP tunables, 100
network card, second, setting up, 30
networking in boot process, 349
network monitoring. *See* Nagios tool
Network Time Protocol (NTP), 322
NFS performance optimization, 105
NIC bonding, setting up, 24–26
NIC teaming, and installation program, 8
nice command, adjusting process priority
        with, 89–90
ni performance category (top utility), 48
noatime option (XFS), 126
noninterruptible hang, 378
Noop scheduler (I/O scheduler), 97
normal processes, priority of, 88–89
notail option (ReiserFS), 128
nr_pdflush_threads parameter, 93
NRPE
  configuring Nagios server to use,
        154–155
  configuring on monitored server,
        152–154
nss_ldap module (LDAP), 201, 228
nsswitch.conf file, configuring to find
        LDAP services, 228–229
ntp.conf file
  driftfile parameter, 328
  listing, 323
  logfile statement, 328
  restrict settings, 328
  synchronization interval, configuring,
        324
ntpdate command, 325
ntpd (NTP daemon), 291–292, 327–328
NTP (Network Time Protocol), 322
ntpq command, 326
ntpq -p command, 326

NTP time server
  client, configuring, 325–326
  customizing
    drift file, 327
    log file, 328
    security restrictions, applying,
        328–329
  description of, 321–323
  pulling or pushing time, 324–325
  stand-alone, configuring, 323–324
  synchronization status, checking,
        326–327
ntptrace command, 326

■O

open-iscsi solution (Linux), 173
OpenLDAP
  commands, 201
  configuration files, 201
  configuring, 202
  database, adding information to,
        215–217
  installing, 202
  modules, 201
  server, configuring
    apt-get purge slapd command, 205
    dpkg-reconfigure slapd command,
        203–206
    slapd.conf file, 207–215
  slapd daemon, 201
  slurpd daemon, 201
  utilities
    ldapdelete command, 222
    ldapmodify command, 221
    ldappasswd command, 223
    overview of, 220–221
  verifying configuration with ldapsearch
        command, 217–220
open source SAN. *See* SAN
openssl command, 284
OpenVPN
  certificate authority, configuring,
        305–308
  client keys, creating, 310–311
  copying keys to client, 312
  Diffie-Hellman parameters, generating,
        311–312

installing, 303
server keys, creating, 308–310
openvpn command, 314
/opt/drbl/sbin/drbl-client-switch command, 37–38
/opt/drbl/sbin/drblpush -i command, 32
/opt/drbl/sbin/select-in-client command, 38
optimizing file systems
Ext2/Ext3
analyzing and repairing, 119–124
creating, 116–119
mounting, 119
overview of, 116
ReiserFS, 128–130
XFS
management of, 126
organization of, 124–125
setting properties, 125–126
utilities, 127–128
optimizing performance. *See* performance optimization
outbound mail
for local user, processing, 254
Postfix and, 251
for remote system user, processing, 254
undeliverable, processing, 255

P

page size, default, in memory, 57
pam_ldap module (LDAP), 201
PAM (Pluggable Authentication Modules), configuring for LDAP authentication, 223–228
parameters for Samba configuration as primary domain controller, 242
Partition Disk screen, 13
Partition Disks interface, 17, 21
partitions
boot, creating, 12
logical, for RAID setup, 5
troubleshooting, 365–368
passwords
for LDAP administrator, 202
in LDAP environment, changing, 223
lost administrator, dealing with, 380–381

performance baselining, 80
performance monitoring
CPU, analyzing performance of, 51–57
memory problems, finding, 57–65
network, 73–80
overview of, 45
storage, 65–73
top utility
CPU monitoring with, 46–49
memory monitoring with, 49–50
output from, 45
process monitoring with, 50–51
performance optimization
CPU
adjusting process priority with nice command, 89–90
overview of, 87–89
SMP environments, 90–91
thread scheduler, 87, 88
memory
configuring huge pages, 92–93
inter-process communication, 94–96
overview of, 91–92
write cache, 93–94
network
generic, 106
kernel parameters, tuning, 98–100
overview of, 98
Samba and NFS, 105–106
TCP acknowledgements, 102–103
TCP read and write buffers, 101–102
TCP Syn queue, 103–105
TCP tunables, 100–101
overview of, 83
storage
I/O scheduler, 96–98
overview of, 96
read requests, tuning, 98
testing changes to settings before applying, 85–87
permissions, applying to local directory for Samba, 232
pickup daemon, 251
PKI (public key infrastructure)
advantages of, 321
for VPN, 305

Pluggable Authentication Modules (PAM),
    configuring for LDAP authentica-
    tion, 223–228
plug-ins available in Nagios, 144
pmap command, 63–65
POP3 server, setting up, 279–280
POSIX standard, 290
postdrop command, 251
Postfix MTA
    configuring
        components, 262–263
        dpkg-reconfigure command, 257–262
        global settings, 264–266
        for handling inbound and outbound
            mail, 251–255
        initial settings, 256–257
        master daemon, 263–264
        overview of, 250–251
        simple mail server, 267–268
        for using lookup tables, 269–273
    management tools, 273–274
post-installation tasks
    multipathing, setting up, 26–27
    NIC bonding, setting up, 24–26
primary domain controllers, Samba serv-
    ers as, 241–243
problem, identifying, 344–350
/proc/drbd file, 184
process files, slapd.conf file, 211
process monitoring with top utility, 50–51
process priority, adjusting with nice com-
    mand, 89–90
procmail MDA, 278–279
/proc/net/iet/volume file, 171
ps utility, 62
public IP address, and VPN connection,
    316
public key infrastructure (PKI)
    advantages of, 321
    for VPN, 305
public/private key pairs, 282
pulling time, 324–325
purging database and slapd configuration,
    205
pushing time, 324–325
pvdisplay command, 369
pvscan command, 368

Q
Qpopper, 279–280

R
RAID
    setting up at installation, 4–5
    software-based
        creating at installation, 9–16
        creating LVM logical volumes on top
            of, 16–22
read requests,
    reordering, 114
    tuning, 98
realm, 330
real-time processes, priority of, 88
receiving e-mail
    Cyrus IMAPd, 275–278
    overview of, 274
    procmail, 278–279
    Qpopper, 279–280
recipient_canonical lookup table, config-
    uring Postfix to use, 271
redundancy
    See also RAID
    in enterprise environment, 2
    NIC bonding and, 24
    in storage area network, 2
reference clocks, 324
reinstalling Grub, 361
reiserfsck command, 380
ReiserFS file system
    description of, 6, 116, 128–130
    repairing, 380
relocated lookup table, configuring Postfix
    to use, 271
remounting file system, 110
reordering read and write requests, 114
repairing
    Ext2/Ext3 file system
        debugfs utility, 122–124
        dumpe2fs and tune2fs utilities,
            120–122
        e2fsck utility, 120
    ReiserFS file system, 380
Reporting section (Nagios), 159
Rescue a Broken System option, 353–356

restarting Nagios tool with configuration, 151
restoredisk option (Clonezilla), 40
runlevel scripts, order of, 347–349
runnable process, 51
run queue, 51

■S

Samba performance optimization, 105–106
Samba servers
    integrating in Active Directory, 244–245
    integrating with LDAP
        configuring secure connections, 239
        connecting Samba to LDAP, 238–239
        preparing LDAP, 237–238
        preparing Samba, 236–237
        specifying where to put objects, 240
    overview of, 231
    as primary domain controllers, 241–243
    setting up
        applying permissions to local directory, 232
        defining share, 232–234
        local directory to share, creating, 232
        overview of, 231
        testing access to share, 235–236
        user account, creating, 235
SAN (storage area network)
    accessing with iSCSI, 169
    cluster configuration, backing up, 187–191
    cluster resources, configuring, 180–187
    connection to, 2–3
    DRBD
        monitoring, 168–169
        setting up, 164–165
        starting, 166–167
    hardware requirements for, 163
    Heartbeat, configuring, 175–179
    iSCSI, configuring, 169–172
    iSCSI initiator, configuring, 173–175
    software components needed for creating, 162
    software for, installing, 163
    STONITH, configuring, 191–193
savedisk option (Clonezilla), 40
scheduling process of CPU, 87–88

schema files, slapd.conf file, 211
schema of LDAP, 198–200
Secure Sockets Layer (SSL) protocol
    certificate authority
        creating, 284–289
        need for, 283–284
    key pairs, 282
security options
    See also authentication
    AppArmor
        components of, 290–291
        creating and managing profiles, 294–299
        installing and starting, 293–294
        monitoring status of, 299–302
        overview of, 290
        permissions, 293
        updating profiles, 299
    cryptography
        certificate authority, creating, 284–289
        certificate authority, need for, 283–284
        key pairs, 282
        overview of, 281
        SSL and, 282
    for VPN, 303
security restrictions, applying to NTP time server, 328–329
SELinux, 290
sender_canonical lookup table, configuring Postfix to use, 271
Sendmail, Postfix mail server compared to, 250
server certificates, creating, 284–289
server hardware for enterprise network installation, 2
server keys (OpenVPN), creating, 308–310
servers
    See also Samba servers
    Clonezilla imaging
        assigning directory for, 35
        clients for cloning, configuring, 36–38
        cloning clients, 39–43
        configuring, 36
        Diskless Remote Boot in Linux, 30–35
        setting up, 29

DHCP, setting up, 33–35
Kerberos
   configuring, 332–336
   starting and creating administrative
      user account, 337–338
   user accounts, adding, 338
   verifying KDC is operational, 338–339
mail, configuring, 249, 267–268
NTP time
   client, configuring, 325–326
   customizing, 327–329
   description of, 321–323
   pulling or pushing time, 324–325
   stand-alone, configuring, 323–324
   synchronization status, checking,
      326–327
POP3, setting up, 279–280
synchronizing time between, 322–323
VPN, 304–305
web, and Nagios tool, 131
Service Detail window (Nagios), 156
services for Nagios tool to monitor, defin-
     ing, 144–148
shared memory, 94–96
shared storage. *See* SAN
shmall setting, 95
shmmax setting, 95
shmmni setting, 95
si performance category (top utility), 49
slab memory, 60
slabtop utility, 61
slapd.conf file
   ACLs, 214–215
   contents of, 207–211
   description of, 201
   logging, 213–214
   schema and process files, 211
   startup parameters, 211–213
slapd daemon (OpenLDAP), 201
slurpd daemon (OpenLDAP), 201
smbclient command, 235
smbclient -L localhost command, 234
smbpasswd command, 231, 235
smbpasswd -W command, 239
SMP environment. *See* symmetric
     multiprocessing (SMP) kernel
     environment

smtpd process, 253–255
snapshot technology for backing up files, 5
software
   Diskless Remote Boot in Linux
     configuring, 32–33
     installing, 31–32
   RAID
     creating at installation, 9–16
     creating LVM logical volumes on top
       of, 16–22
     implementing, 4–5
   virtualization, creating installation con-
     figuration using, 4
SSH VPN, 303
SSL (Secure Sockets Layer) protocol
   certificate authority
     creating, 284–289
     need for, 283–284
   key pairs, 282
stack trace, dumping
   interruptible hangs, 375–377
   noninterruptible hangs, 378
stand-alone NTP time server, configuring,
     323–324
starting
   AppArmor, 294
   DRBD, 166–167
   installation, 8
   iSCSI target, 170
   Kerberos server, 337–338
startup parameters, slapd.conf file,
     211–213
stash file for Kerberos server, creating, 336
stat command, 110
stats command, 112
STONITH, configuring, 191–193
storage
   I/O scheduler
     description of, 96
     optimizing, 97–98
   monitoring performance of, 65–73
   optimizing performance of, 96
   read requests, tuning, 98
storage area network. *See* SAN
st performance category (top utility), 49
stratums, 322–323
superblocks, 112–113

swap memory, 57

switching off barriers, 114

symmetric multiprocessing (SMP) kernel environment
description of, 88
optimizing, 90–91

synchronization status, NTP, checking, 326–327

synchronizing time between servers, 322–323

sy performance category (top utility), 48

sysctl command, 84, 85

/sys/kernel/security/apparmor/profiles file, 300

sysvconfig tool, 172

sysvconfig utility, 89

■T

Tactical Monitor Overview window (Nagios), 155

target ID of iSCSI target, 171

taskset command, 90–91

TCP acknowledgements, 102–103

tcp_keepalive_intvl parameter, 104

tcp_keepalive_time parameter, 104

tcp_max_syn_backlog parameter, 103

TCP read and write buffers, 101–102

tcp_synack_retries parameter, 104

TCP Syn queue, 103–105

TCP tunables, 100–101

testing
access to Samba share, 235–236
changes to settings before applying, 85–87
LDAP client connectivity, 230

thread scheduler, 87–88

Ticket Granting Ticket (TGT), 330

tickless kernel, 52

time command, 80, 86

time periods for Nagios tool, defining, 149–151

TLS (Transport Layer Security), 282

top utility
CPU cycles and, 89
CPU monitoring with, 46–49
Last used cpu (SMP) option, 54
memory monitoring with, 49–50

output from, 45

process monitoring with, 50–51

tools
See also Nagios tool; troubleshooting tools
debugfs, 110–111, 122–124, 378
debugreiserfs, 129–130
dumpe2fs, 120–122
e2fsck, 120
fsck.reiserfs, 128
management, Postfix MTA, 273–274
man –k xfs, 127
Multidisk, 15
OpenLDAP
ldapdelete command, 222
ldapmodify command, 221
ldappasswd command, 223
overview of, 220–221
sysvconfig, 172
tune2fs, 120–122
XFS file system, 127–128

Transport Layer Security (TLS), 282

transport lookup table, configuring Postfix to use, 272

trivial-rewrite daemon, 253–255

troubleshooting
chroot environment and, 357
file systems
Ext3, accessing damaged, 378–380
ReiserFS, 380
Grub
loading manually, 362–364
reinstalling, 361
identifying problem, 344–350
kernel
interruptible hang, 375–377
noninterruptible hang, 378
lost administrator password, 380–381
LVM logical volumes
boot problems, 368–373
device not activated automatically, 374–375
excluding devices for, 374
master boot record, 364
overview of, 343
partitions, 365–368

troubleshooting tools

init=/bin/bash, 351–353
Knoppix Rescue CD, 357–360
overview of, 351
Rescue a Broken System option, 353–356
trusted root certificate authority, 283
tun device, adding to VPN server, 315
tune2fs utility, 120–122
tuning CPU
adjusting process priority using nice command, 89–90
overview of, 87–89
SMP environments, 90–91
thread scheduler, 87–88

U

unconfined command, 301
Universal Time Coordinated (UTC), 322
updating AppArmor profiles, 299
Upstart, 347
user accounts
for Kerberos server, adding, 338
for Samba, creating, 235
user authentication for Nagios tool, 132–134
user mailboxes, managing, 277–278
us performance category (top utility), 48
UTC= setting, 322
UTC (Universal Time Coordinated), 322
utilities. *See* tools

V

van Vugt, Sander, *Beginning Ubuntu Server Administration,* 131
/var/lib/ldap/DB_CONFIG file, 204
/var/run/slapd/slapd.args file, 211
Venema, Wietse, 251
versions of Ubuntu Server, 64- compared to 32-bit, 7
vgdisplay command, 370
vgscan command, 370
virtualization software, creating installation configuration using, 4
virtual lookup table, configuring Postfix to use, 272
virtual memory, 91
Virtual Private Network server. *See* VPN server

vmstat -s command
CPU performance and, 52, 57
vmstat utility
active and inactive memory information, 58
cpu section, 55
disk performance and, 67– 69
sample mode, 55, 57, 68
swap information, 58
VPN
See also VPN server
normal configuration of, 304–305
public key infrastructure for, 305
VPN server
See also OpenVPN
configuring, 313–316
description of, 303
Linux VPN client, configuring, 316–319
Windows VPN client, configuring, 320

W

wa parameter (top utility), 90
wa performance category (top utility), 48
web servers, and Nagios tool, 131
winbind package, 245–246
Windows VPN client, configuring, 320
workstation accounts for Samba, creating, 243
write cache, optimizing, 93–94
write requests, reordering, 114

X

X.509 standard, 282
xfsctl function, 125
xfsdump command, 127
XFS file system
description of, 6, 124
management of, 126
organization of, 124–125
setting properties, 125–126
utilities, 127–128
xfs_freeze command, 128
xfs_growfs command, 125–127
xfs_info command, 125
xfs_repair command, 127
xfs_rtcp command, 127
xinetd, running Qpopper through, 279

You Need the Companion eBook

Your purchase of this book entitles you to buy the companion PDF-version eBook for only $10. Take the weightless companion with you anywhere.

We believe this Apress title will prove so indispensable that you'll want to carry it with you everywhere, which is why we are offering the companion eBook (in PDF format) for $10 to customers who purchase this book now. Convenient and fully searchable, the PDF version of any content-rich, page-heavy Apress book makes a valuable addition to your programming library. You can easily find and copy code—or perform examples by quickly toggling between instructions and the application. Even simultaneously tackling a donut, diet soda, and complex code becomes simplified with hands-free eBooks!

Once you purchase your book, getting the $10 companion eBook is simple:

❶ Visit **www.apress.com/promo/tendollars/**.

❷ Complete a basic registration form to receive a randomly generated question about this title.

❸ Answer the question correctly in 60 seconds, and you will receive a promotional code to redeem for the $10.00 eBook.

2855 TELEGRAPH AVENUE | SUITE 600 | BERKELEY, CA 94705

Offer valid through 6/09.